Auguste Comte, Frederic Harrison

**The Positive Philosophy of Auguste Comte**

Vol. II.

Auguste Comte, Frederic Harrison

**The Positive Philosophy of Auguste Comte**
*Vol. II.*

ISBN/EAN: 9783337081546

Printed in Europe, USA, Canada, Australia, Japan

Cover: Foto ©Thomas Meinert / pixelio.de

More available books at **www.hansebooks.com**

BOHN'S PHILOSOPHICAL LIBRARY

# THE POSITIVE PHILOSOPHY OF AUGUSTE COMTE

VOL. II.

### GEORGE BELL & SONS

LONDON: YORK STREET, COVENT GARDEN
AND NEW YORK, 66, FIFTH AVENUE
CAMBRIDGE: DEIGHTON, BELL & CO.

# THE
# POSITIVE PHILOSOPHY
## OF
# AUGUSTE COMTE

FREELY TRANSLATED AND CONDENSED BY
HARRIET MARTINEAU

WITH AN INTRODUCTION BY
FREDERIC HARRISON

IN THREE VOLUMES

VOL. II.

LONDON
GEORGE BELL & SONS
1896

CHISWICK PRESS:—CHARLES WHITTINGHAM AND CO.
TOOKS COURT, CHANCERY LANE, LONDON.

# CONTENTS.

## BOOK V.
## BIOLOGY.
### CHAPTER I.
#### GENERAL VIEW OF BIOLOGY.

|   | PAGE |
|---|---|
| Opposite starting-points in philosophy | 1 |
| Starting-point of Physiology | 2 |
| Its present imperfection | 3 |
| Its field | 3 |
| Relation to Medicine | 3 |
| Its object | 5 |
| Idea of Life | 5 |
| De Blainville's definition | 7 |
| Definition of Biology | 9 |
| Means of investigation | 11 |
| OBSERVATION | 12 |
| Artificial apparatus | 12 |
| Chemical exploration | 13 |
| EXPERIMENT | 13 |
| By affecting the organism | 14 |
| By affecting the Medium | 14 |
| Comparative experiment | 15 |
| Pathological investigation | 16 |
| COMPARISON | 18 |
| Five kinds of comparison | 21 |
| Comparison of parts of the same organism | 22 |
| Of phases of the same organism | 23 |
| Of different organisms | 23 |
| Relation of Biology to other sciences | 26 |
| To Chemistry | 26 |
| To Physics | 28 |
| To Astronomy | 29 |
| To Mathematics | 33 |
| Use of scientific fictions | 37 |

| | PAGE |
|---|---|
| Condition and prospects of the science | 38 |
| Requisite Education | 39 |
| Art of Classification | 40 |
| Influence of Biology upon the Positive Spirit | 41 |
| Distribution of the science | 44 |
| Where to begin | 46 |

## CHAPTER II.

### ANATOMICAL PHILOSOPHY.

| | |
|---|---|
| Development of Statical biology | 48 |
| Process of discovery of the tissues | 48 |
| Combination with Comparative anatomy | 50 |
| Elements and Products | 50 |
| Vitality of the organic fluids | 53 |
| Classification of the tissues | 55 |
| ORGANIC: Cellular tissue | 55 |
| Dermous tissue | 56 |
| Sclerous tissue | 57 |
| Kystous tissue | 57 |
| ANIMAL: Muscular and nervous tissues | 57 |
| Limitation of the inquiry | 58 |

## CHAPTER III.

### BIOTAXIC PHILOSOPHY.

| | |
|---|---|
| Comparative anatomy of vegetables and animals | 60 |
| Animal anatomy our subject | 61 |
| Division of the Natural Method | 61 |
| Natural groups | 61 |
| Co-ordination of them | 62 |
| Three laws of co-ordination | 63 |
| Question of permanence of organic species | 64 |
| Two logical conditions of the study | 68 |
| Subordination of characteristics | 68 |
| Procedure, in use of the Natural Method | 69 |
| Division of animal and vegetable kingdom | 70 |
| Hierarchy of the animal kingdom | 71 |
| Attribute of symmetry | 72 |
| Division of Duplicate animals | 73 |
| Division of Articulated animals | 73 |
| Consideration of the envelope | 73 |
| Natural Method applied to the Vegetable Kingdom | 74 |
| Difficulty of co-ordination | 74 |

CONTENTS. vii

## CHAPTER IV.
### ORGANIC OR VEGETATIVE LIFE.

|   | PAGE |
|---|---|
| Condition of Dynamical Biology | 78 |
| Vital phenomena: their division | 79 |
| Theory of Organic Media | 79 |
| Exterior conditions of Life | 80 |
| Mechanical conditions: Weight | 80 |
| Pressure | 81 |
| Motion and rest | 82 |
| Thermological action | 82 |
| Light, Electricity, etc. | 83 |
| Molecular conditions | 84 |
| Air and water | 84 |
| Study of Specifics | 85 |
| History of Physiology | 85 |
| Philosophical character of Physiology | 88 |
| Division of the study | 89 |
| Two functions of the organic life | 89 |
| Results of organic action | 91 |
| State of composition and decomposition | 92 |
| Vital heat | 92 |
| Electrical state | 93 |
| Production and development of living bodies | 93 |
| Decline of the organism | 94 |

## CHAPTER V.
### THE ANIMAL LIFE.

|   | PAGE |
|---|---|
| Transition from the inorganic to the organic | 98 |
| Primitive nervous properties | 98 |
| Relation of the animal to the organic life | 98 |
| To inorganic philosophy | 99 |
| Properties of tissue | 100 |
| Sensibility | 101 |
| Irritability | 101 |
| Present state of analysis of animality | 103 |
| Movement | 103 |
| Exterior Sensation | 105 |
| Interior Sensation | 107 |
| Mode of action of animality | 107 |
| Intermittence | 108 |
| Sleep | 108 |
| Habit | 109 |
| Need of activity | 111 |
| Association of the animal functions | 111 |

## CHAPTER VI.

### INTELLECTUAL AND MORAL OR CEREBRAL FUNCTIONS.

|   | PAGE |
|---|---|
| Short-coming of Descartes | 113 |
| History till Gall's time | 114 |
| Positive theory of Cerebral functions | 115 |
| Its proper place | 115 |
| Vices of Psychological systems | 115 |
| Method: Interior Observation | 116 |
| Doctrine: Relation between the Affective and Intellectual faculties | 118 |
| Brutes and Man | 119 |
| Theory of the *I* | 119 |
| Reason and Instinct | 120 |
| Basis of Gall's doctrine | 122 |
| Divisions of the brain | 123 |
| Subdivision | 125 |
| Objections | 126 |
| Necessity of human actions | 126 |
| Answered | 127 |
| Hypothetical distribution of faculties | 128 |
| Needed improvements | 129 |
| Anatomical basis | 129 |
| Physiological analysis of faculties | 130 |
| Examination of historical cases | 131 |
| Pathological and Comparative analysis | 132 |
| Laws of action | 134 |
| Intermittence and continuity | 134 |
| Association | 134 |
| Unity of the brain and nervous system | 135 |
| Imperfect state of Phrenology | 136 |
| Present state of Biology | 136 |
| Retrospect of Natural Philosophy | 137 |

# BOOK VI.

## SOCIAL PHYSICS.

### CHAPTER I.

#### NECESSITY AND OPPORTUNENESS OF THIS NEW SCIENCE.

| | |
|---|---|
| Proposal of the subject | 139 |
| Conditions of Order and Progress | 140 |
| The theological polity | 143 |
| Criterion of social doctrine | 144 |
| Failure of the Theological polity | 144 |

|   |   |
|---|---|
| The Metaphysical polity | 148 |
| Becomes obstructive | 150 |
| Dogma of Liberty of Conscience | 151 |
| Dogma of Equality | 155 |
| Dogma of the Sovereignty of the People | 156 |
| Dogma of National Independence | 156 |
| Inconsistency of the Metaphysical doctrine | 157 |
| Notion of a state of Nature | 157 |
| Adhesion to the worn-out | 159 |
| Recurrence to war | 160 |
| Principle of Political Centralization | 160 |
| The Stationary doctrine | 164 |
| Dangers of the critical period | 167 |
| Intellectual anarchy | 167 |
| Destruction of public morality | 169 |
| Private morality | 171 |
| Political corruption | 173 |
| Low aims of political questions | 176 |
| Fatal to Progress | 177 |
| Fatal to Order | 178 |
| Incompetence of political leaders | 179 |
| Advent of the Positive Philosophy | 182 |
| Logical coherence of the doctrine | 183 |
| Its effect on Order | 184 |
| Its effect on Progress | 187 |
| Anarchical tendencies of the scientific class | 191 |
| Conclusion | 192 |

## CHAPTER II.

### PRINCIPAL PHILOSOPHICAL ATTEMPTS TO CONSTITUTE A SOCIAL SCIENCE.

|   |   |
|---|---|
| History of Social Science | 194 |
| Aristotle's "Politics" | 197 |
| Montesquieu | 198 |
| Condorcet | 201 |
| Political economy | 203 |
| Growth of historical study | 208 |

## CHAPTER III.

### CHARACTERISTICS OF THE POSITIVE METHOD IN ITS APPLICATION TO SOCIAL PHENOMENA.

|   |   |
|---|---|
| Infantile state of social science | 211 |
| The Relative superseding the Absolute | 213 |
| Presumptuous character of the existing political spirit | 214 |
| Prevision of social phenomena | 217 |

## CONTENTS.

| | PAGE |
|---|---|
| Spirit of Social Science | 218 |
| Statical study | 219 |
| Social Organization | 220 |
| Political and social concurrence | 221 |
| Interconnection of the social organism | 223 |
| Order of statical study | 226 |
| Dynamical study | 227 |
| Social continuity | 228 |
| Produced by natural laws | 228 |
| Notion of Human perfectibility | 232 |
| Limits of political action | 234 |
| Social phenomena modifiable | 235 |
| Order of modifying influences | 237 |
| Means of Investigation in Social Science | 241 |
| Direct Means | 241 |
| Observation | 241 |
| Experiment | 245 |
| Comparison | 247 |
| Comparison with inferior animals | 248 |
| Comparison of co-existing states of society | 249 |
| Comparison of consecutive states | 251 |
| Promise of a fourth method of investigation | 256 |

## CHAPTER IV.

### RELATION OF SOCIOLOGY TO THE OTHER DEPARTMENTS OF POSITIVE PHILOSOPHY.

| | |
|---|---|
| Relation to Biology | 259 |
| Relation to Inorganic philosophy | 263 |
| Man's action on the external world | 266 |
| Necessary Education | 266 |
| Mathematical preparation | 267 |
| Pretended theory of chances | 268 |
| Reaction of Sociology | 269 |
| As to doctrine | 270 |
| As to Method | 271 |
| Speculative rank of Sociology | 274 |

## CHAPTER V.

### SOCIAL STATICS, OR THEORY OF THE SPONTANEOUS ORDER OF HUMAN SOCIETY.

| | |
|---|---|
| Three aspects | 275 |
| 1. The Individual | 275 |
| 2. The Family | 281 |
| The Sexual relation | 283 |
| The Parental relation | 286 |

CONTENTS.  xi

|  | PAGE |
|---|---|
| 3. Society | 289 |
| Distribution of employments | 291 |
| Inconveniences | 293 |
| Basis of the true theory of government | 294 |
| Elementary subordination | 295 |
| Tendency of society to government | 297 |

## CHAPTER VI.

### SOCIAL DYNAMICS; OR THEORY OF THE NATURAL PROGRESS OF HUMAN SOCIETY.

|  | |
|---|---|
| Scientific view of Human Progression | 299 |
| Course of Man's social development | 300 |
| Rate of progress | 301 |
| *Ennui* | 302 |
| Duration of human life | 303 |
| Increase of Population | 305 |
| The order of evolution | 307 |
| Law of the Three Periods | 309 |
| The Theological period | 310 |
| Intellectual influence of the Theological philosophy | 312 |
| Social influences of the Theological philosophy | 316 |
| Institution of a speculative class | 317 |
| The Positive stage | 319 |
| Attempted union of the two philosophies | 320 |
| The Metaphysical Period | 323 |
| Co-existence of the three Periods in the same mind | 325 |
| Corresponding material development | 326 |
| Primitive military life | 326 |
| Primitive Slavery | 327 |
| The Military *régime* provisional | 328 |
| Affinity between the Theological and Military *régime* | 329 |
| Affinity between the Positive and Industrial spirit | 331 |
| Intermediate *régime* | 332 |

# THE POSITIVE PHILOSOPHY OF AUGUSTE COMTE.

## BOOK V.

## BIOLOGY.

### CHAPTER I.

#### GENERAL VIEW OF BIOLOGY.

THE study of the external world and of Man is the eternal business of philosophy; and there are two methods of proceeding; by passing from the study of Man to that of external nature, or from the study of external nature to that of Man. Whenever philosophy shall be perfect, the two methods will be reconciled: meantime, the contrast of the two distinguishes the opposite philosophies,—the theological and the positive. We shall see hereafter that all theological and metaphysical philosophy proceeds to explain the phenomena of the external world from the starting-point of our consciousness of human phenomena; whereas, the positive philosophy subordinates the conception of Man to that of the external world. All the multitude of incompatibilities between the two philosophies proceed from this radical opposition. If the consideration of Man is to prevail over that of the universe, all phenomena are inevitably attributed to *will*,—first natural, and then outside of nature; and this constitutes the theological system. On the contrary, the direct study of the universe suggests and developes the great idea of

*Opposite starting-points in philosophy.*

the *laws* of nature, which is the basis of all positive philosophy, and capable of extension to the whole of phenomena, including at last those of Man and Society. The one point of agreement among all schools of theology and metaphysics, which otherwise differ without limit, is that they regard the study of Man as primary, and that of the universe as secondary,—usually neglecting the latter entirely. Whereas, the most marked characteristic of the positive school is that it founds the study of Man on the prior knowledge of the external world.

Starting-point of Physiology. This consideration affects physiology further than by its bearing on its encyclopedical rank. In this one case the character of the science is affected by it. The basis of its positivity is its subordination to the knowledge of the external world. Any multitude of facts, however well analysed, is useless as long as the old method of philosophizing is persisted in, and physiology is conceived of as a direct study, isolated from that of inert nature. The study has assumed a scientific character only since the recent period when vital phenomena began to be regarded as subject to general laws, of which they exhibit only simple modifications. This revolution is now irreversible, however incomplete and however imperfect have been the attempts to establish the positive character of our knowledge of the most complex and individual of physiological phenomena; especially that of the nerves and brain. Yet, unquestionable as is the basis of the science, its culture is at present too like that to which men have been always accustomed, pursued independently of mathematical and inorganic philosophy, which are the only solid foundations of the positivity of vital studies.

There is no science with regard to which it is so necessary to ascertain its true nature and scope; because we have not only to assign its place in the scale, but to assert its originality. On the one hand, metaphysics strives to retain it; and on the other, the inorganic philosophy lays hold of it, to make it a mere outlying portion of its scientific domain. For more than a century, during which biology has endeavoured to take its place in the hierarchy of fundamental sciences, it has been bandied between metaphysics and physics; and the strife can be ended only by the decision of positive philosophy, as to what position shall be occupied by the study of living bodies.

The present backwardness of the science is explained by the extreme complexity of its phenomena, and its recent date. That complexity forbids the hope that biological science can ever attain a perfection comparable to that of the more simple and general parts of natural philosophy: and, from its recent date, minds which see in every other province the folly of looking for first causes and modes of production of phenomena, still carry these notions into the study of living bodies. For more than a century intelligent students have in physics put aside the search after the mystery of weight, and have looked only for its laws; yet they reproach physiology with teaching us nothing of the nature of life, consciousness, and thought. It is easy to see how physiology may thus be supposed to be far more imperfect than it is; and if it be, from unavoidable circumstances, more backward than the other fundamental sciences, it yet includes some infinitely valuable conceptions, and its scientific character is far less inferior than is commonly supposed.

*Its present imperfection.*

We must first describe its domain.

There is no doubt that the gradual development of human intelligence would, in course of time, lead us over from the theological and metaphysical state to the positive by a series of logical conceptions. But such an advance would be extremely slow; and we see, in fact, that the process is much quickened by a special stimulus of one sort or another. Our historical experience, which testifies to every great advance having been made in this way, shows that the most common auxiliary influence is the need of application of the science in question. Most philosophers have said that every science springs from a corresponding art;—a maxim which, amidst much exaggeration, contains solid truth, if we restrict it, as we ought, to the separation of each science from the theological and metaphysical philosophy which was the natural product of early human intelligence. In this view it is true that a double action has led to the institution of science, the arts furnishing posi-

*Its field.*

*Relation to Medicine.*

tive data, and then leading speculative researches in the direction of real and accessible questions. But there is another side to this view. When the science has once reached a certain degree of extension, the progress of speculative knowledge is checked by a too close connection of theory with practice. Our power of speculation, limited as it is, still far surpasses our capacity for action: so that it would be radically absurd to restrict the progress of the one to that of the other. The rational domains of science and art are, in general, perfectly distinct, though philosophically connected: in the one we learn to know, and therefore to foreknow; in the other to become capable, and therefore to act. If science springs from art, it can be matured only when it has left art behind. This is palpably true with regard to the sciences whose character is clearly recognized. Archimedes was, no doubt, deeply aware of it when he apologized to posterity for having for the moment applied his genius to practical inventions. In the case of mathematics and astronomy we have almost lost sight of this truth, from the remoteness of their formation; but, in the case of physics and of chemistry, at whose scientific birth we may almost be said to have been present, we can ourselves testify to their dependence on the arts at the outset, and to the rapidity of their progress after their separation from them. The first series of chemical facts were furnished by the labours of art; but the prodigious recent development of the science is certainly due, for the most part, to the speculative character that it has assumed.

These considerations are eminently applicable to physiology. No other science has been closely connected with a corresponding art, as biology has with medical art,—a fact accounted for by the high importance of the art and the complexity of the science. But for the growing needs of practical medicine, and the indications it affords about the chief vital phenomena, physiology would have probably stopped short at those academical dissertations, half literary, half metaphysical, studded with episodical adornments, which constituted what was called the science little more than a century ago. The time however has arrived when biology must, like the other sciences, make a fresh start in a purely speculative direction, free from all entanglement with medical or any other art. And when this science and the others shall have attained an abstract completeness, then will arise the further duty, as I have indicated before, of connecting the system of the arts with that of the sciences by an intermediate order of rational conceptions. Meanwhile such an operation would be premature, because the system of the sciences is not completely formed; and, with regard to physiology especially, the first necessity is to separate it from medicine, in order to secure the originality of its scientific character, by constituting organic science as a consequence of inorganic. Since the time of Haller this process has gone on; but with extreme uncertainty and imperfection; so that even now the science is, with a few valuable exceptions, committed to physicians, who are rendered unfit for such a charge both by the eminent importance of their proper business, and by the profound imperfection of their existing education. Physiology is the only science which is not taken possession of by minds exclusively devoted to it. It has not even a regularly assigned place in the best-instituted scientific corporations. This state of things cannot last, the importance and difficulty of the science being considered. If we would not confide the study of astronomy to navigators, we shall not leave physiology to the leisure of physicians. Such an organization as this is a sufficient evidence of the prevalent confusion of ideas about physiological science; and when its pursuit has been duly provided for, that reaction for the benefit of art will ensue which should put to flight all the fears of the timid about the separation of theory from practice. We have seen before how the loftiest truths of science concur to put us in possession of an art; and the verification of this truth, which physics and chemistry have afforded before our eyes, will be repeated in the case of physiology when the science has advanced as far.

Having provided for a speculative view of physiology, we must inquire into its object; *Its object.* and, as the vital laws constitute the essential subject of biology, we must begin by analysing the fundamental idea of *life*.

Before the time of Bichat, this idea was wrapped in a mist of metaphysical abstrac- *Idea of Life.*

tions; and Bichat himself, after having perceived that a definition of life could be founded on nothing else than a general view of phenomena proper to living bodies, so far fell under the influence of the old philosophy as to call life a struggle between dead nature and living nature. The irrationality of this conception consists especially in its suppressing one of the two elements whose concurrence is necessary to the general idea of *life*. This idea supposes, not only a being so organized as to admit of the vital state, but such an arrangement of external influences as will also admit of it. The harmony between the living being and the corresponding *medium* (as I shall call its environment) evidently characterizes the fundamental condition of life; whereas, on Bichat's supposition, the whole environment of living beings tends to destroy them. If certain perturbations of the medium occasionally destroy life, its influence is, on the whole, preservative; and the causes of injury and death proceed at least as often from necessary and spontaneous modifications of the organism as from external influences. Moreover, one of the main distinctions between the organic and the inorganic regions is that inorganic phenomena, from their greater simplicity and generality, are produced under almost any external influences which admit of their existence at all; while organic bodies are, from their complexity, and the variety of actions always preceding, very closely dependent on the influences around them. And the higher we ascend in the ranks of organic bodies, the closer is this dependence, in proportion to the diversity of functions; though, as we must bear in mind, the power of the organism in modifying the influences of the medium rises in proportion. The existence of the being then requires a more complex aggregate of exterior circumstances; but it is compatible with wider limits of variation in each influence taken by itself. In the lowest rank of the organic hierarchy, for instance, we find vegetables and fixed animals which have no effect on the medium in which they exist, and which would therefore perish by the slightest changes in it, but for the very small number of distinct exterior actions required by their life. At the other extremity we find Man, who can live only by the concurrence of the most complex exterior conditions, atmospherical and terrestrial, under various physical and chemical aspects; but, by an indispensable compensation, he can endure, in all these conditions, much wider differences than inferior organisms could support, because he has a superior power of reacting on the surrounding system. However great this power, it is as contradictory to Bichat's view as his dependence on the exterior world. But this notion of Man's independence of exterior nature, and antagonism to it, was natural in Bichat's case, when physiological considerations bore no relation to any hierarchy of organisms, and when Man was studied as an isolated existence. However, the radical vice of such a starting-point for such a study could not but impair the whole system of Bichat's physiological conceptions; and we shall see how seriously the effects have made themselves felt.

Next ensued the abuse, by philosophers, and especially in Germany, of the benefits disclosed by comparative anatomy. They generalized extravagantly the abstract notion of life yielded by the study of the aggregate of organized beings, making the idea of life exactly equivalent to that of spontaneous activity. As all natural bodies are active, in some manner and degree, no distinct notion could be attached to the term; and this abuse must evidently lead us back to the ancient confusion, which arose from attributing life to all bodies. The inconvenience of having two terms to indicate a single general idea should teach us that, to prevent scientific questions from degenerating into a contest of words, we must carefully restrict the term *life* to the only really living beings, —that is, those which are organized,—and not give it a meaning which would include all possible organisms, and all their modes of vitality. In this case, as in all primitive questions, the philosophers would have done wisely to respect the rough but judicious indications of popular good sense, which will ever be the true starting-point of all wise scientific speculation.

I know of no other successful attempt to define life than that of M. de Blainville, proposed in the introduction to his treatise on Comparative Anatomy. He characterizes life as the double interior motion, general and continuous, of com- *De Blainville's definition.*

position and decomposition, which in fact constitutes its true universal nature. I do not see that this leaves anything to be desired, unless it be a more direct and explicit indication of the two correlative conditions of a determinate organism and a suitable medium. This criticism however applies rather to the formula than to the conception; and the conditions are implied in the conception,—the conditions of an organism to sustain the renovation, and a medium to minister to the absorption and exhalation; yet it might have been better to express them. With this modification, the definition is unexceptionable,—enunciating the one phenomenon which is common to all living beings, and excluding all inert bodies. Here we have, in my view, the first elementary basis of true biological philosophy.

It is true, this definition neglects the eminent distinction between the *organic* and the *animal* life, and relates solely to the vegetative life; and it appears to violate the general principle of definitions,—that they should exhibit a phenomenon in the case in which it is most, and not in that in which it is least developed. But the proposed definition is shown, by these very objections, to rest upon a due estimate of the whole biological hierarchy: for the animal life is simply a complementary advancement upon the organic or fundamental life, adapted to procure materials for it by reaction upon the external world, and to prepare or facilitate its acts by sensations, locomotion, etc., and to preserve it from unfavourable influences. The higher animals, and Man especially, are the only ones in which this relation is totally subverted,—the vegetative life being destined to support the animal, which is erected into the chief end and preponderant character of organic existence. But in Man himself, this admirable inversion of the usual order becomes comprehensible only by the aid of a remarkable development of intelligence and sociality, which tends more and more to transform the species artificially into a single individual, immense and eternal, endowed with a constantly progressive action upon external nature. This is the only just view to take of this subordination of the vegetative to the animal life, as the ideal type towards which civilized humanity incessantly tends, though it can never be fully realized. We shall hereafter show how this conception is related to the new fundamental science which I propose to constitute: but in pure biology, the view is unscientific, and can only lead us astray. It is not with the essential properties of humanity that biology is concerned; but with the individual in his relation to other organic beings; and it must therefore rigorously maintain the conception of animal life being subordinated to the vegetative, as a general law of the organic realm, and the only apparent exception to which forms the special object of a wholly different fundamental science. It should be added that, even where the animal life is the most developed, the organic life, besides being the basis and the end, remains common to all the tissues, while, at the same time, it alone proceeds in a necessarily continuous manner,—the animal life, on the contrary, being intermittent. These are the grounds on which M. de Blainville's definition of life must be confirmed, while, nevertheless, we may regard the consideration of animality, and even of humanity, as the most important object of biology.

This analysis of the phenomenon of life will help us to a clear definition of the science which relates to it. We have seen that the idea of life supposes the mutual relation of two indispensable elements,—an organism, and a suitable medium or environment. It is from the reciprocal action of these two elements that all the vital phenomena proceed;—not only the animal, but also the organic. It immediately follows that the great problem of positive biology consists in establishing, in the most general and simple manner, a scientific harmony between these two inseparable powers of the vital conflict, and the act which constitutes that conflict: in a word, in connecting, in both a general and special manner, the double idea of organ and medium with that of function. The idea of function is, in fact, as double as the other; and, if we were treating of the natural history of vital beings, we must expressly consider it so: for, by the law of the equivalence of action and reaction, the organism must act on the medium as much as the medium on the organism. In treating of the human being, and especially in the social state, it would

*Definition of Biology.*

be necessary to use the term *function* in this larger sense: but at present there will be little inconvenience in adopting it in its ordinary sense, signifying organic acts, independently of their exterior consequences.

Biology, then, may be regarded as having for its object the connecting, in each determinate case, the anatomical and the physiological point of view; or, in other words, the statical and dynamical. This perpetual relation constitutes its true philosophical character. Placed in a given system of exterior circumstances, a definite organism must always act in a necessarily determinate manner; and, inversely, the same action could not be precisely produced by really distinct organisms. We may then conclude interchangeably, the act from the subject, or the agent from the act. The surrounding system being always supposed to be known, according to the other fundamental sciences, the double biological problem may be laid down thus, in the most mathematical form, and in general terms: *Given, the organ or organic modification, to find the function or the act; and reciprocally.* This definition seems to me to fulfil the chief philosophical conditions of the science; and especially it provides for that rational prevision, which, as has been so often said, is the end of all true science; an end which abides through all the degrees of imperfection which, in any science, at present prevents its attainment. It is eminently important to keep this end in view in a science so intricate as this, in which the multitude of details tempts to a fatal dispersion of efforts upon desultory researches. No one disputes that the most perfect portions of the science are those in which prevision has been best realized; and this is a sufficient justification of the proposal of this aim, whether or not it shall ever be fully attained. My definition excludes the old division between anatomy and physiology, because I believe that division to have marked a very early stage of the science, and to be no longer sustainable. It was by the simple and easy considerations of anatomy that the old metaphysical view was discredited, and positivity first introduced into biology: but that service once accomplished, no reason remains for the separation; and the division, in fact, is growing fainter every day.

Not only does my definition abstain from separating anatomy from physiology; it joins to it another essential part, the nature of which is little known. If the idea of life is really inseparable from that of organization, neither can be severed, as we have seen, from that of a medium or environment, in a determinate relation with them. Hence arises a third elementary aspect; viz., the general theory of organic media, and of their action upon the organism, abstractedly regarded. This is what the German philosophers of our day confusedly asserted in their notion of an intermediate realm,—of air and water,—uniting the inorganic and organic worlds: and this is what M. de Blainville had in view in what he called the study of exterior modifiers, general and special. Unhappily, this portion which, after anatomy proper, is the most indispensable preliminary of biology, is still so obscure and imperfect that few physiologists even suspect its existence.

The definition that I have proposed aids us in describing not only the object or nature of the science, but its subject, or domain: for, according to this formula, it is not in a single organism, but in all known, and even possible organisms, that biology must endeavour to establish a constant and necessary harmony between the anatomical point of view and the physiological. This unity of subject is one of the chief philosophical beauties of biology; and, in order to maintain it, we must here avow that in the midst of an almost infinite diversity, the study of Man must always prevail, and rule all the rest, whether as starting-point or aim. Our hope, in studying other organisms, is to arrive at a more exact knowledge of Man: and again, the idea of Man is the only possible standard to which we can refer other organic systems. In this sense, and in this only, can the point of view of the antiquated philosophy be sustained by the deeper philosophy which is taking its place. Such is, then, the necessary consolidation of all the parts of biological science, notwithstanding the imposing vastness of its rational domain.

As for the means of investigation in this science,—the first observation that occurs is that it affords a striking confirmation of the   *Means of investigation.*

philosophical law before laid down, of the inevitable increase of our scientific resources in proportion to the complication of the phenomena in question. If biological phenomena are incomparably more complex than those of any preceding science, the study of them admits of the most extensive assemblage of intellectual means (many of them new) and developes human faculties hitherto inactive, or known only in a rudimentary state. The logical resources which are thus obtained will be exhibited hereafter. At present, we must notice the means of direct exploration and analysis of phenomena in this science.

OBSERVATION. First, Observation acquires a new extension. Chemistry admitted the use of all the five senses; but biology is, in this respect, an advance upon chemistry. We can here employ an artificial apparatus to perfect the natural sensations, and especially in the case of sight. Much needing precaution in the use, and very subject to abuse, as is this resource, it will always be eagerly employed. In a statical view, such an apparatus helps us to a much better estimate of a structure whose least perceptible details may acquire a primary importance, in various relations: and, even in the dynamical view, though much less favourable, we are sometimes enabled by these artificial means to observe directly the elementary play of the smallest organic parts, which are the ordinary basis of the principal vital phenomena. Till recently, these aids were limited to the sense of sight, which here, as everywhere else, is the chief agent of scientific observation. But some instruments have been devised in our day to assist the hearing; and, though invented for pathological investigations, they are equally fit for the study of the healthy organism. Though rough at present, and not to be compared to microscopic apparatus, these instruments indicate the improvements that may be made hereafter in artificial hearing. Moreover, they suggest, by analogy, that the other senses, not excepting even touch, may admit of such assistance, hinted to the restless sagacity of explorers by a better theory of the corresponding sensations.

*Artificial apparatus.*

Next, the biologist has an advantage over the chemist in being able to employ the whole of chemical procedures, as a sort of new power, to perfect the preliminary exploration of the subject of his researches, according to the evident rule of philosophy that each doctrine may be converted into a method with regard to those that follow it in the scientific hierarchy; but never with regard to those which precede it. In anatomical observations, especially, as might be foreseen, a happy use is made of chemical procedure, to characterize with precision the different elementary tissues, and the chief products of the organism. In physiological observations also, though they are less favourable to the use of such means, they are of real and notable efficacy,—always supposing, in both cases, that they are used under the guidance of sound philosophy, and not overcharged with the minute numerical details which too often burden the chemical analyses of the organic tissues. One more resource may be mentioned, which was often employed by Bichat to make up for the absence or imperfection of chemical tests; the examination of alimentary effects,—the substances which immediately compose organized bodies being, usually, by their nature, more or less fit for nutrition. In an anatomical view this study may become a useful complement of the other means of investigation.

*Chemical exploration.*

Proceeding to the second class of means,—Experiment cannot but be less and less decisive, in proportion to the complexity of the phenomena to be explored: and therefore we saw this resource to be less effectual in chemistry than in physics; and we now find that it is eminently useful in chemistry in comparison with physiology. In fact, the nature of the phenomena seems to offer almost insurmountable impediments to any extensive and prolific application of such a procedure in biology. These phenomena require the concurrence of so large a number of distinct influences, external and internal, which, however diverse, are closely connected with each other, and yet within narrow limits, that, however easy it may be to disturb or suspend the process under notice, it is beyond measure difficult to effect a determinate perturbation. If too powerful, it would obviate the phenomenon: if too feeble, it would not sufficiently mark the artificial case. And, on the other hand, though intended

EXPERIMENT.

and directed to modify one only of the phenomena, it must presently affect several others, in virtue of their mutual sympathy. Thus, it requires a highly philosophical spirit, acting with extreme circumspection, to conduct physiological experiments at all; and it is no wonder if such experiments have, with a few happy exceptions, raised scientific difficulties greater than those proposed to be solved,—to say nothing of those innumerable experiments which, having no definite aim, have merely encumbered the science with idle and unconnected details.

In accordance with what has been said of the mutual relations of the organism and its environment, we must bear in mind that experiments in physiology must be of two kinds. We must introduce determinate perturbations into the medium as well as the organism; whereas the latter process has alone been commonly attempted. If it is objected that the organism must itself be disturbed by such affection of the medium, the answer is that the study of this reaction is itself a part of the experiment. It should be remarked that experimentation on the organism is much the less rational of the two methods, because the conditions of experiment are much less easily fulfilled. The first rule, that the change introduced shall be fully compatible with the existence of the phenomenon to be observed, is rendered often impracticable by the incompatibility of life with much alteration of the organs: and the second rule,—that the two compared cases shall differ under only one point of view,—is baffled by the mutual sympathy of the organs, which is very different from their harmony with their environment. In both lights, nothing can be imagined more futile in the way of experiment than the practice of vivisection, which is the commonest of all. Setting aside the consideration of the cruelty, the levity, and the bad moral stimulus involved in the case, it must be pronounced absurd; for any positive solution is rendered impossible by the induced death of a system eminently indivisible, and the universal disturbance of the organism under its approach.

*By affecting the organism.*

*By affecting the Medium.* The second class of physiological experiments appears to me much more promising:

—that in which the system of exterior circumstances is modified for a determinate purpose. Scarcely anything has been done in this direction beyond some incomplete researches into the action of artificial atmospheres, and the comparative influence of different kinds of alimentation. We are here better able to circumscribe, with scientific precision, the artificial perturbation we produce; we can control the action upon the organism, so that the general disturbance of the system may affect the observation very slightly; and we can suspend the process at pleasure, so as to allow the restoration of the normal state before the organism has undergone any irreparable change. It is easy to see how favourable, in comparison, these conditions are to rational induction. And to these considerations may be added the one more, that under this method we can observe varying states in one individual; whereas, under the practice of vivisection, we have to observe the normal state in one individual, and the artificial in another. Thus we are justified in our satisfaction that the least violent method of experimentation is the most instructive.

As to the application of experiment in the various degrees of the biological scale;—it is easiest in the lower order of organisms, *Comparative experiment.* because their organs are simpler and fewer, their mutual sympathy is less, and their environment is more definite and less complex; and these advantages, in my opinion, more than compensate for the restriction of the field of experiment. It is true, we are remote from the human type, which is the fundamental unity of biology; and our judgment is thus impaired, especially with regard to the phenomena of animal life: but, on the other hand, we are all the nearer to the scientific constitution proper to inorganic physics, which I consider to be the ultimate destination of the art of experiment. The advantages at the other end of the scale are that the higher the organism, the more is it susceptible of modification, both from its own complexity and from the greater variety of external influences involved;—every advantage bringing with it, as we have seen, an increase of difficulty.

No one will suppose, I trust, that from anything I have said I have the slightest desire to undervalue the use of experiment in biology, or to slight such achievements as Harvey's experiments on circulation; Haller's on irritability; part of Spallanzani's on digestion and generation; Bichat's on the triple harmony between the heart, the brain, and the lungs in the superior animals; those of Legallois on animal heat; and many analogous efforts which, seeing the vast difficulty of the subject, may rival the most perfect investigations in physics. My object is simply to rectify the false or exaggerated notions of the capacity of the experimental method, misled by its apparent facility to suppose it the best method of physiological research; which it is not. One consideration remains in this connection; the consideration of the high scientific destination of pathological investigation, regarded as offering, in biology, the real equivalent of experimentation, properly so called.

*Pathological Investigation.* Precisely in the case in which artificial experimentation is the most difficult, nature fulfils the conditions for us; and it would surely be mistaking the means for the end to insist on introducing into the organism perturbations of our own devising, when we may find them taking place without that additional confusion which is caused by the use of artificial methods. Physiological phenomena lend themselves remarkably to that spontaneous experimentation which results from a comparison of the normal and abnormal states of the organism. The state of disease is not a radically different condition from that of health. The pathological condition is to the physiological simply a prolongation of the limits of variation, higher or lower, proper to each phenomenon of the normal organism; and it can never produce any entirely new phenomenon. Therefore, the accurate idea of the physiological state is the indispensable ground of any sound pathological theory; and therefore, again, must the scientific study of pathological phenomenon be the best way to perfect our investigations into the normal state. The gradual invasion of a malady, and the slow passage from an almost natural condition to one of fully marked disease, are far from being useless preliminaries, got rid of by the abrupt introduction of what may be called the violent malady of direct experiment: they offer, on the contrary, inestimable materials to the biologist able to put them to use. And so it is also in the happy converse case, of the return, spontaneous or contrived, to health, which presents a sort of verification of the primitive analysis. Moreover, the direct examination of the chief phenomenon is not obscured, but much elucidated, by this natural process. And again, it may be applied directly to Man himself, without prejudice to the pathology of animals, and even of vegetables. We may enjoy our power of turning our disasters to the profit of our race: and we cannot but deplore the misfortune that our great medical establishments are so constituted as that little rational instruction is obtained from them, for want of complete observations and duly prepared observers.

Here, as elsewhere, the distinction holds of the phenomena belonging to the organism or to the medium; and here, as before, we find the maladies produced from without the most accessible to inquiry. Pathological inquiry is also more suitable than experimental, to the whole biological series: and thus it answers well to extend our observations through the entire hierarchy, though our object may be the study of Man; for his maladies may receive much light from a sound analysis of the derangements of other organisms,—even the vegetable, as we shall see when we treat of the comparative process.

Again, pathological analysis is applicable, not only to all organisms, but to all phenomena of the same organism; whereas direct experimentation is too disturbing and too abrupt to be ever applied with success to certain phenomena which require the most delicate harmony of a varied system of conditions. For instance, the observation of the numerous maladies of the nervous system offers us a special and inestimable means of improving our knowledge of the laws of intellectual and moral phenomena, imperfect as are yet our qualifications for using them. There remains one other means of knowledge under this head; the examination of exceptional organizations, or cases of monstrosity. As might be anticipated, these organic anomalies were the last to pass over from the gaze of a barren curiosity to the investigation of science; but we are now learning to refer them to the laws of the regular organism, and to subject them to pathological procedures, regarding such exceptions as true maladies, of a deeper and more obscure origin than others, and of a more incurable nature;—considerations which, of course, reduce their scientific value. This resource shares with pathology the advantage of being applicable through the whole range of the biological system.

It is still necessary to insist that, in either method of experimentation, direct or indirect, artificial or natural, the elementary rules should be kept in view; first, to have a determinate aim; that is, to seek to illustrate an organic phenomenon, under a special aspect; and, secondly, to understand beforehand the normal state, and its limits of variation. In regard to the more advanced sciences, it would seem puerile to recommend such maxims as these; but we must still insist on them in biology. It is through neglect of them that all the observations yet collected on the derangements of the intellectual and moral phenomena have yielded scarcely any knowledge of their laws. Thus, whatever may be the value of the most suitable method of experimentation, we must ever remember that here, as elsewhere, and more than elsewhere, pure observation must always hold the first rank, as casting light, primarily, on the whole subject, which it is proposed to examine afterwards, as a special study, with a determinate view, by the method of experimentation.

COMPARISON. In the third place, we have to review the method of Comparison, which is so specially adapted to the study of living bodies, and by which, above all others, that study must be advanced. In Astronomy, this method is necessarily inapplicable: and it is not till we arrive at Chemistry that this third means of investigation can be used; and then, only in subordination to the two others. It is in the study, both statical and dynamical, of living bodies, that it first acquires its full development; and its use elsewhere can be only through its application here.

The fundamental condition of its use is the unity of the principal subject, in combination with a great diversity of actual modifications. According to the definition of life, this combination is eminently realized in the study of biological phenomena, however regarded. The whole system of biological science is derived, as we have seen, from one great philosophical conception; the necessary correspondence between the ideas of organization and those of life. There cannot be a more perfect fundamental unity of subject than this; and it is unnecessary to insist upon the almost indefinite variety of its modifications,—statical and dynamical. In a purely anatomical view, all possible organisms, all the parts of each organism, and all the different states of each, necessarily present a common basis of structure and of composition, whence proceed successively the different secondary organizations which constitute tissues, organs, and systems of organs, more or less complicated. In the same way, in a physiological view, all living beings, from vegetable to man, considered in all the acts and periods of their existence, are endowed with a certain common vitality, which is a necessary basis of the innumerable phenomena which characterize them in their degrees. Both these aspects present as most important, and really fundamental, what there is in common among all the cases; and their particularities as of less consequence; which is in accordance with the great prevalent law, that the more general phenomena overrule the less. Thus broad and sound is the basis of the comparative method, in regard to biology.

At the first glance the immensity of the science is overwhelming to the understanding, embracing as it does all organic and vital cases, which it appears impossible ever to reduce within the compass of our knowledge: and no doubt, the discouragement hence arising is one cause of the backwardness of biological philosophy. Yet the truth is that this very magnitude affords, not an obstacle, but a facility to the perfecting of the science, by means of the luminous comparison which results from it, when once the human mind becomes familiar enough with the conditions of the study to dispose its materials so as to illustrate each other. The science could make no real progress while Man was studied as an isolated subject. Man must necessarily be the type; because he is the most complete epitome of the whole range of cases: Man, in his adult and normal state, is the representative of the great scientific unity, whence the successive terms of the great biological series recede, till they terminate in the simplest organizations, and the most imperfect modes of existence. But the science would remain in the most defective state in regard to Man himself, if it were not pursued through a perpetual comparison, under all possible aspects, of the first term with all inferior ones, till the simplest was reached: and then, back again, through the successive complications which occur between the lowest type and the highest. This is the most general, the most certain, the most effectual method of studying physiological as well as anatomical phenomena. Not only is there thus a greater number of cases known, but each case is much better understood by their approximation. This would not be the case, and the problem would be embarrassed instead of simplified, if there were not a fundamental resemblance among the whole series, accompanied by gradual modifications, always regulated in their course: and this is the reason why the comparative method is appropriate to biology alone, of all the sciences, except, as we shall see hereafter, in social physics.

Complete and spontaneous as this harmony really is, no philosopher can contemplate without admiration the eminent art by which the human mind has been aided to convert into a potent means what appeared at first to be a formidable difficulty. I know no stronger evidence of the force of human reason than such a transformation affords. And in this case, as in every other in which primordial scientific powers are concerned, it is the work of the whole race, gradually developed in the course of ages, and not the original product of any isolated mind,—however some moderns may be asserted to be the creators of comparative biology. Between the primitive use that Aristotle made of this method in the easiest cases,—as in comparing the structure of Man's upper and lower limbs,—to the most profound and abstract approximations of existing biology, we find a very extensive series of intermediate states, constantly progressive, among which history can point out individually only labours which prove what had been the advance in the spirit of the comparative art at the corresponding period, as manifested by its larger and more effectual application. It is evident that the comparative method of biologists was no more the invention of an individual than the experimental method of the physicists.

There are five principal heads under which biological comparisons are to be classed. *Five kinds of comparison.*

1. Comparison between the different parts of the same organism.
2. Comparison between the sexes.
3. Comparison between the various phases presented by the whole of the development.
4. Comparison between the different races or varieties of each species.
5. Lastly, and pre-eminently, Comparison between all the organisms of the biological hierarchy.

It must be understood that the organism is always to be supposed in a normal state. When the laws of that state are fully established, we may pass on to pathological comparison, which will extend the scope of those laws: but we are not yet advanced enough in our knowledge of normal conditions to undertake anything beyond. Moreover, though comparative pathology would be a necessary application of biological science, it cannot form a part of that science, but rather belongs to the future medical science, of which it must form the basis.—Again, biological comparison can take place only between the organisms, and not between them and their medium. When such comparison comes to be instituted, it will be, not as biological science, but as a matter of natural history.

The spirit of biological comparison is the same under all forms. It consists in regarding all cases as radically analogous in respect to the proposed investigation, and in representing their differences as simple modifications of an abstract type; so that secondary differences may be connected with the primary according to uniform laws; these laws constituting the biological philosophy by which each determinate case is to be explained. If the question is anatomical, Man, in his adult and normal state, is taken for the fundamental unity, and all other organizations as successive simplifications, descending from the primitive type, whose essential features will be found in the remotest cases, stripped of all complication. If the question is physiological, we seek the fundamental identity of the chief phenomenon which characterises the function proposed, amidst the graduated modifications of the series of comparative cases, till we find it isolated, or nearly so, in the simplest case of all; and thence we may trace it back again, clothed in successive complications of secondary qualities. Thus, the theory of analogous existences, which has been offered as a recent innovation, is only the necessary principle of the comparative method, under a new name. It is evident that this method must be of surpassing value when philosophically applied: and also that, delicate as it is, and requiring extreme discrimination and care in its estimate and use, it may be easily converted into a hindrance and embarrassment, by giving occasion to vicious speculations on analogies which are only apparent.

Of the five classes specified above, three only are so marked as to require a notice here: the comparison between the different parts of the same organism; between the different phases of each development; and between the distinct terms of the great hierarchy of living bodies.

Comparison of parts of the same organism. The method of comparison began with the first of these. Looking no further than Man, no philosophical mind can help being struck by the remarkable resemblance that his different chief parts bear to each other in many respects,—both as to structure and function. First, all the tissues, all the apparatus, in as far as they are organized and living, offer those fundamental characteristics which are inherent in the very ideas of organization and life, and to which the lowest organisms are reduced. But, in a more special view, the analogy of the organs becomes more and more marked as that of the functions is so; and the converse; and this often leads to luminous comparisons, anatomical and physiological, passing from the one to the other, alternately. This original and simple method of comparison is by no means driven out by newer processes. It was thus, for instance, that Bichat, whose subject was Man only, and adult Man, discovered the fundamental analogy between the mucous and the cutaneous systems, which has yielded so much advantage to both biology and pathology. And again, with all M. de Blainville's mastery of the principle of the comparative method, we cannot doubt the sufficiency of the analysis of the human organism to establish the resemblance he exhibited between the skull and the other elements of the vertebral column.

A new order of resources presents itself when we compare the different phases of the same organism. Its chief value is in its offering, on a small scale, and, as it were, under one aspect, the whole series of the most marked organisms of the biological hierarchy; for it is obvious that the primitive state of the highest organism must present the essential characters of the complete state of the lowest; and thus successively,—without, however, compelling us to find the counterpart of every inferior term in the superior organism. Such an analysis of ages unquestionably offers the property of realizing in an individual, that successive complication of organs and functions which characterizes the biological hierarchy, and which, in this homogeneous and compact form, constitutes a special and singular order of luminous comparisons. Useful through all degrees of the scale, it is evidently most so in the case of the highest type, the adult Man, as the interval from the origin to the utmost complexity is in that case the greatest. It is valuable chiefly in the visible ascendant period of life; for we know very little of the fœtal period; and the declining stage, which is in fact only a gradual death, presents little scientific interest: for, if there are many ways of living, there is only one natural way of dying. The rational analysis of death, however, has its own importance, constituting a sort of general corollary, convenient for the verification of the whole body of biological laws.

*Of phases of the same organism.*

The popular notion of comparative biology is that it consists wholly of the last of the methods I have pointed out: and this shows how pre-eminent it is over the others; the popular exaggeration however being mischievous by concealing the origin of the art. The peculiarity of this largest application consists in its being founded on a very protracted comparison of a very extensive series of analogous cases, in which the modification proceeds by almost insensible graduated declension. The two more restricted methods could not offer a series of cases extensive enough to establish, without con-

*Of different organisms.*

firmation, the nature and value of the comparative method, though, that point once fixed, they may then come into unquestionable use. As for the value of the largest application, it demonstrates itself. There is clearly no structure or function whose analysis may not be perfected by an examination of what all organisms offer in common with regard to that structure and function, and by the simplification effected by the stripping away of all accessory characteristics, till the quality sought is found alone, from whence the process of reconstruction can begin. It may even be fairly said that no anatomical arrangement, and no physiological phenomenon, can be really understood till the abstract notion of its principal element is thus reached, by successively attaching to it all secondary ideas, in the rational order prescribed by their greater or less persistence in the organic series. Such a method seems to me to offer, in biology, a philosophical character very like mathematical analysis genuinely applied; when it presents, as we have seen, in every indefinite series of analogous cases, the essential part which is common to all, and which was before hidden under the secondary specialities of each separate case. It cannot be doubted that the comparative art of biologists will produce an equivalent result, up to a certain point; and especially, by the rational consideration of the organic hierarchy.

This great consideration was at first established only in regard to anatomy; but it is yet more necessary in physiology, and not less applicable, except from the difficulty of that kind of observation. In regard to physiological problems particularly, it should be remarked that not only all animal organisms, but the vegetable also, should be included in the comparison. Many important phenomena, and among others those of organic life, properly so called, cannot be analysed without an inclusion of the vegetable form of them. There we see them in their simplest and most marked condition, for it is by the great act of vegetable assimilation that brute matter passes really into the organized state, all ulterior transformations by means of the animal organization being much less marked. And thus, the laws of nutrition, which are of the highest importance, are best disclosed by the vegetable organism.

The method is unquestionably applicable to all organs and all acts, without any exception; but its scientific value diminishes as it is applied to the higher apparatus and functions of the superior organisms, because these are restricted in proportion to their complexity and superiority. This is eminently the case with the highest intellectual and moral functions which below Man disappear almost entirely; or, at least, almost cease to be recognizable below the first classes of the mammifers. We cannot but feel it to be an imperfection in the comparative method that it serves us least where we are most in need of all our resources; but it would be unphilosophical to deprive ourselves, even in this case, of the light which is cast upon the analysis of Man as moral, by the study of the intellectual and affective qualities of the superior animals, and of all others which present such attributes, however imperfect our management of the comparison may yet be. And we may observe that the comparative method finds a partial equivalent in the rational analysis of ages,—thus rendered more clear, extensive, and complete,—for the disadvantages which belong to the same stage of the biological hierarchy.

Thus I have presented the principal philosophical characters of the comparative method. It being the aim of biological study to ascertain the general laws of organic existence, it is plain that no course of inquiry could be more favourable than that which exhibits organic cases as radically analogous, and deducible from each other.

This study of our means of exploration has shown that our resources do increase with the complexity of our subject. The two first methods—of Observation and Experiment—we have seen to acquire a large extension in the case of this science: while the third, before almost imperceptible, becomes, by the nature of the phenomena, wellnigh unbounded in its scope. We have next to examine the true rational position of Biology in the hierarchy of the fundamental sciences; that is, its relation to those that precede it, and to the one which follows it, in order to ascertain what kind and degree of speculative perfection it admits of, and what preliminary training is best adapted to its systematic cultivation. By this inquiry we shall see why we are justified in assigning to it a place between chemistry and social science.

**Relation of Biology to other sciences.** Of the relation of Biology to social science, I need say little here, as I shall have to speak of it at length in the next volume. My task will then be to separate them, rather than to establish their connection, which it is the tendency of our time to exaggerate, through the spontaneous development of natural philosophy. None but purely metaphysical philosophers would at this day persist in classing the theory of the human mind and of society as anterior to the anatomical and physiological study of individual man. We may therefore regard this point as sufficiently settled for the present, and pass on to the relation of Biology to inorganic philosophy.

**To Chemistry.** It is to chemistry that Biology is, by its nature, most directly and completely subordinated. In analyzing the phenomenon of life, we saw that the fundamental acts which, by their perpetuity, characterize that state, consist of a series of compositions and decompositions; and they are therefore of a chemical nature. Though in the most imperfect organisms, vital reactions are widely separated from common chemical effects, it is not the less true that all the functions of the proper organic life are necessarily controlled by those fundamental laws of composition and decomposition which constitute the subject of chemical science. If we could conceive throughout the whole scale the same separation of the organic from the animal life that we see in vegetables alone, the vital motion would offer only chemical conceptions, except the essential circumstances which distinguish such an order of molecular reactions. The general source of these important differences is, in my opinion, to be looked for in the result of each chemical conflict not depending only on the simple composition of the bodies between which it takes place, but being modified by their proper organization; that is, by their anatomical structure. Chemistry must clearly furnish the starting-point of every rational theory of nutrition, secretion, and, in short, all the functions of the vegetative life, considered separately; each of which is controlled by the influence of chemical laws, except for the special modifications belonging to organic conditions. If we now bring in again the consideration, discarded for the moment, of the animal life, we see that it could in no way alter this fundamental subordination, though it must greatly complicate its actual application: for we have seen that the animal life, notwithstanding its vast importance, can never be regarded in biology otherwise than as destined to extend and perfect the organic life, whose general nature it cannot change. Such an intervention modifies, anew and largely, the chemical laws of the purely organic functions, so as to render the effect very difficult to foresee; but not the less do these laws continue to control the aggregate of the phenomena. If, for instance, a change in the nervous condition of a superior organism disturbs a given secretion, as to its energy or even its nature, we cannot conceive that such an alteration can be of a random kind: such modifications, irregular as they may appear, are still submitted to the chemical laws of the fundamental organic phenomenon, which permit certain variations, but interdict many more. Thus, no complication produced by animal life can withdraw the organic functions from their subordination to the laws of composition and decomposition. This relation is so important, that no scientific theory could be conceived of in biology without it; since, in its absence, the most fundamental phenomena might be conceived of as susceptible of arbitrary variations, which would not admit of any true law. When we hear, at this day, on the subject of azote, such a doctrine as that the organism has the power of spontaneously creating certain elementary substances, we perceive how indispensable it still is to insist directly on those principles which alone can restrain the spirit of aberration.

Besides this direct subordination of biology to chemistry, there are relations of method between them. Observation and experimentation being much more perfect in chemistry, they serve as an admirable training for biological inquiry. Again, a special property of chemistry is its developing the art of scientific nomenclature; and it is in chemistry that biologists must study this important part of the positive method, though it cannot, from the complexity of their science, be of so much scientific value as in chemistry. It is on the model of the chemical nomenclature that those systematic denominations have been laid down by which biologists have classified the most simple anatomical arrangements, certain well-defined pathological states, and the most general degrees of the animal hierarchy: and it is by a continued pursuit of the same method that further improvements will be effected.

We thus see why biology takes its place next after chemistry, and why chemical inquiries constitute a natural transition from the inorganic to the organic philosophy.

To Physics. The subordination of biology to Physics follows from its relation to Chemistry: but there are also direct reasons, relating both to doctrine and method, why it should be so.

As to doctrine,—it is clear that the general laws of one or more branches of Physics must be applied in the analysis of any physiological phenomenon. This application is necessary in the examination of the medium, in the first place; and the analysis of the medium is required to be very exact, on account of the strong effect of its variations on phenomena so easily modified as those of the organism. And next, the organism itself is no less dependent on those laws, relating as they do to weight, heat, electricity, etc. It is obvious that if biology is related to chemistry through the organic life, it is related to physics by the animal life,—the most special and noble of the sensations, those of sight and hearing, requiring for the starting-point of their investigation an application of optics and acoustics. The same remark holds good in regard to the theory of utterance, and the study of animal heat and the electric properties of the organism. It remains to be wished that the biologists would study and apply these laws themselves, instead of committing the task to physicists: but they have hitherto followed too much the example of the physicists, who, as we have seen, have committed the application of mathematical analysis in their own science to the geometers; whereas, it cannot be too carefully remembered that if the more general sciences are independent of the less general, which, on the other hand, must be dependent on them, the students of the higher must be unfit, in virtue of that very independence, to apply them to a more complex science, whose conditions they cannot sufficiently understand. If the case was clear in regard to the intrusion of the geometers into physics, it is yet more so with regard to the intrusion of the physicists into biology; on account of the more essential difference in the nature of the two sciences. The biologists should qualify themselves for the application of the preceding sciences to their own, instead of looking to the physicists for guidance which can only lead them astray.

In regard to Method, biology is indebted to physics for the most perfect models of observation and experimentation. Observations in physics are of a sufficient complexity to serve as a type for the same method in biology, if divested of their numerical considerations, which is easily done. Chemistry however can furnish an almost equally good model in simple observation. It is in experimentation that biologists may find in physics a special training for their work. As the most perfect models are found in the study of physics, and the method is singularly difficult in physiology, we see how important the contemplation of the best type must be to biologists. Such is the nature of the dependence, as to doctrine and method, of biology on physics. We turn next to its relations with Astronomy; and first, with regard to doctrine.

The relation of physiology to astronomy is more important than is usually supposed. I mean something more than the impossibility of understanding the theory of weight, and its effects upon the organism, apart from the consideration of general gravitation. I mean, besides, and more specially, that it is impossible to form a scientific conception of the conditions of vital existence without taking into the account the aggregate astronomical elements that characterize the planet which is the home of that vital existence. We shall see more fully, in the next volume, how humanity is affected by these astronomical conditions; but we must cursorily review these relations in the present connection.

*To Astronomy.*

The astronomical data proper to our planet are, of course, statical and dynamical. The biological importance of the statical conditions is immediately obvious. No one questions the importance to vital existence of the mass of our planet in comparison with that of the sun, which determines the intensity of gravity; or of its form, which regulates the direction of the force; or of the fundamental equilibrium and the regular oscillations of the fluids which cover the greater part of its surface, and with which the existence of living beings is closely implicated; or of its dimensions, which limit the indefinite multiplication of races, and especially the human; or of its distance from the centre of our system, which chiefly determines its temperature. Any sudden change in one or more of these conditions would largely modify the phenomena of life. But the influence of the dynamical conditions of astronomy on biological study is yet more important. Without the two conditions of the fixity of the poles as a centre of rotation, and the uniformity of the angular velocity of the earth, there would be a continual perturbation of the organic media which would be incompatible with life. Bichat pointed out that the intermittence of the proper animal life is subordinate in its periods to the diurnal rotation of our planet; and we may extend the observation to all the periodical phenomena of any organism, in both the normal and pathological states, allowance being made for secondary and transient influences. Moreover, there is every reason to believe that, in every organism, the total duration of life and of its chief natural phases depends on the angular velocity proper to our planet; for we are authorized to admit that, other things being equal, the duration of life must be shorter, especially in the animal organism, in proportion as the vital phenomena succeed each other more rapidly. If the earth were to rotate much faster, the course of physiological phenomena would be accelerated in proportion; and thence life would be shorter; so that the duration of life may be regarded as dependent on the duration of the day. If the duration of the year were changed, the life of the organism would again be affected: but a yet more striking consideration is that vital existence is absolutely implicated with the form of the earth's orbit, as has been observed before. If that ellipse were to become, instead of nearly circular, as eccentric as the orbit of a comet, both the medium and the organism would undergo a change fatal to vital existence. Thus the small eccentricity of the earth's orbit is one of the main conditions of biological phenomena, almost as necessary as the stability of the earth's rotation; and every other element of the annual motion exercises an influence, more or less marked, on biological conditions, though not so great as the one we have adduced. The inclination of the plane of the orbit, for instance, determines the division of the earth into climates, and, consequently, the geographical distribution of living species, animal and vegetable. And again, through the alternation of seasons, it influences the phases of individual existence in all organisms; and there is no doubt that life would be affected if the revolution of the line of the nodes were accelerated; so that its being nearly immoveable has some biological value. These considerations indicate how necessary it is for biologists to inform themselves accurately, and without any intervention, of the real elements proper to the astronomical constitution of our planet. An inexact knowledge will not suffice. The laws of the limits of variation of the different elements, or, at least, a scientific analysis of the chief grounds of their permanence, are essential to biological investigation; and these can be obtained only through an acquaintance with astronomical conceptions, both geometrical and mechanical.

It may at first appear anomalous, and a breach of the encyclopedical arrangement of the sciences, that astronomy and biology should be thus immediately and eminently connected, while two other sciences lie between. But, indispensable as are physics and chemistry, astronomy and biology are, by their nature, the two principal branches of natural philosophy. They, the complements of each other, include in their rational harmony the general system of our fundamental conceptions. The solar system and Man are the extreme terms within which our ideas will for ever be included. The system first, and then Man, according to the positive course of our speculative reason: and the reverse in the active process: the laws of the system determining those of Man, and remaining unaffected by them. Between these two poles of natural philosophy the laws of physics interpose, as a kind of complement of the astronomical laws; and again, those of chemistry, as an immediate preliminary of the biological.

Such being the rational and indissoluble constitution of these sciences, it becomes apparent why I insisted on the subordination of the study of Man to that of the system, as the primary philosophical characteristic of positive biology.

Though in the infancy of the human mind, when it was in its theological state, and in its youthful metaphysical stage, the order of these sciences was reversed, there was a preparation for the true view. Through all the fanciful notions of the ancient philosophy about the physiological influence of the stars, we discern a strong though vague perception of some connection between vital and celestial phenomena. Like all primitive intuitions of the understanding, this one needed only rectification by the positive philosophy; under the usual condition, however, of being partially overthrown in order to be reorganized. But modern students, finding no astronomical conditions in the course of their anatomical and physiological observations, have discarded the idea of them altogether,—as if it were ever possible for facts to bear immediate testimony to the conditions without which they could not exist, and which do not admit of a moment's suspension! Such an order of primitive conditions is however now established beyond dispute. In order to prevent any return to vicious or exaggerated notions about the physiological influence of the stars, it is enough to bear in mind two considerations: first, that the astronomical conditions of vital existence are comprised within our own planetary system; and secondly, that they relate, not directly to the organism, but to its environment, affecting as they do the constitution of our globe.

In regard to method,—the importance of astronomical study to biologists consists, as in other cases, in its offering the most perfect model of philosophizing on any phenomena whatever; the importance of this example becoming greater in proportion to the complexity of the subordinate science, on account of the stronger temptation to discursive and idle inquiries offered by the latter. The more difficult their researches become, the more sedulous should physiologists be to refresh their positive forces at the source of positive knowledge; and, in the contemplation of the few general and indisputable conceptions which constitute this lofty science, to be on their guard against the baseless notions of a vital principle, vital forces, and entities of that character. Hitherto, all advance in positivity in biology has been obtained at the expense of its dignity, which has always been implicated with an imaginary origin of life, of sensibility, etc.: but when physiologists have learned from their study of gravitation and other primary laws how to confine themselves to true science, their subject will rise to the highest elevation that positivity admits of,—that rational prevision of events which is, as I have so often said, the end of true science:—an end to be aimed at in biology, as it is perfectly fulfilled in astronomy.

Here, too, must biologists learn the character of sound scientific hypothesis. This method is eminently wanted in so complex a study as physiology; but it has been as yet used with very little effect. The way is, undoubtedly, to determine the organ from the function, or the function from the organ. It is permissible to form the most plausible hypothesis as to the unknown function of a given organ, or the concealed organ of a manifest function. If the supposition be in harmony with existing knowledge, if it be held provisionally, and if it be capable of a positive verification, it may contribute to the progress of discovery, and is simply a use of a right of the human mind, exercised as in astronomy. The only eminent example known to me of sound hypothesis in biology is that of M. Broussais, in proposing the mucous membrane of the alimentary canal as the seat of so-called essential fevers. Whether he was mistaken or not, is not the question. His hypothesis being open to unquestionable confirmation or subversion, it gave a great impulse to the study of pathology in a positive manner: and it will stand in the history of the human mind, as the first example of the spontaneous introduction of a sound hypothetical method into the positive study of living beings: a method derived from the region of astronomy.

It remains to consider the relation of biology to mathematics.

The encroachments of the pure geometers upon the domain of biology have been at- | To mathematics.

tended with the same mischief, but in an aggravated form, that we have witnessed in the case of other sciences. This mischief has led physiologists to repudiate mathematics altogether, and open an impassable gulf between themselves and the geometers. This is a mistake; inasmuch as their science cannot be severed from that which is the basis of the whole of natural philosophy; and it is only through the admission of this that they can maintain the originality and independence of their scientific labours. The rational study of nature proceeds on the ground that all phenomena are subject to invariable laws, which it is the business of philosophical speculation to discover. It is needless to prove that on any other supposition, science could not exist, and our collections of facts could yield no result. In the phenomena of living bodies, as in all others, every action proceeds according to precise, that is, mathematical laws, which we should ascertain if we could study each phenomenon by itself. The phenomena of the inorganic world are, for the most part, simple enough to be calculable: those of the organic world are too complex for our management: but this has nothing to do with any difference in their nature. And this is the view which both geometers and biologists should bear in mind.

If in astronomy our calculations are baffled when we pass beyond two or three essential conditions, it is evident how impracticable they must be amidst the inextricable complications of physiology. And again, this complexity prevents our ever effecting a mathematical disclosure of the elementary laws of the science. This excludes all idea of this method of philosophizing in biology; for these laws are no otherwise accessible than by the immediate analysis of their numerical effects. Now, whichever way vital phenomena are looked at, they present such endless and incessant variations in their numbers, that geometers are baffled as completely as if those degrees were entirely arbitrary. Even numerical chemistry is inapplicable to bodies whose molecular composition varies incessantly; and this is precisely the distinguishing character of living organisms. However hurtful may have been the incursions of the geometers, direct and indirect, into a domain which it is not for them to cultivate, the physiologists are not the less wrong in turning away from mathematics altogether. It is not only that without mathematics they could not receive their due preliminary training in the intervening sciences: it is further necessary for them to have geometrical and mechanical knowledge, to understand the structure and the play of the complex apparatus of the living, and especially the animal organism. Animal mechanics, statical and dynamical, must be unintelligible to those who are ignorant of the general laws of rational mechanics. The laws of equilibrium and motion are, as we saw when treating of them, absolutely universal in their action, depending wholly on the energy, and not at all on the nature of the forces considered: and the only difficulty is in their numerical application in cases of complexity. Thus, discarding all idea of a numerical application in biology, we perceive that the general theorems of statics and dynamics must be steadily verified in the mechanism of living bodies, on the rational study of which they cast an indispensable light. The highest orders of animals act, in repose and motion, like any other mechanical apparatus of a similar complexity, with the one difference of the mover, which has no power to alter the laws of motion and equilibrium. The participation of rational mechanics in positive biology is thus evident. Mechanics cannot dispense with geometry; and besides, we see how anatomical and physiological speculations involve considerations of form and position, and require a familiar knowledge of the principal geometrical laws which may cast light upon those complex relations.

In regard to Method, the necessity of recurring to a perfect model of reasoning, the more earnestly in proportion to the complexity of the science concerned, is applicable in regard to Mathematics, as to Astronomy; only with still greater urgency. In mathematics we find the primitive source of rationality; and to mathematics must the biologists resort for means to carry on their researches. If biologists have hitherto not done this, but contented themselves with what is called logic, apart from all determinate reasoning, much of the fault is chargeable upon the indifference of geometers about duly organizing the whole of mathematical knowledge. The imperfect and inadequate character of the elementary treatises on mathematics that have hitherto been given to the world quite accounts for the neglect of the fundamental logical properties of mathematical science by even intelligent minds. It accounts also for the exaggerations of some philosophers, who maintain that, far from preparing the intellectual organ for the rational interpretation of nature, a mathematical education rather tends to develop a spirit of sophistical argumentation and illusory speculation. Such an abuse, however, cannot affect the real value of mathematics as a means of positive education; but rather exhibits the necessity of a philosophical renovation of the whole system of mathematical instruction. Whatever advantage can be attributed to logic in directing and strengthening the action of the understanding is found in a higher degree in mathematical study, with the immense added advantage of a determinate subject, distinctly circumscribed, admitting of the utmost precision, and free from the danger which is inherent in all abstract logic,—of leading to useless and puerile rules, or to vain ontological speculations. The positive method, being everywhere identical, is as much at home in the art of reasoning as anywhere else: and this is why no science, whether biology or any other, can offer any kind of reasoning, of which mathematics does not supply a simpler and purer counterpart. Thus, we are enabled to eliminate the only remaining portion of the old philosophy which could even appear to offer any real utility; the logical part, the value of which is irrevocably absorbed by mathematical science. Hither, then, must biologists come, to study the logical art so as to apply it to the advancement of their difficult researches. In this school must they learn familiarly the real characters and conditions of scientific evidence, in order to transfer it afterwards to the province of their own theories. The study of it here, in the most simple and perfect cases, is the only sound preparation for its recognition in the most complex.

The study is equally necessary for the formation of intellectual habits; for obtaining an aptitude in forming and sustaining positive abstractions, without which the comparative method cannot be used in either anatomy or physiology. The abstraction which is to be the standard of comparison must be first clearly formed, and then steadily maintained in its integrity, or the analysis becomes abortive: and this is so completely in the spirit of mathematical combinations, that practice in them is the best preparation for it. A student who cannot accomplish the process in the more simple case may be assured that he is not qualified for the higher order of biological researches, and must be satisfied with the humbler office of collecting materials for the use of minds of another order. Hence arises another use of mathematical training;—that of testing and classifying minds, as well as preparing and guiding them. Probably as much good would be done by excluding the students who only encumber the science by aimless and desultory inquiries, as by fitly instituting those who can better fulfil its conditions.

There seems no sufficient reason why the use of scientific fictions, so common in the hands of geometers, should not be introduced into biology, if systematically employed, and adopted with sufficient sobriety. In mathematical studies, great advantages have arisen from imagining a series of hypothetical cases, the consideration of which, though artificial, may aid the clearing up of the real subject, or its fundamental elaboration. This art is usually confounded with that of hypotheses; but it is entirely different; inasmuch as in the latter case the solution alone is imaginary; whereas in the former, the problem itself is radically ideal. Its use can never be in biology comparable to what it is in mathematics: but it seems to me that the abstract character of the higher conceptions of comparative biology renders them susceptible of such treatment. The process would be to intercalate, among different known organisms, certain purely fictitious organisms, so imagined as to facilitate their comparison, by rendering the biological series more homogeneous and continuous: and it might be that several might hereafter meet with more or less of a realization among organisms hitherto unexplored. It may be possible, in the present state of our knowledge of living bodies, to conceive of a new organism capable of fulfilling certain given conditions of existence. However that may be, the

*Use of scientific fictions.*

collocation of real cases with well-imagined ones, after the manner of geometers, will doubtless be practised hereafter, to complete the general laws of comparative anatomy and physiology, and possibly to anticipate occasionally the direct exploration. Even now, the rational use of such an artifice might greatly simplify and clear up the ordinary system of pure biological instruction. But it is only the highest order of investigators who can be entrusted with it. Whenever it is adopted, it will constitute another ground of relation between biology and mathematics.

We have now gone over all those grounds,—both of doctrine and of method. Of the three parts of mathematics, Mechanics is connected with biology in the scientific point of view; and geometry in the logical: while both rest upon the analytical theories which are indispensable to their systematic development.

This specification of the relations of biology determines its rank in the hierarchy of sciences. From this again we learn the kind and degree of perfection of which biology is susceptible; and, more directly, the rational plan of preliminary education which it indicates.

*Condition and prospects of the science.* If the perfection of a science were to be estimated by the means of its pursuit, biology would evidently excel all others; for we can concentrate upon it the whole of the resources of observation and of reasoning offered by all the others, together with some of high importance appropriate to itself. Yet, all this wealth of resources is an insufficient compensation for the accumulated obstacles which beset the science. The difficulty is not so much in its recent passage into the positive state as in the high complexity of its phenomena. After the wisest use of all our resources, this study must ever remain inferior to all the departments of inorganic philosophy, not excepting chemistry itself. Still, its speculative improvement will be greater than might be supposed by those who are unaware how incomplete and barren is the accumulation of observations and heterogeneous conceptions which now goes by the name of the science. All that has yet been done should be regarded as a preliminary operation,—an ascertainment and trial of means, hitherto provisional, but henceforth to be organized. Such an organization having really taken place among a few qualified investigators, the state of the science may be regarded as very satisfactory. As for the direct establishment of biological laws, the few positive ideas that we have obtained justify the expectation that the science of living bodies may attain to a real co-ordination of phenomena, and therefore to their prevision, to a greater or smaller extent.

As for the requisite education,—as it comprehends the study of the preceding sciences, from mathematics downwards, it is clearly of a more extensive and difficult order than any hitherto prescribed. But the time saved from the useless study of words, and from futile metaphysical speculations, would suffice for all the purposes of the regenerated science, which discards these encumbrances. Requisite Education.

If, next, we look at the reaction of the science on the education of the general mind, the first thing that strikes us is that the positive study of Man affords to observers the best test and measure of the mental power of those who pursue the study. In other sciences, the real power of the inquirer and the value of his acquisitions are concealed from popular estimate by the scientific artifices which are requisite for the pursuit; as in the case of mathematics, whose hieroglyphic language is very imposing to the uninitiated: so that men of extremely small ability, rendering very doubtful services, have obtained a high reputation for themselves and their achievements. But this can hardly take place in biology; and the preference which popular good sense has accorded to the study of Man as a test of scientific intelligence is therefore well-grounded. Here the most important phenomena are common to all; and the race may be said to concur in the study of Man: and, the more difficult and doubtful the ascertainment of general laws in so complex a science, the higher is the value of individual and original meditation. When these laws become better known, this originality will yield some of its value to the ability which will then be requisite for their application. The moral world will, under all future, as under all past circumstances, regard the knowledge of human nature as the most indubitable sign, and the commonest measure, of true intellectual superiority.

The first intellectual influence of the science is in perfecting, or rather developing, two of the most important of our elementary powers, which are little required by the preceding sciences;—the arts of comparison and of classification, which, however necessary to each other, are perfectly distinct. Of the first, I have said enough; and of the second I shall speak hereafter; so that I have now only to indicate its function in biology.

*Art of Classification.* The universal theory of philosophical classifications, necessary not only to aid the memory but to perfect scientific combinations, cannot be absent from any branch of natural philosophy: but it is incontestable that the full development of the art of classification was reserved for biological science. As we have seen before, each of our elementary powers must be specially developed by that one of our positive studies which requires its most urgent application, and which, at the same time, offers it the most extended field. Under both aspects, biology tends, more than any other science, to favour the spontaneous rise of the general theory of classifications. First, no other so urgently claims a series of rational classifications, on account both of the multiplicity of distinct but analogous beings, and of the necessity of organizing a systematic comparison of them in the form of a biological hierarchy; and next, the same characteristics which demand these classifications facilitate their spontaneous establishment. The multiplicity and complexity are not, as might at first appear, obstacles to the systematic arrangement of subjects: on the contrary, they are aids, as the diversity of their relations offers a greater number of analogies, more extensive and easy to lay hold of. This is the reason why the classification of animals is superior to that of vegetables; the greater variety and complexity of animal organisms affording a better hold for the art of classifying. And thus we see that the very difficulties of the science are of a nature at once to require and permit the most marked and spontaneous development of the general art of classification; and hither must the student in every other department of science resort, to form his conceptions of this all-important method. Here alone can geometers, astronomers, physicists, and even chemists learn the formation of natural groups, and their rational co-ordination; and yet more, the general principle of the subordination of characteristics, which constitutes the chief artifice of the method. The biologists alone, at this day, can be in habitual possession of clear and positive ideas in these three relations.—Each of the fundamental sciences has, as we have already so often seen, the exclusive property of specially developing some one of the great logical procedures of which the whole positive method is composed; and it is thus that the more complex, while dependent on the simpler, react on their superiors by affording them new rational powers and instruments. In this view of the hierarchical character and unity of the system of human knowledge, it becomes clear that the isolation still practised in the organization of our positive studies is as hurtful to their special progress as to their collective action upon the intellectual government of the human race.

Looking now to the higher function of this science,—its influence upon the positive spirit, as well as method,—we have only to try it by the test proposed before;—its power of destroying theological conceptions in two ways:— by the rational prevision of phenomena, and by the voluntary modification of them which it enables Man to exercise. As the phenomena of any science become more complex, the first power decreases, and the other increases, so that the one or the other is always present to show, unquestionably, that the events of the world are not ruled by supernatural will, but by natural laws. Biological science eminently answers to this test. While its complexity allows little prevision, at present, in regard to its phenomena, it supplies us with a full equivalent, in regard to theological conceptions, in the testimony afforded by the analysis of the conditions of action of living bodies. The natural opposition of this species of investigation to every kind of theological and metaphysical conception is particularly remarkable in the case of intellectual and affective

*Influence of Biology upon the Positive spirit.*

phenomena,—the positivism of which is very recent, and which, with the social phenomena that are derived from them, are the last battle-ground, in the popular view, between the positive philosophy and the ancient. In virtue of their complexity, these phenomena are precisely those which require the most determinate and extensive concurrence of various conditions, exterior and interior; so that the positive study of them is eminently fitted to expose the futility of the abstract explanations derived from the theological or metaphysical philosophy. Hence, we easily understand the marked aversion which this study is privileged to arouse among different sects of theologians and metaphysicians. As the labours of anatomists and physiologists disclose the intimate dependence of moral phenomena on the organism and its environment, there is something very striking in the vain efforts of followers of the old philosophies to harmonize with these facts the illusory play of supernatural influences or psychological entities. Thus has the development of biological science put the positive philosophy in possession of the very stronghold of the ancient philosophy. The same effect becomes even more striking in the other direction, from biological phenomena being, beyond all others, susceptible of modification from human intervention. We have a large power of affecting both the organism and its environment, from the very considerable number of the conditions which concur in their existence: and our voluntary power of disturbing phenomena, of suspending, and even destroying them, is so striking as to compel us to reject all idea of a theological or metaphysical direction. As in the other case, of which indeed it is a mere extension, this effect is most particularly marked in regard to moral phenomena, properly so called, which are more susceptible of modification than any others. The most obstinate psychologist could not well persist in maintaining the sovereign independence of his intellectual entities, if he would consider that the mere standing on his head for a moment would put a complete stop to the course of his own speculations. Much as we may wish that, in addition to these evidences, we had that of an extensive power of scientific prevision in biology, such a power is not needed for the conclusions of popular good sense. This prevision is not always baffled: and its success in a few marked cases is sufficient to satisfy the general mind that the phenomena of living bodies are subject, like all others, to invariable natural laws, which we are prevented from interpreting in all cases only by their extreme complexity.

But, moreover, positive biology has a special conquest of its own over the theological and metaphysical systems, by which it has converted an ancient dogma into a new principle. In chemistry the same thing occurred when the primitive notion of absolute creation and destruction was converted into the precise conception of perpetual decomposition and recomposition. In Astronomy, the same thing occurred when the hypothesis of final causes and providential rule gave place to the view of the solar system as the necessary and spontaneous result of the mutual action of the principal masses which compose it. Biology, in its close connection with astronomy, has completed this demonstration. Attacking, in its own way, the elementary dogma of final causes, it has gradually transformed it into the fundamental principle of the conditions of existence, which it is the particular aptitude of biology to develope and systematize. It is a great error in anatomists and physiologists,—an error fatal both to science and theology, —to endeavour to unite the two views. Science compels us to conclude that there is no organ without a function, and no function without an organ. Under the old theological influences, students are apt to fall into a state of anti-scientific admiration when they find the conditions and the fulfilment coincide,—when, having observed a function, anatomical analysis discloses a statical position in the organism which allows the fulfilment of the function. This irrational and barren admiration is hurtful to science, by habituating us to suppose that all organic acts are effected as perfectly as we can imagine, thus repressing the expansion of our biological speculations, and inducing us to admire complexities which are evidently injurious: and it is in direct opposition to religious aims, as it assigns human wisdom as the rule and even the limit of the divine, which, if such a parallel is to be established, must often appear to be the inferior of the two. Though we cannot imagine radically new organisms, we can, as I showed in my suggestion about the use of scientific fictions, conceive of organizations which should differ distinctly from any that are known to us, and which should be incontestably superior to them in certain determinate respects. The philosophical principle of the conditions of existence is in fact simply the direct conception of the necessary harmony of the statical and the dynamical analyses of the subject proposed. This principle is eminently adapted to the science of biology, which is continually engaged in establishing a harmony between the means and the end; and nowhere else, therefore, is seen in such perfection, that double analysis, statical and dynamical, which is found everywhere.

These, then, are the philosophical properties of positive biology. To complete our review of the science as a whole, we have only to note briefly the division and rational co-ordination of its parts.

*Distribution of the science.* It does not fall within the scope of this work to notice several branches of positive biological knowledge, which are of extreme importance in their own place, but secondary in regard to the principles of positive philosophy. We have no concern here with pathology, and the corresponding medical art; nor with natural history, and the corresponding art of the education of organisms. These are naturally, and not untruly, called biological studies: but we must here confine the term strictly to the speculative and abstract researches which are the foundation of the science. The interior distribution of the science, thus regarded, is this.

The speculative and abstract study of the organism must be divided, first, into statics and dynamics; according as we are seeking the laws of organization or those of life: and again, statical biology must be divided into two parts, to which M. de Blainville has given the name, in regard to animals, of *zootomy* and *zootaxy*, according as we study the structure and composition of individual organisms, or construct the great biological hierarchy which results from the comparison of all known organisms. It would be easy to modify M. de Blainville's terms so as to make them common to animals and vegetables. Dynamical biology, to which we may give the name *bionomy*, as the end and aim of the whole set of studies, evidently admits of no analogous subdivision. The general name of Biology thus includes the three divisions, biotomy, biotaxy, and pure bionomy, or physiology properly so called.

Their definition exhibits their necessary dependence; and thereby determines also their philosophical co-ordination. While it is universally allowed that anatomical ideas are indispensable to physiological studies, because the structure must be known before its action can be judged of, the subordination of bionomy to biotaxy is not so well understood. Yet it is easy to see that the place of any organism in the scale must be known before its aggregate phenomena can be effectually studied: and again, the consideration of this hierarchy is indispensable to the use of that grandest instrument of all — the comparative method. Thus, from every point of view, the double relation of dynamical to statical biology is unquestionable.

The two divisions of statical biology are less clearly marked; and it even appears as if, in regard to them, we were involved in a vicious circle: for if, on the one hand, the rational classification of living beings requires the antecedent knowledge of their organization, it is certain, on the other hand, that anatomy itself, like physiology, cannot be studied, in regard to all organisms, without an antecedent formation of the biological hierarchy. Thus we must admit a consolidation of the respective advancements of biotomic and biotaxic studies, through their intimate connection. In such a case, as a separation and determinate co-ordination are required by our understandings, it appears to me that we cannot hesitate to make a dogmatic arrangement,—placing the theory of organization before that of classification,—for the last is absolutely dependent on the first; while the first could meet some wants, though in a restricted way, without the second. In a word, none but known organisms can be classified; whereas they all can and must be studied, to a certain extent, without being mutually compared. And again, there is no reason why, in a systematic exposition of anatomical philosophy, we should not borrow directly from biotaxy its construction of the organic hierarchy; an anticipation which involves much less inconvenience than severing the complete study of structure.—However, it must be always borne in mind that any system will have to undergo a general revision, with a view to bringing out the essential relations of its parts: the relations, not only of the two sections of statical biology, but of both to the dynamical. This consideration goes far to diminish the importance assigned to these questions of priority: and the only reason why such a revision appears more necessary in biology than in the other sciences is, that there is a profounder accordance between its departments than we find in theirs.

The interior distribution of these three departments is determined, as usual, by the order of dependence of phenomena, on the ground of their relative generality. Thus, the theory of the organic life precedes that of the animal: and the theory of the highest functions and organs of Man terminates the biological system.

*Where to begin.* It has often been a question whether, in studying each organ and function in the whole scale, it is best to begin at the one end or the other;—to begin with Man or the simplest known organism. I do not consider this question so all-important as it is often supposed, as all qualified inquirers admit the necessity of using the two methods alternately, whichever is taken first: but I think that a distinction should be made between the study of the organic and that of the animal life. The functions of the first being chemical, it is less necessary to begin with Man; and I think there may be a scientific advantage in studying the vegetable organism first, in which that kind of functions is the more pure and more marked, and therefore the more easily and completely studied: but every investigation, anatomical or physiological, relating to animal life, must be obscure if it began elsewhere than with Man, who is the only being in which such an order of phenomena is immediately intelligible. It is evidently the obvious state of Man, more and more degraded, and not the indecisive state of the sponge, more and more improved, that we should pursue, through the animal series, when we are analysing any of the constituent characters of animality. If we seem to be by this procedure deserting the ordinary

## CONCLUSION OF REVIEW.

course of passing from the most general and simple subject to the most particular and complex, it is only to conform the better to the philosophical principal which prescribes that every course, and which leads us from the most known subjects to the least known. In all cases but this, the usual course is the fittest in biological studies.

Here we conclude our review of biological science as a whole. The extent to which I have carried out the survey will allow us to consider its separate portions very briefly. In doing so, I shall follow the order just laid down, passing from the simple considerations of pure anatomy to that positive study of the phenomena of the intellect and the affections, as the highest part of human nature, which will carry us over from biology to Social Physics,—the final object of this work.

# CHAPTER II.

### ANATOMICAL PHILOSOPHY.

*Development of Statical biology.* IT was during the second half of the last century that Daubenton and Vicq-d'Azyr achieved the extension of the statical study of living bodies to the whole of known organisms; and the lectures and writings of Cuvier carried on, and spread abroad, the regenerating influence of this great view. But, indispensable as was this conception to the development of anatomical science, it could not complete the character of statical biology without the aid and addition of Bichat's grand idea of the general decomposition of the organism into its various elementary tissues; the high philosophical importance of which appears to me not yet to be worthily appreciated.

The natural development of comparative anatomy would, no doubt, have disclosed this analysis to us sooner or later: but how slow the process would have been we may judge by what we see of the reluctance of comparative anatomists to abandon the exclusive study of systems of organs while unable to deny the preponderant importance of the study of the tissues. Of all changes, those which relate to method are the most difficult of accomplishment; and perhaps there is no example of their resulting spontaneously from a regular advance under the old methods, without a direct impulsion from a new original conception, energetic enough to work a revolution in the system of study. Biology must, from its great complexity, be more dependent on such a necessity than any other science.

*Process of discovery of the tissues.* Though zoological analysis furnishes the best means of separating the various organic tissues, and especially of giving precision to the true philosophical sense of this great notion, pathological analysis offered a more direct and rapid way to suggest the first idea of such a decomposition, even regarding the human organism alone. When pathological anatomy had been once founded by Morgagni, it was evident that in the best-marked maladies no organ is ever entirely diseased, and that the alterations are usually confined to some of its constituent parts, while the others preserve their normal condition. In no other way could the distinction of the elementary tissues have been so clearly established. By the co-existence in one organ of sound and impaired tissues, and, again, by different organs being affected by similar maladies, in virtue of the disease of a common tissue, the analysis of the chief anatomical elements was spontaneously indicated, at the same time that the study of the tissues was shown to be more important than that of the organs. It is not consistent with my objects to go further into this: but it was necessary to show that we owe to pathological analysis the perception of this essential truth. It was Pinel who suggested it to Bichat, by his happy innovation of studying at once all the diseases proper to the different mucous membranes. Bichat then, while knowing nothing of the study of the organic hierarchy, carried off from the students of comparative anatomy the honour of discovering the primitive idea which is most indispensable of all to the general advancement of anatomical philosophy. His achievement consisted in rationally connecting with the normal condition a notion derived from the pathological condition, in virtue probably of the natural reflection that if the different tissues of the same organ could each be separately diseased in its own way, they must have, in their healthy condition, distinct modes of existence, of which the life of the organ is really composed. This principle was entirely overlooked before Bichat published the treatise in which he established the most satisfactory *à posteriori* development of it: and it is now placed beyond all question. The only matter of regret is that, in creating a wholly new aspect of anatomical science, Bichat did not better mark its spirit by the title he gave it. If he had called it *abstract* or *elementary* instead of *general* anatomy, he would have indicated its philosophical function, and its relation to other anatomical points of view.

The anatomical philosophy began to assume its definitive

Combination with Comparative anatomy. character from the very recent time when the human mind learned to combine the two great primitive ideas of the organic hierarchy, and of Bichat's discovery, which applies the universal conception to the statical study of living bodies. These combined ideas are necessarily the subject of our present examination. Putting aside the irrational distinctions, still too common among biologists, of many different kinds of anatomy, we must here recognize only one scientific anatomy, chiefly characterized by the philosophical combination of the comparative method with the fundamental notion of the decomposition of the organs into tissues. It is apparently strange that, after Bichat's discovery, comparative anatomists, with Cuvier at their head, should have persisted in studying organic apparatus in its complex state, instead of beginning with the investigation of the tissues, pursuing the analysis of the laws of their combinations into organs, and ending with the grouping of those organs into apparatus, properly so called: but not even Cuvier's great name can now prevent the application of the comparative method to the analysis of tissues, throughout the whole biological hierarchy. The work, though at present neither energetically nor profoundly pursued, is begun, and will reform the habitual direction of anatomical speculation.

Bichat's studies related to Man alone; and his method of comparison bore only upon the simplest and most restricted cases of all; the comparison of parts and that of ages. His principle must, therefore, necessarily undergo some transformations, to fit it for a more extensive application. The most important of these improvements, especially in a logical view, appears to me to consist in the great distinction introduced by M. de Blainville between the true anatomical *elements* and the simple *products* of the organism, which Bichat had confounded. We saw before the importance of this distinction in the chemical study of organic substances: and we meet it again now, face to face, as an anatomical conception.

Elements and Products.

We have seen that life, reduced to the simplest and most general notion of it, is characterized by the double continuous motion of absorption and exhalation, owing to the reciprocal action of the organism and its environment, and adapted to sustain during a certain time, and within certain limits of variation, the integrity of the organization. It results from this that, at every instant of its existence, every living body must present, in its structure and composition, two very different orders of principles: absorbed matters in a state of assimilation, and exhaled matters in a state of separation. This is the ground of the great anatomical distinction between organic elements and organic products. The absorbed matters, once completely assimilated, constitute the whole of the real materials of the organism. The exhaled substances, whether solid or fluid, become, from the time of their separation, foreign to the organism, in which they cannot generally remain long without danger. Regarded in a solid state, the true anatomical elements are always necessarily continuous in tissue with the whole of the organism: and again, the fluid elements, whether stagnant or circulating, remain in the depths of the general tissue, from which they are equally inseparable: whereas the products are only deposited, for a longer or shorter time, on the exterior or interior surface of the organism. The differences are not less characteristic, in a dynamical view. The true elements alone must be regarded as really living: they alone participate in the double vital motion: and they alone grow or decrease by absorption or exhalation. Even before they are finally excreted, the products are already essentially dead substances, exhibiting the same conditions that they would manifest anywhere else, under similar molecular influences.

The separation of the elements from the products is not always easy to effect when, as frequently happens, they combine in the same anatomical arrangement to concur in the same function. All products are not, like sweat, urine, etc., destined to be expelled without further use in the organic economy. Several others, as saliva, the gastric fluid, bile, etc., act as exterior substances, and in virtue of their chemical composition in preparing for the assimilation of the organic materials. It is difficult to fix the precise moment when these bodies cease to be products and become elements;—the moment, that is, when they pass from the inorganic to the organic state,—from death to life. But these difficulties arise from the imperfection of our analysis, and not from any uncertainty in the principle of separation. It may be observed however that there are circumstances in which products, and particularly among the solids, are closely united to true anatomical elements in the structure of certain apparatus, to which they supply essential means of improvement. Such are, for instance, the greater number of epidermic productions, the hair, and eminently the teeth. But even in this case, a sufficiently delicate dissection, and a careful analysis of the whole of the function will enable us to ascertain, with entire precision, how much is organic and how much inorganic in the proposed structure. Such an investigation was not prepared for when Bichat confounded the teeth with the bones, and concluded the epidermis and the hair to be tissues, of a piece with the cutaneous tissue; but the rectification which ensued was all-important, as enabling us to define the idea of tissue or *anatomical element*, which is the preferable term. It was through comparative anatomy that the rectification took place; for the study of the biological series showed that the inorganic parts which in Man appear inseparable from the essential apparatus are in fact only simple means of advancement, gradually introduced at assignable stages of the ascending biological series.

If we assert that in the order of purely anatomical speculations, the study of products must be secondary to that of elements, it will not be supposed that we undervalue the study of products. This study is of extreme importance in physiology, whose principal phenomena would be radically unintelligible without it; and without it pathological knowledge must come to a stand. As results, they indicate organic alterations; and as modifiers, they exhibit the origin of a great number of those alterations. In fact, the knowledge of them is much promoted by their separation from the anatomical elements, which withdraw the attention of biologists from the real claims of the whole class of products.

The consideration of products being once dismissed to its proper place, anatomical analysis has assumed its true character of completeness and clearness. Thus we may undertake now what was before impossible—an exact enumeration of anatomical elements. And again, these tissues can be classified according to their true general relations; and may even be reduced to a single tissue, modified by determinate laws. These two are the other chief transformations undergone by the great anatomical theory of Bichat, through the application of the comparative method: and these two we now proceed to review.

The first is connected with the great question of the vitality of the organic fluids, about which our ideas are far from being, I think, sufficiently settled. Every living body consists of a combination of solids and fluids, the respective proportions of which vary, according to the species, within very wide limits. The very definition of the vital state supposes this conjunction; for the double motion of composition and decomposition which characterizes life could not take place among solids alone; and, on the other hand, a liquid or gaseous mass not only requires a solid envelope, but could admit of no real organization. If the two great primitive ideas of Life and Organization were not inseparable, we might imagine the first to belong to fluids, because they are so readily modified; and the other to solids, as alone capable of structural formation: and here, under another view, we should find the necessary harmony of the two elements. The comparison of types in the biological series confirms, in fact, the general rule that the vital activity increases with the preponderance of fluid elements in the organism; while a greater persistence of the vital state attends the preponderance of solids. This has long been regarded as a settled law by philosophical biologists, in studying the series of ages alone. These considerations seem to show that the controversy about the vitality of fluids rests, like many other famous controversies, on a vicious proposal of the problem, since such a mutual relation of the solids and the fluids excludes at once both humourism and solidism. Discarding, of course, the products from the question, there can be no doubt that the fluid elements of the organism manifest a life as real as that of the solids. The founders of modern pathology, in their reaction against the old humourism, have not paid

*Vitality of the organic fluids.*

sufficient attention, in the theory of diseases, to the direct and spontaneous alterations of which the organic fluids, especially the blood, are remarkably susceptible, in virtue of the complexity of their composition. It would appear, from a philosophical point of view, very strange if the most active and susceptible of the anatomical elements did not participate, primarily or consecutively, in the perturbations of the organism. But, on the other hand, it is not less certain that the fluids, animal and vegetable, cease to live as soon as they have quitted the organism; as, for instance, the blood after venesection. They then lose all organization, and are in the condition of products. The vitality of the fluids, considered separately, constitutes them an ill-defined, and therefore interminable, question.

A truly positive inquiry however arises out of the question—the inquiry as to which of the immediate principles of a fluid are vital; for it cannot be admitted that all are so indiscriminately. Thus, the blood being chiefly composed of water, it would be absurd to suppose such an inert vehicle to participate in the life of the fluid; but then, which of the other constituents is the seat of life? Microscopic anatomy gives us the answer,—that it resides in the globules, properly so called, which are at once organized and living. However valuable such a solution would be, it can be regarded at present only as an attempt; for it is admitted that these globules, though determinate in form, shrink more and more as the arterial blood passes through an inferior order of vessels,—that is, as it approaches its incorporation with the tissues; and that, at the precise moment of assimilation, there is a complete liquefaction of the globules. It would thus appear that we must cease to regard the blood as living at the very moment when it accomplishes its chief act of vitality. Before any decision can be made, we must have the counter proof,—the acknowledgment that true globules are exclusively characteristic of living fluids, in opposition to those which, as simple products, are essentially inert, and hold in suspension various solids, which make them difficult to be distinguished from true globules, notwithstanding the determinate form of the latter. Microscopical observations are too delicate, and sometimes deceptive, to admit at present of the irreversible establishment of this essential point of anatomical doctrine.

The statical study of living bodies would form but a very incomplete introduction to the dynamical, if the fluids were left out of the investigation of the organic elements, however much remains to be desired in our knowledge of them. The omission of them in Bichat's treatise leaves a great gap. Still, as the anatomy of solids must always take precedence of that of fluids, Bichat chose the true point of departure, though he did not undertake the whole subject. It must be added that the examination of the fluids is so much the more difficult of the two as to be wellnigh impracticable. In an anatomical sense, it is impracticable: and the two only methods,—microscopical and chemical examination,—are impaired by the rapid disorganization which ensues when the fluids quit the organism. The chemical method is in itself the more valuable of the two: but, besides that the chemists habitually confound the elements and the products, they have always examined the former in a more or less advanced state of decomposition: and, being unaware of this, they have offered only the most false and incoherent notions of the molecular constitution of the organized fluids. In such a state of things, it is only by a full preparation, from the study of the solid elements, that anything can be done in the study of the fluids. It is almost needless to say that by the same rule which prescribes this order, we should study fluids in the order of their increasing liquefaction,—taking the fatty substances first, then the blood and other liquids, and lastly the vaporous and gaseous elements, which will always be the least understood.

The order of inquiry being thus settled, the next subject is the rational classification of the tissues, according to their anatomical filiation. It was not by such a study as Bichat's,—of Man alone,—that anything certain could become known of such obscure differences as those of the fundamental tissues. In order to obtain such knowledge the study of the whole biological series is indispensable.

*Classification of the tissues.*

The first piece of knowledge thus obtained is that the cellular tissue is the

*Organic. Cellular tissue.*

primitive and essential web of every organism; it being the only one that is present through the whole range of the scale. The tissues which appear in Man so multiplied and distinct lose all their characteristic attributes as we descend the series, and tend to merge entirely in the general cellular tissue, which remains the sole basis of vegetable, and perhaps of the lowest animal organization. This fact harmonizes well with the philosophical account of the basis of life, in its last degree of simplicity; for the cellular tissue is eminently fitted, by its structure, for absorption and exhalation. At the lower end of the series, the living organism, placed in an unvarying medium, does nothing but absorb and exhale by its two surfaces, between which are ever oscillating the fluids destined for assimilation, and those which result from the contrary process. For so simple a function as this the cellular tissue suffices. It remained to be ascertained under what laws the original tissue becomes gradually modified so as to engender all the others, with those attributes which at first disguise their common derivation: and this is what Comparative anatomy has begun to establish, with some distinctness.

The characteristic modifications of the tissue are of two prominent classes: the first, more common and less profound, are limited to the simple structure: the other class, more special, and more profound, affect the composition itself.

Of the first order the prominent case is that of the dermous tissue, properly so called, which is the basis of the general organic envelope, exterior and interior. The modification here is mere condensation, differently marked, in regard to animal organisms, according as the surface is, as in exterior surfaces, more exhalant than absorbent, or, as in interior surfaces, more absorbent than exhalant. Even this first transformation is not rigorously universal; and we must ascend the scale a little way to find it clearly characterized. Not only in some of the lowest of the animal organisms, are the exterior and interior essentially alike, so that the two surfaces may be interchanged, but, if we go a little lower, we find no anatomical distinction between the en-

*Dermous tissue.*

velope and the whole of the organism, which is uniformly cellular.

By an increasing condensation of the parent tissue, three distinct but inseparable tissues proceed from the derma, all of which are destined to an important, though passive office in the animal economy, either as envelopes protecting the nervous organs, or as auxiliaries of the locomotive apparatus. These are the fibrous, cartilaginous, and bony tissues, ranged by Bichat in their rational order, and named by M. Laurent, in their combination, the *sclerous* tissue. The different degrees of consolidation here arise from the deposition in the cellular network of a heterogeneous substance, organic or inorganic, the extraction of which leaves no doubt as to the nature of the tissue. When, on the other hand, by a last direct condensation, the original tissue becomes itself more compact, without being incrusted by a foreign substance, we recognize a new modification, in which impermeability becomes compatible with suppleness, which is the characteristic of the serous, or (as M. Laurent calls it) the *kystous* tissue, the office of which is to interpose between the various mobile organs, and to contain liquids, both circulating and stagnant.

<small>Sclerous tissue.</small>

<small>Kystous tissue.</small>

The second order of transformations exhibits two secondary kinds of tissue which distinguish the animal organism, and which appear at about the same degree of the scale—the muscular and the nervous tissues. In each there is an anatomical combination of the fundamental tissue with a special organic element, semi-solid and eminently vital, which, having long gone by the name of *fibrine* in the first case, has suggested the corresponding name of *neurine* (given us by M. de Blainville) for the other. Here the transformation of the parent tissue is so complete, that it would be difficult to establish, and yet more to detect it in the higher organisms; but the analogies of comparative anatomy leave no doubt, and only make us wish that we could understand with more precision the mode of anatomical union of the muscular and nervous substances with the cellular tissue.

<small>ANIMAL. Muscular and nervous tissues.</small>

Passing on to the chief subdivision of each of the

secondary tissues, the first consideration is of the general position, which is always related to a modification, greater or smaller, of the structure itself. Comparative analysis shows us that in the case of both the muscular and the nervous system, the organization of the tissue becomes more special and elevated, exactly in proportion to its deeper position between the exterior and interior surfaces of the animal envelope. Thence arises the rational division of each of these systems into superficial and profound. This distinction is more especially remarkable with regard to the nervous system, arranged, first, in the form of filaments, and afterwards that of ganglions, with or without external apparatus.

This is the family of tissues, the study of which forms the basis of anatomical analysis. It would be departing from my object to inquire into the laws of composition under which the ascent is made from this primary study to that of porous substances, and thence on to the theory of the organs, and then to that of systems of organs, which would lead us on to physiological analysis. I have fulfilled the aim of this section in exhibiting the methodical connection of the four degrees of anatomical speculation, about which no real uncertainty exists.

*Limitation of the inquiry.* Deeper than this we cannot go. The last term in our abstract, intellectual decomposition of the organism is the idea of tissue. To attempt the passage from this idea to that of molecule, which is appropriate to inorganic philosophy, is to quit the positive method altogether: and those who do so, under the fancy that they may possibly establish a notion of organic molecules, and who give that vain search the name of transcendental anatomy, are in fact imitating the chemists in a region into which Chemistry must enter in its own shape where admissable at all, and are asserting in other words that, as bodies are formed of indivisible molecules, animals are formed of animalcules. This is simply an attempt, in the old spirit, to penetrate into the nature of existences, and to establish an imaginary analogy between orders of phenomena which are essentially heterogeneous. It is little creditable to the scientific spirit of our time that this aberration should call for exposure and rebuke, and that it should need to be asserted that the idea of tissue is, in organic speculation, the logical equivalent of the idea of molecule in inorganic speculation.

We here find ourselves in possession of a sufficient basis of anatomical science, while we need yet a more complete and profound combination of the ideas of comparative and textural anatomy. This want will be supplied when we become universally familiarized with the four analytical degrees, complementary to each other, which must henceforth be recognized and treated as the basis of anatomical speculation.

# CHAPTER III.

### BIOTAXIC PHILOSOPHY.

AFTER the statical analysis of living bodies, there must be a hierarchical co-ordination of all known, or even possible organisms, in a single series, which must serve as a basis for the whole of biological speculations. The essential principles of this philosophical operation are what I have now to point out.

*Comparative anatomy of vegetables and animals.* We have already seen that it is the distinction of biological science to have developed the theory of classifications, which, existing in all sciences, attains its perfection when applied to the complex attributes of the animal organisms. In all ages, the vegetable organism was the direct subject of biological classification; but it was pursued on the principles furnished by the consideration of animals, whence the type was derived which guided philosophical speculation in the case. It could not be otherwise, so marked and incontestable as are the distinctions among animal organisms: and even the zoological classification of Aristotle, imperfect as it is, is infinitely superior to anything which could then have been attempted with regard to vegetables. This natural original classification has been rather rectified than changed by the labours of modern times; while that of vegetables has met with an opposite fate. As a fact, the first successful attempts in the animal region long preceded the establishment of the true principles of classification; whereas, it was only by a laborious systematic application of these principles that it has been possible, even within a century, to effect any rational co-ordination in the vegetable region, so little marked, in comparison, are the distinctions in the latter case. The natural result was that the animal realm, used as a type, became more and more attended to, till the improvements in zoological classification have gone so far as perhaps to lead us to fear that the vegetable organism, owing to its great simplicity, can never become subject to a much better classification than that in which it was left in the last century. The labours of the reformers of that time are very far indeed from having been useless; only, what they undertook for the vegetable kingdom has turned rather to the profit of the animal;—an inevitable circumstance, since the property which rendered the animal kingdom the natural type of the taxonomical series must adapt it to receive all the improvements arising from the general principles of the theory. The character of the theory could not but remain incomplete, however, as long as the vegetable classification continued to be regarded as the chief end of the research; and the classification became rational only when it was seen that the vegetable region was the further end of the series, in which the most complex animal organism must hold the first place; an order of arrangement under which the vegetable organism will be more effectually studied than it ever was while made an object of exclusive investigation. All that is needed is that naturalists should extend to the whole series the anatomical and physiological considerations which have been attached too exclusively to animal organisms; and this will certainly be done now that the human mind is fairly established at the true point of view, commanding the fundamental theory of natural classification.

These prefatory remarks indicate our theme. We must have the whole series in view; but the animal region must be our immediate and explicit subject,—both as furnishing the rational bases of the general theory of classification, and as exhibiting its most eminent and perfect application. *Animal anatomy our subject.*

The subject divides itself into two parts: the formation of natural groups, and their hierarchical succession;—a division necessary for purposes of study, though the two parts ultimately and logically coalesce. *Division of the natural method.*

In contemplating the groups, the process is to class together those species which pre- *Natural groups.*

sent, amidst a variety of differences, such essential analogies as to make them more like each other than like any others,—without attending, for the present, to the gradation of the groups, or to their interior distribution. If this were all, the classification must remain either doubtful or arbitrary, as the circumscription of each group could seldom be done so certainly as inevitably to include or exclude nothing that might not belong to another group: and great discordance was therefore observed in the early division into *orders, families,* and even *genera*. But the difficulty disappears on the foundation of the fundamental hierarchy, which rigorously assigns its place to each species, and clearly defines the ideas of *genera, families,* and *classes,* which henceforth indicate different kinds of decomposition, effected through certain modifications of the principle which graduates the whole series. The animal realm, especially in its higher parts, is as yet the only one in which the successive degrees have admitted a fully scientific description. The rough classification into natural groups was an indispensable preparation for the marshalling into a series of the immeasurable mass of materials presented by nature. The groups being thus separated, and the study of the irinterior distribution postponed, the innumerable throng of organic existences became manageable. This great benefit has misled botanists into the supposition that the formation of these groups is the most scientific part of the natural method,—otherwise than as a preliminary process. The regular establishment of natural families offers, no doubt, great facilities to scientific study, by enabling a single case to serve for a whole group: but this is a wholly different matter from the value of the natural method, regarded as it must henceforth be, as the highest rational means of the whole study, statical and dynamical, of the system of living bodies; and the great condition of which is that the mere position assigned to each body makes manifest its whole anatomical and physiological nature, in its relation to the bodies which rank before or after it. These properties could never belong to any mere establishment of natural families, if they could be grouped with a perfection which is far from being possible; for the

Co-ordination of them.

arbitrary arrangement of the families, and the indeterminate decomposition of each of them into species, would destroy all aptitude for comprehensive anatomical or physiological comparison, and open the way for that search after partial and secondary analogies which we see to be so mischievous in the study of the vegetable kingdom at this day.

The Natural Method, then, is philosophically characterized by the general establishment of the organic hierarchy, reduced, if desired, to the rational co-ordination of genera and even of families, the realization of which is found only in the animal region; and there only in an initiatory state. And the co-ordination proceeds under three great laws, which are these: first, that the animal species present a perpetually increasing complexity, both as to the diversity, the multiplicity, and the speciality of their organic elements, and as to the composition and augmenting variety of their organs and systems of organs. Secondly: that this order corresponds precisely, in a dynamical view, with a life more complex and more active, composed of functions more numerous, more varied, and better defined. Thirdly: that the living being thus becomes, as a necessary consequence, more and more susceptible of modification, at the same time that he exercises an action on the external world, continually more profound and more extensive. It is the union of these three laws which rigorously fixes the philosophical direction of the biological hierarchy, each one dissipating any uncertainty which might hang about the other two. Hence results the possibility of conceiving of a final arrangement of all living species in such an order as that each shall be always inferior to all that precede it, and superior to all that follow it, whatever might otherwise, from its nature, be the difficulty of ever realizing the hierarchical type to such a degree of precision as this.

*Three laws of co-ordination.*

All adequate inquirers are now agreed upon this conception as the starting-point of biological speculation; and I need not therefore stop to take notice of any prior controversies, except one, which is noticeable from its having tended to illustrate and advance the principle of the natural method. I refer to the discussion raised by Lamarck, and maintained, though in an imperfect manner, by Cuvier, with regard to the general permanence of organic species. The first consideration in this matter is, that whatever may be the final decision of this great biological question, it can in no way affect the fundamental existence of the organic hierarchy. Instead of there being, as Lamarck conjectured, no real zoological series, all animal organisms being identical, and their characteristics due to external circumstances, we shall see, by a closer examination, that the hypothesis merely presents the series under a new aspect, which itself renders the existence of the scale more clear and unquestionable than before; for the whole zoological series would then become, in fact and in speculation, perfectly analogous to the development of the individual; at least, in its ascending period. There would be simply a long determinate succession of organic states, gradually deduced from each other in the course of ages by transformations of growing complexity, the order of which, necessarily linear, would be precisely comparable to that of the consecutive metamorphoses of hexapod insects, only much more extended. In brief, the progressive course of the animal organism, which is now only a convenient abstraction, adapted to facilitate thought by abridging discourse, would thus be converted into a real natural law. This controversy, then, in which Lamarck showed by far the clearer and profounder conception of the organic hierarchy, while Cuvier, without denying, often misconceived it, leaves, in fact, wholly untouched the theory of the biological series, which is quite independent of all opinion about the permanence or variation of living species.

*Question of permanence of organic species.*

The only attribute of this series which could be affected by this controversy is the continuity or discontinuity of the organic progression: for, if we admit Lamarck's hypothesis, in which the different organic states succeed each other slowly by imperceptible transitions, the ascending series must evidently be conceived of as rigorously continuous; whereas, if we admit the stability of living species, we must lay down as a fundamental principle the discontinuousness of the series, without pretending, either, to limit, *à priori*, in any way the small elementary intervals. This is the question to be considered; and thus restricted, the discussion is of extreme importance to the general advancement of the Natural Method, which will be, in fact, much more clearly described if we are able to regard the species as essentially stable, and the organic series therefore as composed of distinctly separate terms, even at its highest stages of development; for the idea of *species*, which is the principal biotaxic unity, would no longer allow any scientific definition, if we must admit the indefinite transformation of different species into each other, under the sufficiently-prolonged influence of circumstances sufficiently intense. However certain might be the existence of the biological hierarchy, we should have almost insurmountable difficulty in realizing it; and this proves to us the high philosophical interest which belongs to this great question.

Lamarck's reasoning rested on the combination of these two incontestable but ill-described principles: first, the aptitude of any organism (and especially an animal organism) to be modified to a conformity to the exterior circumstances in which it is placed, and which solicit the predominant exercise of some special organ, corresponding to some faculty become requisite; and secondly, the tendency of direct and individual modifications to become fixed in races by hereditary transmission, so that they may increase in each new generation, if the environment remains unaltered. It is evident that if this double property is admitted without restriction, all organisms may be regarded as having been produced by each other, if we only dispose the environment with that freedom and prodigality so easy to the artless imagination of Lamarck. The falseness of this hypothesis is now so fully admitted by naturalists that I need only briefly indicate where its vice resides.

We need not stop to object to the immeasurable time required for each system of circumstances to effect such an organic transformation; nor yet to expose the futility of imagining organic environments, purely ideal, which are out of all analogy with existing media. We may pass on to the consideration that the conjecture rests on a deeply erroneous notion of the nature of the living organism. The organism and the medium must doubtless be mutually related; but it does not follow that either of them produces the other. The question is simply of an equilibrium between two heterogeneous and independent powers. If all possible organisms had been placed in all possible media, for a suitable time, the greater number of them would necessarily disappear, leaving those only which were accordant with the laws of the fundamental equilibrium; and it is probably by a series of eliminations like this that a biological harmony has become gradually established on our globe, where we see such a process now for ever going on. But the whole conception would be overthrown at once if the organism could be supposed capable of modification, *ad infinitum*, by the influence of the medium, without having any proper and indestructible energy of its own.

Though the solicitation of external circumstances certainly does change the primitive organization by developing it in some particular direction, the limits of the alteration are very narrow: so that, instead of wants creating faculties, as Lamarck would have us believe, those wants merely develop the powers to a very inconsiderable degree, and could have no influence at all without a primitive tendency to act upon. The disappearance of the superior races of animals before the encroachments of Man shows how limited is the power of the organism to adapt itself to an altered environment; even the human barbarian gives way to civilized Man: and yet the power of adaptation is known to be greatest in the highest organisms, whereas the hypothesis of Lamarck would require the fact to be the other way. In a statical view, too, this conception would compel us to regard the introductory animal as containing, at least in a rudimentary state, not only all the tissues, (which might be admissible, reducible as they are to the cellular tissue,) but all the organs and systems of organs; which is incompatible with anatomical comparison. Thus, in every view is Lamarck's conception condemned: and it even tends to destroy the philosophical balance between the two fundamental ideas of organization and life, by leading us to suppose most life where there is least organization. The lesson that we may learn from it is to study more effectually the limits within which, in each case, the medium may modify the organism, about which a very great deal remains to be learned: and meantime, there can scarcely be a doubt, especially after the luminous exposition of Cuvier, that species remain essentially fixed through all exterior variations compatible with their existence.

Cuvier's argument rests upon two chief considerations, complementary to each other;—the permanence of the most ancient known species; and the resistance of existing species to the most powerful modifying forces: so that, first, the number of species does not diminish; and next, it does not increase. We go back for evidence to the descriptions of Aristotle, twenty centuries ago: we find fossil species, identical with those before our eyes: and we observe in the oldest mummies even the simple secondary differences which now distinguish the races of men. And, as to the second view, we derive evidence from an exact analysis of the effects of domestication on races of animals and vegetables. Human intervention, affording, as it does, the most favourable case for alteration of the organism, has done nothing more, even when combined with change of locality, than alter some of the qualities, without touching any of the essential characters of any species; no one of which has ever been transformed into any other. No modification of race, nor any influences of the social state, have ever varied the fundamental and strongly marked nature of the human species. Thus, without straying into any useless speculations about the origin of the different organisms, we rest upon the great natural law that living species tend to perpetuate themselves indefinitely, with the same chief characteristics, through any exterior changes compatible with their existence. In non-essentials the species is modified within certain limits, beyond which it is not modified but destroyed. To know thus much is good: but we must remember that it teaches us nothing, with any completeness, of the kind of influence exercised by the medium on the organism. The rational theory of this action remains to be formed: and the laying down the question was the great result of the Lamarck controversy, which thus rendered an eminent service to the progress of sound biological philosophy.

We may now proceed on the authorized conception that the great biological series is necessarily discontinuous. The transitions may ultimately become more gradual, by the discovery of intermediate organisms, and by a better directed study of those already known: but the stability of species makes it certain that the series will always be composed of clearly distinct terms separated by impracticable intervals. It now appears that the preceding examination was no needless digression, but an inquiry necessary to establish, in the hierarchy of living bodies, this characteristic property, so directly involved in the rational establishment of the hierarchy itself.

*Two logical conditions of the study.* Having surveyed the two great conceptions of Natural Groups, and the biological series, which together constitute what is called the Natural Method, we must now notice two great logical conditions of the study. The first, or primordial, is the principle of the subordination of characters: the other, the final, prescribes the translation of the interior characters into exterior, which, in fact, results from a radical investigation of the same principle.

*Subordination of characteristics.* From the earliest use of the natural method, even before the investigation had passed on from the natural groups to the series of them, it was seen that the taxonomic characters must be not only numbered but weighed, according to the rules of a certain fundamental subordination which must exist among them. The only subordination which is strictly scientific, and free from all arbitrary intermixture, is that which results from a comparative analysis of the different organisms: this analysis is of recent date, and even yet is adequately applied only in the animal region; and thus the subordination was no more than barely conceived of before the institution of comparative anatomy, and the weighing of attributes is closely connected with the conception of the organic hierarchy. The subordination of taxonomic characters is effected by measuring their respective importance according to the relation of the corresponding organs to the phenomena which distinguish the species under study,—the phenomena becoming more special as we descend to smaller subdivisions. In short, here as elsewhere, the philosophical task is to establish a true harmony between statical conditions and dynamical properties; between ideas of life and ideas of organization, which should never be separated in our scientific studies but in order to their ulterior combination. Thus our aim, sometimes baffled but always hopeful, is to subordinate the taxonomic characters to each other, without the admission of anything arbitrary into any arrangement of importance. We thus meet with gaps in our schedules which we should avoid, or be insensible to, under an arbitrary system; but we may subdue our natural impatience under this imperfection by accustoming our mind to regard rational classification as a true science, continually progressive, always perfectible, and therefore always more or less imperfect, like all positive science.

In conducting the process of comparison, the characters must be admitted without restriction, in virtue of their positive rationality, however inconvenient to manage and difficult to verify. *Procedure, in use of the Natural Method.* This is the foundation of the proposed classification. The next step is to discard from the collection those whose verification would be too difficult, substituting for them some customary equivalents. Without this second process, which is as yet inadequately appreciated, the passage from the abstract to the concrete would be inextricably embarrassed. The anatomist and physiologist may be satisfied with a definition of groups which will not suit the zoologist, and still less the naturalist. The kind of transformations required is easily specified. First, it is clear how important it is to discard the characters which are not permanent, and those which do not belong to the various natural modifications of the species under study. They can be admitted only as provisional attributes till true equivalents, permanent and common, have been discovered. But the very nature of the problem indicates that the aim of the chief substitution should be to replace all the interior characters by exterior: and it is this which constitutes the main difficulty, and, at the same time, the highest perfection of this final operation. When such a condition is fulfilled, on the basis of a rational primitive classification, the natural method is irrevocably constituted, in the plenitude of its various essential properties, as we now find it in the case of the animal kingdom.

This transformation appears to be necessarily possible; for, as a chief characteristic of animality is action upon the external world and corresponding reaction, the most important primitive phenomena of animal life must take place at the surface of separation between the organism and its environment; and considerations with regard to this envelope, its form, consistence, etc., naturally furnish the principal distinctions of the different animal organizations. The interior organs, which have no direct and continuous relation to the medium, will always be of the highest importance among vegetative phenomena, the primitive and uniform basis of all life: but they are of secondary consequence in considering the degrees of animality; so that the interior part of the animal envelope, by which various materials for use are elaborated, is less important, in a taxonomic point of view, than the exterior part, which is the seat of the most characteristic phenomenon. Accordingly, the transformation of interior into exterior zoological characters is not merely an ingenious and indispensable artifice, but a simple return from the distraction of an overwhelming mass of facts to a direct philosophical course of investigation. When therefore we see a recourse to inferior characteristics in the study of the animal series, we must recognize the truth that not only is the classification as yet unfinished, but that the operation is imperfectly conceived of; that the inquirer has not ascended, through sound biological analysis, to the original source of analogies empirically discovered.

After thus ascertaining the nature of the Natural Method, we must, before quitting the subject, glance at the mode of its application in the co-ordination of the biological series, condensed into its principal masses.

*Division of animal and vegetable kingdoms.* The most general division of the organic world is into the animal and vegetable kingdoms; a division which remains as an instance of thorough discontinuity, in spite of all efforts to represent it as an artificial arrangement. The deeper we go in the study of the inferior animals, the more plainly we perceive that locomotion, partial at least, and a corresponding degree of general sensibility, are the predominant and uniform characters of the entire animal series. These two attributes are even more universal in the animal kingdom than the existence of a digestive canal, which is commonly regarded as its chief exclusive characteristic; a predominance which would not have been assigned to this attribute of the organic life but for its being an inevitable consequence, and therefore an unquestionable test, of the double property of locomotion and sensibility; to which we must, in consequence, assign the first place. Such a transformation, however, relates only to moveable animals; so that for the rest, we should have still to seek some other yet more general indication of universal animality, if we must despair of finally discovering in it every direct anatomical condition of these two animal properties. As for the case of certain gyrating plants which appear to manifest some signs of these properties, our imperfect analysis of their motions discloses no true character of animality, since we can discover no constant and immediate relation with either exterior impressions or the mode of alimentation.

Next to the division of the two organic kingdoms comes the question of the rational hierarchy of the animal kingdom, by itself. *Hierarchy of the animal kingdom.* In the place of the irrational considerations, so much relied on formerly, of abode, mode of nutrition, etc., we now rest upon the supreme consideration of the greater or less complexity of the organism, of its relative perfection, speciality, elevation; in short, of the degree of animal *dignity*, as M. Jussieu has well expressed it. The next preparatory step was in the anatomical field, to determine the successive degrees of animality proper to the different organs. The combination of the two great inquiries,—into the bases of the zoological hierarchy as residing in the organization, and into the rank of the organs in their relation to life,—has furnished, since the beginning of this century, the first direct and general sketch of a definitive graduation of the animal kingdom. Henceforth, it became admitted that, as the nervous system constitutes the most animal of the anatomical elements, the classification must be directed by it; other organs, and, yet more, inorganic conditions, being recurred to only on the failure of the chief in the most special subdivisions; and the substitutes being employed according to their decreasing animality. Whatever share other zoologists may have contributed by their labours to the formation of this theory, it is to M. de Blainville that the credit of it especially belongs: and it is by his classification that we must proceed in estimating the application of the Natural Method to the direct construction of the true animal hierarchy.

*Attribute of symmetry.* The happiest innovation which distinguishes this zoological system is that it attributes a high taxonomic importance to the general form of the animal envelope, which had before been neglected by naturalists, and which offers the most striking feature, in regard to description, in the symmetry which is the prevailing character of the animal organism. We must here reserve the case of the non-symmetrical animals; and this shows that the idea is insufficiently analysed as yet. The principle is perhaps saved, or the difficulty distanced, by the fact that in these animals no trace can be discovered of a nervous system; but there is a sufficient want of precision and clearness to mark this as a case reserved for further analysis. We shall not wonder at this imperfection if we remember how erroneous were the notions, no further back than two generations ago, about very superior orders of animals,—the whole of the radiated, a part of the mollusks, and even of the lower articulated animals. Among the orders thus restricted, there are two kinds of symmetry, the most perfect of which relates to a plane, and the other to a point, or rather to an axis: hence the further classification of animals into the duplicate and the radiated. It is impossible to admire too much the exactness with which an attribute, apparently so unimportant, corresponds with the aggregate of the highest biological comparisons, which are all found spontaneously converging towards this simple and luminous distinction. Still it remains empirical in its preponderance; and we yet need a clear and rational explanation, both physiological and anatomical, of the extreme necessary inferiority of the radiated to the duplicate animals, which, by their nature, must be nearer to Man, the fundamental unity in zoology.

Taking the duplicate animals, or *artiozoaries*, their order is again divided according to the consistence of the envelope,—whether it is hard or soft,—and therefore more or less fit for locomotion.  *Division of duplicate animals.* This is, in fact, a protraction of the last consideration, as symmetry must be more marked in the case of a hard than of a soft covering. The two great attributes of animality,—locomotion and sensation,—establish profound and unquestionable differences, anatomical and physiological, between these two cases; and we may easily connect them rationally with this primitive distinction, and perceive how they exhibit inarticulated animals as necessarily inferior to the articulated.

The articulated animals must next be distinguished into two great classes, according to the mode of articulation; whether under *Division of articulated animals.* the envelope, by a bony skeleton, or a cartilaginous one, in the lowest degrees; or whether the articulation is external, by the consolidation of certain horny parts of the envelope, alternating with the soft parts. The inferiority of this latter organization, especially with regard to the high functions of the nervous system, must be seen at a glance. It is observable that the more imperfect development of this eminently animal system always coincides with a fundamental difference in the position of its central part, which is always above the digestive canal in vertebrated animals, and below it in those which have an external articulation.

The rational hierarchy of the chief organisms in the upper part of the animal series is, then, composed of the three great classes;—the vertebrated animals, those which are articulated externally, and the mollusks; or, in scientific language, the *osteozoaries*, the *entomozoaries*, and the *malacozoaries*.

Glancing, finally, at the division of the first of these classes, I may remark that all former descriptions and definitions may  *Consideration of the envelope.*

merge in the consideration of the envelope. It will be enough here to refer merely to the secondary view of the envelope,—that of the inorganic productions which separate it from its environment. M. de Blainville has shown us how the descent from Man, through all the mammifera, the birds, reptiles, amphibious animals, and fishes, is faithfully represented by the consideration of a cutaneous surface furnished with hair, feathers, scales, or left bare. The same determining importance of the envelope is perceived in the next order of animals, in which the descent is measured by the increasing number of pairs of locomotive appendages, from the hexapods to the myriapods, and even to the apodes, which are at the lower extremity.

It is not consistent with the object of this Work to go further into a description of the animal hierarchy. My aim in giving the above details has been to fix the reader's attention on my preliminary recommendation to study the present co-ordination of the animal kingdom as an indispensable concrete explanation of the abstract conceptions which I had offered, in illustration of the natural method. We must pass by, therefore, all speculations and studies which belong to zoological philosophy, and merely observe that there is one portion of the fundamental system which remains to be constituted, and the general principles of which are as yet only vaguely perceived;—I mean the rational distribution of the species of each natural genus. This extreme and delicate application of the taxonomic theory would have been inopportune at an earlier stage of the development of the science: but the time has arrived for it to be undertaken now.

*Natural method applied to the Vegetable kingdom.* We cannot but see that the natural method does not admit of anything like the perfection in the vegetable kingdom that it exhibits in even the lower stages of the animal. The families may be regarded as established, though in an empirical way; but their natural co-ordination remains almost entirely arbitrary, for want of a hierarchical principle by which to subordinate them rationally. The idea *Difficulty of co-ordination.* of animality yields a succession of degrees, deeply marked, so as to supply the basis of a true animal hierarchy: but there is nothing of the kind in our conception of vegetable existence. The intensity in this region is not always equal; but the character of vegetable life is homogeneous;—it is always assimilation and the contrary, continuous, and issuing in a necessary reproduction. The mere differences of intensity in such phenomena cannot constitute a true vegetable scale, analogous to the animal; and the less because the gradation is owing at least as much to the preponderant influence of external circumstances as to the characteristic organization of each vegetable. Thus, we have here no sufficient rational basis for a hierarchical comparison. A second obstacle ought to be noticed,—serious enough, though of less importance than the first;—that each vegetable is usually an agglomeration of distinct and independent beings. The case does not resemble that of the polypus formation. In the compound structure of the lowest animal orders a scientific definition is still possible. There is a vital basis common to all the animal structures which are otherwise independent of each other: but in the vegetable case, it is a mere agglomeration, such as we can often produce by grafting, and where the only common elements are inorganic parts, aiding a mechanical consolidation. There is no saying, in the present state of our knowledge, how far such a system may extend, without being limited by any organic condition, as it seems to depend on purely physical and chemical conditions, in combination with exterior circumstances. Faintly marked as the original organic diversity is by nature, it is evident how all rational subordination of the vegetable families in a common hierarchy is impeded by the coalescent tendency just noticed.

The principal division which is the starting-point of M. Jussieu's classification is the only beginning of a true co-ordination in the vegetable kingdom. It consists in distinguishing the vegetables by the presence or the absence of seminal leaves; and when they are present, by their having several or only one. For the successive passage from those which have several to those that have none may be regarded as a continuous descent, like that of the biological series, though less marked. Such a view has been verified by the investigation of the organs of nutrition, according to the discovery of Desfontaines,—as yet the only eminent example of a large and happy application of comparative anatomy to the vegetable organism. By this concurrence of the two modes of comparison,—of the reproductive and nutritive arrangements,—this proposition has taken its rank among the most eminent theorems of natural philosophy. But this beginning of a hierarchy remains obviously insufficient,—the numerous families in each of the three divisions remaining under a purely arbitrary arrangement, which we can hardly hope to convert into a rational one. The interior distribution of species, and even of genera, within each family must be radically imperfect, as the requisite taxonomical principles cannot be applied to their arrangement till the difficulty of the co-ordination of the families,—a difficulty much less, but as yet insurmountable, —has been overcome. The Natural Method has, therefore, as yet yielded no other result, as to the vegetable kingdom, than the more or less empirical establishment of families and genera. We cannot be surprised that it has not yet excluded the use of artificial methods, and above all that of Linnæus,—true as it is that, up to our time, the co-ordination of the vegetable kingdom was the field for the application of the Natural Method. It should ever be remembered, however, that the Natural Method is not merely a means of classification, but an important system of real knowledge as to the true relations of existing beings: so that even if it should be disused for the purposes of descriptive botany, it would not the less be of high value for the study of plants, the comparative results of which would be fixed and combined by it. In the present condition and prospects of the science, as to the establishment of a vegetable series, we must take the whole vegetable kingdom together as the last term of the great biological series,—as the last of the small number of essential modes of organization which (when the subdivisions are disregarded) are markedly separated from each other in the classification that gives us the logical command of the study of living beings. Applied first to the vegetable kingdom, the natural method is now seen to be the means by which the animal realm, the type of all our knowledge of organic life, is to be perfected. To whatever orders of phenomena natural classification is to be applied, here its theory must first be studied; and hence it is that biological science bears so important a part in the advancement of the whole of the positive method. It is much that a considerable progress has been made in ranging, in a due order of dignity, the immense series of living beings, from Man to the simplest plant: but, moreover, this theory of classification is an indispensable element of the whole positive method; an element which could not have been developed in any other way, nor even otherwise appreciated.

## CHAPTER IV.

#### ORGANIC OR VEGETATIVE LIFE.

Condition of Dynamical Biology.
WE have to pass on to dynamical biology, which is very far indeed from having attained the clearness and certainty of the statical department of the science. Important as are the physiological researches of recent times, they are only preliminary attempts, which must be soundly systematized before they can constitute a true dynamical biology. The minds which are devoted to mathematical, astronomical, and physical studies are not of a different make from those of physiologists; and the sobriety of the former classes, and the extravagance of the latter, must be ascribed to the definite constitution of the simpler sciences and the chaotic state of physiology. The melancholy condition of this last is doubtless owing in part to the vicious education of those who cultivate it, and who go straight to the study of the most complex phenomena without having prepared their understandings by the practice of the most simple and positive speculation: but I consider the prevalent license as due yet more to the indeterminate condition of the spirit of physiological science. In fact, the two disadvantages are one; for if the true character of the science were established, the preparatory education would immediately be rectified.

This infantine state of physiology prescribes the method of treating it here. I cannot proceed, as in statical biology, to an analytical estimate of established conceptions. I can only examine, in pure physiology, the notions of method; that is, the mode of organization of the researches necessary to the ascertainment of the laws of vital phenomena. The progress of biological philosophy depends on the distinct and rational institution of physiological questions, and not on attempts, which must be premature, to resolve them. Conceptions relating to method are always important in proportion to the complexity of the phenomena in view: therefore are they especially valuable in the case of vital phenomena; and above all, while the science is in a nascent state.

Though all vital phenomena are truly interconnected, we must, as usual, decompose them, for purposes of speculative study, into those of greater and those of less generality. *Vital phenomena: their division.* This distinction answers to Bichat's division into the organic or vegetative life, which is the common basis of existence of all living bodies; and animal life, proper to animals, but the chief characters of which are clearly marked only in the higher part of the zoological scale. But, since Gall's time, it has become necessary to add a third division,—the positive study of the intellectual and moral phenomena which are distinguished from the preceding by a yet more marked speciality, as the organisms which rank nearest to Man are the only ones which admit of their direct exploration. Though, under a rigorous definition, this last class of functions may doubtless be implicitly included in what we call the animal life, yet its restricted generality, the dawning positivity of its systematic study, and the peculiar nature of the higher difficulties that it offers, all indicate that we ought, at least for the present, to regard this new scientific theory as a last fundamental branch of physiology; in order that an unseasonable fusion should not disguise its high importance, and alter its true character. These, then, are the three divisions which remain for us to study, in our survey of biological science.

Before proceeding to the analysis of organic or vegetative life, I must say a few words on the theory of organic media, without considering which, there can be no true analysis of vital phenomena. *Theory of Organic Media.*

This new element may be said to have been practically introduced into the science by that controversy of Lamarck, already treated of, about the variation of animal species through the prolonged influence of external circumstances. It is our business here to exclude from the researches thus introduced, everything but what concerns physiology properly so called, reduced to the abstract theory of the living organism. We have seen that the vital state supposes the necessary and permanent concurrence of a certain aggregate of external actions with the action of the organism itself: it is the exact analysis of these conditions of existence which is the object of the preliminary theory of organic media; and I think it should be effected by considering separately each of the fundamental influences under which the general phenomenon of life occurs. It cannot be necessary to point out the importance of the study of this half of the dualism which is the condition of life: but I may just remark on the evidence it affords of the subordination of the organic to the inorganic philosophy; the influence of the medium on the organism being an impracticable study as long as the constitution of the medium is not exactly known.

*Exterior conditions of Life.* The exterior conditions of the life of the organism are of two classes,—physical and chemical; or, in other words, mechanical and molecular. Both are indispensable; but the first may be considered, from their more rigorous and sensible permanence, the most general,—if not as to the different organisms, at least as to the continued duration of each of them.

*Mechanical conditions. Weight.* First in generality we must rank the action of Weight. There is no denying that Man himself must obey, whether as weight or projectile, the same mechanical laws that govern every other equivalent mass: and by reason of the universality of these laws, weight participates largely in the production of vital phenomena, to which it is sometimes favourable, sometimes opposed, and scarcely ever indifferent. There is great difficulty in the analysis of its effects, because its influence cannot be suspended or much modified for the purpose; but we have ascertained something of them, both in the normal and the pathological states of the organism. In the lower, the vegetable portion of the scale, the physiological action of weight is less varied but more preponderant, the vital state being there extremely simple and least removed from the inorganic condition. The laws and limits of the growth of vegetables appear to depend essentially on this influence, as is proved by Mr. Knight's experiments on germination, as modified by a quicker or slower motion of rotation. Much higher organisms are subject to analogous conditions, without which we could not explain, for instance, why the largest animal masses live constantly in a fluid sufficiently dense to support almost their whole weight, and often to raise it spontaneously. However, the superior part of the animal series is least fit for the ascertainment of the physiological influence of weight, from its concurrence with a great number of heterogeneous actions: but this again enables us to study it in a variety of vital operations: for there is scarcely a function, organic, animal, or even intellectual, in which we may not point out the indispensable intervention of weight, which specially manifests itself in all that relates to the stagnation or movement of fluids. It is therefore much to be regretted that a subject so extended and important has not been studied in a rational spirit and method.

The next mechanical condition,—pressure, liquid or gaseous,—is an indirect consequence of weight. Some few scientific results have here been obtained, from the facility with which pressure may be modified by artificial or natural circumstances. There are limits in the barometrical scale, outside of which no atmospherical animal,—Man or any other,—can exist. We cannot so directly verify such a law in the case of aquatic animals: but it would seem that in proportion to the density of the medium must be the narrowness of the vertical limits assignable to the abode of each species. Of the relation between these intervals and the degree of organization, it must be owned, however, that we have no scientific knowledge, our ideas being, in fact, wholly confused as to the inferior organisms, and especially in the vegetable kingdom. Though, through many difficulties and complexities, the science is in a merely nascent state, some inquiries, such as those relating to the influence of atmospheric pressure on the venous circulation, and recent observations on its co-operation in the mechanism of standing and moving, etc., show that biologists are disposed to study this order of questions in a rational manner.

*Pressure.*

**Motion and rest.** Among the physical conditions, and perhaps first among them, the physiological influence of motion and rest should be investigated. Amidst the confusion and obscurity which exist on this subject, I think we may conclude that no organism, even the very simplest, could live in a state of complete immobility. The double movement of the earth, and especially its rotation, may probably be as necessary to the development of life as to the periodical distribution of heat and light. Too much care, however, cannot be taken to avoid confounding the motion produced by the organism itself with that by which it is affected from without; and the analysis had therefore better be applied to communicated than spontaneous motion. And as rotary motion tends, by the laws of mechanics, to disorganize any system, and therefore, eminently, to trouble its interior phenomena, it is this kind of motion which may be studied with the best result; for which object we should do well to investigate, in a comparative way, the modifications undergone by the principal functions from the organism being made to rotate in such a gradual variety as is compatible with a normal state. The attempt has as yet been made only with plants, and for another purpose; while, in the case of the superior animals, including Man, we have only incomplete and disjointed observations, scarcely transcending mere popular notions.

**Thermological action.** After the mechanical influences, we reach one which affects structure—the thermological action of the medium. It is the best known of all: for nothing is plainer than that life can exist only within certain limits of the thermometrical scale, and that there are limits affecting every family, and even every living race; and again, that the distribution of organisms over our globe takes place in zones sufficiently marked, as to differences of heat, to furnish thermometrical materials to the physicists, in a general way. But, amidst the multitude of facts in our possession, all the essential points of rational doctrine are still obscure and uncertain. We have not even any satisfactory series of observations about the thermometrical intervals corresponding to the different organic conditions;—much less any law relating to such a harmony, which has never, in fact, been connected with any other essential biological character. This great gap exists as much with regard to the successive states of the same organism as to the scale of organisms. The necessary revision might be best applied first to the lowest states; as the egg and the lowest organisms appear able to sustain wider differences of temperature than those of a higher order: and several philosophical biologists have even believed that life may have been always possible on our planet, notwithstanding the different systems of temperature through which its surface has successively passed. On the whole, the sum of our analyses may seem to disclose, amidst many anomalies, a general law: that the vital state is so subordinated to a determinate thermometrical interval, as that this interval perpetually diminishes as life becomes more marked,—in the case both of the individual and of the series. If even this general law is not yet scientifically established, it may be supposed how ignorant we are of the modifications produced in the organism by variations of external temperature, within the limits compatible with life. There has even been much confusion between the results of abrupt and gradual changes of temperature, though experiment has shown that graduation vastly expands the limits within which the human organism can exist; and again, between the influence of external, and the organic production of vital heat. This last great error shows that even the laying down the question remains to be done. The same thing may be said of the other exterior conditions, such as light and electricity, of which all that we know in this connection is that they exert a permanent influence needful for the production and support of life. Besides the confusion and uncertainty of our observations, we have to contend with the inferiority of our knowledge of those branches of physics, and with the mischief of the baseless hypotheses which we before saw to infest the study of them. While physicists talk of fluids and ethers, avowing that they do so in an artificial sense, for purposes of convenience, physiologists speak of them as the real principles of two orders of exterior actions indispensable to the vital state. Till

*Light, Electricity, etc.*

reform becomes substantial and complete in the study of light and electricity, these will remain the exterior conditions of vitality of which our knowledge is the most imperfect.

*Molecular conditions.* Passing on from the physical to the chemical conditions of the medium, we find our amount of knowledge scarcely more satisfactory. In strict generality, this study relates to the physiological in-
*Air and Water.* fluence of air and water, the mingling of which, in various degrees, constitutes the common medium necessary to vitality. As M. de Blainville remarked, they must not be considered separately, as in a physical or chemical inquiry, but in that mixture which varies only in the proportions of its elements. This might be anticipated from our knowledge of the chemical constitution of living bodies, the essential elements of which are found only in the combination of air and water: but we have physiological evidence also, which shows that air deprived of moisture, and water not aerated, are fatal to vital existence. In this view there is no difference between atmospheric and aquatic beings, animal and vegetable, but the unequal proportion of the two fluids; the air, in the one case, serving as a vehicle for vaporized water; and the water, in the other case, conveying liquefied air. In both cases, water furnishes the indispensable basis of all the organic liquids: and the air the essential elements of nutrition. We know that the higher mammifera, including Man, perish when the air reaches a certain degree of dryness, as fishes do in water which has been sufficiently deprived of air by distillation. Between these extreme terms there exists a multitude of intermediaries in which moister conditions of air and more aerated states of water correspond with determinate organisms; and the observation of Man in the different hygrometrical states of atmospheres shows how, in the individual case, physiological phenomena are modified within the limits compatible with the vital state. If we may say that the question has been laid down in this inquiry, it is only in a vague and obscure way. Besides our ignorance of the varying proportions, we have none but the most confused notions about the way in which each fluid participates in the support of life. Oxygen is the only element of the air about

which we have made any intelligent inquiry, while physiologists entertain the most contradictory notions about azote: and the uncertainty and obscurity are still greater with regard to water. In this state of infancy, it can be no wonder that the science offers as yet no law as to the influence of the medium on the organism—even in regard to the question whether a certain condition of existence becomes more or less inevitable as the organism rises in the scale.

The study of the influence of specifics does not enter here, on account, of course, of the absence of generality; but it should be just pointed out that, reduced as is the number of substances called specifics, there are still enough,—as aliments, medicines, and poisons,—to afford a hint of what might be learned by an exploration of them, in regard to the harmony between the organic world and the inorganic. The very quality of their operation, that it is special and discontinuous, and therefore not indispensable, indicates the experimental method in this case, as being certain, well circumscribed, and very various. This study may then be regarded as a needful appendix, completing the preliminary biological doctrine which I have called that of organic media, and offering resources which are proper to it, and cannot be otherwise obtained. Unhappily, this complement is in even a more backward state than the more essential portions, notwithstanding the multitude of observations, unconnected and unfinished, already assembled in this path of research.

*Study of specifics.*

If such is the state of preliminary knowledge, it is clear how little has yet been learned of the laws of life themselves. The inquiry has gone through revolutions, as other questions have, before reaching the threshold of positivity, in our day. From the impulse given by Descartes, the illustrious school of Boerhaave arose in physiology, which exaggerated the subordination of biology to the simpler parts of natural philosophy so far as to assign to the study of life the place of appendix to the general system of inorganic physics. From the consequent reaction against this absurdity arose the theory of Stahl, which may be considered the most scientific formula of the metaphysical state of physiology.

*History of Physiology.*

The struggle has since lain between these two schools,—the strength of the metaphysical one residing in its recognition of physiology as a distinct science, and that of the physico-chemical, in its principle of the dependence of the organic on the inorganic laws, as daily disclosed more fully by the progress of science. The effect of this improved knowledge has been to modify the conceptions of metaphysical physiology: the formula of Barthez, for instance, representing a further departure from the theological state than that of Stahl; as Stahl's already did than that of Van Helmont, though the same metaphysical entity might be in view when Van Helmont called it the *archeus*, and Stahl the *soul*, and Barthez the *vital principle*. Stahl instituted a reaction against the physico-chemical exaggerations of Boerhaave; but Barthez established, in his preliminary discourse, the characteristics of sound philosophizing, and exposed the necessary futility of all inquisition into causes and modes of production of phenomena, reducing all real science to the discovery of their laws. For want of the requisite practice in the positive method, the scheme of Barthez proved abortive; and, after having proposed his conception of a vital principle as a mere term to denote the unknown cause of vital phenomena, he was drawn away by the prevalent spirit of his time to regard the assumed principle as a real and complex existence, though profoundly unintelligible. Ineffectual as his enterprise proved, its design with regard to the advancement of positive science cannot be mistaken. The progressive spirit is still more marked in the physiological theory of Bichat, though we find entities there too. These entities however show a great advance, as a determinate and visible seat is assigned to them. The vital forces of Bichat however still intervene in phenomena, like the old specific entities introduced into physics and chemistry, in their metaphysical period, under the name of faculties or occult virtues, which Descartes so vigorously hunted down, and Molière so happily ridiculed. Such is the character of the supposed *organic sensibility*, by which, though a mere term, Bichat endeavoured to *explain* physiological phenomena, which he thus merely reproduced under another name: as when, for instance, he thought he had accounted for the successive flow of different liquids in one canal by saying that the organic sensibility of the canal was successively in harmony with each fluid, and in antipathy to the rest. But for his untimely death however, there can be no doubt that he would have issued into an entire positivity. His treatise on General Anatomy, though appearing a very few years after his treatise on Life and Death, is a great advance upon it; and even in the construction of his metaphysical theory of vital forces he certainly first introduced, under the title *properties of tissue*, a conception of the highest value, destined to absorb all ontological conceptions, and to prepare for the entire positivity of the elementary notions of physiology. The thing required is to substitute *properties* for *forces*; and Bichat's treatment of tissue fulfilled this condition with regard to a very extensive class of effects: and thus his theory, while it amended the metaphysical doctrine of Stahl and Barthez, opened the way to its entire reformation by presenting at once the germ and the example of purely positive conceptions. This is now the state of physiological philosophy in the minds of the majority of students; and the conflict between the schools of Stahl and Boerhaave,—between the metaphysical and the physico-chemical tendency,—remains at the point to which it was brought up by the impulse communicated by Bichat. It would be hopeless to look to the oscillations of this antagonism for an advance in science. If the one doctrine prevailed, science would be in a state of retrogression; if the other, in a state of dissolution; as in our social condition, in the conflict of the two political tendencies, the retrograde and the revolutionary. The progress of physiology depends on the growth of positive elementary conceptions, such as will remand to the domain of history the controversy from which nothing more is to be expected. Abundant promise of such an issue now appears: the two schools have annulled each other; and the natural development of the science has furnished means for its complete institution to be begun. This I look upon as the proper task of the existing generation of scientific men, who need only a better training to make them adequate to it. If, from its complexity, physiology has been later than other sciences in its rational formation, it may reach its maturity more rapidly from the ground having been cleared by the pursuit of the anterior sciences. Many delays were occasioned in their case by transitory phases which were not understood in the earlier days of positivity, and which need never again arrest experienced investigation. It may be hoped that physiologists will spare their science the useless and humbling delay in the region of metaphysical hypothesis which long embarrassed the progress of physics.

Philosophical character of Physiology. The true philosophical character of physiology consists, as we have seen, in establishing an exact and constant harmony between the statical and the dynamical points of view,—between the ideas of organization and of life,—between the notion of the agent and that of the act; and hence arises the obligation to reduce all abstract conceptions of physiological *properties* to the consideration of elementary and general phenomena, each of which conveys the idea of a determinate seat. In other words, the reduction of *functions* to corresponding *properties* must be regarded as the simple consequence of decompounding the general life into the different functions,—discarding all notions about *causes*, and inquiring only into *laws*. Bichat's conception of the properties of tissue contains the first germ of this renovated view; but it only indicates the nature of the philosophical operation, and contains no solution of the problem. Not only is there a secondary confusion between the properties of tissue and simple physical properties, but the principle of the conception is vitiated by the irrational distinction between the properties of tissue and vital properties; for no property can be admitted in physiology without its being at once vital and belonging to tissue. In endeavouring to harmonize the different degrees of physiological and of anatomical analysis, we may lay down the philosophical principle that the idea of *property* which indicates the last term of the one must correspond with *tissue*, which is the extreme term of the other; whilst the idea of *function*, on the other hand, corresponds to that of *organ*: so that the successive ideas of function and of property present a gradation of thoughts similar to that which exists between the ideas of organ and of tissue, except that the one relates to the act and the other to the agent. This relation appears to me to constitute an incontestable and important rule in biological philosophy; and on it we may establish the first great division among physiological properties. We have seen how in anatomy there is a division between the fundamental, generating tissue, the cellular, and the secondary tissues which result from the combination of certain substances with this original web; and in the same way must physiological properties be divided into two groups,—the one comprising the general properties which belong to all the tissues, and which constitute the proper life of the cellular tissue; and the other, the special properties which characterize its most marked modifications,—that is, the muscular and nervous tissues. This division, indicated by anatomy, strikingly agrees with the great physiological distinction between the organic or vegetative and the animal life; as the first order of properties must afford the basis of that general life, common to all organized beings, to which vegetable existence is reduced; while the second relates exclusively to the special life of animated beings. Such a correspondence at once makes the principle more unquestionable, and facilitates the application of the rule. Division of the study.

If we look at what has been done, towards the construction of this fundamental theory, we shall find that it is fairly accomplished with regard to the secondary, or animal tissues,—all the general phenomena of animal life being unanimously connected with irritability and sensibility,—these being considered as attributes each of a definite tissue: and thus, the most marked case is the best understood. But the other division,—the properties which are wholly general, belonging to the universal life, are far more important, as underlying the others; and an extreme confusion and divergence exist with regard to them. No clear and satisfactory conception of the second class can be formed while the first is left in obscurity; and thus, the science remains in a purely provisional state,—its development having taken place in an order inverse to that which its nature requires.

The functions which belong to the vegetative life are two,—the antagonism of which corresponds to the definition of life itself: Two functions of the organic life.

first, the interior *absorption* of nutritive materials from the surrounding medium; whence results, after their assimilation, final nutrition; and secondly, the *exhalation* of molecules, which then become foreign bodies, to be parted with, or disassimilated, as nutrition proceeds. It appears to be an error to make digestion and circulation characteristics of animality; as we certainly find them here in the fundamental sense of both. Digestion is properly a preparation of aliment for assimilation; and this takes place in a simple and almost unvaried manner in vegetable organisms: and circulation, though nothing like what it is in animals, where there is a central organ to effect it, is not less essential in vegetative life,—the lowest organism showing the continual motion of a fluid holding in suspension or dissolved, matters absorbed or thrown out; and this perpetual oscillation, which does not require a system of vessels to itself, but may take place through the cellular tissue, is equally indispensable to animal and vegetable existence. These, then, are the two great vegetative processes, performed by properties which are provisionally supposed (after the analysis of M. de Blainville, which is open to some objection) to be three,—hygrometricity, capillarity, and retractility. This analysis shows clearly that the actions which constitute vegetable life are simply physico-chemical phenomena; physical as to the motion of the molecules inwards and outwards; and chemical in what relates to the successive modifications of these different substances. Under the first aspect, they depend on the properties, hygrometrical, capillary, and retractile, of the cellular tissue: under the second, and much more obscure at present, they relate to the molecular action which its composition admits. This is the spirit in which the analysis of organic phenomena should be instituted; whereas that of animal phenomena should be regarded from a wholly different point of view, as we shall see hereafter.

The study of this vegetative life is not even yet rationally organized. We have seen that, in the anatomical view, the vegetable kingdom is regarded as the last term of an unique series,—the various degrees of which differ, for the most part, more widely from each other than any one of them from this extreme term. The same conception should direct physiological speculations on the organic life, analyzed uniformly for all living beings: but this has not hitherto been even attempted. Till it is accomplished, no essential point of physiological doctrine can be established, however able may be the investigations carried on, and however valuable the materials supplied. It may be alleged that the phenomena relating to general life may be studied in the broadest simplicity in vegetable organisms: but it is no more possible in physiology than in anatomy to interpret the extreme cases in the scale by each other without having passed through the intermediate degrees: and the dynamical case is the more difficult of the two: so that the isolated study of the organic life in vegetables cannot illustrate that of the higher order of animals. And one natural consequence of this irrational isolation of the vegetable case is that chemists and physicists have engrossed researches which properly belong to biologists alone. The comparative method, which we have seen to be the characteristic resource of biological philosophy, has not as yet been duly introduced into the general study of organic life, though it is at once more indispensable, and more completely applicable than in the case of animal life. If it were consistent with the character of this Work, we could point out gaps at almost every step, and about the simplest phenomena, which must shock any inquiring mind:—the darkness, doubts, and differences about digestion; and again about gaseous digestion, or respiration;—in regard to which the most contradictory opinions are held:—divergences about the simplest preliminary phenomena of vegetative life, which show how much has to be done before we can undertake any direct investigation into the phenomena of assimilation and the converse process.

We shall find ourselves even further from satisfaction if we turn from the consideration of the *functions* of organic life to those more compound phenomena which are usually confounded with them, but which M. de Blainville has taught us to distinguish as *results* from the action of, not one organ or set of organs, as in the case of function, but of the simultaneous action of all the principal organs. Of these results, the

*Results of organic action.*

**State of composition and decomposition.**

most immediate and necessary is the continuous state of composition and decomposition which characterizes the vegetative life. Ignorant as we are of assimilation and secretion, the very questions cannot have been as yet suitably laid down. No one has thought, for instance, of instituting an exact chemical comparison between the total composition of each organism and the corresponding system of alimentation; nor, conversely, between the exhaled products and the whole of the agents which had supplied or modified them; so that we can give no precise scientific account of the general phenomenon of the composition and decomposition of every organism as a necessary consequence of the concurrence of the different functions. We have at present only incomplete and disjointed materials, which have never been referred to any general fact.

**Vital heat.**

It is acknowledged now that all organisms have, more or less, the character which used to be ascribed to only the highest, of sustaining a determinate temperature, notwithstanding variations of heat in their environment; and this is a second result of the whole of the vegetative functions, which almost always co-exists with the first. But this important study is not only in a backward state, but ill-conceived. Besides the error before noticed, of confounding vital heat with the temperature of the medium, the fundamental character of the phenomenon appears to me to have been misconceived. Its modification by the animal functions can never be understood till it has been studied in its primitive universal manifestation in all living bodies, each of which represents a chemical centre, able to maintain its temperature against external influences, within certain limits, as a necessary consequence of the phenomena of composition and decomposition. This is doubtless the point of view from which the positive study of vital heat must be regarded; and to consider it under the modifications of animal life, is to place the accessory before the principal, and to propose views which are merely provisional, if not erroneous. In the most recent works upon this leading subject, the organic foundations are, it is true, more carefully considered: but the investigation cannot be said to be duly instituted as long as the vegetable organism is not regularly introduced into it.

These remarks are even more applicable to the electrical study of living bodies. Here we find again, and with aggravation, the confusion between organic action and external influence, as well as the aberrations remarked on in physics about ethers and electric fluids. Here, too, we meet with the error observed upon in the last case, about the physiological origin of the phenomenon. And here, again, we are bound to conclude that a permanent electrization is ascribable to acts of composition and decomposition, notwithstanding the electrical variations of the medium. And again we find that the animal functions can only modify, by accelerating or augmenting, more or less, the fundamental phenomenon. But the electrical analysis of the organism is yet further than the thermological from being conceived of and pursued in a rational view.

*Electrical state.*

Next follow the general phenomena which result in a less direct and necessary manner from the whole of the vegetative functions:—the production and development of living bodies.

Notwithstanding the original investigations of Harvey and of Haller, with regard to the superior animals, this investigation may be considered, owing to its complexity, to be more in the rear of a positive institution than any of the preceding. The tendency to search for causes and modes of production of phenomena, instead of for their laws, has acted with fatal effect here; and, amidst every kind of deficiency, the main cause of the obscurity of the case is, undoubtedly, that students have occupied themselves in looking for what cannot be found. However, the labours of anatomists and zoologists have evidently prepared the way for a more rational study. It is even worthy of remark that some students who were most bent on the search into causes have been led on by the spread of the positive spirit, to spend their efforts on inquiries into ovology and embryology, which are assuming a more scientific character every day. Still, the preliminary requisite for the formation of doctrine,—a fundamental analysis,

*Production and development of living bodies.*

—remains unfulfilled; and the ascertainment of the laws of production and development is not, therefore, to be attempted at present. In the lowest departments of the scale, the multiplication of organisms takes place by a simple prolongation of any part of the parent mass, which is almost homogeneous; and in this extreme case, we understand the phenomenon to be analogous to every other kind of reproduction of the primitive cellular tissue. In the higher degrees of the scale, we are in the dark from the moment we depart from immediate observation; and when the simplest previsions are so radically uncertain and even erroneous as in this case, the science may be pronounced to be in a state of infancy, notwithstanding the imposing appearance of the mass of works accumulated for its illustration.

The comparative method has been applied in a yet more incomplete way to the phenomena of organic development. The question has never yet been laid down under a form common to all organisms, including the vegetable. The grave error is still committed of studying the development in the animal cases alone; so that the most eminently animal of the systems, the nervous, is represented as the first to appear in the embryo of the higher orders,—a supposition adverse to the institution of any really general conception of the theory of development, and in direct opposition to one of the most constant laws of biological philosophy,—the perpetual accordance between the chief phases of the individual evolution and the most marked successive degrees of the organic hierarchy; for in this last view the nervous tissue is seen to be the latest and most special transformation of the primitive tissue. The preliminary analysis of organic development is, then, still far from being conceived of in a rational spirit, governed by the high philosophical intention of reconciling, as much as possible, the various essential aspects of the science of living bodies.

*Decline of the organism.* To be complete, this analysis should evidently be followed by the inverse, and yet correlative study of the decline of the organism, from its maturity to its death. The general theory of death is certainly in a very backward state, since the ablest physiological researches on this subject have usually related to violent or accidental death; considered, too, in the highest organisms exclusively, and affecting functions and systems of organs of an essentially animal nature. As for the deterioration of the organic life, we have yet attained to only one initiatory philosophical glimpse, which exhibits it as a necessary consequence of life itself, by the growing predominance of the movement of exhalation over that of absorption, whence results gradually an exaggerated consolidation of the organism which was originally almost fluid, a process which, in the absence of more rapid influences, tends to produce a state of desiccation incompatible with all vital phenomena. Valuable, however, as is such a glimpse, it serves only to characterize the true nature of the question, by indicating the general direction of the researches which it requires. The important considerations relative to animal life could not be rationally introduced into such a subject till this preliminary doctrine shall have been established; as in regard to all the other points of view before examined.

Summary as this review has been, we have seen enough to be authorized to conclude that the backward state of physiological science is owing mainly to the vicious training of physiologists, and the irrational institution of their habitual labours. The circulation of the blood, the first general fact which gave birth to positive physiology; and the laws of the fall of bodies, the first acquisition of sound physics, are discoveries almost absolutely contemporaneous; and yet, what an immense inequality there is now in the progress of two sciences setting out from so similar a disclosure! Such a difference cannot be attributed wholly to the greater complexity of physiological phenomena, and must have depended much also on the scientific spirit which directed their general study, to the level of which the greater number of those who cultivate it have been unable to rise. The phenomena of the vegetative life obviously require, both for their analysis and their explanation, an intimate combination of the leading notions of inorganic philosophy with physiological considerations, obtained through a thorough familiarity with the preliminary laws relating to the structure and classification of living bodies. Now, each of these inseparable conditions is, in our day, the separate property of a particular order of positive investigators. Hence we have, on the one hand, the supposed organic chemistry, a bastard study, which is only a rough first sketch of vegetable physiology, undertaken by inquirers who know nothing of the true subject of their labours: and, on the other hand, vague, incoherent, and partly metaphysical doctrines, of which physiology has been chiefly constituted by minds almost entirely destitute of the most indispensable preliminary ideas. The barren anarchy which has resulted from so vicious an organization of scientific labour would be enough of itself to testify to the direct utility of the general, and yet positive point of view which characterizes the foregoing survey.

## CHAPTER V.

#### THE ANIMAL LIFE.

IT was only by a late and long-prepared effort that the human mind could attain that state of abstraction and physiological generality necessary for the comprehension of all vital beings,—from Man to the vegetable,—as one series. It is only in our own day that a point of view so new and so difficult has been established; and as yet, among only the most advanced minds, even as regards the simplest general aspects of biology,—in the statical study of the organism. It is not at all surprising that physiological comparison should have been first applied to the animal functions, because they first suggest its importance and possibility, however clearly it may afterwards appear that the organic life at once requires and admits a larger and more indispensable application of the comparative method. Looking more closely, however, into this evident existing superiority of animal over organic physiology, we must bear in mind the distinction between the two elementary aspects of every positive study,—the analysis of phenomena and their explanation. It is only with regard to the first that the animal life has been in reality better explored than the organic. It is not possible that the explanation of the most special and complex phenomena should be more advanced than that of the most simple and general, which serve as a basis to the others. Such a state of the science would be in opposition to all the established laws of the human mind.

However imperfect the theory of organic phenomena still is, it is unquestionably conceived in a more scientific spirit than we find in any explanations of animal physiology. We have seen that the vegetative phenomena approach most nearly to the inorganic; and that the school of Boerhaave sinned only in exaggeration, proceeding from in-

*Transition from the inorganic to the organic.* — sufficient knowledge; and it must be by this time evident that this is the link between the inorganic and the biological philosophy, by which we are enabled to regard the whole of natural philosophy as forming a homogeneous and continuous body of doctrine. By a natural consequence, a wholly different view must be taken of the rational theories of animal life: that is, of the phenomena of irritability and sensibility, which offer no basis of analogy with inorganic phenomena. With regard to sensibility, no one will question this: and, as to irritability,—though contraction may be seen as a movement occasioned by heat, and, yet more, by electricity, these phenomena must be carefully separated from the contractile effect of the irritable fibre which is a product of the nervous action; and especially when it is voluntary. Irritability is as radically foreign to the inorganic world as sensibility; with which, too, it is inseparably connected. *Primitive nervous properties.* — This double property is, then, strictly primitive in the secondary tissues, and therefore no more a subject of explanation than weight, heat, or any other fundamental physical property. Whenever we have a true theory of animal life, it will be by comparing all the general phenomena which are connected with this double property, according to their preparatory analysis, in order to discover their laws; that is, as in all other cases, their constant relations, both of succession and similitude. This will be done in order to the usual end of obtaining a rational prevision; the subject here being the mode of action of a given animal organism, placed in determinate circumstances; or, reciprocally, the animal arrangement that may be induced by any given act of animality. All attempts to explore the nature of sensibility and irritability are mere hindrances in the way of this final aim, by drawing off our attention from the laws of animality in a vain search after what can never be found.

*Relation of the animal to the organic life.* — The true relation of the animal to the organic life must throughout be carefully kept in mind. This relation is double. The organic life first serves as the basis of the animal; and then as its general end and object. We have dwelt enough on the first, if even any one would think of contesting that, in order to move and feel, the animal must first live; and that the fundamental vegetative life could not cease without extinguishing the other. As for the second relation, it is evident that the phenomena of irritability and sensibility are directed by the general needs of the organic life, which they serve by procuring better materials, and by guarding against unfavourable influences. Even the intellectual and moral functions have usually no other primitive office. Without such a destination, these properties would either destroy the organism or themselves perish. It is only in the human species, and even there only under a high degree of civilization, that any kind of inversion of this order can be conceived of. In that case, the vegetative life is essentially subordinated to the animal, the development of which it is alone destined to aid; and this, it seems to me, is the noblest scientific notion that we can form of humanity, distinct from animality:—a transformation which can be safely considered as possible only by transferring to the whole species, or at least to society, the primitive end which, in the case of animals, is limited to the individual, or, at the utmost, to the family, as we shall see hereafter. It is only among a small number of men, and it is very far indeed from being a just matter of expectation from the whole species, that the intellect can acquire such a preponderance in the whole of the organism as to become the end and object of human existence. An exception so special, and so easy to explain in the case of Man, cannot alter the universality of a consideration verified by the whole animal kingdom, wherein the animal life is seen to be always destined to perfect the organic. It is only by a scientific abstraction, necessary for purposes of progress, that we can provisionally conceive of the first as isolated from the second, which is, strictly speaking, inseparable from it under the double aspect just exhibited. Thus, as the positive theory of animality must continually rest on that of general vitality, it is indissolubly combined with the whole of inorganic philosophy, which furnishes the basis of organic physiology. In a secondary sense, the same dependence exists. We admitted, while reviewing mathematical philosophy, that the laws of

*To inorganic philosophy.*

equilibrium and motion operate among all orders of phenomena, being absolutely universal. Among physiological phenomena we find them accordingly; and, when contraction is produced by the irritability of the muscular fibre, all the phenomena of animal mechanics which result, whether for rest or locomotion, are dependent on the general laws of mechanics. In an inverse way the same thing takes place with regard to the functions of sensibility, in which the inorganic philosophy must intervene in connection with the primitive impression on the sentient extremities, carefully distinguished from its transmission by the nervous filament, and its perception by the cerebral organ. This impression acts through an intermediate physical apparatus, optical, acoustic, or other, the study of which according to appropriate physical laws, constitutes a chief element of the positive analysis of the phenomenon. Not only must we use the knowledge already established, but we want, for our analysis, further progress in it, and even the creation of new doctrines, as the theory of flavours, and yet more of odours, in regard to the mode of propagation of which there are doubtless several general laws, of a purely inorganic character, remaining to be established. In investigating these connections between biology and inorganic science, we find again what we saw before, that chemistry is spontaneously related to vegetable physiology, and physics especially to animal physiology; though neither could be altogether dispensed with in either department, where they are required, more or less, in combination.

*Properties of tissue.* Our ideas of the double properties of irritability and sensibility cannot be truly scientific till each is irreversibly assigned to a corresponding tissue. Bichat conceived of all tissues as necessarily sensitive and irritable, but in different degrees;—an error which was natural or inevitable at a time when so little was known of tissue in the way of anatomical analysis, but one which, if maintained now, would hand over the whole science to the physico-chemical school, and efface all real distinction between the inorganic and organic departments of natural philosophy. Rational biology requires that the two properties should be inherent in determinate tissues,—themselves modifications, profound and distinctly marked, of the primitive cellular tissue,—that our anatomical data may be in harmony with the physiological; in other words, that the elementary ideas of tissue and of property should be in perfect correspondence. The scientific character of physiology in this direction is essentially defective among biologists in general. But the new explorations continually made show us how it was that Bichat was misled. He considered it proved that sensibility existed where there were no nerves: but further investigation proves that the systems of sensibility were erroneously attributed to an organ deprived of nerves, instead of being referred to the simultaneous injury of neighbouring nerves; or that the nervous tissue existed, though it was difficult to find. If cases apparently contradictory still remain, it would be obviously absurd to reject on their account a conception required by the principles of rational physiology, and founded on unquestionable cases, by far more numerous and decisive than those which still seem to be exceptional. This consideration should be applied to different organisms, as well as to the different tissues of the human organism. The animals supposed to be without nerves, on which the metaphysical school has insisted so much, disappear as comparative anatomy enables us to generalize more and more the idea of nervous tissue, and to detect it in the inferior organisms. It is thus, for instance, that it has been recently found in several radiated animals. The time has come for its being established as a philosophical axiom that nerves are necessary for any degree of sensibility, the apparent exceptions being left as so many anomalies to be resolved by the future progress of anatomical analysis.

*Sensibility.*

The same process must be instituted with the common notions of irritability, which are still ruled by Bichat's theory. He supposed, for instance, that the contractions of the heart were determined, independently of all nervous action, by the immediate stimulus of the flow of the blood towards it; whereas, it is now established that a provision of nerves is as indispensable to the irritability of this muscle as of any other; and generally, that the great distinction laid down by Bichat, between organic and animal contractility, must be abandoned.

*Irritability.*

All irritability is then necessarily animal; that is, it requires a corresponding nervous provision, whatever may be the immediate centre from which the nervous action proceeds. Much illustration of this subject is needed for its scientific use, though not for the logical sanction of a principle already placed beyond dispute. We need this further enlightenment, not only in regard to the use of the modern distinction made by many physiologists between the sensory and the motory nerves, though such a question has considerable philosophical importance; but much more in regard to another consideration, more direct and more eminent, in regard to which we are in a state of most inconvenient uncertainty and obscurity: I mean the scientific distinction which must be maintained, sooner or later, between the voluntary and involuntary motions. The doctrine of Bichat had the advantage of representing this difference, which we see, in fact, to have furnished him with his chief arguments; whereas, now that we insist on irritability being of one kind only, and dependent on a nervous provision, we find ourselves involved in a very delicate fundamental difficulty, the solution of which is however indispensable, to enable us to understand how all motions must not be indistinctly voluntary. For this solution we must obtain—what we certainly have not as yet— an exact co-ordination of anatomical differences with incontestable physiological differences. There can be no question that such a phenomenon as the voluntary movements of the locomotive muscles while that of the cardiac muscle remains absolutely involuntary, must admit of analysis, however difficult it may be. Here then we find a chasm among the very principles of the science, by which the positive theory of irritability is much perplexed, certain as is its principle. In almost all cases the ablest anatomist is unable to decide otherwise than by the fact itself, if any definite motion is necessarily voluntary or involuntary; which affords sufficient proof of the absence of any real law in the case. The solution will probably be obtained by an analysis of the intermediate motions, as we may call them,—those which, involuntary at first, end in becoming voluntary; or the reverse. These cases, which are very common, appear to me eminently fit to prove that the distinction between voluntary and involuntary motions arises from no radical difference of muscular irritability, but only from the mode, and perhaps the degree of innervation, modified by long habit. If this be as generally true as it seems to be in some cases of acquired control, it must be supposed that the most involuntary motions, which are those most indispensable to life, would have been susceptible of voluntary suspension (not even excepting the motions of the heart) if their incessant rigorous necessity had not hindered the contraction of suitable habits in their case. While we conclude it to be probable that the difference between the two kinds of motion proceeds indirectly from the action of the entire nervous system upon the muscular system, we cannot help perceiving how greatly science stands in need of a thorough new examination into this obscure fact.

This brief survey shows us the general imperfection of the study of animality. We shall find that even in the department of the primitive analysis of its general phenomena, in which it appears so superior to that of the organic life, it is very far indeed from being yet fit for exploration by positive laws. *Present state of analysis of animality.*

In regard to irritability, first,—the mechanism of no animal movement has yet been satisfactorily analysed,—all the chief cases being still the subject of radical controversy among equally qualified physiologists. We retain a vicious distinction among movements, contrary to all mechanical judgment,—a distinction between the general motion which displaces the whole mass, and the partial motions which subserve the organic life,—as for the reception of aliment, or the expulsion of any residuum, or the circulation of fluids; yet the first order are partial, though their object is unlike that of the second; for, in a mechanical view, the organism allows of no others. By the great laws of motion, the animal can never displace its centre of gravity by interior motion, without co-operation from its environment, any more than a steam-carriage which should work without friction on a horizontal plane, turning its wheels without result. The movements which produce locomotion are not *Movement.*

mechanically different from those, for instance, which carry food along the alimentary canal;—the difference is in the apparatus, which, for locomotion, consists of exterior appendages, so disposed as to cause a reaction in the medium, which produces the displacement of the whole body. Certain mollusks furnish an illustration of this, when they change their place by means of contractions of the cardiac muscle, or of intestinal muscles. The simplest notions of animal mechanics being thus obscured and corrupted in their origin, it is no wonder that the physiologists still dispute about the mechanism of the circulation, and most of the means of locomotion, as leaping, flying, swimming, etc. In the way in which they proceed, they are remote from any mutual understanding, and the most opposite opinions may be maintained with equal plausibility. It needs but a word to suggest to those who have attended to what has gone before, that this extreme imperfection results from the inadequate and faulty education of physiologists, who are too often ignorant of the inorganic science which is here directly involved. The complexity of the animal apparatus, and the impossibility of bringing the primitive moving powers under any mathematical theory, will for ever forbid the application of numerical methods: but the great laws of equilibrium and motion are applicable, through all varieties of apparatus, and are the same in animal mechanics, or celestial, or industrial, or any other mechanics whatever. Some physiologists, finding their difficulty, have handed over their study to the geometers and physicists; and these, with their habits of numerical precision, and their ignorance of anatomy, have brought out only absurd results. The remedy is, as we know, in the work being consigned to physiologists, duly prepared by a sufficient training in inorganic science. The study of animal sounds, or phonation, for instance, cannot be carried on to any purpose without such knowledge as physicists have of the theory of sound; and the general production of the voice, and the differences of utterance among animals, require for their explanation a knowledge at once of acoustics and anatomy; and speech itself requires this preparation no less, while demanding other requisites with it. It is to be hoped that all experience, in each department of scientific inquiry, will convince students more and more of the folly and mischief of the anarchical parcelling out of natural philosophy; but the physiologists are those who, above all, must see the need of a better organization of scientific labour,—so remarkable as is the subordination of their particular science to all that have gone before.

The analysis of the phenomena of sensibility is not more satisfactory than that of irritability: and even less so, if we leave out of the account the great knowledge that we have obtained, by anatomical study, of the corresponding organs; a knowledge which, however, must here be connected with physiology. The least imperfect part of this study relates to the simple exterior sensations. The phenomenon of sensation is composed of three elements, as we have seen: the impression of the external agent or the nervous extremities, by the aid of some physical apparatus; the transmission by the nervous fibre; and the reception by the cerebral organ. The first of these suggests, like the mechanical facts we have been considering, the immediate dependence of the phenomenon on the laws of the inorganic world; as the relation of the theory of visions to optics: of the theory of hearing to acoustics, in all that concerns the mode of action proper to the apparatus of sight and hearing. And yet, more expressly than even in the case of mechanics, have these theories been delivered into the hands of the physicists, who, again, bring out results from their treatment of them which are manifestly absurd. The only difference between this case and the preceding is that the metaphysicians have kept a longer hold upon this part of animal physiology,—the theory of sensations having been abandoned to them till a very recent time. It was not, indeed, till Gall imparted his ever-memorable impulse to the investigation, that physiologists claimed this department at all. It is no wonder, therefore, that the positive theory of sensations is less well conceived, and more recent, than that of motion; and naturally more imperfect, independently of its superior difficulty, and the backwardness of those branches of physics to which it relates. The simplest modifications of the phenomenon of

*Exterior sensation.*

vision and of hearing cannot as yet be referred with certainty to determinate organic conditions; as, for instance, the adjustment of the eye to see distinctly at very various distances; a faculty which the physiologists have allowed the physicists to attribute to various circumstances of structure, always illusory or inadequate, the physiologists the while playing the part of critics, instead of appropriating a study which belongs exclusively to them. Even the limits of the function are usually very vaguely defined: that is, the kind of exterior notions furnished by each sense, abstracted from all intellectual reflection, is rarely circumscribed with any distinctness. Thus it is no wonder if we are still ignorant of almost all positive laws of sight and hearing, and even of smell and taste.—The only point of doctrine, or rather of method, that we may consider to have attained any scientific stability, is the fundamental order in which the different kinds of sensations should be studied: and this notion has been supplied by comparative anatomy rather than by physiology. It consists in classifying the senses by their increasing speciality,—beginning with the universal sense of contact, or touch, and proceeding by degrees to the four special senses, taste, smell, sight, and finally, hearing. This order is rationally determined by the analysis of the animal series, as the senses must be considered more special and of a higher kind in proportion as they disappear from the lower degrees of the zoological scale. It is remarkable that this gradation coincides with the degree of importance of the sensation in regard to sociality, if not to intelligence. Unhappily, it measures yet more evidently the increasing imperfection of the theory.—We ought not to pass over the luminous distinction introduced by Gall between the passive and the active state of each special sense. An analogous consideration to this, but more fundamental, would consist, it seems to me, in distinguishing the senses themselves as active and passive, according as their action is, from their nature, voluntary or involuntary. This distinction seems very marked in the case of sight and hearing; the one requiring our free participation, to a certain extent, while the other affects us without our will, or even our consciousness. The more vague, but more profound influence that music exercises over us, compared with that of painting, seems to be chiefly attributable to such a diversity. An analogous difference, but less marked, exists between taste and smell.

There is a second class of sensations, forming the natural transition from the study of the sensations to that of the affective and intellectual functions, which all physiologists, since the time of Cabanis, and yet more, of Gall, have found it necessary to admit, to complete the study of the sensations. They are the interior sensations which relate to the satisfaction of the natural wants; and, in a pathological state, the pains produced by bodily alteration. These are still more indispensable than the first to the perfection of the organic life; and, though they procure no direct notions of the external world, they radically modify, by their intense and continuous action, the general course of intellectual operations, which are, in most animal species, entirely subordinated to them. This great department of the theory of sensations is even more obscure and unadvanced than the foregoing. The only positive notion which is fairly established in regard to it is that the nervous system is indispensable to both kinds of sensibility. *Interior sensation.*

Once again we see how the extreme imperfection of doctrine here is owing to the imperfection of method; and that again, as before, to the inadequate preparation of the inquirers to whom the study belongs. It is a great thing, however, to have withdrawn the subject from the control of the metaphysicians; and some labours of contemporary physiologists authorize us to hope that the true spirit of the inquiry is at length entered into; and that the study of the sensations will be directed, as it ought to be, to develope the radical accordance between anatomical and physiological analysis.

Having reviewed the two orders of animal functions, we must consider the complementary part of the theory of animality;—the ideas about the mode of action which are common to the phenomena of irritability and sensibility. It is true, these ideas belong also to intellectual and moral phenomena; but we must review them here, to complete our delineation of the chief aspects of the study of animal life. *Mode of action of animality.*

The considerations about such mode of action naturally divide themselves into two classes: the one relating to the function of either motion or sensation, separately; and the other to the association of the two functions. The first may relate to either the mode or the degree of the animal phenomenon. Following this order, the first theory that presents itself is that of the intermittence of action, and consequently, that of habit, which results from it. Bichat was the first who pointed out the intermittent character of every animal faculty, in contrast with the continuousness of vegetative phenomena. The double movement of absorption and exhalation which constitutes life could not be suspended for a moment without determining the tendency to disorganization: whereas, every act of irritability or sensibility is necessarily intermittent, as no contraction or sensation can be conceived of as indefinitely prolonged; so that continuity would imply as great a contradiction in animal life as interruption in the organic. All the progress made, during the present century, in physiological anatomy, has contributed to the perfecting of this theory of intermittence. Rationally understood, it applies immediately to a very extensive and important class of animal phenomena; that is, to those which belong to the different degrees of sleep. The state of sleep thus consists of the simultaneous suspension, for a certain time, of the principal actions of irritability and sensibility. It is as complete as the organization of the superior animals admits when it suspends all motions and sensations but such as are indispensable to the organic life,—their activity being also remarkably diminished. The phenomenon admits of great variety of degrees, from simple somnolence to the torpor of hybernating animals. But this theory of sleep, so well instituted by Bichat, is still merely initiated, and presents many fundamental difficulties, when we consider the chief modifications of such a state, even the organic conditions of which are very imperfectly known, except the stagnation of the venous blood in the brain, which appears to be generally an indispensable preliminary to all extended and durable lethargy. It is easy to conceive how the prolonged activity of the animal functions in a waking state may, by the law of intermittence, occasion a proportional suspension: but it is not so easy to see why the suspension should be total when the activity has been only partial. Yet we see how profound is the sleep, intellectual and muscular, induced by fatigue of the muscles alone in men who, while awake, have given very little exercise to their sensibility, interior, or even exterior. We know still less of incomplete sleep; especially when only a part of the intellectual or affective organs, or of the locomotive apparatus is torpid; whence arise dreams and various kinds of somnambulism. Yet such a state has certainly its own general laws, as well as the waking state. Some experiments, not duly attended to, perhaps justify the idea that, in animals, in which the cerebral life is much less varied, the nature of dreams becomes, to a certain point, susceptible of being directed at the pleasure of the observer, by the aid of external impressions produced, during sleep, upon the senses whose action is involuntary; and especially smell. And in the case of Man, there is no thoughtful physician who, in certain diseases, does not take into the account the habitual character of the patient's dreams, in order to perfect the diagnosis of maladies in which the nervous system is especially implicated: and this supposes that the state is subject to determinate laws, though they may be unknown. But, however imperfect the theory of sleep may still be, in these essential respects, it is fairly constituted upon a positive basis of its own; for, looked at as a whole, it is *explained*, according to the scientific acceptation of the term, by its radical identity with the phenomena of partial repose offered by all the elementary acts of the animal life. When the theory of intermittence is perfected, we shall, I imagine, adopt Gall's view of connecting it with the sympathy which characterizes all the organs of animal life, by regarding the two parts of the symmetrical apparatus as alternately active and passive, so that their function is never simultaneous: and this, as much in regard to the external senses as the intellectual organs. All this, however, deserves a fresh and thorough investigation.

The theory of Habit is a sort of necessary appendix to that of intermittence; and, like

Habit.

it, due to Bichat. A continuous phenomenon would be, in fact, capable of persistence, in virtue of the law of inertia; but intermittent phenomena alone can give rise to habits, properly so called: that is, can tend to reproduce themselves spontaneously through the influence of a preliminary repetition, sufficiently prolonged at suitable intervals. The importance of this animal property is now universally acknowledged among able inquirers, who see in it one of the chief bases of the gradual perfectibility of animals, and especially of Man. Through this it is that vital phenomena may, in some sort, participate in the admirable regularity of those of the inorganic world, by becoming, like them, periodical, notwithstanding their greater complexity. Thence also results the transformations,—optional up to a certain point of inveteracy of habit, and inevitable beyond that point,—of voluntary acts into involuntary tendencies. But the study of habit is no further advanced than that of intermittence, in regard to its analysis: for we have paid more attention hitherto to the influence of habits once contracted than to their origin, with regard to which scarcely any scientific doctrine exists. What is known lies in the department of natural history, and not in that of biology. Perhaps it may be found, in the course of scientific study, that we have been too hasty in calling this an animal property, though the animal structure may be more susceptible of it. In fact, there is no doubt that inorganic apparatus admits of a more easy reproduction of the same acts after a sufficient regular and prolonged reiteration, as I had occasion to observe in regard to the phenomenon of sound; and this is essentially the character of animal habit. According to this view, which I commend to the attention of biologists, and which, if true, would constitute the most general point of view on this subject, the law of habit may be scientifically attached to the law of inertia, as geometers understand it in the positive theory of motion and equilibrium.

In examining the phenomena common to irritability and sensibility under the aspect of their activity, physiologists have to examine the two extreme terms,—exaggerated action, and insufficient action, in order to determine the intermediate normal degree: for the study of intermediate cases can never be successfully undertaken till the extreme cases which comprehend them have been first examined.

The need of exercising the faculties is certainly the most general and important of all those that belong to the animal life: we may even say that it comprehends them all, if we exclude what relates merely to the organic life. The existence of an animal organ is enough to awaken the need immediately. We shall see, in the next volume, that this consideration is one of the chief bases that social physics derives from individual physiology. Unhappily this study is still very imperfect with regard to most of the animal functions, and to all the three degrees of their activity. To it we must refer the analysis of all the varied phenomena of pleasure and pain, physical and moral. The case of defect has been even less studied than that of excess; and yet its scientific examination is certainly not less important, on account of the theory of *ennui*, the consideration of which is so prominent in social physics,—not only in connection with an advanced state of civilization, but even in the roughest periods, in which, as we shall see hereafter, *ennui* is one of the chief moving springs of social evolution. As for the intermediate degree, which characterizes health, welfare, and finally happiness, it cannot be well treated till the extremes are better understood. The only positive principle yet established in this part of physiology is that which prescribes that we should not contemplate this normal degree in an absolute manner, but in subordination to the intrinsic energy of the corresponding faculties; as popular good sense has already admitted, however difficult it may be practically to conform to the precept in social matters, from the unreflecting tendency of every man to erect himself into a necessary type of the whole species.

Need of activity.

We have now only to notice, further, the third order of considerations; the study of the association of the animal functions.

This great subject should be divided into two parts, relating to the *sympathies*, to which Bichat has sufficiently drawn the attention of physiologists, and the *synergies*, as Barthez

Association of the animal functions.

has called them, which are at present too much neglected. The difference between these two sorts of vital association corresponds to that between the normal and the pathological states: for there is synergy whenever two organs concur simultaneously in the regular accomplishment of any function; whereas sympathy supposes a certain perturbation, momentary or permanent, partial or general, which has to be stopped by the intervention of an organ not primarily affected. These two modes of physiological association are proper to the animal life, any appearance to the contrary being due to the influence of animal over organic action. The study is fairly established on a rational basis; the physiologists of our time seeming to be all agreed as to the nervous system being the necessary agent of all sympathy; and this is enough for the foundation of a positive theory. Beyond this, we have only disjointed though numerous facts. The study of the synergies, though more simple and better circumscribed, does not present, as yet, a more satisfactory scientific character, either as to the mutual association of the different motions, or as to the different modes of sensibility; or as to the more general and complex association between the phenomena of sensibility and those of irritability. And yet this great subject leads directly to the most important theory that physiology can finally present,—that of the fundamental unity of the animal organism, as a necessary result of a harmony between its various chief functions. Here alone it is that, taking each elementary faculty in its normal state, we can find the sound theory of the *Ego*, so absurdly perverted at present by the vain dreams of the metaphysicians: for the general sense of the *I* is certainly determined by the equilibrium of the faculties, the disturbance of which impairs that consciousness so profoundly in many diseases.

## CHAPTER VI.

### INTELLECTUAL AND MORAL, OR CEREBRAL FUNCTIONS

THE remaining portion of biological philosophy is that which relates to the study of the affective and intellectual faculties, which leads us over from individual physiology to Social Physics, as vegetative physiology does from the inorganic to the organic philosophy.

While Descartes was rendering to the world the glorious service of instituting a complete system of positive philosophy, the reformer, with all his bold energy, was unable to raise himself so far above his age as to give its complete logical extension to his own theory by comprehending in it the part of physiology that relates to intellectual and moral phenomena. After having instituted a vast mechanical hypothesis upon the fundamental theory of the most simple and universal phenomena, he extended in succession the same philosophical spirit to the different elementary notions relating to the inorganic world; and finally subordinated to it the study of the chief physical functions of the animal organism. But, when he arrived at the functions of the affections and the intellect, he stopped abruptly, and expressly constituted from them a special study, as an appurtenance of the metaphysico-theological philosophy, to which he thus endeavoured to give a kind of new life, after having wrought far more successfully in sapping its scientific foundations. We have an unquestionable evidence of the state of his mind in his celebrated paradox about the intelligence and instincts of animals. He called brutes automata, rather than allow the application of the old philosophy to them. Being unable to pursue this method with Man, he delivered him over expressly to the domain of metaphysics and theology. It is difficult to see how he could have done otherwise, in the then existing

*Shortcoming of Descartes.*

state of knowledge: and we owe to his strange hypothesis, which the physiologists went to work to confute, the clearing away of the partition which he set up between the study of animals and that of Man, and consequently, the entire elimination among the higher order of investigators, of theological and metaphysical philosophy. What the first contradictory constitution of the modern philosophy was, we may see in the great work of Malebranche, who was the chief interpreter of Descartes, and who shows how his philosophy continued to apply to the most complex parts of the intellectual system the same methods which had been shown to be necessarily futile with regard to the simplest subjects. It is necessary to indicate this state of things because it has remained essentially unaltered during the last two centuries, notwithstanding the vast progress of positive science, which has all the while been gradually preparing for its inevitable transformation. The school of Boerhaave left Descartes's division of subjects as they found it: and if they, the successors of Descartes in physiology, abandoned this department of it to the metaphysical method, it can be no wonder that intellectual and moral phenomena remained, till this century, entirely excluded from the great scientific movement originated and guided by the impulse of Descartes. The growing action of the positive spirit has been, during the whole succeeding interval, merely critical,—attacking the inefficacy of metaphysical studies,—exhibiting the perpetual reconciliation of the naturalists on points of genuine doctrine, in contrast to the incessant disputes of various metaphysicians, arguing still, as from Plato downwards, about the very elements of their pretended science: this criticism itself relating only to results, and still offering no objection to the supremacy of metaphysical philosophy, in the study of Man, in his intellectual and moral aspects. It was not till our own time that modern science, with the illustrious Gall for its organ, drove the old philosophy from this last portion of its domain, and passed on in the inevitable course from the critical to the organic state, striving in its turn to treat in its own way the general theory of the highest vital functions. However imperfect the first attempts, the thing is

*History till Gall's time.*

done. Subjected for half a century to the most decisive tests, this new doctrine has clearly manifested all the indications which can guarantee the indestructible vitality of scientific conceptions. Neither enmity nor irrational advocacy has hindered the continuous spread, in all parts of the scientific world, of the new system of investigation of intellectual and moral man. All the signs of the progressive success of a happy philosophical revolution are present in this case.

The positive theory of the affective and intellectual functions is therefore settled, irreversibly, to be this:—it consists in the experimental and rational study of the phenomena of interior sensibility proper to the cerebral ganglions, apart from all immediate external apparatus. These phenomena are the most complex and the most special of all belonging to physiology; and therefore they have naturally been the last to attain to a positive analysis; to say nothing of their relation to social considerations, which must be an impediment in the way of their study. This study could not precede the principal scientific conceptions of the organic life, or the first notions of the animal life; so that Gall must follow Bichat: and our surprise would be that he followed him so soon, if the maturity of his task did not explain it sufficiently. The grounds of my provisional separation of this part of physiology from the province of animal life generally are—the eminent differences between this order of phenomena and those that have gone before,—their more direct and striking importance,—and, above all, the greater imperfection of our present study of them. This new body of doctrine, thus erected into a third section of physiology, will assume its true place within the boundaries of the second when we obtain a distincter knowledge of organic, and a more philosophical conception of animal physiology. We must bear in mind what the proper arrangement should be,—this third department differing much less from the second than the second differs from the first. *Positive theory of Cerebral functions.*

*Its proper place.*

We need not stop to draw out any parallel or contrast between phrenology and psychology. Gall has fully and clearly exposed the *Vices of Psychological systems.*

powerlessness of metaphysical methods for the study of intellectual and moral phenomena: and in the present state of the human mind, all discussion on this subject is superfluous. The great philosophical cause is tried and judged; and the metaphysicians have passed from a state of domination to one of protestation,—in the learned world at least, where their opposition would obtain no attention but for the inconvenience of their still impeding the progress of popular reason. The triumph of the positive method is so decided that it is needless to devote time and effort to any demonstration, except in the way of instruction: but, in order to characterize, by a striking contrast, the true general spirit of phrenological physiology, it may be useful here to analyse very briefly the radical vices of the pretended physiological method, considered merely in regard to what it has in common in the principal existing schools;—in those called the French, the German, and (the least consistent and also the least absurd of the three) the Scotch school:—that is, as far as we can talk of schools in a philosophy which, by its nature, must engender as many incompatible opinions as it has adepts gifted with any degree of imagination. We may, moreover, refer confidently to these sects for the mutual refutation of their most essential points of difference.

Method. Interior Observation. As for their fundamental principle of *interior observation*, it would certainly be superfluous to add anything to what I have already said about the absurdity of the supposition of a man seeing himself think. It was well remarked by M. Broussais, on this point, that such a method, if possible, would extremely restrict the study of the understanding, by necessarily limiting it to the case of adult and healthy Man, without any hope of illustrating this difficult doctrine by any comparison of different ages, or consideration of pathological states, which yet are unanimously recognized as indispensable auxiliaries in the simplest researches about Man. But, further, we must be also struck by the resolute interdict which is laid upon all intellectual and moral study of animals, from whom the psychologists can hardly be expecting any *interior observation*. It seems rather strange that the philosophers who have so attenuated this immense subject should be those who are for ever reproaching their adversaries with a want of comprehensiveness and elevation. The case of animals is the rock on which all psychological theories have split, since the naturalists have compelled the metaphysicians to part with the singular expedient imagined by Descartes, and to admit that animals, in the higher parts of the scale at least, manifest most of our affective, and even intellectual faculties, with mere differences of degree; a fact which no one at this day ventures to deny, and which is enough of itself to demonstrate the absurdity of these idle conceptions.

Recurring to the first ideas of philosophical common sense, it is at once evident that no function can be studied but with relation to the organ that fulfils it, or to the phenomena of its fulfilment: and, in the second place, that the affective functions, and yet more the intellectual, exhibit in the latter respect this particular characteristic,— that they cannot be observed during their operation, but only in their results,—more or less immediate, and more or less durable. There are then only two ways of studying such an order of functions; either determining, with all attainable precision, the various organic conditions on which they depend,—which is the chief object of phrenological physiology; or in directly observing the series of intellectual and moral acts,—which belongs rather to natural history, properly so called: these two inseparable aspects of one subject being always so conceived as to throw light on each other. Thus regarded, this great study is seen to be indissolubly connected on the one hand with the whole of the foregoing parts of natural philosophy, and especially with the fundamental doctrines of biology; and, on the other hand, with the whole of history,—of animals as well as of man and of humanity. But when, by the pretended psychological method, the consideration of both the agent and the act is discarded altogether, what material can remain but an unintelligible conflict of words, in which merely nominal entities are substituted for real phenomena? The most difficult study of all is thus set up in a state of isolation, without any one point of support in the most simple and perfect sciences, over which it is yet proposed to give it a majestic sovereignty: and in this all psychologists agree, however extreme may be their differences on other points.

*Doctrine. Relation between the Affective and Intellectual faculties.*

About the method of psychology or ideology, enough has been said. As to the doctrine, the first glance shows a radical fault in it, common to all sects,—a false estimate of the general relations between the affective and the intellectual faculties. However various may be the theories about the preponderance of the latter, all metaphysicians assert that preponderance by making these faculties their starting-point. The intellect is almost exclusively the subject of their speculations, and the affections have been almost entirely neglected; and, moreover, always subordinated to the understanding. Now, such a conception represents precisely the reverse of the reality, not only for animals, but also for Man: for daily experience shows that the affections, the propensities, the passions, are the great springs of human life; and that, so far from resulting from intelligence, their spontaneous and independent impulse is indispensable to the first awakening and continuous development of the various intellectual faculties, by assigning to them a permanent end, without which—to say nothing of the vagueness of their general direction—they would remain dormant in the majority of men. It is even but too certain that the least noble and most animal propensities are habitually the most energetic, and therefore the most influential. The whole of human nature is thus very unfaithfully represented by these futile systems, which, if noticing the affective faculties at all, have vaguely connected them with one single principle, sympathy, and, above all, self-consciousness, always supposed to be directed by the intellect. Thus it is that, contrary to evidence, Man has been represented as essentially a reasoning being, continually carrying on, unconsciously, a multitude of imperceptible calculations, with scarcely any spontaneity of action, from infancy upwards. This false conception has doubtless been supported by a consideration worthy of all respect,—that it is by the intellect that Man is modified and improved; but science requires, before all things, the reality of any views, independently of their desirableness;

and it is always this reality which is the basis of genuine utility. Without denying the secondary influence of such a view, we can show that two purely philosophical causes, quite unconnected with any idea of application, and inherent in the nature of the method, have led the metaphysicians of all sects to this hypothesis of the supremacy of the intellect. The first is the radical separation which it was thought necessary to make between brutes and man, and which would have been effaced at once by the admission of the preponderance of the affective over the intellectual faculties; and the second was the necessity that the metaphysicians found themselves under, of preserving the unity of what they called the *I*, that it might correspond with the unity of the *soul*, in obedience to the requisitions of the theological philosophy, of which metaphysics is, as we must ever bear in mind, the final transformation. But the positive philosophers, who approach the question with the simple aim of ascertaining the true state of things, and reproducing it with all positive accuracy in their theories, have perceived that, according to universal experience, human nature is so far from being single that it is eminently multiple; that is, usually induced in various directions by distinct and independent powers, among which equilibrium is established with extreme difficulty when, as usually happens in civilized life, no one of them is, in itself, sufficiently marked to acquire spontaneously any considerable preponderance over the rest. Thus, the famous theory of the *I* is essentially without a scientific object, since it is destined to represent a purely fictitious state. There is, in this direction, as I have already pointed out, no other real subject of positive investigation than the study of the equilibrium of the various animal functions,—both of irritability and of sensibility,—which marks the normal state, in which each of them, duly moderated, is regularly and permanently associated with the whole of the others, according to the laws of sympathy, and yet more of synergy. The very abstract and indirect notion of the *I* proceeds from the continuous sense of such a harmony; that is, from the universal accordance of the entire organism. Psychologists have attempted in vain to make

*Brutes and Man.*

*Theory of the I.*

out of this idea, or rather sense, an attribute of humanity exclusively. It is evidently a necessary result of all animal life; and therefore it must belong to all animals, whether they are able to discourse upon it or not. No doubt a cat, or any other vertebrated animal, without knowing how to say "I," is not in the habit of taking itself for another. Moreover, it is probable that among the superior animals the sense of personality is still more marked than in Man, on account of their more isolated life; though if we descended too far in the zoological scale we should reach organisms in which the continuous degradation of the nervous system attenuates this compound sense, together with the various simple feelings on which it depends.

Reason and Instinct.

It must not be overlooked that though the psychologists have agreed in neglecting the intellectual and moral faculties of brutes, which have been happily left to the naturalists, they have occasioned great mischief by their obscure and indefinite distinction between intelligence and instinct, thus setting up a division between human and animal nature which has had too much effect even upon zoologists to this day. The only meaning that can be attributed to the word *instinct*, is any spontaneous impulse in a determinate direction, independently of any foreign influence. In this primitive sense, the term evidently applies to the proper and direct activity of any faculty whatever, intellectual as well as affective; and it therefore does not conflict with the term *intelligence* in any way, as we so often see when we speak of those who, without any education, manifest a marked talent for music, painting, mathematics, etc. In this way there is instinct, or rather, there are instincts in Man, as much or more than in brutes. If, on the other hand, we describe *intelligence* as the aptitude to modify conduct in conformity to the circumstances of each case,—which, in fact, is the main practical attribute of *reason*, in its proper sense,—it is more evident than before that there is no other essential difference between humanity and animality than that of the degree of development admitted by a faculty which is, by its nature, common to all animal life, and without which it could not even be conceived to exist.

Thus the famous scholastic definition of Man as a *reasonable animal* offers a real no-meaning, since no animal, especially in the higher parts of the zoological scale, could live without being to a certain extent reasonable, in proportion to the complexity of its organism. Though the moral nature of animals has been but little and very imperfectly explored, we can yet perceive, without possibility of mistake, among those that live with us and that are familiar with us,—judging of them by the same means of observation that we should employ about men whose language and ways were previously unknown to us,—that they not only apply their intelligence to the satisfaction of their organic wants, much as men do, aiding themselves also with some sort of language; but that they are, in like manner, susceptible of a kind of wants more disinterested, inasmuch as they consist in a need to exercise their faculties for the mere pleasure of the exercise. It is the same thing that leads children or savages to invent new sports, and that renders them, at the same time, liable to *ennui*. That state, erroneously set up as a special privilege of human nature, is sometimes sufficiently marked, in the case of certain animals, to urge them to suicide, when captivity has become intolerable. An attentive examination of the facts therefore discredits the perversion of the word *instinct* when it is used to signify the fatality under which animals are impelled to the mechanical performance of *acts* uniformly determinate, without any possible modification from corresponding circumstances, and neither requiring nor allowing any education, properly so called. This gratuitous supposition is evidently a remnant of the automatic hypothesis of Descartes. Leroy has demonstrated that among mammifers and birds this ideal fixity in the construction of habitations, in the seeking of food by hunting, in the mode of migration, etc., exists only in the eyes of closet-naturalists or inattentive observers.

After thus much notice of the radical vice of all psychological systems, it would be departing from the object of this work to show how the intellectual faculties themselves have been misconceived. It is enough to refer to the refutation by which Gall and Spurzheim have introduced their labours: and I would particularly point out the philosophical demonstration by which they have exhibited the conclusion that sensation, memory, imagination, and even judgment,—all the scholastic faculties, in short,—are not, in fact, fundamental and abstract faculties, but only different degrees or consecutive modes of the same phenomenon, proper to each of the true elementary phrenological functions, and necessarily variable in different cases, with a proportionate activity. One virtue of this admirable analysis is that it deprives the various metaphysical theories of their one remaining credit,—their mutual criticism, which is here effected, once for all, with more efficacy than by any one of the mutually opposing schools.

Again, it would be departing from the object of this portion of our work to judge of the doctrines of the schools by their results. What these have been we shall see in the next volume; the deplorable influence on the political and social condition of two generations of the doctrines of the French school, as presented by Helvetius, and of the German psychology, with the ungovernable *I* for its subject; and the impotence of the Scotch school, through the vagueness of what it called its doctrines, and their want of mutual connection. Dismissing all these for the present, we must examine the great attempt of Gall, in order to see what is wanting in phrenological philosophy to form it into the scientific constitution which is proper to it, and from which it is necessarily still more remote than organic, and even animal physiology.

Basis of Gall's doctrine.
Two philosophical principles, now admitted to be indisputable, serve as the immovable basis of Gall's doctrine as a whole: viz., the innateness of the fundamental dispositions, affective and intellectual, and the plurality of the distinct and independent faculties, though real acts usually require their more or less complex concurrence. Within the limits of the human race, all cases of marked talents or character prove the first; and the second is proved by the diversity of such marked cases, and by most pathological states,—especially by those in which the nervous system is directly affected. A comparative observation of the higher animals would dispel all doubt, if any existed in either case. These two principles,—aspects of a single fundamental concep-

tion,—are but the scientific expression of the results of experience, in all times and places, as to the intellectual and moral nature of Man,—an indispensable symptom of truth, with regard to all parent ideas, which must always be connected with the spontaneous indications of popular reason, as we have seen in preceding cases in natural philosophy. Thus, besides all guidance from analogy, after the study of the animal life, we derive confirmation from all the methods of investigation that physiology admits; from direct observation, experiment, pathological analysis, the comparative method and popular good sense,—all of which converge towards the establishment of this double principle. Such a collection of proofs secures the stability of this much of phrenological doctrine, whatever transformations other parts may have to undergo. In the anatomical view, this physiological conception corresponds with the division of the brain into a certain number of partical organs, symmetrical like those of the animal life, and, though more contiguous and mutually resembling than in any other system, and therefore more adapted both for sympathy and synergy, still distinct and mutually independent, as we were already aware was the case with the ganglions appropriate to the external senses. In brief, the brain is no longer an organ, but an apparatus of organs, more complex in proportion to the degree of animality. The proper object of phrenological physiology thence consists in determining the cerebral organ appropriate to each clearly marked, simple disposition, affective or intellectual; or, reciprocally, which is more difficult, what function is fulfilled by any portion of the mass of the brain which exhibits the anatomical conditions of a distinct organ. The two processes are directed to develope the agreement between physiological and anatomical analysis which constitutes the true science of living beings. Unfortunately, our means are yet further from answering our aims than in the two preceding divisions of the science.

The scientific principle involved in the phrenological view is that the functions, affective and intellectual, are more elevated, more human, if you will, and at the same time less ener-

Divisions of the brain.

getic, in proportion to the exclusiveness with which they belong to the higher part of the zoological series, their positions being in portions of the brain more and more restricted in extent, and further removed from its immediate origin,—according to the anatomical decision that the skull is simply a prolongation of the vertebral column, which is the primitive centre of the entire nervous system. Thus, the least developed and anterior part of the brain is appropriated to the characteristic faculties of humanity; and the most voluminous and hindmost part to those which constitute the basis of the whole of the animal kingdom. Here we have a new and confirmatory instance of the rule which we have had to follow in every science; that it is necessary to proceed from the most general to the more special attributes, in the order of their diminishing generality. We shall meet with it again in the one science which remains for us to review; and its constant presence, through the whole range, points it out as the first law of the dogmatic procedure of the positive spirit.

A full contemplation of Gall's doctrine convinces us of its faithful representation of the intellectual and moral nature of Man and animals. All the psychological sects have misconceived or ignored the pre-eminence of the affective faculties, plainly manifest as it is in all the moral phenomena of brutes, and even of Man; but we find this fact placed on a scientific basis by the discovery that the affective organs occupy all the hinder and middle portion of the cerebral apparatus, while the intellectual occupy only the front portion, which, in extreme cases, is not more than a fourth, or even a sixth part of the whole. The difference between Gall and his predecessors was not in the separation of the two kinds of faculties, but that they assigned the brain to the intellectual faculties alone, regarding it as a single organ, and distributing the passions among the organs pertaining to the vegetative life,—the heart, the liver, etc. Bichat supported this view by the argument of the sympathies of these organs, under the excitement of the respective passions; but the variableness of the seat of sympathy, according to native susceptibility or to accident, is a sufficient answer to such a plea, and teaches us simply the importance of considering the influence exercised by the state of the brain upon the nerves which supply the apparatus of the organic life.

Next comes the subdivision established by Gall and Spurzheim in each of these two orders. The affective faculties are divided into the propensities, and the affections or sentiments, the first residing in the hindmost and lowest part of the brain; and the other class in the middle portion. The intellectual faculties are divided into the various perceptive faculties, which together constitute the range of observation: and the small number of reflective faculties, the highest of all, constituting the power of combination, by comparison and co-ordination. The upper part of the frontal region is the seat of these last, which are the chief characteristic attribute of human nature. There is a certain deficiency of precision in this description; but, besides that we may expect improving knowledge to clear it up, we shall find, on close examination, that the inconvenience lies more in the language than in the ideas. The only language we have is derived from a philosophical period when all moral and even intellectual ideas were shrouded in a mysterious metaphysical unity, which allows us now no adequate choice of terms.

*Subdivision.*

Taking the ordinary terms in their literal sense, we should misconceive the fundamental distinction between the intellectual faculties and the others. When the former are very marked, they unquestionably produce real inclinations or propensities, which are distinguished from the inferior passions only by their smaller energy. Nor can we deny that their action occasions true emotions or sentiments, more rare, more pure, more sublime than any other, and, though less vivid than others, capable of moving to tears; and is testified by so many instances of the rapture excited by the discovery of truth, in the most eminent thinkers that have done honour to their race—as Archimedes, Descartes, Kepler, Newton, etc. Would any thoughtful student take occasion, by such approximations, to deny all real distinction between the intellectual and affective faculties? The wiser conclusion to be drawn from the case is that we must reform our philosophical language, to raise it, by rigorous precision, to the dignity of scientific language. We may say as much about the subdivision of the affective faculties into propensities and sentiments, the distinction being, though less marked, by no means less real. Apart from all useless discussion of nomenclature, we may say that the real difference has not been clearly seized. In a scientific view, it would suffice to say that the first and fundamental class relates to the individual alone, or, at most, to the family, regarded successively in its principal needs of preservation,—such as reproduction, the rearing of young, the mode of alimentation, of habitation, etc. Whereas, the second more special class supposes the existence of some social relations, either among individuals of a different species, or especially between individuals of the same species, apart from sex, and determines the character which the tendencies of the animal must impress on each of these relations, whether transient or permanent. If we keep this distinctive character of the two classes in view, it will matter little what terms we use to indicate them, when once they shall have acquired a sufficient fixedness, through rational use.

These are the great philosophical results of Gall's doctrine, regarded, as I have now presented it, apart from all vain attempts to localize in a special manner the cerebral or phrenological functions. I shall have to show how such an attempt was imposed upon Gall by the necessities of his glorious mission: but, notwithstanding this unfortunate necessity, the doctrine embodies already a real knowledge of human and brute nature very far superior to all that had ever been offered before.

Objections. Necessity of human actions. Among the innumerable objections which have been aimed at this fine doctrine,—considered always as a whole,—the only one which merits discussion here is the supposed necessity of human actions. This objection is not only of high importance in itself, but it casts new light back upon the spirit of the theory; and we must briefly examine it from the point of view of positive philosophy.

When objectors confound the subjection of events to invariable laws with their necessary exemption from modification, they lose sight of the fact that phenomena become susceptible of modification in proportion to their complexity. The only irresistible action that we know of is that of weight, which takes place under the most general and simple of all natural laws. Answered. But the phenomena of life and acts of the mind are so highly complex as to admit of modification beyond all estimate; and, in the intermediate regions, phenomena are under control precisely in the order of their complexity. Gall and Spurzheim have shown how human action depends on the combined operation of several faculties; how exercise develops them; how inactivity wastes them; and how the intellectual faculties, adapted to modify the general conduct of the animal according to the variable exigencies of his situation, may overrule the practical influence of all his other faculties. It is only in mania, when disease interferes with the natural action of the faculties, that fatality, or what is popularly called irresponsibility, exists. It is therefore a great mistake to accuse cerebral physiology of disowning the influence of education or legislation, because it fixes the limits of their power. It denies the possibility, asserted by the ideology of the French school, of converting by suitable arrangements, all men into so many Socrates, Homers, or Archimedes; and it denies the ungovernable energy of the *I*, asserted by the German school; but it does not therefore affect Man's reasonable liberty, or interfere with his improvement by the aid of a wise education. It is evident indeed that improvement by education supposes the existence of requisite predispositions: and that each of them is subject to determinate laws, without which they could not be systematically influenced; so that it is, after all, cerebral physiology that is in possession of the philosophical problem of education. Furthermore, this physiology shows us that men are commonly of an average constitution; that is, that, apart from a very few exceptional organizations, every one possesses in a moderate degree all the propensities, all the sentiments, and all the elementary aptitudes, without any one faculty being remarkably preponderant. The widest field is thus open for education, in modifying in almost any direction organisms so flexible, though the degree of their development may remain of that average amount which consists very well with social harmony; as we shall have occasion to see hereafter.

*Hypothetical distribution of faculties.* A much more serious objection to Gall's doctrine arises out of the venturesome and largely erroneous localization of the faculties which he thought proper to propose. If we look at his position, we shall see that he merely used the right, common to all natural philosophers, of instituting a scientific hypothesis, in accordance with the theory on that subject which we examined in connection with Physics. He fulfilled the conditions of this theory; his subject being, not any imaginary fluids, ether or the like, but tangible organs, whose hypothetical attributes admit of positive verifications. Moreover, none of those who have criticised his localization could have proposed any less imperfect, or, probably, so well indicated. The advice of prudent mediocrity, to abstain from hypothesis, is very easy to offer; but if the advice was followed, nothing would ever be done in the way of scientific discovery. It is doubtless inconvenient to have to withdraw or remake, at a subsequent period, the hypotheses to which a science owes its existence, and which, by that time, have been adopted by inferior inquirers with a blinder and stronger faith than that of the original proposers: but there is no use in dwelling upon a liability which arises from the infirmity of our intelligence. The practical point for the future is that strong minds, prepared by a suitable scientific education, should plant themselves on the two great principles which have been laid down as the foundation of the science, and thence explore the principal needs of cerebral physiology, and the character of the means by which it may be carried forwards. Nor need there be any fear that the science will be held back by such a method. Nothing prevents us, when reasoning, as geometers do, upon indeterminate seats, or positions supposed to be indeterminate, from arriving at real conclusions, involving actual utility, as I hope to show, from my own experience, in the next volume; though it is evident that it will be a great advantage to the exactness and efficacy of our conclusions, whenever the time arrives for the positive determination of the cerebral organs. Meantime it is clear that we owe to Gall's hypothetical localization our view of the necessity of such a course; and that if he had confined himself to the high philosophical generalities with which he has furnished us, he would never have constituted a science, nor formed a school; and the truths which we see to be inestimable would have been strangled in their birth by a coalition of hostile influences.

We see what is the philosophical character of cerebral physiology. We must next inquire what are the indispensable improvements that it demands.

Needed improvements.

First, we want a fundamental rectification of all the organs and faculties, as a necessary basis for all further progress. Taking an anatomical view of this matter, we see that the distribution of organs has been directed by physiological analyses alone,—usually imperfect and superficial enough,—instead of being subjected to anatomical determinations. This has entitled all anatomists to treat such a distribution as arbitrary and loose, because, being subject to no anatomical consideration about the difference between an organ and a part of an organ, it admits of indefinite subdivisions, which each phrenologist seems to be able to multiply at will. Though the analysis of functions no doubt casts much light on that of organs, the original decomposition of the whole organism into systems of organs, and those again into single organs, is not the less independent of physiological analysis, to which, on the contrary, it must furnish a basis. This is established in regard to all other biological studies; and there is no reason why cerebral inquiries should be an exception. We do not need to see the digestive, or the respiratory apparatus in action, before anatomy can distinguish them from each other: and why should it be otherwise with the cerebral apparatus? The anatomical difficulties are no doubt much greater, on account of the resemblance and proximity of the organs in the cerebral case: but we must not give up this indispensable analysis for such a reason as that. If it were so, we must despair of conferring a special scientific character on phrenological doctrine at all; and we must abide by those generalities alone which I have just laid down. When we propose to develope the harmony between the anatomical

Anatomical basis.

and the physiological analysis of any case, it is supposed that each has been separately established, and not that the one can be copied from the other. Nothing therefore can absolve the phrenologists from the obligation to pursue the analysis of the cerebral system by a series of vigorous anatomical labours, discarding for the time all ideas of function, or, at most, employing them only as auxiliary to anatomical exploration. Such a consideration will be most earnestly supported by those phrenologists who perceive that, in determining the relative preponderance of each cerebral organ in different subjects, it is not only the bulk and weight of the organ that has to be taken into the account, but also its degree of activity, anatomically estimated, by, for instance, the energy of its partial circulation.

Next, following a distinct but parallel order of ideas, there must be a purely physiological analysis of the various elementary faculties; and in this analysis, which has to be harmonized with the other, every anatomical idea must be, in its turn, discarded. The position of phrenology is scarcely more satisfactory in this view than any other, for the distinction between the different faculties, intellectual and even affective, and their enumeration are conceived of in a very superficial way, though incomparably more in the positive spirit than any metaphysical analyses. If metaphysicians have confounded all their psychological notions in an absurd unity, it is probable that the phrenologists have gone to the other extreme in multiplying elementary functions. Gall set up twenty-seven; which was, no doubt, an exaggeration to begin with. Spurzheim raised the number to thirty-five; and it is liable to daily increase for want of a rational principle of circumscription for the regulation of the easy enthusiasm of popular explorers. Unless a sound philosophy interposes, to establish some order, we may have as many faculties and organs as the psychologists of old made entities. However great may be the diversity of animal natures, or even of human types, it is yet to be conceived, (as real acts usually suppose the concurrence of several fundamental faculties,) that even a greater multiplicity might be represented by a very small

*Physiological analysis of faculties.*

number of elementary functions of the two orders. If, for instance, the whole number were reduced to twelve or fifteen well-marked faculties, their combinations, binary, ternary, quaternary, etc., would doubtless correspond to many more types than can exist, even if we restricted ourselves to distinguishing, in relation to the normal degree of activity of each function, two other degrees,—one higher and the other lower. But the exorbitant multiplication of faculties is not in itself so shocking as the levity of most of the pretended analyses which have regulated their distribution. In the intellectual order, especially, the aptitudes have been usually ill-described, apart from the organs: as when a mathematical aptitude is assigned on grounds which would justify our assigning a chemical aptitude, or an anatomical aptitude, if the whole bony casket had not been previously parcelled off into irremoveable compartments. If a man could do sums according to rules quickly and easily, he had the mathematical aptitude, according to those who do not suspect that mathematical speculations require any superiority of intellect. Though the analysis of the affective faculties, which are so much better marked, is less imperfect, there are several instances of needless multiplication in that department.

To rectify or improve this analysis of the cerebral faculties, it would be useful to add to the observation of Man and society a physiological estimate of the most marked individual cases,—especially in past times. The intellectual order, which most needs revision, is that which best admits of this procedure. If, for instance, it had been applied to the cases of the chief geometers, the absurd mistake that I have just pointed out could not have been committed; for it would have been seen what compass and variety of faculties are required to constitute mathematical genius, and how various are the forms in which that genius manifests itself. One great geometer has shone by the sagacity of his inventions; another by the strength and extent of his combinations; a third by the happy choice of his notations, and the perfection of his algebraic style, etc. We might discover, or at least verify, all the real fundamental

*Examination of historical cases.*

intellectual faculties by the scientific class alone. In an inferior degree it would be the same with an analogous study of the most eminent artists. This consideration, in its utmost extent, is connected with the utility of the philosophical study of the sciences, under the historical as well as the dogmatical point of view, for the discovery of the logical laws concerned: the difference being that in this last case, we have first to determine the elementary faculties, and not the laws of their action: but the grounds must be essentially analogous.

Phrenological analysis has, then, to be reconstituted; first in the anatomical, and then in the physiological order; and finally, the two must be harmonized; and not till then can phrenological physiology be established upon its true scientific basis. Such a procedure is fairly begun, as we have seen, with regard to the two preceding divisions of our science; but it is not yet even conceived of in relation to cerebral physiology, from its greater complexity and more recent positivity.

Pathological and Comparative analysis. The phrenologists must make a much more extensive use than hitherto of the means furnished by biological philosophy for the advancement of all studies relating to living bodies: that is, of pathological, and yet more of comparative analysis. The luminous maxim of M. Broussais, which lies at the foundation of medical philosophy,—that the phenomena of the pathological state are a simple prolongation of the phenomena of the normal state, beyond the ordinary limits of variation,—has never been duly applied to intellectual and moral phenomena: yet it is impossible to understand anything of the different kinds of madness, if they are not examined on this principle. Here, as in a former division of the science, we see that the study of malady is the way to understand the healthy state. Nothing can aid us so well in the discovery of the fundamental faculties as a judicious study of the state of madness, when each faculty manifests itself in a degree of exaltation which separates it distinctly from others. There has been plentiful study of monomania; but it has been of little use, for want of a due connection and comparison with the normal state. The works that have appeared on the subject have been more literary than scientific; those who have had the best opportunity for observation have been more engaged in governing their patients than in analysing their cases; and the successors of Pinel have added nothing essential to the ameliorations introduced by him, half a century ago, in regard to the theory and treatment of mental alienation. As for the study of animals, its use has been vitiated by the old notions of the difference between instinct and intelligence. Humanity and animality ought reciprocally to cast light upon each other. If the whole set of faculties constitutes the complement of animal life, it must surely be that all that are fundamental must be common to all the superior animals, in some degree or other: and differences of intensity are enough to account for the existing diversities,—the association of the faculties being taken into the account, on the one hand, and, on the other, the improvement of Man in society being set aside. If there are any faculties which belong to Man exclusively, it can only be such as correspond to the highest intellectual aptitudes: and this much may appear doubtful if we compare, in an unprejudiced way, the actions of the highest mammifers with those of the least developed savages. It seems to me more rational to suppose that power of observation and even of combination exists in animals, though in an immeasurably inferior degree;—the want of exercise, resulting chiefly from their state of isolation, tending to benumb and even starve the organs. Much might be learned from a study of domestic animals, though they are far from being the most intelligent. Much might be learned by comparing their moral nature now with what it was at periods nearer to their first domestication; for it would be strange if the changes that they have undergone in so many physical respects had been unaccompanied by variations in the functions which more easily than any others admit of modification. The extreme imperfection of phrenological science is manifest in the pride with which Man, from the height of his supremacy, judges of animals as a despot judges of his subjects; that is, in the mass, without perceiving any inequality in them worth noticing. It is not the less certain that, surveying the whole animal hierarchy, the principal orders of this hierarchy sometimes differ more from each other, in intellectual and moral respects, than the highest of them vary from the human type. The rational study of the mind and the ways of animals has still to be instituted, nothing having yet been done but in the way of preparation. It promises an ample harvest of important discovery directly applicable to the advancement of the study of Man, if only the naturalists will disregard the declamation of theologians and metaphysicians about their pretended degradation of human nature, while they are, on the contrary, rectifying the fundamental notion of it by establishing, rigorously and finally, the profound differences which positively separate us from the animals nearest to us in the scale.

Laws of action.

The two laws of action,—intermission and association,—require much more attention than they have yet received in connection with cerebral physiology. The law of intermittence is eminently applicable to the functions of the brain,—the symmetry of the organs being borne in mind. But this great subject requires a new examination, seeing that it is requisite for science to reconcile their evident intermittence with the perfect continuity that seems to be involved in the connection which mutually unites all our intellectual operations, from earliest infancy to extreme decrepitude, and which cannot be interrupted by the deepest cerebral perturbations, provided they are transient. This question, for which metaphysical theories allowed no place, certainly offers serious difficulties: but its positive solution must throw great light upon the general course of intellectual acts. As for the association of the faculties, in sympathy or synergy, the physiologists begin to understand its high importance, though its general laws have not yet been scientifically studied. Without this consideration, the number of propensities, sentiments, or aptitudes would seem to be susceptible of any degree of multiplication. For one instance, investigators of human nature have been wont to distinguish various kinds of courage, under the names of civil, military, etc., though the original disposition to brave any kind of danger must always be uniform, but more or less directed by the understanding. No doubt, the martyr who

Intermittence and continuity.

Association.

endures the most horrible tortures with unshaken fortitude rather than deny his convictions, and the man of science who undertakes a perilous experiment after having calculated the chances, might fly in the field of battle if compelled to fight for a cause in which they felt no interest; but not the less is their kind of courage the same as that of the brave soldier. Apart from inequalities of degree, there is no other difference than the superior influence of the intellectual faculties. Without the diverse cerebral synergies, either between the two great orders of faculties, or between the different functions of each order, it would be impossible to analyse the greater proportion of mental actions; and it is in the positive interpretation of each of them by such association that the application of phrenological doctrine will chiefly consist, when such doctrine shall have been scientifically erected. When the elementary analysis shall have been instituted, allowing us to pass on to the study of these compound phenomena, we may think of proceeding to the more delicate inquiry whether, in each cerebral organ, a distinct part is not especially appropriate to the establishment of these synergies and sympathies. Some pathological observations have given rise to this suspicion,—the grey substance of the brain appearing more inflamed in those perturbations which affect the phenomena of the will, and the white in those which relate to intellectual operations.

If our existing phrenology isolates the cerebral functions too much, it is yet more open to reproach for separating the brain from the whole of the nervous system. *Unity of the brain and nervous system.* Bichat taught us that the intellectual and affective phenomena, all-important as they are, constitute, in the whole system of the animal economy, only an intermediate agency between the action of the external world upon the animal through sensorial impressions, and the final reaction of the animal by muscular contractions. Now, in the present state of phrenological physiology, no positive conception exists with regard to the relation of the series of cerebral acts to this last necessary reaction. We merely suspect that the spinal marrow is its immediate organ. Even if cerebral physiology carefully comprehended the whole of the nervous system, it would still, at present, separate it too much from the rest of the economy. While rightly discarding the ancient error about the seat of the passions being in the organs of the vegetative life, it has too much neglected the great influence to which the chief intellectual and moral functions are subject from other physiological phenomena; as Cabanis pointed out so emphatically, while preparing the way for the philosophical revolution which we owe to Gall.

We have now seen how irrational and narrow is the way in which intellectual and moral physiology is conceived of and studied: and that till this is rectified, the science, which really appears not to have advanced a single step since its institution, cannot make any true progress. We *Imperfect state of Phrenology.* see how it requires, above even the other branches of physiology, the preparation of scientific habits, and familiarity with the foregoing departments of natural philosophy; and how, from its vicious isolation, it tends to sink to the level of the most superficial and ill-prepared minds, which will make it the groundwork of a gross and mischievous quackery, if the true scientific inquirers do not take it out of their hands. No inconveniences of this kind, however, should blind us to the eminent merits of a conception which will ever be one of the principal grounds of distinction of the philosophy of the nineteenth century, in comparison with the one which preceded it.

*Present state of Biology.* Looking back, on the completion of this survey of the positive study of living bodies, we see that, imperfect as it is, and unsatisfactory as are the parts which relate to life, compared with those which relate to organization, still the most imperfect have begun to assume a scientific character, more or less clearly indicated, in proportion to the complexity of the phenomena.

We have now surveyed the whole system of natural philosophy, from its basis in mathematical, to its termination in biological philosophy. Notwithstanding the vast interval embraced by these two extremities, we have passed through the whole by an almost insensible gradation, finding nothing hypothetical in the transition, through chemistry, from inorganic to organic philosophy, and verifying as we proceeded the rigorous continuity of the system of the natural sciences. That system, though comprehending all existing knowledge, is, however, still incomplete, leaving a wide area to the retrograde influence of the theologico-metaphysical philosophy, to which it abandons a whole order of ideas, the most immediately applicable of all. There is yet wanting, to complete the body of positive philosophy, and to organize its universal preponderance, the subjection to it of the most complex and special phenomena of all,—those of humanity in a state of association. I shall therefore venture to propose the new science of *Social Physics*, which I have found myself compelled to create, as the necessary complement of the system. This new science is rooted in biology, as every science is in the one which precedes it; and it will render the body of doctrine complete and indivisible, enabling the human mind to proceed on positive principles in all directions whatever, to which its activity may be incited. Imperfect as the preceding sciences are, they have enough of the positive character to render this last transformation possible: and when it is effected, the way will be open for their future advancement, through such an organization of scientific labour as must put an end to the intellectual anarchy of our present condition.

# BOOK VI.

## SOCIAL PHYSICS.

### CHAPTER I.

#### NECESSITY AND OPPORTUNENESS OF THIS NEW SCIENCE.

IN the five foregoing parts of this work, our investigation proceeded on an ascertained and undisputed scientific basis; and our business was to exhibit the progress made in each science; to free it from entanglement with the ancient philosophy; and to show what further improvements might be anticipated. Our task is a different, and a much harder one, in the case of the sixth and last science that I am about to treat of. The theories of Social science are still, even in the minds of the best thinkers, completely implicated with the theologico-metaphysical philosophy; and are even supposed to be, by a fatal separation from all other science, condemned to remain so involved for ever. The philosophical procedure which I have undertaken to carry through becomes more difficult and bold, from this point onwards, without at all changing its nature or object; and it must so far present a new character as it must henceforth be employed in creating a wholly new order of scientific conceptions, instead of judging, arranging, and improving such as already existed.

It is not to be expected that this new science can be at once raised to a level with even the most imperfect of those which we have been reviewing. All that can be rationally proposed in our day is to recognize the character of positivity in social as in all other science, and to ascertain the chief bases on which it is founded; but this is enough, as I hope to show, to satisfy our most urgent intellectual necessities, and even the most imperative needs of immediate social practice. In its scientific connection with the rest of this work, all that I can hope to do is to exhibit the general considerations of the case, so as to resolve the intellectual anarchy which is the main source of our moral anarchy first, and then of the political, which I shall treat of only through its originating causes. *Proposal of the subject.* The extreme novelty of such a doctrine and method renders it necessary, before entering upon the immediate subject, to set forth the importance of such a procedure, and the futility of the chief attempts which have been indirectly made to investigate social science. However unquestionable may be the need of such science, and the obligation to discover it, the best minds have not yet attained a point of view from which they can estimate its depth and breadth and true position. In its nascent state every science is implicated with its corresponding art; and remains implicated with it, as we have seen, the longer in proportion to the complexity of the phenomena concerned. If biological science, which is more advanced than social, is still too closely connected with the medical art, as we have seen that it is, we cannot be surprised that men are insensible to the value of all social speculations which are not immediately connected with practical affairs. We cannot be surprised at any obstinacy in repelling them, as long as it is supposed that by rejecting them, society is preserved from chimerical and mischievous schemes: though experience has abundantly shown that the precaution has never availed, and that it does not now prevent our being daily invaded by the most illusory proposals on social matters. It is in deference to as much as is reasonable in this apprehension that I propose to state, first, how the institution of a science of Social Physics bears upon the principal needs and grievances of society, in its present deplorable state of anarchy. Such a representation may perhaps convince men worthy of the name of statesmen that there is a real and eminent utility in labours of this kind, worthy of the anxious attention of men who profess to devote themselves to the task of resolving the alarming revolutionary constitution of modern societies.

From the point of view to which we have been raised by our study of the preceding sciences, we are able to survey the social situation of our own time in its fullest extent and broadest light; and what we see is that there is a deep and widely-spread anarchy of the whole intellectual system, which has been in this state of disturbance during the long interregnum, resulting from the decline of the theologico-metaphysical philosophy. At the present time, the old philosophy is in a state of imbecility; while the development of the positive philosophy, though always proceeding, has not yet been bold, broad, and general enough to comprehend the mental government of the human race. We must go back through that interregnum to understand truly the present floating and contradictory state of all great social ideas, and to perceive how society is to be delivered from the peril of dissolution, and brought under a new organization, more consistent and more progressive than that which once rested on the theological philosophy. When we have duly observed the powerlessness of conflicting political schools, we shall see the necessity of introducing an entirely new spirit into the organization of society, by which these useless and passionate struggles may be put an end to, and society led out of the revolutionary state in which it has been tossed for three centuries past.

**Conditions of Order and Progress.** The ancients used to suppose Order and Progress to be irreconcilable: but both are indispensable conditions in a state of modern civilization; and their combination is at once the grand difficulty and the main resource of every genuine political system. No real order can be established, and still less can it last, if it is not fully compatible with progress: and no great progress can be accomplished if it does not tend to the consolidation of order. Any conception which is so devoted to one of these needs as to prejudice the other, is sure of rejection, sooner or later, as mistaking the nature of the political problem. Therefore, in positive social science, the chief feature must be the union of these two conditions, which will be two aspects, constant and inseparable, of the same principle. Throughout the whole range of science, thus far, we have seen that the conditions of combination and of progress are originally identical: and I trust we shall see, after looking into social science in the same way, that ideas of Order and Progress are, in Social Physics, as rigorously inseparable as the ideas of Organization and Life in Biology: from whence indeed they are, in a scientific view, evidently derived.

The misfortune of our actual state is that the two ideas are set up in radical opposition to each other,—the retrograde spirit having directed all efforts in favour of Order, and anarchical doctrine having arrogated to itself the charge of Social Progress; and, in this state of things, the reproaches exchanged between the respective parties are only too well merited by both. In this vicious circle is society now confined; and the only issue from it is by the undisputed preponderance of a doctrine equally progressive and hierarchical. The observations which I have to make on this subject are applicable to all European societies, which have, in fact, all undergone a common disorganization, though in different degrees, and with various modifications, and which cannot be separately reorganized, however they may be for a time restrained; but I shall keep the French nation chiefly in view, not only because the revolutionary state has been most conspicuous in them, but because they are, in all important respects, better prepared, in spite of appearances, than any other, for a true reorganization.

Among the infinite variety of political ideas which appear to be striving in society, there are in fact only two orders, the mingling of which in various proportions occasions the apparent multiplicity: and of these two, the one is really only the negation of the other. If we wish to understand our own condition, we must look at it as the result and last term of the general conflict undertaken, for three centuries past, for the gradual demolition of the old political system. So regarding it, we see that whereas, for above half a century, the irremediable decay of the old system has proved the necessity of founding a new one, we have not been sufficiently aware of the need to have formed an original and direct conception, adequate to the purpose; so that our theoretical ideas have remained inferior to our practical necessities, which, in a healthy state of the social organism, they habitually anticipate, to prepare for their regular and peaceable satisfaction. Though the political movement could not but have changed its nature, from that time forward, becoming organic instead of critical, yet, for want of a basis in science, it has proceeded on the same old ideas that had actuated the past struggle; and we have witnessed the spectacle of defenders and assailants alike endeavouring to convert their old weapons of war into instruments of reorganization, without suspecting the inevitable failure which must ensue to both parties. Such is the state that we find ourselves in now. All ideas of order in the political world are derived from the old doctrine of the theological and military system, regarded especially in its catholic and feudal constitution: a doctrine which from our point of view in this work, represents the theological state of social science: and, in the same way, all ideas of progress are still derived from the purely negative philosophy which, issuing from protestantism, assumed its final form and development in the last century, and which, applied to social affairs, constitutes the metaphysical state of politics. The different classes of society range themselves on the one side or the other, according to their inclination for conservatism or amelioration. With every new uprising of a social difficulty, we see the retrograde school proposing, as the only certain and universal remedy, the restoration of the corresponding part of the old political system; and the critical school referring the evil exclusively to the destruction of the old system not being complete. We do not often see the two doctrines presented without modification. They so exist only in purely speculative minds. But when we see them in monstrous alliance, as we do in all degrees of existing political opinion, we cannot but know that such an alliance cannot yield any virtue which its elements do not contain, and that it can only exhibit their mutual neutralization. We must here, it is clear, regard the theological and the metaphysical politics separately, in the first place, that we may afterwards understand their present antagonism, and form an estimate of the futile combinations into which men have endeavoured to force them.

Pernicious as the theological polity may be in our day, no true philosopher will ever forget that it afforded the beneficent guardianship under which the formation and earliest development of modern societies took place. But it is equally incontestable that, for three centuries past, its influence among the most advanced nations has been essentially retrograde, notwithstanding some partial services. We need not go into any discussion of its doctrine, in order to ascertain its powerlessness for future service: for it is plain that a polity that could not hold its ground before the natural progress of intelligence and of society can never again serve as a basis of social order. The historical analysis which I shall have to offer of the causes that have dissolved the Catholic and feudal system will show, better than any argument, how radical and irretrievable is the decay. The theological school explains the fact, as far as it can, by fortuitous and, we might almost say, personal causes: and, when they will no longer suffice, resorts to its common supposition, of a mysterious caprice of Providence which has allotted to social order a season of probation, of which no account can be given, either as to its date or its duration, or even its character. A contemplation of historical facts however shows that all the great successive modifications of the theological and military system have, from the beginning and increasingly, tended to the complete elimination of a *régime* which, by the fundamental law of social evolution, could never be more than provisional, however indispensable. And if any efforts to restore the system could achieve a temporary success, they would not bring back society to a normal state, but would merely restore the very situation which compelled the revolutionary crisis, by obliging it to set about the work of destruction again, with more violence, because the *régime* has altogether ceased to be compatible with progress in the most essential respects. While avoiding all controversy on so plain a case, I must briefly present a new view which appears to me to point out the simplest and surest criterion of the value of any social doctrine, and which emphatically condemns the theological polity.

Regarded from the logical point of view, the problem

*The theological polity.*

**Criterion of social doctrine.** of our social reorganization seems to me reducible to this one condition: to construct rationally a political doctrine which, in the whole of its active development, shall be always fully consequent on its own principles. No existing doctrines approach to a fulfilment of this condition: all contain, as indispensable elements, numerous and direct contradictions on the greater number of important points. It may be laid down as a principle that the doctrine which furnishes accordant solutions on the various leading questions of polity, without failing in this one respect in the course of application, must, by this indirect test alone, be recognized as sufficiently adapted to reorganize society; since this intellectual reorganization must mainly consist in re-establishing harmony in the troubled system of our social ideas. When such a regeneration shall have been accomplished in an individual mind (and in that way it must begin), its generalization, sooner or later, is secure; for the number of minds cannot increase the difficulty of the intellectual convergence, but only defer the success. We shall hereafter find how great is the superiority of the positive philosophy in this view; because, once extended to social phenomena, it must connect the different orders of human ideas more completely than could be done in any other way.

**Failure of the theological polity.** The accomplishment of this great logical condition might be expected from the theological polity above all others, because its doctrine is limited to co-ordinating a system so clearly defined by its long application, and so fully developed in all its essential parts, that it may well be supposed secure from all serious inconsistency. The retrograde school accordingly extols habitually, as its characteristic attribute, the perfect coherence of its ideas, in contrast with the contradictions of the revolutionary school. Yet, though the theological polity is less inconsistent than the metaphysical, it shows a daily increasing tendency to concessions of the most radical importance, directly contrary to all its essential principles. This is evidence enough of the futility of a doctrine which does not even possess the one quality most spontaneously correspondent to its nature. The old political system is seen to be destroyed as soon as its most devoted adherents have lost the true general sentiment of it: and this may now be observed, not only in active practice, but among purely speculative minds of a high order, which are unconsciously modified by the irresistible influences of their age. If examples are desired, we need only bring the retrograde doctrine into comparison with the elements of modern civilization. There can be no doubt that the development of the sciences, of industry, and even of the fine arts, was historically the principal, though latent cause, in the first instance, of the irretrievable decline of the theological and military system. At present, it is the ascendancy of the scientific spirit which preserves us from any real restoration of the theological spirit; as, again, the industrial spirit, in its perpetual extension, constitutes our best safeguard against any serious recurrence of the military or feudal spirit. Whatever may be the names given to our political struggles, this is the real character of our social antagonism. Now, amidst this state of things, do we hear of such a thing as any government, or even any school, seriously proposing a systematic repression of science, industry and art? Do not all powers (with an eccentric exception here and there) claim the honour of encouraging their progress? Here we have the first inconsistency of the retrograde polity, annulling its own project of a restoration of the past: and though the inconsistency is less apparent than some others, it must be regarded as the most decisive of all, because it is more universal and more instinctive than any other. Napoleon Bonaparte himself, the hero of retrogression in our time, set himself up, in all sincerity, as the protector of industry, art, and science. Purely speculative minds, though more easily separating themselves from any prevalent tendency, have escaped no better from the influence of their times. How many have been the attempts, for instance, for two centuries past, on the part of some of the most eminent minds, to subordinate reason to faith, according to the theological formula; reason itself being made the supreme judge of such a submission, and thus evidencing the contradictory character of the proposition! The most eminent thinker of the Catholic school, the illustrious De Maistre, bore involuntary testimony to the necessity of his time when he endeavoured, in his principal work, to re-establish the papal supremacy on historical and political reasonings, instead of ordaining it by divine right, which is the only ground appropriate to such a doctrine, and the only ground he would have proposed in any age but one in which the general state of intelligence precluded such a plea. Instances like these may spare us further illustration.

As for more direct inconsistencies, more striking, though less profound, and comprehended within the present times, we see in every sect of the retrograde school a direct opposition to some fundamental part of their common doctrine. Perhaps the only point on which there is now any unanimity in that school is in the consent to break up the very basis of the catholic and feudal system, by surrendering the division between the spiritual and temporal power; or, what comes to the same thing, acquiescing in the subordination of the spiritual to the temporal authority. In this respect, the kings are showing themselves as revolutionary as their peoples; and the priests have ratified their own degradation, in catholic countries no less than protestant. If their desire is to restore the old system, their first step must be to unite the innumerable sects which have sprung out of the decline of Christianity; but every attempt of the sort has failed through the blind and obstinate determination of the governments to retain the supreme direction of the theological power, the centralization of which they thus render impossible. Napoleon only showed an exaggerated copy, in his violent inconsistencies, of what many princes had done before him: and after his fall, when the sovereigns of Europe united to set up a power in opposition to revolutionary tendencies, they usurped the attributes of the old spiritual authority, and exhibited the spectacle of a high council composed of heretic chiefs, and governed by a schismatic prince. After this, it was manifestly impossible to introduce the papal power into the alliance, in any way whatever. Such instances of the postponement of religious principles to temporal convenience are not new; but they show how the main idea of the old political system has ceased to preponderate in the minds of the very persons who undertook to restore it. The divisions in the retrograde school have been of late apparent under all circumstances, whether of success or defeat. Any temporary success ought to rally all dissentients, in a school which boasts of the unity of its doctrine: yet, through a long course of years we have witnessed successive, and more and more serious schisms among the subdivisions of the triumphant party. The advocates of catholicism and those of feudality have quarrelled: and the latter have split into partisans of aristocracy and defenders of royalty. Under the completest restored supremacy, the schisms would only break out again, with more violence, through the incompatibility of the existing social state with the old political system. The vague assent to its general principles which is yielded in a speculative sense, must give way in their application; and every practical development must engender further divisions: and this is the scientific description of any theory which is incompatible with the facts.

When the retrograde party is reduced to the rank of an opposition, it has recourse to the principles of the revolutionary doctrine. This has been the case repeatedly during the last three centuries, when that party has been put upon the defensive. Thus we see the Catholics in England, and yet more in Ireland, asserting the claim of liberty of conscience, while still clamouring for the repression of Protestantism in France, Austria, and elsewhere. Again, when the sovereigns of Europe invoked the aid of the peoples to put down Napoleon, they surrendered their retrograde doctrine, and testified to the power of the critical, as that which was really influencing civilized society, even though they were proposing, all the while, to effect the restoration of the ancient polity. We have seen something even more wonderful since that struggle. We have seen the retrograde party taking possession of the whole body of critical doctrine, endeavouring to systematize it for its own uses, and sanctioning all its anarchical consequences; trying to set up the catholic and feudal *régime* by the very means which have destroyed it; and believing that a mere change in the person of the sovereign would intercept the consequences of a political movement which they had done nothing to modify.[1] This is simply a new way of signing a political

[1] This was written during the reign of Louis Philippe, and the administration of M. Guizot.

abdication, however the ability of those who do it may be extolled.—We need not look further for illustrations of the pregnant fact that a polity which is the type of unity and permanence has been full of schisms, and now contains elements directly incompatible with its fundamental principles; and that, as when we find De Maistre reproaching Bossuet with mistaking the nature of catholicism, and then himself falling into inconsistencies, the party of Order is proposing to re-establish that which is not comprehended by its most illustrious defenders.

*The Metaphysical polity.* Turning now to the Metaphysical polity, we must first observe and carefully remember that its doctrine, though exclusively critical, and therefore revolutionary, has still always had the virtue of being progressive, having, in fact, superintended the chief political progress accomplished during the last three centuries, which must be, in the first instance, essentially negative. What this doctrine had to do was to break up a system which, having directed the early growth of the human mind and society, tended to protract that infantile period; and thus, the political triumph of the metaphysical school was a necessary preparation for the advent of the positive school, for which the task is exclusively reserved of terminating the revolutionary period by the formation of a system uniting Order with Progress. Though the metaphysical system, considered by itself, presents a character of direct anarchy, an historical view of it, such as we shall take hereafter, shows that, considered in its origin, and in its antagonism to the old system, it constitutes a necessary provisional state, and must be dangerously active till the new political organization which is to succeed it is ready to put an end to its agitations.

The passage from one social system to another can never be continuous and direct. There is always a transitional state of anarchy which lasts for some generations at least; and lasts the longer the more complete is the renovation to be wrought. The best political progress that can be made during such a period is in gradually demolishing the former system, the foundations of which had been sapped before. While this inevitable process is going on, the elements of the new system are taking form as political institutions, and the reorganization is stimulated by the experience of the evils of anarchy. There is another reason why the constitution of the new system cannot take place before the destruction of the old; that without that destruction no adequate conception could be formed of what must be done. Short as is our life, and feeble as is our reason, we cannot emancipate ourselves from the influence of our environment. Even the wildest dreamers reflect in their dreams the contemporary social state: and much more impossible is it to form a conception of a true political system, radically different from that amidst which we live. The highest order of minds cannot discern the characteristics of the coming period till they are close upon it; and before that, the incrustations of the old system will have been pretty much broken away, and the popular mind will have been used to the spectacle of its demolition. The strongest head of all antiquity is an example of this. Aristotle could not conceive of a state of society that was not founded on slavery, the irrevocable abolition of which took place some centuries after him.— These considerations are illustrative of our own times, for which all former transition periods were merely a preparation. Never before was the destined renovation so extensive and so thorough; and never before, therefore, was the critical preparatory period so protracted and so perilous. For the first time in the history of the world, the revolutionary action is attached to a complete doctrine of methodical negation of all regular government. Such being the origin of the existing critical doctrine, we can explain the services which that doctrine has hitherto rendered, and the obstacles which it now opposes to the reorganization of modern society. We shall see hereafter how each of its principal dogmas has sprung out of some corresponding decay in the old social order; a decay which then proceeded all the faster for the opposition having become a dogma. The misfortune of the case lies in the doctrine which was thus necessarily relative to the old system coming by degrees to be supposed absolute: but we may leave it to those who desire it to blame the political conduct of our fathers, without whose energetic perseverance we should not have found ourselves at our present stage of progress, or have been able to conceive of the better polity that is approaching. The absolute or metaphysical spirit was necessary to direct the formation of the critical and anti-theological doctrine, which needed all possible energy to overthrow the great ancient system; and this energy could no otherwise be imparted to the dogmas of the critical philosophy. The necessity and the fact of the case are obvious enough: but not the less must we deplore the consequence,—that the energy imparted to the anarchical principle has gone on to impede the institution of the very political order for which it came to prepare the way. When, in the natural course of events, any doctrine has become hostile to the purposes it was destined to serve, it is evidently done with; and its end, or the close of its activity, is near. We have seen that the retrograde or theological polity has become as disturbing as the metaphysical or revolutionary: if we find also that the latter, whose office was to aid progress, has become obstructive, it is clear that both doctrines are worn out, and must soon be replaced by a new philosophy.—This condition of the metaphysical polity is a matter so serious that we must dwell upon it a little, to see how so provisional an influence can have produced the appearance of a new and stable system.

The spirit of revolutionary polity is to erect into a permanency the temporary action which it prompts. For instance, being in antagonism with ancient order, its tendency is to represent all government as being the enemy of society, and the duty of society to be to keep up a perpetual suspicion and vigilance, restricting the activity of government more and more, in order to guard against its encroachments, so as to reduce it at length to mere functions of police, in no way participating in the supreme direction of collective action and social development. This was the inevitable action by which the social evolution was brought about: and it is our misfortune that it now remains as an obstacle to the reorganization that we need. As the process could not but occupy several centuries, the power that wrought it must needs be invested with something definitive and absolute in the popular view, which cannot look far beyond

*Becomes obstructive.*

the present: and it was well that it was so; for the old system could not have been deprived of its directing powers, if they had not been stripped off from the governments, and assumed by the polity which had arisen to supersede them.

Regarding the doctrine in a more special view, it is clear that its most important principle is the right of free inquiry, or the dogma of unbounded liberty of conscience; involving the immediate consequences of the liberty of the press, or of any other mode of expression, and of communication of opinions. This is the rallying-point of the revolutionary doctrine, to which all orders of minds have come up,—the proud and the humble, the wise and the weak,—those whose other opinions were compatible with this dogma, and those who unconsciously held views of an opposite order. The impulse of this emancipation was irresistible; and the revolutionary contagion was, in this one respect, universal. It is a chief characteristic of the mind of society in this century. The most zealous partisans of the theological polity are as apt as their adversaries to judge by their personal knowledge; and those who, in their writings, set up as defenders of spiritual government, recognize, like the revolutionists whom they attack, no other supreme authority than that of their own reason. Now if we look at what is the real meaning of this dogma of the universal and absolute right of inquiry, we shall find that it is the mere abstract expression (such as is common in metaphysics) of the temporary state of unbounded liberty in which the human mind was left by the decay of the theological philosophy, and which must last till the social advent of the positive philosophy. Such an embodiment of the fact of the absence of intellectual regulation powerfully concurred in expediting the dissolution of the old system. The formula could not but appear absolute at the time, because no one could foresee the scope of the transitional state which it marked; a state which is even now mistaken by many enlightened minds for a definitive one. Negative as we now see this dogma to be, signifying release from old authority while waiting for the necessity of positive science, (a necessity which

*Dogma of liberty of conscience.*

already puts liberty of conscience out of the question in astronomy and physics, etc.,) the absolute character supposed to reside in it gave it energy to fulfil its revolutionary destination; enabled philosophers to explore the principles of a new organization; and, by admitting the right of all to a similar research, encouraged the discussion which must precede and effect the triumph of those principles. Whenever those principles shall have become established, the right of free inquiry will abide within its natural and permanent limits: that is, men will discuss, under appropriate intellectual conditions, the real connection of various consequences with fundamental rules uniformly respected. Till then, the opinions which will hereafter bring understandings into submission to an exact continuous discipline by embodying the principles of the new social order can appear only as simple individual thoughts, produced in virtue of the right of free inquiry; since their final supremacy can result in no other way than from the voluntary assent of numbers, after the freest discussion. I shall enter further into this subject hereafter: and what I have said will, I hope, prevent any one being shocked by my general appreciation of the revolutionary dogma of free inquiry, as it is plain that without it this book would never have been written.

Indispensable and salutary as it has been, this dogma can never be an organic principle: and, moreover, it constitutes an obstacle to reorganization, now that its activity is no longer absorbed by the demolition of the old political order. In any case, private or public, the state of inquiry can evidently be only provisional, indicating the condition of mind which precedes and prepares for a final decision, towards which our reason is always tending, even when it is renouncing old principles, in order to form new ones. It is taking the exception for the rule when we set up, as a natural and permanent state, the precarious situation which belongs to the period of transition; and we ignore the deepest necessities of human reason when we would protract that scepticism which is produced by the passage from one mode of belief to another, and which is, in our need of fixed points of conviction, a kind of morbid perturbation which cannot be prolonged beyond the corresponding crisis without serious danger. To be always examining and never deciding would be regarded as something like madness in private conduct: and no dogmatic consecration of such conduct in all individuals could constitute any perfection of social order, with regard to ideas which it is much more essential, and much more difficult to establish beyond the reach of dispute. There are very few persons who consider themselves fit to sit in judgment on the astronomical, physical, and chemical ideas which are destined to enter into social circulation; and everybody is willing that those ideas should direct corresponding operations; and here we see the beginnings of intellectual government. Can it be supposed that the most important and the most delicate conceptions, and those which by their complexity are accessible to only a small number of highly-prepared understandings, are to be abandoned to the arbitrary and variable decisions of the least competent minds? If such an anomaly could be imagined permanent, a dissolution of the social state must ensue, through the ever-growing divergence of individual understandings, delivered over to their disorderly natural impulses in the most vague and easily perverted of all orders of ideas. The speculative inertia common to most minds, and perhaps, to a certain extent, the wise reserve of popular good sense, tend, no doubt, to restrict such political aberrations: but these are influences too feeble to root out the pretension of every man to set himself up as a sovereign arbiter of social theories;—a pretension which every intelligent man blames in others, with a reservation, more or less explicit, of his own personal competency. Now the intellectual reorganization cannot proceed amidst such a state of things, because the convergence of minds requires the renunciation by the greater number of their right of individual inquiry on subjects above their qualifications, and requiring, more than any others, a real and permanent agreement. Then again, the unbridled ambition of ill-prepared intellects rushes in among the most complex and obscure questions: and these disturbances, though they must finally neutralize each other, make terrible devastation in the interval; and each one that is destroyed makes way for another; so that the issue of these controversies is a perpetual aggravation of the intellectual anarchy.

No association whatever, even of the smallest number of individuals, and for the most temporary objects, can subsist without a certain degree of reciprocal confidence, intellectual and moral, among its members, each one of whom has incessantly to act upon views which he must admit on the faith of some one else. If it is so in this limited case, there is something monstrous in proposing the opposite procedure in the case of the whole human race, each one of whom is at an extreme distance from the collective point of view, and is the last person of the whole number fit to judge of the rules by which his personal action should be directed. Be the intellectual development of each and all what it may, social order must ever be incompatible with a perpetual discussion of the foundations of society. Systematic toleration can exist only with regard to opinions which are considered indifferent or doubtful, as we see in that aspect of the revolutionary spirit which takes its stand on Protestantism, where the innumerable Christian sects are too weak to pretend to spiritual dominion, but where there is as fierce an intolerance about any common point of doctrine or discipline as in the Romish Church itself. And when the critical doctrine was, at the beginning of the French Revolution, supposed to be organic, we know how the directors of the movement strove to obtain a general assent, voluntary or forced, to the dogmas of the revolutionary philosophy, which they regarded as the bases of social order, and therefore above controversy. We shall see hereafter what are the due limits of the right of free inquiry, in a general way, and in regard to our own social period. It is enough to observe here that political good sense has adopted, to express the first requisite of all organization, that fine axiom of the Catholic Church; *in necessary things, unity: in doubtful things, liberty: in all things, charity:*—a maxim which admirably proposes the problem, without, however, suggesting the principles by which it must be solved, and that unity attained which would be a mere illusion if it did not result, in the first instance, from free discussion.

The dogma which ranks next in importance to that of

free inquiry is that of Equality; and in the same way, it is taken to be absolute when it is only relative, and permanent, while it expresses merely the position of minds employed in breaking up the old system. It is an immediate consequence of liberty of conscience, which brings after it the most fundamental equality of all,—that of intelligence. The supposition of its being absolute was not less necessary in this case than the former: for, if all social classification had not been systematically disallowed, the old corporations would have preserved their sway, from the impossibility of their conceiving of any other classification. To this day we have no sufficiently distinct notion ourselves of such an arrangement as would be truly appropriate to a new state of civilization. When the dogma of equality had achieved the overthrow of the old polities, it could not but become an obstacle to any reorganization, because its activity must then be directed against the bases of any new classification whatever; for, of course, any classification must be incompatible with the equality that was claimed for all. Since the abolition of slavery, there has been no denial, from any quarter, of the right of every man (innocent of strong anti-social conduct) to expect from all others the fulfilment of the conditions necessary to the natural development of his personal activity, suitably directed: but beyond that undisputed right, men cannot be made, because they are not, equal, nor even equivalent; and they cannot therefore possess, in a state of association, any identical rights beyond the great original one. The simple physical inequalities which fix the attention of superficial observers are much less marked than intellectual and moral differences; and the progress of civilization tends to increase these more important differences, as much as to lessen the inferior kind: and, applied to any assemblage of persons thus developed, the dogma of equality becomes anarchical, and directly hostile to its original destination.

Dogma of Equality.

The second result of the dogma of liberty of conscience is the Sovereignty of the people: and, like the former, it wrought at first the double service of destroying the old *régime* and preparing for a new one. Till the final system could be

Dogma of the Sovereignty of the People.

constituted, the only safeguard against the renewed supremacy of the old one was in the setting up of provisional institutions, which the peoples claimed the absolute right to change at will. It was only by means of the doctrine of popular sovereignty that that succession of political endeavours could take place which must precede the installation of a true system of government, whenever the intellectual renovation of society shall be sufficiently advanced to settle the conditions and natural extent of the different sovereignties. Meanwhile, in discharging its function, this dogma proves its revolutionary character before our eyes, by opposing all reorganization, condemning, as it does, all the superior to an arbitrary dependence on the multitude of the inferior, by a kind of transference to the peoples of the divine right which had become the opprobrium of kings.

*Dogma of National Independence.* The revolutionary spirit of the critical doctrine manifests itself no less clearly when we look at international relations. The necessity of order being in this case more equivocal and obscure, the absence of all regulating power has been more ingenuously declared than in other cases. When the ancient spiritual power was politically annulled, the dissolution of European order followed spontaneously from the principle of liberty of conscience; and the most natural papal function was at an end. Till the new social organization shall show us the law by which the nations shall become once more connected, the metaphysical notions of national isolation, and therefore of mutual non-intervention, must prevail; and they will be regarded as absolute till it appears how they defeat their own end. As all attempts at European co-ordination must otherwise be directed by the ancient system, we owe to the doctrine of national independence our rescue from the monstrous arrangement of the most civilized nations being politically subordinated to the least advanced, because the latter were least changed from their ancient state, and would be sure therefore to be placed at the head of such an association. But, if such a doctrine were more than provisional, the nations would sink below their state in the Middle Ages; and at the very time when they are marked out, by an ever-growing resemblance, for an association more extensive, and, at the same time more regular, than that which was proposed by the old catholic and feudal system. It is clear that when the dogma of national isolation has fulfilled its function of separating the nations, in order to a preparation for a new union, its further action must be as purely anarchical as that of its predecessors.

A brief notice of the logical inconsistency of the revolutionary doctrine will conclude our preliminary review of it.

This inconsistency is more radical and more manifest than in the case of the retrograde or theological doctrine; but it does not imply so utter a condemnation; not only on account of its recent formation, but because such a vice does not prevent its fulfilling its critical office. Notwithstanding profound differences, the adversaries of the old polity found no difficulty in uniting for successive partial demolitions about which they were agreed, postponing till their period of success their contests about the ulterior developments of their doctrine; a course which would be impossible in the case of any organic operation, in which each part must be considered in its relation to the whole. Thus far only, however, can the inconsistency be tolerated. When once the whole of any doctrine becomes hostile to its original purposes, it is condemned: and this is true of the metaphysical doctrine, which at once opposes the progress it professed to aid, and sustains the foundations of the political system it proposed to destroy. *Inconsistency of the Metaphysical doctrine.*

Its culminating point was at the most marked period of the first French Revolution, when it was, by an unavoidable illusion, taken to be the principle of social reorganization. It was then seen in its best aspect of consistency and power; and then it was that, the ancient system being disposed of, its vices became apparent. It showed itself hostile to all social reorganization, and became actually retrograde in its character by setting itself up in violent opposition to the movement of modern civilization. For one illustration, look at the strange metaphysical notion of a supposed state of nature, which was to be the primitive and invariable type of every social state. This doctrine is not to be attri- *Notion of a state of Nature.*

buted to Rousseau alone. It is that of all philosophers, in all times and countries, who have unconsciously concurred in developing the revolutionary metaphysical doctrine which Rousseau, by his urgent dialectics, only pushed to its real conclusions. His doctrine, which represents a state of civilization as an ever-growing degeneracy from the primitive ideal type, is common to all modern metaphysicians; and we shall see hereafter that it is only the metaphysical form of the theological dogma of the degradation of the human race by original sin. According to such a principle, all political reformation must be regarded as destined to re-establish that primitive state: and what is that but organizing a universal retrogradation, though with progressive intentions? The applications of this doctrine have been in conformity to its philosophical constitution. When it was necessary to replace the feudal and catholic *régime*, men did not fix their contemplation on the social future, but summoned up their imperfect remembrances of a very distant past, trying to substitute for a decrepit system a more ancient and decrepit system still, but, for that very reason, nearer to the primitive type. Instead of a worn-out catholicism, they proposed a sort of metaphysical polytheism, at the same time that, in polity, they desired to replace the Middle Age system by the radically inferior *régime* of the Greeks and Romans. The very elements of modern civilization, the only possible germs of a new social state, were endangered by barbaric condemnation of the industrial and artistic advancement of modern society, in the name of primitive virtue and simplicity. Even the scientific spirit, which is the only principle of intellectual organization, was stigmatized as tending to institute an aristocracy of knowledge which was as incompatible as any other aristocracy with the original equality that was to be set up again. Lavoisier was the martyr of this state of opinion; and it is his case that will illustrate the period to our remotest posterity. It is useless for the metaphysical school to represent such results as portentous or eccentric incidents. Their legitimate descent from the revolutionary polity is evident and certain; and we should witness a repetition of them if it were possible (which it is not) for this polity to become prevalent again. The tendency to social retrogradation, under the idea of returning to the primitive state, so thoroughly belongs to the metaphysical polity, that the new sects who, in their brief day, have most haughtily censured the revolutionary imitation of Greek and Roman types, have unconsciously reproduced the same error in a far more marked way by striving to re-establish the confusion between the temporal and spiritual power, and extolling, as the highest social perfection, a return to the Egyptian or Hebrew theocracy, founded on fetichism, disguised under the name of pantheism.

As the metaphysical doctrine was the issue of the theological, and destined to modify it, it was a matter of course that it should vindicate the general foundations of the old system, even after having destroyed its chief conditions of existence. *Adhesion to the worn-out.* Every reformer, for three centuries past, while urging the development of the critical spirit further than his predecessors, assumed to set immutable bounds to it; deriving his limitations from the old system. All the absolute rights proclaimed as the basis of the new doctrine were guaranteed by a sort of religious consecration, in the last resort; and this was indispensable, if their efficacy was not to be impaired by continual discussion. It was always with an invocation of the principles of the old polity on their lips that the reformers proceeded to demolish the spiritual and temporal institutions in which they were embodied; and the whole *régime* fell through the conflict of its chief elements. Hence there arose, in the intellectual region, a Christianity more and more attenuated or simplified, and reduced at last to that vague and impotent theism which, by a monstrous conjunction of terms, metaphysicians have entitled *Natural Religion*, as if all religion were not necessarily supernatural. The pretension to direct a social reorganization by this strange conception is merely a recurrence to the old principle that social order must rest on a theological basis. This is now the most fatal inconsistency of the revolutionary school; and while armed with such a concession, the advocates of catholicism will always have an incontestable logical superiority over the irrational defamers of the old faith, who proclaim the need of a religious organization, and yet disallow all the necessary conditions.

It is clear that society would be condemned to a perpetuity of the intellectual anarchy which characterizes it at present if it were to be for ever made up of minds which admit the want of a theological *régime* on the one hand, while, on the other, they reject its principal conditions of existence; and those who thus acknowledge themselves incapable have no right to discredit the only rational way to reorganization which remains open, and by which every other order of human conceptions has been happily retrieved and established. The social application of the positive philosophy remains as the resource, and the only resource, after the failure of both the preceding systems.

Recurrence to war.
In its temporal application the inconsistency of the metaphysical doctrine is as conspicuous as in the spiritual. It strives to preserve, if not the feudal, at least the military spirit, in which the feudal had its origin. The French nation did, it is true, in their revolutionary enthusiasm, proscribe war from that time forward: but when the armed coalition of the retrograde forces of Europe brought out an immense amount of energy for self-defence, for the sake of the progressive movement, the sentiment, which was grounded on no principle, soon disappeared, and France was distinguished by the most conspicuous military activity, invested with its most oppressive characteristics. The military spirit is in fact so congenial with the critical doctrine that any pretext will serve for its indulgence: as for instance, when it is proposed to regulate by war the action of the more advanced nations upon the less advanced. The true logical consequence of this would be a universal uproar; but, happily, the nature of modern civilization saves us from danger. The tendency of the critical *régime* in this respect is shown by the perpetual endeavours of the various sections of the revolutionary school to reinstate the memory of the man who, of all others, strove for political retrogradation, by wasting an enormous amount of power in the restoration of the military and theological system.

Principle of Political Centralization.
Before quitting the subject of the inconsistencies of this school, I must, in justice, point out one more contradiction which, as being of a progressive character, is honourable to those

most advanced minds which entertain it, and which alone understand its necessity, opposed as it is to the dogmas of independence and isolation which constitute the spirit of the critical school. I refer to the principle of political centralization. The two parties seem here to have changed sides. The retrograde doctrine, notwithstanding its proud pretensions to order and unity, preaches the distribution of political centres, in the secret hope of preserving the old system yet a while longer among the most backward of the populations, by keeping them aloof from the general centres of civilization; while the revolutionary policy, on the other hand, proud of having withstood, in France, the coalition of the old powers, discards its own maxims to recommend the subordination of the secondary to the principal centres by which such a noble stand has already been made, and which must become a most valuable auxiliary of reorganization. Thus alone can the reorganization be, in the first place, restricted to a choice population. In brief, the revolutionary school alone has understood that the increasing anarchy of the time, intellectual and moral, requires, to prevent a complete dislocation of society, a growing concentration of political action, properly so called.

Thus, after three centuries, employed in the necessary demolition of the ancient *régime*, the critical doctrine shows itself as incapable of other application, and as inconsistent as we have now seen it to be. It is no more fit to secure Progress, than the old doctrine to maintain Order. But, feeble as they are apart, they actually sustain each other by their very antagonism. It is universally understood that neither can ever again achieve a permanent triumph: but, so strong is the apprehension of even the temporary preponderance of either, that the general mind, for want of a more rational point of support, employs each doctrine in turn to restrain the encroachments of the other. This miserable oscillation of our social life must proceed till a real doctrine, as truly organic as progressive, shall reconcile for us the two aspects of the great political problem. Then, at last, the two opposite doctrines will disappear for ever in the new conception that will be seen to be completely adapted to fulfil the destination of both. Often has each party, blinded by some temporary success, believed that it had annihilated the other; and never has the event failed to mock the ignorant exultation. The critical doctrine seemed to have humbled for ever the catholic-feudal school; but that school arose again. Napoleon thought he had accomplished a retrograde reaction; but the very energy of his efforts caused a reaction in favour of revolutionary principles. And thus society continues to vibrate between conflicting influences; and those influences continue to exist only by their mutual neutralization. For that purpose only, indeed, are they now ever applied. Neither could be spared before the advent of the state which is to succeed them. Without the one, we should lose the sentiment of Order, and without the other, that of Progress: and the keeping alive this sentiment, on either hand, is the only practical efficacy which now remains to them. Feeble as the conception must be, in the absence of any principle which unites the two requisites, it is preserved by the presence of the two decaying systems; and they keep before the minds of both philosophers and the public the true conditions of social reorganization, which otherwise our feeble nature might misconceive or lose sight of. Having the two types before us, we see the solution of the great problem to be, to form a doctrine which shall be more organic than the theological, and more progressive than the metaphysical.

The old political system can be no pattern for a *régime* suitable to a widely different civilization; but we are not under the less obligation to study it, in order to learn what are the essential attributes of all social organization, which must reappear in an improved state in the future. The general conception of the theological and military system even seems to me to have passed too much out of sight. And, as to the Critical system, there can be no question of its affording, by its progressive character, and its exposure of the preceding *régime*, a most valuable stimulus to society to seek for something better than mere modifications of systems that have failed. The common complaint that it renders all government impossible, is a mere avowal of impotence on the part of those who utter it. Whatever are its imperfections, it fulfilled for a time one of the two requisites: its abolition would in no way assist the reestablishment of Order; and no declamations against the revolutionary philosophy will affect the instinctive attachment of society to principles which have directed its political progress for three centuries past, and which are believed to represent the indispensable conditions of its future development. Each of its dogmas affords an indication of how the improvement is to be effected. Each expresses the political aspect of certain high moral obligations which the retrograde school, with all its pretensions, was compelled to ignore, because its system had lost all power to fulfil them. In this way, the dogma of Free Inquiry decides that the spiritual reorganization must result from purely intellectual action, providing for a final voluntary and unanimous assent, without the disturbing intervention of any heterogeneous power. Again, the dogmas of Equality and the Sovereignty of the people devolve on the new powers and classes of society the duty of a public-spirited social conduct, instead of working the many for the interests of the few. The old system practised these moralities in its best days; but they are now maintained only by the revolutionary doctrine, which it would be fatal to part with till we have some substitute in these particular respects; for the effect would be that we should be delivered over to the dark despotism of the old system;—to the restorers of religions, for instance, who, if proselytism failed, would have recourse to tyranny to compel unity, if once the principle of free inquiry were lost from among us.

It is useless to declaim against the critical philosophy, and to deplore, in the name of social order, the dissolving energy of the spirit of analysis and inquiry. It is only by their use that we can obtain materials for reorganization; materials which shall have been thoroughly tested by free discussion, carried on till general conviction is secured. The philosophy which will arise out of this satisfaction of the public reason will then assign the rational limits which must obviate the abuse of the analytical spirit, by establishing that distinction in social matters, between the field of reasoning and that of pure observation, which we have found already marked out in regard to every other kind of science.

Though consigned, by the course of events, to a negative doctrine for awhile, society has never renounced the laws of human reason: and when the proper time arrives, society will use the rights of this reason to organize itself anew, on principles which will then have been ascertained and estimated. The existing state of no-government seems necessary at present, in order to that ascertainment of principles; but it does not at all follow, as some eccentric individuals seem to think, that the right of inquiry imposes the duty of never deciding. The prolonged indecision proves merely that the principles which are to close the deliberation are not yet sufficiently established. In the same way, because society claims the right of choosing and varying its institutions and governing powers, it by no means follows that the right is for ever to be used in choosing and varying, when its indefinite use shall have become injurious. When the right conditions shall have been ascertained, society will submit its choice to the rules which will secure its efficacy; and in the interval, nothing can be more favourable to future order than that the political course should be kept open, to admit of the free rise of the new social system. As it happens, the peoples have, thus far, erred on the side of too hasty a desire for reorganization, and a too generous confidence in every promise of social order, instead of having shown the systematic distrust attributed to the revolutionary doctrine by those whose worn-out claims will not bear discussion. There is more promise of political reorganization in the revolutionary doctrine than in the retrograde, though it is the supreme claim of the latter to be the safeguard of social Order.

The Stationary doctrine. Such is the vicious circle in which we are at present confined. We have seen what is the antagonism of two doctrines that are powerless apart, and have no operation but in neutralizing each other. They have lost their activity as preponderating influences, and are seen now in the form of political debate, which they daily direct by the one furnishing all the essential ideas of government, and the other the principles of opposition. At shorter and shorter intervals, a partial and transient superiority is allowed to the one or the other, when its antagonist threatens danger. Out of these oscillations a third opinion has arisen, which is constructed out of their ruins, and takes its station between them. I suppose we must give the name of Doctrine to this intermediate opinion, bastard and inconsistent as is its character; for it is presented by very earnest doctors, who urge it upon us as a type of the final political philosophy. We must call it the Stationary Doctrine; and we see it, in virtue of that quality, occupying the scene of politics, among the most advanced people, for above a quarter of a century. Essentially provisional as it is, the Stationary school naturally serves as a guide to society in preserving the material order, without which a true doctrine could not have its free growth. It may be necessary for our weakness that the leaders of this school should suppose that they have a doctrine which is destined to triumph; but whatever benefits arise from their action are much impaired by the mistake of supposing our miserable transition state a permanent type of the social condition. The stationary polity not only contains inconsistencies, but it is itself inconsistency erected into a principle. It acknowledges the essential principles of the other systems, but prevents their action. Disdainful of Utopias, it proposes the wildest of them all;—that of fixing society for ever in a contradictory position between retrogradation and regeneration. The theory serves to keep in check the other two philosophies; and this may be a good: but, on the other hand, it helps to keep them alive; and it is, in so far, an obstacle to reorganization. When I present my historical review of society, I shall explain the special assemblage of social conditions which gave England her parliamentary monarchy, so lauded by the school of mixed doctrine, but in fact, an exceptional institution, whose inevitable end cannot be very far off. When we enter upon that analysis, we shall see how great is the error of philosophers and statesmen when they have taken up a singular and transient case as the solution of the revolutionary crisis of modern societies, and have endeavoured to transplant on the European continent a purely local system, which would be deprived in the process of its very roots: for it is an organized Protestantism which is its main spiritual basis in England. The expectation attached to this single specious aspect of the stationary doctrine will make a future examination of it important; and we shall then see how hopeless is the constitutional metaphysics of the balance of powers, judged by that instance which serves as the common ground of such social fictions. After all the vast efforts made to nationalize elsewhere the stationary compromise, it has never succeeded anywhere but in its native land; and this proves its powerlessness in regard to the great social problem. The only possible result is that the mischief should pass from the acute to the chronic state, becoming incurable by the recognition as a principle of the transient antagonism which is its chief symptom. Its principal merit is that it admits the double aspect of the social problem, and the necessity of reconciling Order and Progress: but it introduces no new idea; and its recognition amounts therefore to nothing more than an equal sacrifice, when necessary, of the one and the other. The order that it protects is a merely material order; and it therefore fails in that function precisely in crises when it is most wanted. On the other hand, this function continues to be attributed to royalty, which is the only power of the old polity that is still active: now, the balance which is instituted by the stationary doctrine surrounds the royal power with bonds that are always tightening, while declaring that royal power to be the chief basis of the government. It is only a question of time when the function of sovereignty, thus embarrassed, shall cease, and the pretended balance be destroyed. This parliamentary polity serves the cause of progress no better than that of order: for, as it proposes no new principle, the restraints which it puts upon the revolutionary spirit are all derived from the ancient system, and therefore tend to become more and more retrograde and oppressive. An example of this is, the restrictions on the right of election; restrictions always derived from irrational material conditions, which, being arbitrary in their character, oppress and irritate, without answering their proposed purpose, and leave the multitude of the excluded much more offended than the small number of the privileged are gratified.

There is no need to say more in this place of the mixed

or Stationary doctrine, which is, in fact, only a last phase of the metaphysical polity. The reader cannot but see that a theory so precarious and subaltern, so far from being able to reorganize modern society, can only regulate, by protracting, the political conflict, and discharge the negative office of preventing kings from retrograding and peoples from destroying. Whatever the value of this service may be, we cannot expect regeneration to be accomplished by means of impediments.

We have now seen the worth of these three systems. To complete our conviction of the need of a better, we must briefly notice the chief social dangers which result from the deplorable protraction of such an intellectual condition, and which must, from their nature, be aggravated from day to day. The dangers are imputable to all the three systems; though the revolutionary and stationary systems assume that the blame of our disorders rests with the retrograde school: but they are certainly no less guilty; for, powerless to discover the remedy, they protract the mischief, and embarrass the treatment. And again, the discordance between the movements of governments and of their peoples is to be attributed quite as much to the hostile spirit of the directing power as to the anarchical tendency of popular opinions. The social perturbations, the aspect of which we are about to examine, proceed no less from the kings than from their peoples, with this aggravated disgrace,—that it seems as if the solution ought to emanate from the kings. *Dangers of the critical period.*

The first, the most fatal, and the most universal consequence of this situation is the alarming and ever-widening extent of the intellectual anarchy which all acknowledge, however they may differ about its cause and termination. This evil is charged almost exclusively on the revolutionary philosophy; and that school too readily admits the charge. But, as we have seen, that doctrine does not prohibit decision, when the requisite grounds are ascertained: and it is the stationary theory that ought to bear the blame of the absence of those grounds: and yet more the retrograde, which is chargeable with urging the restoration of the *Intellectual anarchy.*

same worn-out principles which, by their decrepitude, have caused all this anarchy. The stationary school does not want to hear of any such principles, and interdicts them; and the retrograde school insists that the old ones will do over again. So that, if the revolutionary school first encouraged the anarchy, the other two protract it.

Of all questions, there are none which have so much claim as social problems to be consigned to a small number of choice minds which shall have been prepared by a high order of discipline and instruction for the investigation of questions so complex and so mixed up with human passions. Such is, at least, the natural state of the human mind, in contrast with which its condition in revolutionary periods may be regarded as, in a manner, pathological, however inevitable. The social malady must be very serious when we see all manner of persons, however inferior their intelligence, and however unprepared, stimulated, in the highest manner, and from day to day, to cut the knot of the most intricate political questions, without any guidance or restraint. The wonder is, not that the divergence of opinion is what it is, but that any points of agreement at all are left amidst all this dissolution of social maxims. The evil has reached such a point that all political opinions, though of course derived from one of the three schools, differ through so many degrees as to become individual;— through all degrees, in fact, that the combination of three orders of vicious principles admits of. Except on occasion of emergency, where there is a temporary coalition (amidst which each one usually hopes to have his own way) it becomes more and more difficult to make even a very small number of minds adhere to a plain and explicit profession of political faith. This inability to co-operate prevails in all the three camps,—as we ought carefully to observe: and each party has often, in its ingenuous moments, bitterly deplored the intense disagreement with which it supposed itself to be especially afflicted; whereas, the others were no better organized; and the chief difference in the three cases was that each was most acutely sensible of its own misery.

In countries where this intellectual anarchy has been sanctioned by the political preponderance of Protestantism, the divergences have been more multiplied than elsewhere, without being less serious. It could not but be so from the tendency of the general mind, in its then infantile state, to use its new emancipation to plunge into the indefinite discussion of religious opinions—(the most vague and discordant of all),—in the absence of a restraining spiritual authority. In the United States, for instance, there are hundreds of Christian sects, radically discordant, and incessantly parting off into opinions which are really little more than individual, which it is impossible to classify, and which are really becoming implicated with innumerable political differences. The nations which, like the French, have escaped the treacherous stage of Protestantism, and have passed at once from the Catholic to the fully revolutionary state, were not, on that account, entirely exempt from the intellectual anarchy inherent in any prolonged exercise of the absolute right of free individual inquiry. All that can be said is that their aberrations, without being less anti-social, have a less vague character, and are less in the way of the final reorganization. They arise, take possession for awhile of even healthy and well-trained intellects, and then give place to others that have their day, and in their turn are superseded. In our time, we hear of proposals, entertained here and there even by men who know what positive science is in some one department of study, which it is a shock to one's hopes to see so advocated; proposals, for instance, to abolish money and recur to a state of barter; to destroy the great capitals in order to restore rural innocence; to have a fixed rate of wages, and the same rate for every kind of labour, and so forth. Such opinions are daily given out, side by side with those which are the most philosophical and the most carefully elaborated; and none have any chance of being established under the rule of any intellectual discipline whatever, though the wise are compromised with the foolish in the eyes of public reason. The inevitable result of such a chronic epidemic is the gradual destruction of the public *morale*, which is not sustained, among the generality of men, so much by *Destruction of* the direct sentiment as by habit, guided by *public morality*. the uniform assent of individual wills to invariable and general rules, adapted to fix, on every serious occasion, the true idea of the public good. So complex is the nature of social questions that there is much that is to be said on all sides; and there is no institution, however indispensable, which does not involve serious and numerous inconveniences, more or less partial and transient; and, on the other hand, there is no Utopia so wild as not to offer some incontestable advantages: and few are the minds which are not so preoccupied by ideas, or stimulated by passion, as to be able to contemplate at once all the aspects of any social subject. Thus it is that almost all the great maxims of public morality are condemned on account of their salient faults, while their determining grounds are hidden till exhibited by an exact analysis, which must in many cases be extremely delicate. Thus, again, it is that all true moral order is incompatible with the existing vagabond liberty of individual minds, if such license were to last; for the great social rules which should become customary cannot be abandoned to the blind and arbitrary decision of an incompetent public without losing all their efficacy. The requisite convergence of the best minds cannot be obtained without the voluntary renunciation, on the part of most of them, of their sovereign right of free inquiry, which they will doubtless be willing to abdicate, as soon as they have found organs worthy to exercise appropriately their vain provisional supremacy. If it is so in problems of science, there is every reason to expect it in the more difficult questions of social principle. Meanwhile, all vague notions of public good, degenerating into an indistinct philanthropy, must succumb to the energetic forces of a highly stimulated selfishness. In the daily course of our political conflicts we see accordingly the most conscientious men taxing each other with wickedness and folly; and, on every serious occasion, the most opposite doctrines maintained by persons equally worthy of confidence: and, while all deep and steady conviction is thus rendered impossible, no true political morality can be hoped for by those who desire it most.

This public demoralization has, it must be admitted, been sensibly retarded, in our time, by the preponderance of that revolutionary doctrine which has borne the imputation of causing it; for the revolutionary party, progressive in character, could not but be animated, more than the others, by sincere convictions, which, in their depth and activity, must tend to restrain, and even annihilate, individual selfishness. This was especially remarkable during the season when the revolutionary doctrine was, by a general illusion, supposed to be destined to reorganize society. Under the impulse of this persuasion, the strongest social devotedness that can shed honour upon contemporary history was manifested. But this could be only for a time. As the illusion disappeared, the convictions which arose from it became first weakened, and then mingled with the influences of the stationary, and even the retrograde polity: and though they are still of a higher order than those which are inspired by the other doctrines, and especially among the young, they have not energy to resist the dissolving action of the revolutionary philosophy, even among its own advocates; so that this philosophy now contributes, almost as much as its two antagonists, to the spread of political demoralization.

Private morality is, happily, much less dependent on established opinions. Other conditions enter into this case; and in the commonest questions, natural sentiment is far more operative than in public relations. Disorganizing influences are strongly counteracted by the continuous amelioration of our manners, through a more equable intellectual development, by a juster sense and more familiar taste for the various fine arts, and by the gradual improvement of social conditions in consequence of steady industrial progress. The common rules of domestic and personal morality have guarded private life longer than political from the invasion of disorganizing influences, and the intrusion of individual analysis. But the time has arrived for these inevitable disturbances, long concealed, to manifest their dangerous activity. So long ago as the first rise of the revolutionary state, this deleterious influence on morality, properly so called, began with a serious innovation on the institution of Marriage, which would have been radically changed, by the permission of divorce in Protestant countries, if public decency and private good sense had not, up to this time,

*Private morality.*

weakened the pernicious effects of theologico-metaphysical extravagances. Still, private morality could be reached only through the destruction of political morals: and now, that barrier being broken through, the dissolving action threatens domestic, and even personal morality, which is the necessary foundation of every other. Whichever way we look at it, whether as to the relations of the sexes, to those of ages, or of conditions, it is clear that the elements of all social life are directly compromised by a corrosive discussion which is not directed by true principles, and which brings into question, without the possibility of solution, even the least important ideas of duty. Even the Family, which, amidst the fiercest revolutionary tumults, had been on the whole respected, has been assailed in our day in its very foundations, by attacks on the hereditary principle and on marriage. We have even seen the commonest principle of personal morality, the subjection of the passions to reason, denied by pretended reformers who, in defiance of all experience and such positive science as we have, have proposed as a fundamental dogma of their regenerated morality, the systematic dominion of the passions, which they have striven, not to restrain, but to excite by the strongest stimulants. These speculations have so far penetrated social life, that any one is now at liberty to make an easy merit of the most turbulent passions; so that, if such license could last, insatiable stomachs might at length get to pride themselves on their own voracity. It is in vain for the retrograde school to throw the blame of all this on the revolutionary school. The censure rests upon themselves, inasmuch as they have persisted in extolling, as the only intellectual bases of social duty, principles which have betrayed their impotence in this very case; for, if theological conceptions are, in truth, the immutable bases of future as well as past morality, how is it that they now fail to obviate such license? What are we to think of the attempt to shore up by laborious artifices, the religious principles which are proposed, after they have lost their strength, as the only supports of moral order? No supreme function can be assigned to convictions that have themselves given way before the development of human reason, which is not likely to use its mature power to reconstruct the bonds which it broke through in the efforts of its youth. It is remarkable that the license I have spoken of has been proposed by the ardent restorers of religious theories, in their exasperation against all positive philosophy; and this has, for some time past, been the case with Protestant, no less than Catholic advocates. So far from furnishing bases for morality, domestic or personal, religious convictions have long tended to its injury, both by hindering its erection on more solid foundations among those who are free from their control, and by being insufficient for their own subjects, without the active intervention of a sacerdotal authority; that authority meanwhile perpetually losing its hold over the more advanced populations, and being more and more absorbed by the care of its own preservation, instead of venturing upon any unpopular scheme of discipline. Daily experience shows that the ordinary morality of religious men is not, at present, in spite of our intellectual anarchy, superior to that of the average of those who have quitted the churches. The chief practical tendency of religious convictions is, in our present social life, to inspire an instinctive and insurmountable hatred against all who have emancipated themselves, without any useful emulation having arisen from the conflict. Thus the chief assaults, direct and indirect, on private as well as public morality, are as strictly imputable to the stationary, and yet more to the retrograde, than to the revolutionary philosophy, which is commonly made to bear all the blame. It is indeed but too evident that the three doctrines are almost equally powerless to restrain the development of individual selfishness, which grows bolder, from day to day, in clamouring for the license of the least social passions, in the name of universal intellectual anarchy.

The second characteristic of our condition follows from the first. It is the systematic corruption which is set up as an indispensable instrument of government. *Political corruption.* The three doctrines bear their share, though it may be an unequal one, in this disgraceful result, because all exclude, as we have seen, true political convictions. Amidst the absence, or the discredit, of general ideas, which have now no power to command genuine acts, there is no other daily resource for the maintenance of even a rough and precarious order than an appeal, more or less immediate, to personal interests. Such an influence is scarcely ever needed with men of deep convictions. Even in the lower order of characters, human nature is rarely so debased as to allow a course of political conduct in opposition to any strong convictions; and such contrariety, if persevered in, would soon paralyse the faculties. In the scientific class, in which philosophical convictions are at present most common and best marked, active corruption is scarcely practicable, though minds are there much of the same quality as they are elsewhere. Thus, exceptional cases apart, the rapid spread of a corruption which avails itself of the half-convictions that are prevalent in the political world must be attributed mainly to the undecided and fluctuating state in which social ideas are kept by the intellectual anarchy of our time. Not only does this disorder of minds permit the political corruption: it even requires it, as the only means of obtaining any sort of practical convergence, such as is necessary for the mere preservation of the social state in its grossest interests: and we must prepare ourselves for the continuous extension of the evil, as long as intellectual anarchy goes on destroying all strong political conviction. Rulers and the ruled are alike guilty in regard to this vice: the rulers by their disdain of all social theory; by their repression of mind, and by their application of the instrument which they cannot dispense with to their own, instead of the general interest; and the ruled by their acceptance of the proffered corruption, and by their intellectual condition rendering the use of it inevitable. If individuals cannot co-operate on any other ground than that of private interest, they have no right to complain that governments take the same ground to procure the assistance that they cannot dispense with, during a period in which it is scarcely possible to see clearly what the public good really consists in. All that can be said for such a state of things is that matters would be worse if individual eccentricities were not somewhat restrained by personal interest, in the absence of better influences; and that it is the natural result of the situation to which it applies, and therefore certainly destined to disappear whenever society shall begin to admit of a better discipline. Till then we must expect to see this miserable expedient more and more resorted to; as is proved by the constant experience of all peoples living under a prolonged constitutional or representative *régime*, as we now call it, always compelled to organize in this manner a certain material discipline in the midst of a complete intellectual, and therefore moral anarchy. All that we have a right to require is that governments, instead of welcoming this disastrous necessity, and making an eager use of the facilities it offers, should set themselves to favour, systematically, by all the means at their command, the great philosophical elaboration through which modern society may enter upon a better course.

By corruption, I do not mean only direct venality, nor yet the holding of honorary distinctions which are merely flattering to the vanity. The scope offered to various kinds of ambition is a more corrupting influence. In some countries this had been carried so far, in the form of creation of offices, that nations are farmed by the functionaries of their governments. The danger of such a course is obvious enough; for the number of aspirants, where offices are very numerous, must always largely exceed that of the chosen; and their disappointment must awaken passions anything but favourable to the established *régime*. Moreover, the practice must spread the more it is resorted to; and it will go on extending till the time for social reorganization has arrived. Here, again, all the three schools must share the blame. The Revolutionary school supplied, as we have seen, the dissolving influence which rendered the system of corruption necessary. The Stationary school even sets it up as a type, declaring the equal admission of all to public functions to be the final destination of the general social movement; and aggravating the case by connecting the conditions of order with the mere possession of fortune, however obtained. As for the Retrograde school, with all its pretensions to moral purity, it employs corruption as fatally as the other two, under the special form which it appropriates,—that of systematic hypocrisy. From the opening of the revolutionary period, in the sixteenth century, this system of hypocrisy has been more and more elaborated in practice, permitting the emancipation of all minds of a certain bearing, on the tacit condition that they should aid in protracting the submission of the masses. This was, eminently, the policy of the Jesuits. Thus has the retrograde school suffered under this vice as early as the others; and it cannot but resort to corruption more and more, in proportion to its own opposition to the general movement of the society which it pretends to rule.

This, then, is our state. For want of a moral authority, material order requires the use of either terror or corruption; and the latter is both more durable, less inconvenient, and more accordant with the nature of modern society than the former. But, while admitting the inevitable character of the evil, it is impossible not to lament, bitterly and mournfully, the blindness which prevents the social powers of our time from facilitating to the utmost the philosophical evolution by which alone we can issue into a better state. It seems as if statesmen of all parties were agreed to close this sole avenue of safety by visiting with stupid reprobation all elaboration of social theories. This again, however, is only another consequence of the present state of the most civilized nations; and, as a consequence, not less necessary or characteristic than those that have gone before.

*Low aims of political questions.* The third symptom of our social situation is the growing preponderance of material and immediate considerations in regard to political questions. There is something more concerned here than the ordinary antagonism between theory and practice, aggravated by the weakness of attempts at theory in an infantile period of social science. The repugnance to theory is further attributable to the historical circumstance that when, three centuries ago, the spiritual power was finally annulled or absorbed by the temporal, all lofty social speculations were more and more devolved upon minds which were always pre-occupied by practical affairs. Thus kings and their peoples concurred in exalting the lower order of considerations; and the tendency belonged to all the three schools of polity. If the crowning evil of our time be its intellectual anarchy, it is clear that we cannot too strongly lament this irrational unanimity of the political world in closing the path of progress by proscribing speculative researches. We see the consequences in our experience of the past century. In seeking social reorganization, men have not first looked to the doctrines of a new social order, and then to the corresponding manners; but have gone straight to the construction of institutions, at a time when we have all possible evidence that institutions can be nothing more than provisional, restricted to the most indispensable objects, and having no other relation to the future than such facility as they may afford to the process of political regeneration. The making of institutions in our day consists in parcelling out the old political powers, minutely organizing factitious and complex antagonisms among them, rendering them more and more precarious by submitting them to election for terms; but in no way changing either the general nature of the ancient *régime* or the spirit which worked it. For want of all social doctrine, nothing more has been attempted than restraining the powers thus preserved, till there is every danger of their being altogether annulled, while the principles which were to direct their application were left doubtful and obscure. The pompous name of a Constitution is then given to this piece of work, and it is consecrated to the eternal admiration of posterity. Though the average duration of these constitutions has been at most ten years, each new system, set up on the very ground of the failure of the last, has claimed, under pains and penalties, a general faith in its absolute and indefinite triumph. The only action of such institutions is in preventing all social reorganization by fixing minds on puerile questions of political forms, and by interdicting speculations and philosophical discussions which would disclose the principles of reorganization. By this action, the character of the disease has been concealed as much as possible, and any gradual and specific cure has been almost impracticable. It is strange that minds should be so self-deceived as to disclaim all speculative prejudices while they propose the most absurd of all political Utopias,—the construction of a system of government which rests upon no true social doctrine. Such an absurdity is referrible to the cloudy prevalence of the metaphysical philosophy, which perverts and confuses men's notions in politics, as it did formerly, during its short triumph, in all other orders of human conceptions.

Fatal to Order.  It is not only as an impediment to progress that the preponderance of material conceptions is to be deplored. It is dangerous to order. When all political evils are imputed to institutions instead of to ideas and social manners, which are now the real seat of the mischief; the remedy is vainly sought in changes, each more serious than the last, in institutions and existing powers. The failure of the last change is forgotten; and hopes are concentrated on the next, showing how ineffectual are the lessons of experience when the results are not elucidated by a rational analysis. Such changes must occur, in our progress to a better state. What it is fair to require in regard to them is that they should be recognized as provisional, and be guided by some philosophical consideration of the social question at large. Another consequence of the prevalent preference of institutions to doctrines is, besides its prematurity, its engendering errors of the most serious kind, and of a permanent character, by including in the domain of temporal government what belongs to the spiritual. For their neglect of this grand distinction, the various governments of Europe have been punished by becoming responsible for all the evils of society, whencesoever they might have arisen. The illusion is yet more injurious to society itself through the disturbances and mortifications which it induces. An illustration of the case is presented by the discussions and attacks which have so often menaced the institution of Property. It is impossible to deny that, when all exaggerations are stripped away, an unquestionable amount of evil remains in connection with property, which ought to be taken in hand, and remedied, as far as our modern social state permits. But it is equally evident that the remedy must arise from opinions, customs, and manners, and that political regulations can have no radical efficacy; for the question refers us to public prepossessions and usages which must habitually direct, for the interest of society, the exercise of property, in whose hands soever it may be lodged. We may see here how futile and how blind, and also how disturbing, is this tendency to refer everything to political institutions, instead of fixing expectation on an intellectual and moral reorganization.

Thus we proceed, securing neither order nor progress, while we consider our sufferings to be of a physical, whereas they are really of a moral nature. Modifications of ancient systems have been tried, and have given no relief; and our ideas of political progress are narrowing down to that of a substitution of persons,—the most disgraceful political degradation of all, because, directed by no plan, it tends to subject society to an interminable series of catastrophes. The material order, which is all that is contemplated, is confided to a power which is regarded as hostile, and perpetually enfeebled by a systematic antagonism. The restricted view of each of the agents of such a mechanism prevents their co-operation, except under the immediate alarm of material anarchy, when they suspend their useless controversies till the storm has blown over, when they go on as before, till some catastrophe ensues, taking everybody by surprise, though any one might have foreseen it. In this discarding of social speculation for the sake of material and immediate considerations, we see a fresh indication that intellectual anarchy is the main cause of our social maladies.

A fourth characteristic of our social condition is a natural consequence and complement of the preceding; the incompetence of the minds which occupy the chief political stations, during such a condition of affairs, and even their antipathy to a true reorganization: so that a final, and not less disastrous illusion of modern society is that the solution of the problem may be looked for from those who can do nothing but hinder it. From what we have already seen, we must be aware that the gradual demolition of all social maxims, and, at the same time, the attenuation of political action, must tend to remove elevated minds and superior understandings from such a career, and to deliver over the political world to the rule of charlatanism and mediocrity. The absence of any distinct and large conception of a social

*Incompetence of political leaders.*

future is favourable to the more vulgar forms of ambition; and presumptuous and enterprising mediocrity has never before had so fortunate a chance. While social principles are not even sought, charlatanism will always attract by the magnificence of its promises; and its transient successes will dazzle society, while in a suffering condition, and deprived of all rational hope. Every impulse of noble ambition must turn the best men away from a field of action where there is no chance of scope and permanence, such as are requisite to the carrying out of generous schemes. It is, as M. Guizot has well said, a social period when *men will feebly, but desire immensely.* It is a state of half-conviction and half-will, resulting from intellectual and moral anarchy, offering many obstacles to the solution of our difficulties. It is important, however, not to exaggerate those obstacles. This very state of half-conviction and half-will tends to facilitate by anticipation the prevalence of a true conception of society which, once produced, will have no active resistance to withstand, because it will repose on serious convictions: and at present, the dispersion of social interests tends to preserve the material order which is an indispensable condition of philosophical growth. It would be a mere satirical exaggeration to describe existing society as preferring political quackery and illusion to that wise settlement which it has not had opportunity to obtain. When the choice is offered, it will be seen whether the attraction of deceptive promises, and the power of former habit, will prevent our age from entering, with ardour and steadiness, upon a better course. There are evident symptoms that the choice will be a wise one, though the circumstances of the time operate to place the direction of the movement in hands which are anything but fittest for the purpose. This inconvenience dates from the beginning of the revolutionary period, and is not a new, but an aggravated evil. For three centuries past, the most eminent minds have been chiefly engaged with science, and have neglected politics; thus differing widely from the wisest men in ancient times, and even in the Middle Ages. The consequence of this is that the most difficult and urgent questions have been committed to the class which is essentially one under two names, – the civilians and the metaphysicians, or, under their common title, the lawyers and men of letters, whose position in regard to statesmanship is naturally a subordinate one. We shall see hereafter that, from its origin to the time of the first French Revolution, the system of metaphysical polity was expressed and directed by the universities on the one hand and the great judiciary corporations on the other : the first constituting a sort of spiritual, and the other the temporal power. This state of things is still traceable in most countries of the continent ; while in France, for above half a century, the arrangement has degenerated into such an abuse that the judges are superseded by the bar, and the doctors (as they used to be called) by mere men of letters ; so that now, any man who can hold a pen may aspire to the spiritual regulation of society, through the press or from the professional chair, unconditionally, and whatever may be his qualifications. When the time comes for the constitution of an organic condition, the reign of sophists and declaimers will have come to an end ; but there will be the impediment to surmount of their having been provisionally in possession of public confidence.

The survey that we have made must convince us only too well of the anarchical state of existing society, under its destitution of guiding and governing ideas, and amidst its conflict of opinions and passions, which there is no power in any of the three schools to cure or moderate. As preliminary considerations, these facts are deeply disheartening ; and we cannot wonder that some generous and able, but ill-prepared minds should have sunk into a kind of philosophical despair about the future of society, which appears to them doomed to fall under a gloomy despotism or into mere anarchy, or to oscillate between the two. I trust that the study we are about to enter upon will give rise to a consoling conviction that the movement of regeneration is going on, though quietly in comparison with the apparent decomposition, and that the most advanced of the human race are at the threshold of a social order worthy of their nature and their needs. I shall conclude this introduction by showing what must necessarily be the intellectual character of the salutary philosophy which is to lead us into this better future:

and its dogmatic exposition will follow in the next chapter.

*Advent of the Positive Philosophy.* The preliminary survey which I have just concluded led us necessarily into the domain of politics. We must now return from this excursion, and take our stand again at the point of view of this whole Work, and contemplate the condition and prospects of society from the ground of positive philosophy. Every other ground has been found untenable. The theological and metaphysical philosophies have failed to secure permanent social welfare, while the positive philosophy has uniformly succeeded, and conspicuously for three centuries past, in reorganizing, to the unanimous satisfaction of the intellectual world, all the anterior orders of human conceptions, which had been till then in the same chaotic state that we now deplore, in regard to social science. Contemporary opinion regarded the state of each of those sciences as hopeless till the positive philosophy brought them out of it. There is no reason why it should fail in the latest application, after having succeeded in all the earlier. Advancing from the less complex categories of ideas to the more complex and final one, and comparing with this experience the picture just given of our present social condition, we cannot but see that the political analysis and the scientific concur in demonstrating that the positive philosophy, carried on to its completion, is the only possible agent in the reorganization of modern society. I wish to establish this principle first, and in this place, apart from all considerations about my way of proving my point; so that, if my attempt should be hereafter condemned, no unfavourable inference may be drawn in regard to a method which alone can save society, and that public reason should have nothing to do but to require from happier successors more effectual endeavours in the same direction. In all cases, and especially in this, the method is of even more importance than the doctrine; and it is for this reason that I think it right, before closing my long introduction, to offer, in a brief form, some last prefatory considerations.

This is not the place in which to enter upon any comparison between the positive political philosophy and the other social theories which have been tried; but, while still deferring the scientific appreciation of the positive method, and before quitting the political ground on which I have, for the occasion, taken my stand, I must point out in a direct and general way, the relation of the positive philosophy to the two great necessities of our age.

The ascendancy of a positive social doctrine is secured by its perfect logical coherence in its entire application—a characteristic property which enables us at once to connect the political with the scientific point of view. The positive polity will embrace at once all the essential aspects of the present state of civilization, and will dissolve the deplorable opposition that now exists between the two orders of social needs, the common satisfaction of which will henceforth depend on the same principle. It will impart a homogeneous and rational character to the desultory politics of our day, and it will by the same act connect this co-ordinated present with the whole past, so as to establish a general harmony in the entire system of social ideas, by exhibiting the fundamental uniformity of the collective life of humanity; for this conception cannot, by its nature, be applied to the actual social state till it has undergone the test of explaining, from the same point of view, the continuous series of the chief former transformations of society. It is important to note this difference between the positive principle and that of the two other schools. The critical school treats all times prior to the revolutionary period with a blind reprobation. The retrograde school equally fails in uniting the present with the past, and uniformly disparages the position of modern society during the last three centuries. It is the exclusive property of the positive principle to recognize the fundamental law of continuous human development, representing the existing evolution as the necessary result of the gradual series of former transformations, by simply extending to social phenomena the spirit which governs the treatment of all other natural phenomena. This coherence and homogeneousness of the positive principle is further shown by its operation in not only comprehending all the various social ideas in one whole, but in connecting the system

*Logical coherence of the doctrine.*

with the whole of natural philosophy, and constituting thus the aggregate of human knowledge as a complete scientific hierarchy. We shall see hereafter how this is accomplished, and I mention it now to show how the positive philosophy, finding thus a general fulcrum in all minds, cannot but spread to a universal extension. In the present chaotic state of our political ideas we can scarcely imagine what must be the irresistible energy of a philosophical movement, in which the entire renovation of social science will be directed by the same spirit which is unanimously recognized as effectual in all other departments of human knowledge. Meantime, it finds some points of contact in the most wilful minds, from whence it may proceed to work a regeneration of views. It speaks to every class of society, and to every political party, the language best adapted to produce conviction, while maintaining the invincible originality of its fundamental character. It alone, embracing in its survey the whole of the social question, can render exact justice to the conflicting schools, by estimating their past and present services. It alone can exhibit to each party its highest destination, prescribing order in the name of progress, and progress in the name of order, so that each, instead of annulling, may strengthen the other. Bringing no stains from the past, this new polity is subject to no imputation of retrograde tyranny, or of revolutionary anarchy. The only charge that can be brought against it is that of novelty; and the answer is furnished by the evident insufficiency of all existing theories, and by the fact that for two centuries past its success has been uniform and complete, wherever it has been applied.

*Its effect on Order.* As to its operation upon Order, it is plain that true science has no other aim than the establishment of intellectual order, which is the basis of every other. Disorder dreads the scientific spirit even more than the theological, and, in the field of politics, minds which rebelled against metaphysical hypotheses and theological fictions submit without difficulty to the discipline of the positive method. We even see that while the mind of our day is accused of tending towards absolute scepticism, it eagerly welcomes the least appearance of positive demonstration, however premature and imperfect. The eagerness would be fully as great if the idea were once formed that social science might also be conducted by the positive spirit. The conception of invariable natural laws, the foundation of every idea of order, in all departments, would have the same philosophical efficacy here as elsewhere, as soon as it was sufficiently generalized to be applied to social phenomena, thenceforth referred, like all other phenomena, to such laws. It is only by the positive polity that the revolutionary spirit can be restrained, because by it alone can the influence of the critical doctrine be justly estimated and circumscribed. No longer roused to resistance, as by the retrograde school, and seeing its work done better than by itself, it will merge in a doctrine which leaves it nothing to do or to desire. Under the rule of the positive spirit, again, all the difficult and delicate questions which now keep up a perpetual irritation in the bosom of society, and which can never be settled while mere political solutions are proposed, will be scientifically estimated, to the great furtherance of social peace. By admitting at once that the institutions of modern societies must necessarily be merely provisional, the positive spirit will abate unreasonable expectations from them, and concentrate effort upon a fundamental renovation of social ideas, and consequently of public morals. Instead of indifference being caused by this carrying forward of political aims, there will be a new source of interest in so modifying modern institutions as to make them contributory to the inevitable intellectual and moral evolution. At the same time, it will be teaching society that, in the present state of their ideas, no political change can be of supreme importance, while the perturbation attending change is supremely mischievous, in the way both of immediate hindrance and of diverting attention from the true need and procedure. And again, order will profit by the recognition of the relative spirit of the positive philosophy, which discredits the absolute spirit of the theological and metaphysical schools. It cannot but dissipate the illusion by which those schools are for ever striving to set up, in all stages of civilization, their respective types of immutable government; as when, for instance, they propose to civilize Tahiti by a wholesale importation of Protestantism and a Parliamentary system. Again, the positive spirit tends to consolidate order, by the rational development of a wise resignation to incurable political evils. Negative as is the character of this virtue, it affords an aid under the pains of the human lot which cannot be dispensed with, and which has no place under the metaphysical polity, which regards political action as indefinite. Religious, and especially Christian resignation is, in plain truth, only a prudent temporizing, which enjoins the endurance of present suffering in view of an ultimate ineffable felicity. A true resignation,—that is, a permanent disposition to endure, steadily, and without hope of compensation, all inevitable evils, can proceed only from a deep sense of the connection of all kinds of natural phenomena with invariable laws. If there are (as I doubt not there are) political evils which, like some personal sufferings, cannot be remedied by science, science at least proves to us that they are incurable, so as to calm our restlessness under pain by the conviction that it is by natural laws that they are rendered insurmountable. Human nature suffers in its relations with the astronomical world, and the physical, chemical, and biological, as well as the political. How is it that we turbulently resist in the last case, while, in the others, we are calm and resigned, under pain as signal, and as repugnant to our nature? Surely it is because the positive philosophy has as yet developed our sense of the natural laws only in regard to the simpler phenomena; and when the same sense shall have been awakened with regard to the more complex phenomena of social life, it will fortify us with a similar resignation, general or special, provisional or indefinite, in the case of political suffering. An habitual conviction of this kind cannot but conduce to public tranquillity, by obviating vain efforts for redress, while it equally excludes the apathy which belongs to the passive character of religious resignation, by requiring submission to nothing but necessity, and encouraging the noblest exercises of human activity, wherever the analysis of the occasion opens any prospect whatever of genuine remedy. Finally, the positive philosophy befriends public order by bringing back men's understandings to a normal state through the influence of its method alone, before it has had time to establish any social theory. It dissipates disorder at once by imposing a series of indisputable scientific conditions on the study of political questions. By including social science in the scientific hierarchy, the positive spirit admits to success in this study only well-prepared and disciplined minds, so trained in the preceding departments of knowledge as to be fit for the complex problems of the last. The long and difficult preliminary elaboration must disgust and deter vulgar and ill-prepared minds, and subdue the most rebellious. This consideration, if there were no other, would prove the eminently organic tendency of the new political philosophy.

I have dwelt on this influence of the Positive philosophy, in favour of Order, because it is that which is, as yet, least recognized, while the retrograde and stationary schools continue to found their claims upon that very point. *Its effect on Progress.* There is less mistake about its favourable influence on Progress. In all its applications, the positive spirit is directly progressive; its express office being to increase our knowledge, and perfect the connection of its parts. Even the illustrations of progressions are, at the present day, derived from the positive sciences. Whatever rational idea of social progress (that is, of continuous development, with a steady tendency towards a determinate end,) anywhere exists, should, as we shall hereafter see, be attributed to the unperceived influence of the positive philosophy, in disengaging this great notion from its present vague and fluctuating state by clearly assigning the aim and the general course of progress. Though Christianity certainly bore a part in originating the sentiment of social progress by proclaiming the superiority of the new law to the old, it is evident that the theological polity, proceeding upon an immutable type, which was realized only in the past, must have become radically incompatible with ideas of continuous progression, and manifests, on the contrary, a thoroughly retrograde character. The metaphysical polity, in its dogmatic aspect, has the same incompatibility, though the feeble connection of its doctrines renders it more accessible to the spirit of our time. Indeed, it was only after the decline of that school had begun, that ideas of progress took any general possession of the public mind. Thus the progressive, as well as the organic instinct, is to be developed by the positive philosophy alone.

The only idea of progress which is really proper to the revolutionary philosophy, is that of the continuous extension of liberty; that is, in positive terms, the gradual expansion of human powers. Now, even in the restricted and negative sense in which this is true,—that of the perpetual diminution of obstacles,—the positive philosophy is incontestably superior: for true liberty is nothing else than a rational submission to the preponderance of the laws of nature, in release from all arbitrary personal dictation. Decisions of sovereign assemblies have been called laws by the metaphysical polity, and have been fictitiously regarded as a manifestation of popular will. But no such homage paid to constitutional entities can disguise the arbitrary tendency which marks all the philosophies but the positive. The arbitrary can never be excluded while political phenomena are referred to Will, divine or human, instead of being connected with invariable natural laws; and liberty will remain illusory and precarious, notwithstanding all constitutional artifices, and whatever be the will to which we pay our daily obedience. By substituting the empire of genuine convictions for that of arbitrary will, the positive philosophy will put an end to the absolute liberty of the revolutionary school,—the license of running from one extravagance to another,—and, by establishing social principles, will meet the need at once of order and of progress. The special office of the revolutionary philosophy, that of extinguishing all but the historical existence of the ancient political system, is virtually committed to the positive principle; and, in fact, the power exercised by the critical doctrine in this direction has been owing to its serving the purpose of a provisional organ to the positive philosophy. In other sciences, the critical action, however energetic, is only a collateral consequence of its organic development; and the organic development which is fatal to the old theological system, involves in the same condemnation the metaphysical spirit, which is even the less logical of the two. The most serious difficulty of contemporary politics is the condition of the lower classes; and in this case, the positive philosophy affords practical amelioration most favourable to progress. The revolutionary polity opened only an insurrectionary issue to this difficulty, and merely shifted without solving the question. The question is not settled by opening a way to popular ambition, the gratification of which must be confined to a few, (probably deserters from their class,) and can do nothing to soothe the murmurs of the multitude. The general lot is even aggravated by the excitement of unreasonable hopes, and by the elevation of a few by the chances of the political game. As it is the inevitable lot of the majority of men to live on the more or less precarious fruits of daily labour, the great social problem is to ameliorate the condition of this majority, without destroying its classification, and disturbing the general economy: and this is the function of the positive polity, regarded as regulating the final classification of modern society. We shall have occasion to see hereafter that the mental reorganization, by habitually interposing a common moral authority between the working classes and the leaders of society, will offer the only regular basis of a pacific and equitable reconciliation of their chief conflicts, nearly abandoned in the present day to the savage discipline of a purely material antagonism.

In this brief sketch of the prominent characteristics of the positive polity, we have seen that, notwithstanding its severe estimate of the different existing parties, it commands access to the spirit of each by proving itself adapted to fulfil the aims which each has pursued too exclusively. It can also turn to the profit of its gradual ascendancy all the important incidents of existing society which it could not intercept. Whether in its hour of exultation, the one school manifests its insufficiency; or whether, in the despair of failure, the other shows a disposition to welcome new means of political action; or whether, again, a kind of universal torpor exhibits in its nakedness the aggregate of social needs, the new philosophy can always lay hold of a certain general issue to introduce, by a daily application, its fundamental instruction. In doing this however, we must, it seems to me, lay aside all hope of a real conversion of the retrograde school. Setting aside some happy individual anomalies, such as always exist, and may become more frequent, it remains indisputable that there is such an antipathy, in regard to social questions, between the theological and the positive philosophies, that the one can never estimate the other, and must disappear before it, without being able to undergo any radical modification of its present form. It is, in fact, not Order that the ancient *régime* aims at, but only its own preconception of a unique order, connected with its habits of mind and special interests, outside of which everything appears disorderly, and therefore indifferent. In the midst of its pretended devotion to general order, the retrograde school has often betrayed its tendency to care for the means more than the end. It is through the stationary school, whose love of order is at least more impartial, if not more disinterested, that the positive polity must obtain the access which it could not hope for from the retrograde school. The metaphysical fictions of the parliamentary or constitutional philosophy may have diverted the mind of the stationary school from the true issue; but they have not attained such an ascendancy among the nations of the European continent as to render them deaf to the rational voice of the new philosophy, when it appeals to a school so openly disposed as is the stationary party to establish permanent order, on whatever principles, in modern society. Some useful action may therefore be hoped for through this medium.—Nevertheless, I avow that it is on the revolutionary school alone that, in my opinion, we can expect that the positive polity can exercise a predominant influence, because this school is the only one that is always open to new action on behalf of progress. All its indispensable provisional doctrines will be absorbed by the new philosophy, while all its anarchical tendencies will be extinguished. There will be more explosions of revolutionary doctrine, as long as there are any remains of the retrograde system; for the natural course of events does not wait for our slow philosophical preparation. Whether in virtue of our intellectual condition, or of faults committed by existing governments, such outbreaks will occur; and perhaps they may be necessary to the uprooting of all hope of reconstructing social order on the old basis; but the positive philosophy will have foreseen such conflicts, and will take no part in them, further than to make use of the instruction that they afford. It will not interfere with the last operations of the revolutionary preponderance;—knowing that they are the last. Nor will it paralyse so important a general disposition as that which constitutes the critical spirit, properly so called. By subordinating it for ever to the organic spirit, it will open to it broad political aims; it will afford it employment in destroying all metaphysical and theological interference, using for this end the satirical faculties which produced nothing in the last century, but which may be of a secondary value in influencing the development of the political character that will be finally assigned to each school. On the whole, we may hope that the positive philosophy will find grounds of support among the most advanced sections of the revolutionary school; and, whatever may be the hopes of that school from different political parties, it will be unable to dispense with the scientific superiority of the positive doctrine, which is the certain cause and guarantee of its gradual ascendancy.

It might have been hoped that the renovation we are anticipating would have been largely aided by the scientific class of society, as that which must be most familiar with positive science. But it is not so. At present, the anarchical tendencies of that class appear to be as strong as any. The indifference of scientific men to the most interesting and most urgent of all classes of problems may be partly accounted for by their deep intellectual disgust at the irrational character of the social doctrines of their day; but there are other reasons, even less honourable than this. They are themselves defective in scientific discipline. They abhor generalities, and have a systematic predilection for specialities. Under the idea of an organization of labour, they restrict their several pursuits within the narrowest bounds, without providing for the investigation of general relations; and thus, science becomes a pastime, grounded

*Anarchical tendencies of the scientific class.*

on no adequate preparation. It is not wonderful then that they have no interest in the entire generality which is the indispensable attribute of any philosophy that aspires to the moral government of mankind. Daily experience shows that, when learned bodies are brought into junction, for any political purpose, with sensible men who know nothing of science, but are accustomed to general views, the superiority rests with the latter, even in regard to matters which particularly concern the scientific class. As long as this is the case, the scientific class decrees its own political subordination. Their social sentiment is on a par with their ideas; and their egotism is aggravated by their devotion to specialities, when it ought to be subdued by a mastery of positive science; and would be so, if they could admit its general ideas. This is no fault of individuals among them. It is imputable to the defective scientific education of our time; and all that men of science are censurable for is their dogmatic denial of the need of a better. We must, however, abandon all hope of their co-operation in extending the positive method to the study of social phenomena. If we may anticipate anything in that direction, it must be from a rising generation for whom a more adequate training must be provided, and who will be led by a really scientific education beyond the special and isolated studies to which they now conceive themselves to be destined, and which constitute at present their only idea of scientific pursuit.

Conclusion. I have now presented a view of the chief points of support which the present state of the social world affords to the renovating influence of the new political philosophy. This introduction may appear long; but it will abridge my future labour by furnishing my readers with a kind of rational programme of the conditions of the subject. Yet more, it indicates clearly what is apt to escape the notice of minds habituated to the superficial and irrational treatment of social questions,— the complete political efficacy of the positive philosophy. The high practical utility of the theory I am about to offer cannot be questioned by the haughtiest politician when it has once been demonstrated that the deepest want of modern society is, in its nature, eminently theoretical, and that, consequently, an intellectual, and then a moral reorganization must precede and direct the political.—This mutual relation being established, with a care proportionate to its importance, we must now return,—not again to quit it,—to the strictly scientific point of view of this work, and pursue the study of the phenomena of social physics in a disposition of mind as purely speculative as that in which we surveyed the other fundamental sciences, with no other intellectual ambition than to discover the natural laws of a final order of phenomena, remarkable in the extreme, and never before examined in this way.

Before proceeding, however, to this direct examination, I propose to consider, briefly, the principal philosophical attempts to constitute social science; as a general estimate of this kind will tend to illustrate the nature and spirit of this last great department of positive philosophy.

# CHAPTER II.

### PRINCIPAL PHILOSOPHICAL ATTEMPTS TO CONSTITUTE A SOCIAL SYSTEM.

*History of Social Science.* WE have seen that the complex and special nature of social phenomena is the chief reason why the study has remained imperfect to the last; it being impossible to analyse them till the simpler departments of science were understood, and till the great discovery of cerebral physiology had opened a rational access to their examination. To this main consideration we must now add another, which explains more specially why it has never till now been possible to establish social science on a positive basis. This consideration is, that we have not till now been in possession of a range of facts wide enough to disclose the natural laws of social phenomena.

The first rise of speculative doctrine has always, in all sciences, taken place from the theological method, as I have shown. In the case of the anterior sciences, this did not preclude the formation of a positive theory, when once there had been a sufficient perpetuity of phenomena. The materials were ready before there were observers qualified to make a scientific use of them. But, even if observers had been ready, the phenomena of social life were not ample and various enough in early days to admit of their philosophical analysis. Many and profound modifications of the primitive civilization were necessary to afford a sufficient basis for experiment. We shall see hereafter how indispensable was the operation of the theological philosophy in directing the earliest progress of the human mind and of society. Our present business is to notice the obstacles which it presented to the formation of a true social science. It was not, in fact, till modern political revolutions, and especially the French, had proved the insufficiency of the old political system for the social needs of the age that the great idea of Progress could acquire sufficient firmness, distinctness and generality, to serve a scientific purpose. The direction of the social movement was not determined; and social speculation was embarrassed by fanciful notions of oscillating or circular movements, such as even now cause hesitation in able but ill-prepared minds as to the real nature of human progression. Till it is known in what this progression consists, the fact itself may be disputed; since, from such a point of view, humanity may appear to be doomed to an arbitrary succession of identical phases, without ever experiencing a new transformation, gradually directed towards an end determined by the whole constitution of human nature.

Thus all idea of social progress was interdicted to the philosophers of antiquity, for want of materials of political observation. The most eminent and sagacious of them were subject to the common tendency to suppose the contemporary state of things inferior to that of former times. This supposition was the more natural and legitimate because the philosophical works which contained this view coincided, as to date, with the decline of the Greek and Roman *régime*. This decline, which, in relation to the whole of human history, was in fact progress, could not appear so to the ancients, who did not anticipate what was to come. I have before intimated that the first dawning sense of human progression was inspired by Christianity, which, by proclaiming the superiority of the law of Jesus to that of Moses, gave form to the idea of a more perfect state replacing a less perfect, which had been necessary as a preparation. Though Catholicism[1] was, in this, simply the organ of expression of human reason, the service it thus rendered entitles it not the less, as all true philosophers will agree, to our eternal gratitude. But, apart from the

---

[1] This great idea belongs essentially to Catholicism, from which Protestantism derived it in an imperfect and corrupt manner,—not only by recurring irrationally to the period of the primitive Church, but also by offering for popular guidance the most barbarous and dangerous part of the Scriptures—that which relates to Hebrew antiquity. Mohammedanism pursued the same practice, and thus instituted a mere imitation of Judaic barbarism, without introducing any real amelioration.

mischief of the mysticism and vague obscurity which belong to all applications of the theological method, such a beginning could not possibly suggest any scientific view of social progression: for any such progression was barred at once by the claim of Christianity to be the ultimate stage at which the human mind must stop. The social efficacy of the theological philosophy is now exhausted, and it has become therefore retrograde, as we have seen; but the condition of continuity is an indispensable element in the conception of progress; an idea which would have no power to guide social speculation if it represented progress as limited by its nature to a determinate condition, attained long ago.

It is thus evident that the conception of progress belongs exclusively to the positive philosophy. This philosophy alone can indicate the final term which human nature will be for ever approaching and never attaining; and it alone can prescribe the general course of this gradual development. Accordingly, the only rational ideas of continuous advance are of modern origin, and relate especially to the expansion of the positive sciences which gave birth to them. It may even be worth observing that the first satisfactory view of general progression was proposed by a philosopher whose genius was essentially mathematical; and therefore conversant with the simplest form of the scientific spirit. Whatever may be the value of this observation, it is certain that Pascal was animated by a sense of the progress of the sciences when he uttered the immortal aphorism: "the entire succession of men, through the whole course of ages, must be regarded as one man, always living and incessantly learning." Whatever may have been the actual effect of this first ray of light, it must be admitted that the idea of continuous progress had no scientific consistency, or public regard, till after the memorable controversy, at the beginning of the last century, about a general comparison of the ancients and moderns. In my view, that solemn discussion constitutes a ripe event in the history of the human mind, which thus, for the first time, declared that it had made an irreversible advance. It is needless to point out that the leaders of this great philosophical movement derived all the force of their arguments from the scientific spirit: but it is remarkable that their most illustrious adversaries committed the inconsistency of declaring that they preferred the philosophy of Descartes to that which preceded it.—From this scientific origin the conception spread more and more in a political direction, till, at length, the French revolution manifested the tendency of humanity toward a political system, indeterminate enough, but radically different from the whole system. This was the negative view of social progress; ineffectual in itself, but necessary as a preparation for the advent of the positive philosophy, when it should have made its induction from social phenomena, and ascertained their laws.

Having thus seen how impossible was the formation of social science in ancient times, we are in a condition to appreciate the attempts which were here and there prematurely made. The foregoing analysis shows that the political conditions of the subject are, generally, precisely coincident with the scientific, so as to retard by their competition the possibility of establishing social science on a positive basis. This obstacle has existed even up to our own generation, who can only make a mere beginning in seeking in the past a basis for social science, in virtue of their experience of a revolutionary period, and of their opening perception of the positive principle, as they see it established in the other departments of human knowledge, including that of intellectual and moral phenomena. It would be waste of time, and a departure from my object, to analyse fully the attempts of ancient philosophers to form a political science which was thus clearly impracticable in their day; and I shall therefore merely point out the essential vice of each speculation, thereby justifying the judgment that we have just passed by anticipation, and disclosing the true nature of an enterprise which remains to be begun.

The name of Aristotle first presents itself, his memorable "Politics" being one of the finest productions of antiquity, and furnishing the general type of most of the works on that subject that have followed. This treatise could not possibly disclose any sense of the progressive tendencies of humanity, *Aristotle's "Politics."*

nor the slightest glimpse of the natural laws of civilization; and it was necessarily occupied by metaphysical discussions of the principle and form of government: but it is truly marvellous that any mind should have produced a work so advanced, and even nearer to a positive view than his other works, at a time when political observation was restricted to a uniform and preliminary social state, and when the nascent positive spirit lived feebly in geometry alone. The analysis by which he refuted the dangerous fancies of Plato and his imitators about community of property evidences a rectitude, a sagacity, and a strength which, in their application to such subjects, have been rarely equalled, and never surpassed. Thus much I have said, in the way of homage to the first manifestation of human genius on the great subject of government, notwithstanding the evident influence that it has exercised upon philosophical meditation, from its own day to this.

The works which succeeded need not detain us. They were merely an accumulation of fresh materials, classified by the type that Aristotle had furnished. The next period worth notice is that in which the preponderance of the positive spirit in the study of phenomena caused the first clear comprehension of the meaning of general laws, and in which the idea of human progress began to assume some consistency; and, to find these two conditions in concurrence, we can hardly go further back than the middle of the last century. The first and most important series of works which then presents itself is that of Montesquieu, first, in his treatise on the "Greatness and Decline of the Romans," and afterwards in his "Spirit of Laws." The great strength of this memorable work appears to me to lie in its tendency to regard political phenomena as subject to invariable laws, like all other phenomena. This is manifested at the very outset, in the preliminary chapter, in which, for the first time in the history of the human mind, the general idea of *law* is directly defined, in relation to all, even to political subjects, in the same sense in which it is applied in the simplest positive investigations. The progress of science which had been effected by the labours of Descartes, Galileo and Kepler, a century before, had rendered the

*Montesquieu.*

most advanced minds familiar with an incomplete notion of progress. Montesquieu's conception was a generalization of this incomplete notion: and, instead of denying originality to so eminent a service, we may well be amazed that such a conception should be offered, before the positive method had extended beyond the simplest natural phenomena,—being scarcely admitted into the department of chemistry, and not yet heard of in the study of living bodies. And, in the other view, a man must have been in advance of his time, who could conceive of natural laws as the basis of social speculation and action, while all other able men were talking about the absolute and indefinite power of legislators, when armed with due authority, to modify at will the social state. The very qualities, however, which give its pre-eminence to Montesquieu's work prove to us the impossibility of success in an enterprise so premature in regard to its proposed object, the very conditions of which were still impracticable. The project of the work is not fulfilled in its course; and, admirable as are some of its details, its falls back, like all others, upon the primitive type offered by Aristotle's treatise. We find no reference of social phenomena to the laws whose existence was announced at the outset; nor any scientific selection and connection of facts. The general nature of his practical conclusions seems to show how far the execution of his work was from corresponding with his original intention; for his desultory review of the whole mass of social subjects ends in his setting up, as a universal political type, the English parliamentary system, the insufficiency of which, for the satisfaction of modern social requirements, was not, it is true, so conspicuous in his day as it is now, but still discernible enough, as we shall have occasion to see. It was honourable to Montesquieu's philosophical character, that he steered wide of the metaphysical Utopias which lay in his way, and resorted rather to the narrow anchorage at which he rested; but such a resort, so narrow and so barren, proves that he had wandered away from the course announced by himself. The only part of the book which bears any true marks of sustained positivity is that in which the social influence of permanent local causes,— of that which in political language we may call climate,—

is considered. This view, evidently derived from Hippocrates, manifests a tendency to attach observed phenomena to forces able to produce them, as in natural philosophy; but the aim has failed. The true political influence of climate is misconceived, and usually much exaggerated, through the common error of analysing a mere modification before the main action is fully understood; which is much like trying to determine planetary perturbations before ascertaining the chief gravitations. This error was inevitable under Montesquieu's necessary ignorance of the great social laws, while he was bent upon introducing the positive spirit into the domain of politics. He naturally betook himself to the only class of social speculations which seemed fit for his purpose. Pardonable or unavoidable as was his failure, it is a new evidence of the vast gap which lies open at the outset of the science. Montesquieu did not even perceive, any more than others, the fact which should regulate the whole political theory of climate;—that local physical causes, very powerful in the early days of civilization, lose their force in proportion as human development admits of their being neutralized: —a view which would certainly have occurred to Montesquieu if he had possessed himself of the fundamental notion of human progression before he treated of the political theory of climate. Thus, this great philosopher proposed a grand enterprise which was premature in two senses, and in which he could not but fail,—first, by bringing social phenomena under the operation of the positive spirit before it had been introduced into the system of biological science; and again, in proposing social reorganization during a period marked out for revolutionary action. This explains why a mind so eminent should have exercised, through its very advancement, an immediate influence very inferior to that of a mere sophist, like Rousseau, whose intellectual state, much better adapted to the disposition of his contemporaries, allowed him to constitute himself, with so remarkable a success, the natural organ of the revolutionary movement of the time. It is by our posterity that Montesquieu will be duly estimated, when the extension of the positive philosophy to social speculations will disclose the high value of the precocious attempts which, though doomed to failure, yield the light by which the general question must be laid down.

After Montesquieu, the next great addition to Sociology (which is the term I may be allowed to invent to designate Social Physics) was made by Condorcet, proceeding on the views suggested by his illustrious friend Turgot. Turgot's suggestions with regard to the theory of the perfectibility of human nature were doubtless the basis of Condorcet's speculation exhibited in his "Historical Sketch of the Progress of the Human Mind," in which the scientific conception of the social progression of the race was, for the first time, clearly and directly proposed, with a distinct assertion of its primary importance. The strength of the work lies in its introduction, in which Condorcet exhibits his general idea, and proposes his philosophical project of studying the radical connection of the various social states of mankind. These few immortal pages leave really nothing to be desired in regard to the position of the sociological question at large, which will, in my opinion, rest, through all future time, on this admirable statement. The execution is far from corresponding with the greatness of the project; but no failure in the carrying out can impair the value of the design. The success and the failure may both be easily accounted for by a consideration of the scientific and political knowledge of the time. The expansion of the natural sciences, and especially of chemistry, during the second half of the last century, had thoroughly established in the best minds of the period the idea of positive laws; and the study of living bodies, in the departments of anatomy and taxonomy, if not of physiology, began to assume a truly scientific character. Condorcet's mind was rationally prepared by mathematical study, under the direction of D'Alembert: by his philosophical position in society, he had all the advantage of the expansion of physico-chemical science then taking place; and of the labours of Haller, Jussieu, Linnæus, Buffon and Vicq-d'Azir in the principal departments of biological knowledge; and it was natural that he should conceive the enterprise of carrying into the speculative study of social phenomena the same positive method which, from the time of Descartes, had been regenerating

*Condorcet.*

the entire system of human knowledge. With equal advantages, and his higher order of genius, Montesquieu would, no doubt, have achieved higher results than he has left us. Still, even Condorcet's project was premature, though less so than that of Montesquieu; for a great deficiency remained in the imperfect state of biological knowledge, and especially in the exclusion of intellectual and moral phenomena from treatment by the positive method: and the unfortunate Condorcet did not live to see them assume their proper place. In their absence, he lost himself in wanderings after an indefinite perfectibility, and chimerical and absurd anticipations. Such aberrations, affecting such men, are a lesson to us as to the impossibility of unaided reason overleaping the intervals which have not been steadily explored in the gradual advance of the human mind. As to the political circumstances of the time,—the idea of social progression was certainly more distinct and more firm in Condorcet's than in Montesquieu's time: for the tendency of society to relinquish the ancient social system was becoming evident, though the new system which was to succeed it was but vaguely suspected, even where it was not wholly misconceived. The evil influence of the revolutionary doctrine is singularly exhibited in Condorcet's work, in the form of an inconsistency which must strike every reader. The human race is there represented as having attained a vast degree of perfection at the close of the eighteenth century, while the author attributes an entirely retrogressive influence to almost every doctrine, institution and preponderant power throughout the whole past. Whereas, the total progress accomplished can be nothing else than the result of the various kinds of partial progress realized since the beginning of civilization, in virtue of the gradual onward course of human nature. Such a state of things as Condorcet describes would be nothing else than a perpetual miracle; and it is not to him, therefore, that we can look for any disclosure of the laws of human development, any appreciation of the transitory nature of the revolutionary philosophy, or any general conception of the future of society. Here again we recognize the philosophical superiority of Montesquieu, who, not having

Condorcet's opportunities of estimating the revolutionary spirit, had been able to free his mind from those critical prejudices in regard to the past which formed the views of all around him, and had injured his own earlier speculations. This brief survey of the labours of these great men shows us that the basis of true social science can be fixed only after the revolutionary spirit has begun to decline; and thus the political, as well as the scientific indications of the subject point to our own time as that in which such a science is to be founded. Condorcet gave us a clear exposition of the nature of the enterprise; but the whole accomplishment yet remains to be achieved.

These two attempts are really all that have been made in the right road to social science; for they are the only speculations which have been based on the aggregate of historical facts. I shall have occasion, further on, to notice some attempts which are not worthy to rank with these, and which merely testify to the existing need of social science by showing how various are the directions in which it is sought. On one subject, however, I shall here make a few observations, in order to illustrate further the aim and spirit of my own efforts to constitute a basis for social science. That subject is the nature and object of what is called Political Economy.

We cannot impute to political economists any design to establish social science; for it is the express assertion of the most classical *Political economy.* among them that their subject is wholly distinct from, and independent of general political science. Yet, sincere as they doubtless are in their dogma of isolation, they are no less sincerely persuaded that they have applied the positive spirit to economical science; and they perpetually set forth their method as the type by which all social theories will be finally regenerated. As this pretension has obtained credit enough to procure the establishment of several professorships for this species of instruction, I find myself obliged to explain why it is that I cannot, as would be very desirable, propose to carry on my enterprise from the point reached by these philosophers, but must begin from the beginning. My criticism on political economy in this place is merely for the purpose of showing that it is not the philosophical creation that we want; and I must refer to my exposition as a whole any objectors to my summary estimate of political economy.

It is unfavourable to the philosophical pretensions of the economists that, being almost invariably lawyers or literary men, they have had no opportunity of discipline in that spirit of positive rationality which they suppose they have introduced into their researches. Precluded by their education from any idea of scientific observation of even the smallest phenomena, from any notion of natural laws, from all perception of what demonstration is, they must obviously be incapable of applying, impromptu, a method in which they have had no practice to the most difficult of all analyses. The only philosophical preparation that they can show is a set of vague precepts of general logic, susceptible of no real use; and thus, their conceptions present a purely metaphysical character. There is one great exceptional case which I must at once exempt from this criticism,—that of the illustrious philosopher, Adam Smith, who made no pretension to found a new special science; but merely proposed, (what he admirably achieved) to illustrate some leading points of social philosophy by luminous analyses relating to the division of employments, the function of money, the general action of banks, etc., and other chief portions of the industrial developments of the human race. Though involved, like all his contemporaries, in the metaphysical philosophy, a mind of such quality as his could not, however distinguished in the metaphysical school, be blinded by its illusions, because his preparatory studies had impressed him with a sense of what constitutes a true scientific method, as is clearly proved by the valuable sketches of the philosophical history of the sciences, and of astronomy in particular, which are published among his posthumous works. The economists have no right to claim Adam Smith as their authority while the whole dogmatic part of their science presents a merely metaphysical character, dressed up with special forms and a list of scientific terms, taken bodily from former philosophical expositions,—as, for instance, from the theologico-metaphysical writings of Spinoza. The contemporary history of this so-called science confirms this judgment of its nature. The most certain signs of conceptions being scientific are continuousness and fertility: and when existing works, instead of being the result and development of those that have gone before, have a character as personal as that of their authors, and bring the most fundamental ideas into question; and when, again, the dogmatic constitution provides for no real and sustained progress, but only for a barren reproduction of old controversies, it is clear that we are dealing with no positive doctrine whatever, but merely with theological or metaphysical dissertations. And this is the spectacle which political economy has presented for half a century past. If our economists were really the scientific successors of Adam Smith, they would show us where they had carried on and completed their master's doctrine, and what new discoveries they had added to his primitive surveys; but looking with an impartial eye upon their disputes on the most elementary ideas of value, utility, production, etc., we might imagine ourselves present at the strangest conferences of the scholists of the Middle Ages about the attributes of their metaphysical entities; which indeed economical conceptions resemble more and more, in proportion as they are dogmatized and refined upon. The result is both cases is, but too often, the perversion of the valuable indication of popular good sense, which become confused, inapplicable, and productive only of idle disputes about words. All intelligent men, for instance, understand what is meant by the terms *product* and *producer*; but, from the time that economical metaphysics undertook to define them, the idea of production has become, through vicious generalizations, so indeterminate, that conscientious and clear writers are obliged to use circuitous explanations to avoid the use of terms which have become obscure and equivocal. Such abuse is analogous to that which metaphysics has introduced into the study of the human understanding, with regard, for instance, to the general ideas of analysis and synthesis and the like. The avowal of the economists that their science is isolated from that of social philosophy in general, is itself a sufficient confirmation of my judgment; for it is a universal fact in social, as in biological science, that all the various general aspects of the subject are scientifically one, and rationally inseparable, so that they cannot be illustrated but by each other. Thus, the economical or industrial analysis of society cannot be effected in the positive method, apart from its intellectual, moral, and political analysis, past and present. And thus does the boasted isolation of political economy testify to its being grounded on a metaphysical basis.

This is the dogmatic aspect of the science. But it would be unjust to forget that, looking at this doctrine historically, and more with a political than a scientific view, it constitutes a final essential part of the system of critical philosophy, which has exercised an indispensable, though transitory influence during the revolutionary period. Political Economy has borne an honourable share in this vast intellectual conflict, by thoroughly discrediting the industrial polity of the Middle Ages, which became more and more injurious, in its descent to our time, to the industry which it had once protected. Such is the credit due to Political Economy. Its worst practical fault is that, like the other portions of the metaphysical philosophy, it systematizes anarchy; and the danger is only aggravated by its use of modern scientific forms. It has not been satisfied with criticising, in much too absolute a way, the industrial polity of the old European sovereignties, without which the industrial development of modern times could never have taken place: it goes far beyond this; it sets up as a universal dogma the absence of all regulating intervention whatever as the best means of promoting the spontaneous rise of society; so that, on every serious occasion, this doctrine can respond to urgent practical needs only by the uniform reproduction of this systematic negation. Because it perceives a natural tendency in society to arrange itself in a certain order, not seeing in this a suggestion of an order to be promoted by social arrangements, it preaches an absence of regulation which, if carried out to the limit of the principle, would lead to the methodical abolition of all government. But here we meet the compensating virtue that political economy insists on all human interests being bound up together, and therefore susceptible of a permanent reconciliation. Though this may be simply the expression of the convictions of popular good sense, philosophy owes a tribute of eternal gratitude to the economists for their excellent service in extinguishing the disastrous and immoral prejudice which concluded the amelioration of the condition of some to be obtained by the deterioration of the condition of somebody else; and that the total amount of wealth was always the same; which is as much as denying industrial development altogether. Notwithstanding this great service, political economy has dangerous tendencies through its opposition to the institution of all industrial discipline. As each serious difficulty arises in the course of industrial development, political economy ignores it. In the great question of Machinery this is remarkably illustrated. This is one of the cases of inconvenience inherent in every industrial improvement, from its tendency to disturb, more or less, and for a longer or shorter time, the mode of life of the labouring classes. Instead of recognizing in the urgent remonstrances called forth by this chasm in our social order one of the most eminent and pressing occasions for the application of social science, our economists can do nothing better than repeat, with pitiless pedantry, their barren aphorism of absolute industrial liberty. Without considering that all human questions, practically regarded, are reducible to mere questions of time, they venture to reply to all complaints that, in the long run, all classes, and especially the one most injured on the existing occasion, will enjoy a real and permanent amelioration; a reply which will be regarded as derisive, as long as man's life is incapable of being indefinitely lengthened. Such a doctrine publishes its own weakness by showing its want of relation to the aggregate of our practical needs. Would the copyists who were thrown out of employment by the invention of printing have been completely consoled by being convinced that, in the next generation, there would be an equal number of persons living by printing, and many more in succeeding centuries? Yet such is the consolation habitually offered by political economy; and if there were no other evidence, this inefficiency would prove its unfitness to direct, as it proposes to do, the industrial expansion of modern society. And thus it stands condemned, as to its scientific pretensions, and in spite of some important services, from the political as much as from the scientific point of view.

The temporary predilection of men's minds for political economy is, in truth, a new and strong illustration of the instinctive need which prevails to subject social researches to positive methods; and if that were once done, the interest in political economy would disappear. Various other signs of the times testify to the same disposition, which indeed pervades the whole action of our intelligences. I will refer to only one among the multitude of those signs; but it is one which aids in bringing about the satisfaction of the need. I mean the growing inclination for historical study, and the great improvement in that kind of research within two centuries.

*Growth of historical study.* Bossuet was, unquestionably, the first who proposed to survey, from a lofty point of view, the whole of the past of society. We cannot adopt his explanations, easily derived from theological resources; but the spirit of universality, so thoroughly appreciated, and, under the circumstances, so wonderfully sustained, will always preserve this admirable composition[1] as a model, suggesting the true result of historical analysis;— the rational co-ordination of the great series of human events, according to a single design; which must however be more genuine and complete than that of Bossuet. There is no doubt that this fine piece of instruction has contributed, during both the past and the present century, to the improvement in the character of the chief historical compositions, especially in France and England, and afterwards in Germany. Still, history has more of a literary and descriptive than of a scientific character. It does not yet establish a rational filiation in the series of social events, so as to admit (as in other sciences, and allowing for its greater complexity) of any degree of systematic prevision of their future succession. Perhaps the imputation of rashness cast upon the mere proposal of such a treatment of history is the strongest confirmation we could have of its present unscientific character: for such prevision is everywhere else admitted to be the ultimate scientific test. Another evidence exists in the easy credit daily obtained by misty historical theories which explain nothing, and

---

[1] "Discourse on Universal History."

which testify to the literary and metaphysical bias under which history is studied, by minds unacquainted with the great scientific movement of modern times. Again, another evidence is the dogmatic separation which it is attempted to keep up between history and politics. Still, we must admit the growing taste of our age for historical labours to be a happy symptom of philosophical regeneration, however the inclination may be wasted upon superficial and misleading works, sometimes written with a view to immediate popularity by ministering to the popular taste. One of the most promising incidents of the time is the introduction into the highly metaphysical class of jurists of an historical school which has undertaken to connect, during every period of history, the whole of its legislation with the corresponding state of society.

If the preceding chapter disclosed the destination of the great philosophical creation of which I am treating, the present exhibits its necessity, and the opportuneness of the time. Attempts to constitute a science of society would not have been so obstinate, nor pursued in ways so various, if an instinctive need of it had not been deeply felt. At the same time, the general analysis of the chief efforts hitherto made explains their failure, and convinces us that the whole enterprise remains to be even conceived of in a manner which will secure its accomplishment. Nothing now prevents our going on to the fulfilment of this proposed task, by entering, in the next chapter, on the study of the method in Social Physics. We have so ascertained and cleared our ground, by first taking a survey of our condition from a political point of view, and then reviewing the preparation made, that we are at full liberty to follow the speculative development that will prevail throughout the rest of this book, which will close with the co-ordination between the theory and practice of Social Physics.

# CHAPTER III.

### CHARACTERISTICS OF THE POSITIVE METHOD IN ITS APPLICATION TO SOCIAL PHENOMENA.

IN every science conceptions which relate to method are inseparable from those which relate to the doctrine under consideration. The method has to be so varied in its application, and so largely modified by the complexity and special nature of the phenomena, in each case, that any general notions of method would be too indefinite for actual use. If, therefore, we have not separated the method from the doctrine in the simpler departments of science, much less should we think of doing so when treating of the complex phenomena of social life, to say nothing of the great feature of this last case,—its want of positivity. In the formation of a new science the general spirit of it must be seized before its particular parts can be investigated: that is, we must have some notion of the doctrine before examining the method, and then the method cannot be estimated in any other way than by its use. Thus, I have not to offer a logical exposition of method in social physics before proceeding to the science itself; but I must follow the same plan here as in the case of the anterior sciences,—ascertaining its general spirit, and what are the collective resources proper to it. Though these subjects may be said to belong to the science itself, we may consider them as belonging to the method, as they are absolutely necessary to direct our understandings in the pursuit of this difficult study.

In the higher order of sciences,—in those which are the simplest and the most advanced,— the philosophical definition of each was almost sufficient to characterize their condition and general resources, to which no doubt could attach. But the case is otherwise with a recent and extremely complex study, the very nature of which has to be settled by laborious discussions, which are happily needless in regard to the preceding sciences. In treating of Biology, we found it necessary to dwell upon preparatory explanations which would have seemed puerile in any of the foregoing departments, because the chief bases of a science about which there were still so many disputes must be indisputably settled before it could take rank in the positive series. It is evident that the same process is even more needful, and must be more laborious, in the case of the science of social development, which has hitherto had no character of positivity at all, and which some of the ablest minds of our time sentence never to have any. We must not be surprised then if, after applying here the simplest and most radical ideas of positive philosophy, such as would indeed appear trivial in their formal application to the more advanced sciences, the result should appear to many, even among the enlightened, to constitute too bold an innovation, though the conditions may be no more than the barest equivalent of those which are admitted in every other case.

If we look with a philosophical eye upon the present state of social science, we cannot but recognize in it the combination of all the features of that theologico-metaphysical infancy which all the other sciences have had to pass through. The present condition of political science revives before our eyes the analogy of what astrology was to astronomy, alchemy to chemistry, and the search for the universal panacea to the system of medical studies. We may, for our present purpose, consider the theological and the metaphysical polities together,—the second being only a modification of the first in its relation to social science. Their attributes are the same, consisting, in regard to method, in the preponderance of imagination over observation; and, in regard to doctrine, in the exclusive investigation of absolute ideas; the result of both of which is an inevitable tendency to exercise an arbitrary and indefinite action over phenomena which are not regarded as subject to invariable natural laws. In short, the general spirit of all speculation at that stage is at once ideal in its course, absolute in its conception, and arbitrary in its application; and these are unquestionably the prevailing characteristics of social speculation at present,

*Infantile state of social science.*

regarded from any point of view whatever. If we reverse all the three aspects, we shall have precisely the spirit which must actuate the formation of positive sociology, and which must afterwards direct its continuous development. The scientific spirit is radically distinguished from the theological and metaphysical by the steady subordination of the imagination to observation; and though the positive philosophy offers the vastest and richest field to human imagination, it restricts it to discovering and perfecting the co-ordination of observed facts, and the means of effecting new researches: and it is this habit of subjecting scientific conceptions to the facts whose connection has to be disclosed, which it is above all things necessary to introduce into social researches; for the observations hitherto made have been vague and ill-circumscribed, so as to afford no adequate foundation for scientific reasoning; and they are usually modified themselves at the pleasure of an imagination stimulated by the most fluctuating passions. From their complexity, and their closer connection with human passions, political speculations must be detained longer than any others in this deplorable philosophical condition, in which they are still involved, while simpler and less stimulating sciences have successively obtained emancipation; but we must remember that all other kinds of scientific conception have gone through the same stage, from which they have issued with the more difficulty and delay exactly in proportion to their complexity and special nature. It is, indeed, only in our own day that the more complex have issued from that condition at all, as we saw to be the case with the intellectual and moral phenomena of individual life, which are still studied in a way almost as anti-scientific as political phenomena themselves. We must not, then, consider that uncertainty and vagueness in observation are proper to political subjects. It is only that the same imperfection which has had its day throughout the whole range of speculation is here more intense and protracted; and the same theory which shows how this must be the case gives us full assurance of a philosophical regeneration in this department of science analogous to that which has taken place in the rest, though by means of severer intellectual difficulty, and the embarrassment which may arise from collision with the predominant passions of men; a liability which cannot but stimulate the endeavours of real thinkers.

If we contemplate the positive spirit in its relation to scientific conception, rather than the mode of procedure, we shall find that this philosophy is distinguished from the theologico-metaphysical by its tendency to render relative the ideas which were at first absolute. *The relative superseding the absolute.* This inevitable passage from the absolute to the relative is one of the most important philosophical results of each of the intellectual revolutions which has carried on every kind of speculation from the theological or metaphysical to the scientific state. In a scientific view, this contrast between the relative and the absolute may be regarded as the most decisive manifestation of the antipathy between the modern philosophy and the ancient. All investigation into the nature of beings, and their first and final causes, must always be absolute; whereas the study of the laws of phenomena must be relative, since it supposes a continuous progress of speculation subject to the gradual improvement of observation, without the precise reality being ever fully disclosed: so that the relative character of scientific conceptions is inseparable from the true idea of natural laws, just as the chimerical inclination for absolute knowledge accompanies every use of theological fictions and metaphysical entities. Now, it is obvious that the absolute spirit characterizes social speculation now, wherever it exists, as the different schools are all agreed in looking for an immutable political type, which makes no allowance for the regular modification of political conceptions according to the variable state of civilization. This absolute spirit, having prevailed through all social changes, and their corresponding philosophical divergences, is now so inherent in existing political science that it affords, amidst all its enormous evils, the only means of restraining individual eccentricities, and excluding the influx of arbitrarily variable opinions. Thus, such philosophers as have desired to emancipate themselves from this absolutism, without having risen to the conception of a positive social philosophy, have justly incurred the reproach of representing political ideas as uncertain and even arbitrary in their nature, because they have deprived them of whatever character of consistency they had, without substituting any other. They have even cast a sort of discredit upon all philosophical enterprise in the direction of political science, which, losing its absolutism, seemed to lose its stability, and therefore its morality. A positive sociology, however, would put to flight all these natural, though empirical fears; for all antecedent experience shows that in other departments of natural philosophy, scientific ideas have not become arbitrary by becoming relative, but have, on the contrary, acquired a new consistence and stability by being implicated in a system of relations which is ever extending and strengthening, and more and more restraining all serious aberration. There is therefore no fear of falling into a dangerous scepticism by destroying the absolute spirit, if it is done in the natural course of passing on towards the positive state. Here, as elsewhere, it is characteristic of the positive philosophy to destroy no means of intellectual co-ordination without substituting one more effectual and more extended; and it is evident that this transition from the absolute to the relative offers the only existing means of attaining to political conceptions that can gradually secure an unanimous and permanent assent.

The importance and soundness of these conditions are less conspicuous than they might be, on account of the too close connection which, in social science more than any other, still exists between theory and practice, in consequence of which all speculative and abstract appreciation, however supremely important, excites only a feeble interest and inadequate attention. To show how this confusion results from the imperfection of social science, as the most complex of all, we must look at the existing political spirit in relation to its general application, and not for the moment in relation to the science itself. In this view we *Presumptuous* see that the existing political spirit is marked *character of* by its disposition to exercise an illimitable *the existing* action over the corresponding phenomena, *political spirit.* as it was once supposed possible to do in other departments of philosophy. Men were long in learning that Man's power of modifying phenomena can result only from his knowledge of their natural laws; and in the infancy of each science, they believed themselves able to exert an unbounded influence over the phenomena of that science. As this happened precisely at the period when they had the least power over phenomena, from ignorance of their laws, they rested their confidence on expectations of aid from supernatural agents, or mysterious forces supposed to be inherent in all that they saw. The delusion was protracted, and the growth of true science hindered in proportion, by the increasing complexity of the descending sciences, as each order of phenomena exhibited less generality than the last, and obscured the perception as to what the modifying power of Man really is. Social phenomena are, of course, from their extreme complexity, the last to be freed from this pretension: but it is therefore only the more necessary to remember that the pretension existed with regard to all the rest, in their earliest stage, and to anticipate therefore that social science will, in its turn, be emancipated from the delusion. It still hangs about the class of intellectual and moral phenomena; but otherwise it is now confined to social subjects. There, amidst the dawning of a sounder philosophy, we see statesmen and politicians still supposing that social phenomena can be modified at will, the human race having, in their view, no spontaneous impulsion, but being always ready to yield to any influence of the legislator, spiritual or temporal, provided he is invested with a sufficient authority. We see the theological polity, as before, more consistent than the metaphysical, explaining the monstrous disproportion between slight causes and vast effects, by regarding the legislator as merely the organ of a supernatural and absolute power: and again, we see the metaphysical school following the same course, merely substituting for Providence its unintelligible entities, and especially its grand entity, Nature, which comprehends all the rest, and is evidently only an abstract deterioration of the theological principle. Going further than the theological school in its disdain of the subjection of effects to causes, it escapes from difficulty by attributing observed events to chance, and sometimes, when that method is too obviously absurd, exaggerating ridiculously the influence of the individual mind upon the course of human affairs. The result is the same in both cases. It represents the social action of Man to be indefinite and arbitrary, as was once thought in regard to biological, chemical, physical, and even astronomical phenomena, in the earlier stages of their respective sciences. It is easy to see that true political science would be unacceptable, because it must impose limits on political action, by dissipating for ever the pretension of governing at will this class of phenomena, and withdrawing them from human or superhuman caprice. In close connection with the tendency to absolute conceptions, we must recognize in this delusion the chief intellectual cause of the social disturbance which now exists; for the human race finds itself delivered over, without logical protection, to the ill-regulated experimentation of the various political schools, each one of which strives to set up, for all future time, its own immutable type of government. We have seen what are the chaotic results of such a strife: and we shall find that there is no chance of order and agreement but in subjecting social phenomena, like all others, to invariable natural laws, which shall, as a whole, prescribe for each period, with entire certainty, the limits and character of political action:—in other words, introducing into the study of social phenomena the same positive spirit which has regenerated every other branch of human speculation. Such a procedure is the true scientific basis of human dignity; as the chief tendencies of man's nature thus acquire a solemn character of authority which must be always respected by rational legislation; whereas the existing belief in the indefinite power of political combinations, which seems at first to exalt the importance of Man, issues in attributing to him a sort of social automatism passively directed by some supremacy of either Providence or the human ruler. I have said enough to show that the central difficulty in the task of regenerating political science is to rectify such an error of conception, at a time when our prevailing intellectual habits render it difficult to seize social conceptions in any other than their practical aspect, and when their scientific, and yet more, their logical relations are obscured by the prepossessions of the general mind.

The last of the preliminary considerations that we have to review is that of the scientific prevision of phenomena, which, as the test of true science, includes all the rest. We have to contemplate social phenomena as susceptible of prevision, like all other classes, within the limits of exactness compatible with their higher complexity. Comprehending the three characteristics of political science which we have been examining, prevision of social phenomena supposes first, that we have abandoned the region of metaphysical idealities, to assume the ground of observed realities by a systematic subordination of imagination to observation; secondly, that political conceptions have ceased to be absolute, and have become relative to the variable state of civilization, so that theories, following the natural course of facts, may admit of our foreseeing them; and, thirdly, that permanent political action is limited by determinate laws, since, if social events were always exposed to disturbance by the accidental intervention of the legislator, human or divine, no scientific prevision of them would be possible. Thus, we may concentrate the conditions of the spirit of positive social philosophy on this one great attribute of scientific prevision. This concentration is all the more apt for the purpose of our inquiry, because there is no other view in which the new social philosophy is so clearly distinguished from the old. Events ordered by a supernatural will may leave room for a supposition of revelation; but the very thought of prevision in that case is sacrilegious: and the case is essentially the same when the direction of events is assigned to metaphysical entities, except that it leaves the chance of revelation; the existence of which chance shows that the metaphysical conception is a mere modification of the theological. The old conceptions may evidently be applied to explain opposite facts equally well; and they can never afford the slightest indication of those which are yet future. And, if it be objected that, at all times, a great number of secondary political facts have been considered susceptible of prevision, this only proves that the old philosophy has never been strictly universal, but has always been tempered by an admixture of feeble and imperfect positivism, without

*Prevision of social phenomena.*

more or less of which society could not have held on its course. This admixture has, however, been hitherto insufficient to allow anything worthy the name of prevision,—anything more than a sort of popular forecast of some secondary and partial matters,—never rising above an uncertain and rough empiricism, which might be of some provisional use, but could not in any degree supply the need of a true political philosophy.

Having now ascertained the fundamental position of the problems of political philosophy, and thus obtained guidance as to the scientific aim to be attained, the next step is to exhibit the general spirit of Social Physics, whose conditions we have been deciding.

*Spirit of Social Science.* The philosophical principle of the science being that social phenomena are subject to natural laws, admitting of rational prevision, we have to ascertain what is the precise subject, and what the peculiar character of those laws. The distinction between the Statical and Dynamical conditions of the subject must be extended to social science; and I shall treat of the conditions of social existence as, in biology, I treated of organization under the head of anatomy; and then of the laws of social movement, as in biology of those of life, under the head of physiology. This division, necessary for exploratory purposes, must not be stretched beyond that use: and, as we saw in Biology, that the distinction becomes weaker with the advance of science, so shall we see that when the science of social physics is fully constituted, this division will remain for analytical purposes, but not as a real separation of the science into two parts. The distinction is not between two classes of facts, but between two aspects of a theory. It corresponds with the double conception of order and progress: for order consists (in a positive sense) in a permanent harmony among the conditions of social existence; and progress consists in social development; and the conditions in the one case, and the laws of movement in the other, constitute the statics and dynamics of social physics.—And here we find again the constant relation between the science and the art,—the theory and the practice. A science which proposes a positive study of the laws of order and of progress cannot be charged with speculative rashness by practical men of any intelligence, since it offers the only rational basis for the practical means of satisfying the needs of society, as to order and progress; and the correspondence in this case will be found to be analogous to that which we have seen to exist between biological science and the arts which relate to it,—the medical art especially.—One view of the deepest interest in this connection is that the ideas of order and progress which are in perpetual conflict in existing society, occasioning infinite disturbance, are thus reconciled, and made necessary to each other, becoming as truly inseparable as the ideas of organization and life in the individual being. The further we go in the study of the conditions of human society, the more clearly will the organizing and progressive spirit of the positive philosophy become manifest.

The statical study of sociology consists in the investigation of the laws of action and reaction of the different parts of the social system,—apart, for the occasion, from the fundamental movement which is always gradually modifying them. In this view, sociological prevision, founded upon the exact general knowledge of those relations, acts by judging by each other the various statical indications of each mode of social existence, in conformity with direct observation,- just as is done daily in the case of anatomy. This view condemns the existing philosophical practice of contemplating social elements separately, as if they had an independent existence; and it leads us to regard them as in mutual relation, and forming a whole which compels us to treat them in combination. By this method, not only are we furnished with the only possible basis for the study of social movement, but we are put in possession of an important aid to direct observation; since many social elements which cannot be investigated by immediate observation may be estimated by their scientific relation to others already known. When we have a scientific knowledge of the interior relation of the parts of any science or art; and again, of the relations of the sciences to each other; and again, of the relations of arts to their respective sciences, the observation of certain portions of the scheme enables us to pronounce on the state of other portions, with a true

*Statical study.*

philosophical security. The case is the same when, instead of studying the collective social phenomena of a single nation, we include in the study those of contemporary nations, whose reciprocal influence cannot be disputed, though it is much reduced in modern times, and, as in the instance of western Europe and eastern Asia, apparently almost effaced.

*Social Organization.* The only essential case in which this fundamental relation is misconceived or neglected is that which is the most important of all,—involving, as it does, social organization, properly so called. The theory of social organization is still conceived of as absolute and isolated, independent altogether of the general analysis of the corresponding civilization, of which it can, in fact, constitute only one of the principal elements. This vice is chargeable in an almost equal degree upon the most opposite political schools, which agree in abstract discussions of political systems, without thinking of the coexisting state of civilization, and usually conclude with making their immutable political type coincide with an infantile state of human development. If we ascend to the philosophical source of this error, we shall find it, I think, in the great theological dogma of the Fall of Man. This fundamental dogma, which reappears, in one form or another, in all religions, and which is supported in its intellectual influence by the natural propensity of men to admire the past, tends, directly and necessarily, to make the continuous deterioration of society coincide with the extension of civilization. We have noticed before how, when it passes from the theological into the metaphysical state, this dogma takes the form of the celebrated hypothesis of a chimerical state of nature, superior to the social state, and the more remote, the further we advance in civilization. We cannot fail to perceive the extreme seriousness, in a political as well as a philosophical sense, of an error so completely incorporated with existing doctrines, and so deeply influencing, in an unconscious way, our collective social speculations,—the more disastrously perhaps for not being expressly maintained as a general principle.—If it were so presented, it must immediately give way before sound philosophical discussion; for it is in direct contradiction to many ideas in political philosophy which, without having attained any scientific consistency, are obtaining some intellectual ascendancy, through the natural course of events, or the expansion of the general mind. For instance, all enlightened political writers acknowledge more or less mutual relation between political institutions; and this is the first direct step towards the rational conception of the agreement of the special system of institutions with the total system of civilization. We now see the best thinkers admitting a constant mutual connection between the political and the civil power: which means, in scientific language, that preponderating social forces always end in assuming the direction of society. Such partial advances towards a right view,—such fortunate feeling after the right path, must not, however, induce us to relax in our requirements of a true philosophical conception of that general social agreement which can alone constitute organization. Desultory indications, more literary than scientific, can never supply the place of a strict philosophical doctrine, as we may see from the fact that, from Aristotle downwards, (and even from an earlier period,) the greater number of philosophers have constantly reproduced the famous aphorism of the necessary subordination of laws to manners, without this germ of sound philosophy having had any effect on the general habit of regarding institutions as independent of the coexisting state of civilization,—however strange it may seem that such a contradiction should live through twenty centuries. This is, however, the natural course with intellectual principles and philosophical opinions, as well as with social manners and political institutions. When once they have obtained possession of men's minds, they live on, notwithstanding their admitted impotence and inconvenience, giving occasion to more and more serious inconsistencies, till the expansion of human reason originates new principles, of equivalent generality and superior rationality. We must not therefore take for more than their worth the desultory attempts that we see made in the right direction, but must insist on the principle which lies at the heart of every scheme of social organization,—the necessary participation

*Political and social concurrence.*

of the collective political *régime* in the universal consensus of the social body.

The scientific principle of the relation between the political and the social condition is simply this;—that there must always be a spontaneous harmony between the whole and the parts of the social system, the elements of which must inevitably be, sooner or later, combined in a mode entirely conformable to their nature. It is evident that not only must political institutions and social manners on the one hand, and manners and ideas on the other, be always mutually connected; but, further, that this consolidated whole must be always connected, by its nature, with the corresponding state of the integral development of humanity, considered in all its aspects, of intellectual, moral, and physical activity: and the only object of any political system whatever, temporal or spiritual, is to regulate the spontaneous expansion so as best to direct it towards its determinate end. Even during revolutionary periods, when the harmony appears furthest from being duly realized, it still exists: for without it there would be a total dissolution of the social organism. During those exceptional seasons, the political *régime* is still, in the long run, in conformity with the corresponding state of civilization, as the disturbances which are manifest in the one proceed from equivalent derangements in the other. It is observable that when the popular theory attributes to the legislator the permanent power of infringing the harmony we are speaking of, it supposes him to be armed with a sufficient authority. But every social power, whether called authority or anything else, is constituted by a corresponding assent, spontaneous or deliberate, explicit or implicit, of various individual wills, resolved, from certain preparatory convictions, to concur in a common action, of which this power is first the organ, and then the regulator. Thus, authority is derived from concurrence, and not concurrence from authority, (setting aside the necessary reaction:) so that no great power can arise otherwise than from the strongly prevalent disposition of the society in which it exists: and when there is no strong preponderance, such powers as exist are weak accordingly: and the more extensive the society, the more irresistible is the correspondence. On the other hand, there is no denying the influence which, by a necessary reaction, the political system, as a whole, exercises over the general system of civilization, and which is so often exhibited in the action, fortunate or disastrous, of institutions, measures, or purely political events, even upon the course of the sciences and arts, in all ages of society, and especially the earliest. We need not dwell on this; for no one denies it. The common error, indeed, is to exaggerate it, so as to place the reaction before the primary action. It is evident, considering their scientific relation to each other, that both concur in creating that fundamental agreement of the social organism which I propose to set forth in a brief manner, as the philosophical principle of statical sociology. We shall have to advert repeatedly to the subject of the general correspondence between the political *régime* and the contemporary state of civilization, in connection with the question of the necessary limits of political action, and in the chapter which I must devote to social statics: but I did not think fit to wait for these explanations before pointing out that the political system ought always to be regarded as relative. The relative point of view, substituted for the absolute tendency of the ordinary theories, certainly constitutes the chief scientific character of the positive philosophy in its political application. If, on the one hand, the conception of this connection between government and civilization presents all ideas of political good or evil as necessarily relative and variable (which is quite another thing than being arbitrary), on the other hand, it provides a rational basis for a positive theory of the spontaneous order of human society, already vaguely perceived, in regard to some minor relations, by that part of the metaphysical polity which we call political economy; for, if the value of any political system can consist in nothing but its harmony with the corresponding social state, it follows that in the natural course of events, and in the absence of intervention, such a harmony must necessarily be established.

There are two principal considerations which induce me to insist on this elementary idea of the radical consensus proper to Interconnection of the social organism.

the social organism : first, the extreme philosophical importance of this master-thought of social statics, which must, from its nature, constitute the rational basis of any new political philosophy ; and, secondly, in an accessory way, that dynamical considerations of sociology must prevail throughout the rest of this work, as being at present more interesting, and therefore better understood ; and it is, on that account, the more necessary to characterize now the general spirit of social statics, which will henceforth be treated only in an indirect and implicit way. As all artificial and voluntary order is simply a prolongation of the natural and involuntary order to which all human society tends, every rational political institution must rest upon an exact preparatory analysis of corresponding spontaneous tendencies, which alone can furnish a sufficiently solid basis. In brief, it is our business to contemplate order, that we may perfect it; and not to create it; which would be impossible. In a scientific view, this master-thought of universal social interconnection becomes the consequence and complement of a fundamental idea established, in our view of biology, as eminently proper to the study of living bodies. Not that this idea of interconnection is peculiar to that study : it is necessarily common to all phenomena ; but amidst immense differences in intensity and variety, and therefore in philosophical importance. It is, in fact, true that wherever there is any system whatever, a certain interconnection must exist. The purely mechanical phenomena of astronomy offer the first suggestion of it; for the perturbations of one planet may sensibly affect another, through a modified gravitation. But the relation becomes closer and more marked in proportion to the complexity and diminished generality of the phenomena, and thus, it is in organic systems that we must look for the fullest mutual connection. Hitherto, it had been merely an accessory idea; but then it becomes the basis of positive conceptions ; and it becomes more marked, the more compound are the organisms, and the more complex the phenomena in question,—the animal interconnection being more complete than the vegetable, and the human more than the brute ; the nervous system being the chief seat of the biological interconnection. The idea must therefore be scientifically preponderant in social physics, even more than in biology, where it is so decisively recognized by the best order of students. But the existing political philosophy supposes the absence of any such interconnection among the aspects of society: and it is this which has rendered it necessary for me now to establish the point,—leaving the illustration of it to a future portion of the volume. Its consideration is, in fact, as indispensable in assigning its encyclopædic rank to social science as we before saw it to be in instituting Social Physics a science at all.

It follows from this attribute that there can be no scientific study of society, either in its conditions or its movements, if it is separated into portions, and its divisions are studied apart. I have already remarked upon this, in regard to what is called political economy. Materials may be furnished by the observation of different departments; and such observation may be necessary for that object: but it cannot be called science. The methodical division of studies which takes place in the simple inorganic sciences is thoroughly irrational in the recent and complex science of society, and can produce no results. The day may come when some sort of subdivision may be practicable and desirable; but it is impossible for us now to anticipate what the principle of distribution may be; for the principle itself must arise from the development of the science; and that development can take place no otherwise than by our formation of the science as a whole. The complete body will indicate for itself, at the right season, the particular points which need investigation; and then will be the time for such special study as may be required. By any other method of proceeding, we shall only find ourselves encumbered with special discussions, badly instituted, worse pursued, and accomplishing no other purpose than that of impeding the formation of real science. It is no easy matter to study social phenomena in the only right way,—viewing each element in the light of the whole system. It is no easy matter to exercise such vigilance as that no one of the number of contemporary aspects shall be lost sight of. But it is the right and the only way; and we may perceive in it a clear suggestion that this lofty study should be reserved for the highest order of scientific minds, better prepared than others, by wise educational discipline, for sustained speculative efforts, aided by an habitual subordination of the passions to the reason. There is no need to draw out any lengthened comparison between this state of things as it should be and that which is. And no existing degree of social disturbance can surprise us when we consider how intellectual anarchy is at the bottom of such disturbance, and see how anarchical our intellectual condition appears in the presence of the principle I have laid down.

*Order of statical study.* Before we go on to the subject of social dynamics, I will just remark that the prominent interconnection we have been considering prescribes a procedure in organic studies different from that which suits inorganic. The metaphysicians announce as an aphorism that we should always, in every kind of study, proceed from the simple to the compound: whereas, it appears most rational to suppose that we should follow that or the reverse method, as may best suit our subject. There can be no absolute merit in the method enjoined, apart from its suitableness. The rule should rather be (and there probably was a time when the two rules were one) that we must proceed from the more known to the less. Now, in the inorganic sciences, the elements are much better known to us than the whole which they constitute: so that in that case we must proceed from the simple to the compound. But the reverse method is necessary in the study of Man and of Society; Man and Society as a whole being better known to us, and more accessible subjects of study, than the parts which constitute them. In exploring the universe, it is as a whole that it is inaccessible to us; whereas, in investigating Man or Society, our difficulty is in penetrating the details. We have seen, in our survey of biology, that the general idea of animal nature is more distinct to our minds than the simpler notion of vegetable nature; and that man is the biological unity; the idea of Man being at once the most compound, and the starting-point of speculation in regard to vital existence. Thus, if we compare the two halves of natural philosophy, we shall find that in the one case it is the last degree of composition, and, in the other, the last degree of simplicity, that is beyond the scope of our research. As for the rest, it may obviate some danger of idle discussions to say that the positive philosophy, subordinating all fancies to reality, excludes logical controversies about the absolute value of this or that method, apart from its scientific application. The only ground of preference being the superior adaptation of any means to the proposed end, this philosophy may, without any inconsistency, change its order of proceeding when the one first tried is found to be inferior to its converse:—a discovery of which there is no fear in regard to the question we have now been examining.

Passing on from statical to dynamical sociology, we will contemplate the philosophical conception which should govern our study of the movement of society. *Dynamical study.* Part of this subject is already despatched, from the explanations made in connection with statics having simplified the chief difficulties of the case. And social dynamics will be so prominent throughout the rest of this work, that I may reduce within very small compass what I have to say now under that head.

Though the statical view of society is the basis of sociology, the dynamical view is not only the more interesting of the two, but the more marked in its philosophical character, from its being more distinguished from biology by the master-thought of continuous progress, or rather, of the gradual development of humanity. If I were writing a methodical treatise on political philosophy, it would be necessary to offer a preliminary analysis of the individual impulsions which make up the progressive force of the human race, by referring them to that instinct which results from the concurrence of all our natural tendencies, and which urges man to develope the whole of his life, physical, moral, and intellectual, as far as his circumstances allow. But this view is admitted by all enlightened philosophers; so that I must proceed at once to consider the continuous succession of human development, regarded in the whole race, as if humanity were one. For clearness, we may take advantage of Condorcet's device of supposing a single nation to which we may refer all the consecutive social modifications actually witnessed among distinct peoples. This rational fiction is nearer the reality than we are accustomed to suppose; for, in a political view, the true successors of such or such a people are certainly those who, taking up and carrying out their primitive endeavours, have prolonged their social progress, whatever may be the soil which they inhabit, or even the race from which they spring. In brief, it is political continuity which regulates sociological succession, though the having a common country must usually affect this continuity in a high degree. As a scientific artifice merely, however, I shall employ this hypothesis, and on the ground of its manifest utility.

*Social continuity.* The true general spirit of social dynamics then consists in conceiving of each of these consecutive social states as the necessary result of the preceding, and the indispensable mover of the following, according to the axiom of Leibnitz,—*the present is big with the future.* In this view, the object of science is to discover the laws which govern this continuity, and the aggregate of which determines the course of human development. In short, social dynamics studies the laws of succession, while social statics inquires into those of co-existence; so that the use of the first is to furnish the true theory of progress to political practice, while the second performs the same service in regard to order; and this suitability to the needs of modern society is a strong confirmation of the philosophical character of such a combination.

*Produced by natural laws.* If the existence of sociological laws has been established in the more difficult and uncertain case of the statical condition, we may assume that they will not be questioned in the dynamical province. In all times and places, the ordinary course of even our brief individual life has disclosed certain remarkable modifications which have occurred, in various ways, in the social state; and all the most ancient representations of human life bear unconscious and most interesting testimony to this, apart from all systematic estimate of the fact. Now it is the slow, continuous accumulation of these successive changes which gradually constitutes the social movement, whose steps are ordinarily marked by generations, as the most appreciable elementary variations are wrought by the constant renewal of adults. At a time when the average rapidity of this progression seems to all eyes to be remarkably accelerated, the reality of the movement cannot be disputed, even by those who most abhor it. The only question is about the constant subjection of these great dynamical phenomena to invariable natural laws, a proposition about which there is no question to any one who takes his stand on positive philosophy. It is easy however to establish, from any point of view, that the successive modifications of society have always taken place in a determinate order, the rational explanation of which is already possible in so many cases that we may confidently hope to recognize it ultimately in all the rest. So remarkable is the steadiness of this order, moreover, that it exhibits an exact parallelism of development among distinct and independent populations, as we shall see when we come to the historical portion of this volume. Since, then, the existence of the social movement is unquestionable, on the one hand, and, on the other, the succession of social states is never arbitrary, we cannot but regard this continuous phenomenon as subject to natural laws as positive as those which govern all other phenomena, though more complex. There is in fact no intellectual alternative; and thus it is evident that it is on the ground of social science that the great conflict must soon terminate which has gone on for three centuries between the positive and the theologico-metaphysical spirit. Banished for ever from all other classes of speculation, in principle at least, the old philosophies now prevail in social science alone; and it is from this domain that they have to be excluded, by the conception of the social movement being subject to invariable natural laws, instead of to any will whatever.

Though the fundamental laws of social interconnection are especially verified in this condition of movement, and though there is a necessary unity in this phenomenon, it may be usefully applied, for preparatory purposes, to the separate elementary aspects of human existence, physical, moral, intellectual and, finally, political,—their mutual relation being kept in view. Now, in whichever of these ways we regard, as a whole, the movement of humanity, from the earliest periods till now, we shall find that the various steps are connected in a determinate order; as we shall hereafter see, when we investigate the laws of this succession. I need refer here only to the intellectual evolution, which is the most distinct and unquestionable of all, as it has been the least impeded and most advanced of any, and has therefore been usually taken for guidance. The chief part of this evolution, and that which has most influenced the general progression, is no doubt the development of the scientific spirit, from the primitive labours of such philosophers as Thales and Pythagoras to those of men like Lagrange and Bichat. Now, no enlightened man can doubt that, in this long succession of efforts and discoveries, the human mind has pursued a determinate course, the exact preparatory knowledge of which might have allowed a cultivated reason to foresee the progress proper to each period. Though the historical considerations cited in my former volume were only incidental, any one may recognize in them numerous and indisputable examples of this necessary succession, more complex perhaps, but not more arbitrary than any natural law, whether in regard to the development of each separate science, or to the mutual influence of the different branches of natural philosophy. In accordance with the principles laid down at the beginning of this work, we have already seen in various signal instances, that the chief progress of each period, and even of each generation, was a necessary result of the immediately preceding state; so that the men of genius, to whom such progression has been too exclusively attributed, are essentially only the proper organs of a predetermined movement, which would, in their absence, have found other issues. We find a verification of this in history, which shows that various eminent men were ready to make the same great discovery at the same time, while the discovery required only one organ. All the parts of the human evolution admit of analogous observations, as we shall presently see, though they are more complex and less obvious than that which I have just cited. The natural progression of the arts of life is abundantly evident; and in our direct study of social dynamics we shall find an explanation of the apparent exception of the fine arts, which will be found to oppose no contradiction to the general course of human progression. As to that part of the movement which appears at present to be least reducible to natural laws, the political movement (still supposed to be governed by wills of adequate power), it is clear as in any other case that political systems have exhibited an historical succession, according to a traceable filiation, in a determinate order, which I am prepared to show to be even more inevitable than that of the different states of human intelligence.

The interconnection which we have examined and established in a statical view may aid us in developing the conception of the existence of positive laws in social dynamics. Unless the movement was determined by those laws, it would occasion the entire destruction of the social system. Now, that interconnection simplifies and strengthens the preparatory indications of dynamic order; for, when it has once been shown in any relation, we are authorized to extend it to all others; and this unites all the partial proofs that we can successively obtain of the reality of this scientific conception. In the choice and the application of these verifications, we must remember that the laws of social dynamics are most recognizable when they relate to the largest societies, in which secondary disturbances have the smallest effect. Again, these fundamental laws become the more irresistible, and therefore the more appreciable, in proportion to the advancement of the civilization upon which they operate, because the social movement becomes more distinct and certain with every conquest over accidental influences. As for the philosophical co-ordination of these preparatory evidences, the combination of which is important to science, it is clear that the social evolution must be more inevitably subject to natural laws, the more compound are the phenomena, and the less perceptible therefore the irregularities which arise from individual influences. This shows how inconsistent it is, for instance, to suppose the scientific movement to be subject to positive laws, while the political movement is regarded as arbitrary; for the latter, being more composite, must overrule individual disturbances, and be therefore more evidently predetermined than the former, in which individual genius must have more power. Any paradoxical appearance which this statement may exhibit will disappear in the course of further examination.

If I confined myself strictly to a scientific view, I might satisfy myself with proving the fact of social progression, without taking any notice of the question of human perfectibility. But so much time and effort are wasted in groundless speculation on that interesting question, argued as it is on the supposition that political events are arbitrarily determined, that it may be as well to notice it in passing; and the more, because it may serve as a natural transition to the estimate of the limits of political action.

*Notion of Human perfectibility.* We have nothing to do here with the metaphysical controversy about the absolute happiness of Man at different stages of civilization. As the happiness of every man depends on the harmony between the development of his various faculties and the entire system of the circumstances which govern his life; and as, on the other hand, this equilibrium always establishes itself spontaneously to a certain extent, it is impossible to compare in a positive way, either by sentiment or reasoning, the individual welfare which belongs to social situations that can never be brought into direct comparison: and therefore the question of the happiness of different animal organisms, or of their two sexes, is merely impracticable and unintelligible. The only question therefore is of the effect of the social evolution, which is so undeniable that there is no reasoning with any one who does not admit it as the basis of the inquiry. The only ground of discussion is whether development and improvement,—the theoretical and the practical aspect,—are one; whether the development is necessarily accompanied by a corresponding amelioration, or progress, properly so called. To me it appears that the amelioration is as unquestionable as the development from which it proceeds, provided we regard it as subject, like the development itself, to limits, general and special, which science will be found to prescribe. The chimerical notion of unlimited perfectibility is thus at once excluded. Taking the human race as a whole, and not any one people, it appears that human development brings after it, in two ways, an ever-growing amelioration, first, in the radical condition of Man, which no one disputes; and next, in his corresponding faculties, which is a view much less attended to. There is no need to dwell upon the improvement in the conditions of human existence, both by the increasing action of Man on his environment through the advancement of the sciences and arts, and by the constant amelioration of his customs and manners; and again, by the gradual improvement in social organization. We shall presently see that in the Middle Ages, which are charged with political retrogression, the progress was more political than any other. One fact is enough to silence sophistical declamation on this subject; the continuous increase of population all over the globe, as a consequence of civilization, while the wants of individuals are, as a whole, better satisfied at the same time. The tendency to improvement must be highly spontaneous and irresistible to have persevered notwithstanding the enormous faults,—political faults especially,—which have at all times absorbed or neutralized the greater part of our social forces. Even throughout the revolutionary period, in spite of the marked discordance between the political system and the general state of civilization, the improvement has proceeded, not only in physical and intellectual, but also in moral respects, though the transient disorganization could not but disturb the natural evolution. As for the other aspect of the question, the gradual and slow improvement of human nature, within narrow limits, it seems to me impossible to reject altogether the principle proposed (with great exaggeration, however,) by Lamarck, of the necessary influence of a homogeneous and continuous exercise in producing, in every animal organism, and especially in Man, an organic improvement, susceptible of being established in the race, after a sufficient persistence. If we take the best marked case,—that of intellectual development, it seems to be unquestionable that there is a superior aptitude for mental combinations, independent of all culture, among highly civilized people; or, what comes to the same thing, an inferior aptitude among nations that are less advanced,—the average intellect of the members of those societies being taken for observation. The intellectual faculties are, it is true, more modified than the others by the social evolution: but then they have the smallest relative effect in the individual human constitution: so that we are authorized to infer from their amelioration a proportionate improvement in aptitudes that are more marked and equally exercised. In regard to morals, particularly, I think it indisputable that the gradual development of humanity favours a growing preponderance of the noblest tendencies of our nature, —as I hope to prove further on. The lower instincts continue to manifest themselves in modified action, but their less sustained and more repressed exercise must tend to debilitate them by degrees; and their increasing regulation certainly brings them into involuntary concurrence in the maintenance of a good social economy; and especially in the case of the least marked organisms, which constitute a vast majority. These two aspects of social evolution, then,—the *development* which brings after it the *improvement*,—we may consider to be admitted as facts.

Adhering to our relative, in opposition to the absolute, view, we must conclude the social state, regarded as a whole, to have been as perfect, in each period, as the co-existing condition of humanity and of its environment would allow. Without this view, history would be incomprehensible; and the relative view is as indispensable in regard to progress, as, in considering social statics, we saw it to be in regard to order. If, in a statical view, the various social elements cannot but maintain a spontaneous harmony, which is the first principle of order; neither can any of them help being as advanced, at any period, as the whole system of influences permits. In either case, the harmony and the movement are the result of invariable natural laws which produce all phenomena whatever, and are more obscure in social science merely on account of the greater complexity of the phenomena concerned.

Limits of political action. And, now occurs, as the last aspect of social dynamics, the question of the general limits of political action. No enlightened man can be blind to the necessary existence of such limits, which can be ignored only on the old theological supposition of the legislator being merely the organ of a direct and continuous Providence, which admits of no limits. We need not stop to confute that hypothesis, which has no existence but in virtue of ancient habit of thought. In any case, human action is very limited, in spite of all aids from concurrence and ingenious methods; and it is difficult to perceive why social action should be exempt from this restriction, which is an inevitable consequence of the existence of natural laws. Through all the self-assertions of human pride, every statesman of experience knows well the reality of the bounds prescribed to political action by the aggregate of social influences, to which he must attribute the failure of the greater number of the projects which he had secretly cherished; and perhaps the conviction is most thorough, while most carefully hidden, in the mind of the most powerful of statesmen, because his inability to struggle against natural laws must be decisive in proportion to his implication with them. Seeing that social science would be impossible in the absence of this principle, we need not dwell further upon it, but may proceed to ascertain the fitness of the new political philosophy to determine, with all the precision that the subject admits, what is the nature of these limits, general or special, permanent or temporary.

Two questions are concerned here: first, in what way the course of human development may be affected by the aggregate of causes of variation which may be applied to it; and next, what share the voluntary and calculated action of our political combinations may have among these modifying influences. The first question is by far the most important, both because it is a general principle, which the second is not, and because it is fully accessible, which, again, the second is not.

We must observe, in the first place, that social phenomena may, from their complexity, be more easily modified than any others, *Social phenomena modifiable.* according to the law which was established to that effect in my first volume. Thus, the limits of variation are wider in regard to sociological than any other laws. If, then, human intervention holds the same proportionate rank among modifying influences as it is natural at first to suppose, its influence must be more considerable in the first case than in any other, all appearances to the contrary notwithstanding. This is the first scientific foundation of all rational hopes of a systematic reformation of humanity; and on this ground illusions of this sort certainly appear more excusable than on any other subject. But though modifications, from all causes, are greater in the case of political than of simpler phenomena, still they can never be more than modifications: that is, they will always be in subjection to those fundamental laws, whether statical or dynamical, which regulate the harmony of the social elements, and the filiation of their successive variations. There is no disturbing influence, exterior or human, which can make incompatible elements co-exist in the political system, nor change in any way the natural laws of the development of humanity. The inevitable gradual preponderance of continuous influences, however imperceptible their power may be at first, is now admitted with regard to all natural phenomena; and it must be applied to social phenomena, whenever the same method of philosophizing is extended to them. What then are the modifications of which the social organism and social life are susceptible, if nothing can alter the laws either of harmony or of succession? The answer is that modifications act upon the intensity and secondary operation of phenomena, but without affecting their nature or their filiation. To suppose that they could, would be to exalt the disturbing above the fundamental cause, and would destroy the whole economy of laws. In the political system this principle of positive philosophy shows that, in a statical view, any possible variations can affect only the intensity of the different tendencies belonging to each social situation, without in any way hindering or producing, or, in a word, changing the nature of, those tendencies; and, in the same way, in a dynamical view, the progress of the race must be considered susceptible of modification only with regard to its speed, and without any reversal in the order of development, or any interval of any importance being overleaped. These variations are analogous to those of the animal organism, with the one difference that in sociology they are more complex; and, as we saw that the limits of variation remain to be established in biology, it is not to be expected that sociology should be more advanced. But all we want here is to obtain a notion of the general spirit of the law, in regard both to social statics and dynamics; and looking at it from both points of view, it seems to me impossible to question its truth. In the intellectual order of phenomena, for instance, there is no accidental influence, nor any individual superiority, which can transfer to one period the discoveries reserved for a subsequent age, in the natural course of the human mind; nor can there be the reverse case of postponement. The history of the sciences settles the question of the close dependence of even the most eminent individual genius on the contemporary state of the human mind; and this is above all remarkable in regard to the improvement of methods of investigation, either in the way of reasoning or experiment. The same thing happens in regard to the arts; and especially in whatever depends on mechanical means in substitution for human action. And there is not, in reality, any more room for doubt in the case of moral development, the character of which is certainly determined, in each period, by the corresponding state of the social evolution, whatever may be the modifications caused by education or individual organization. Each of the leading modes of social existence determines for itself a certain system of morals and manners, the common aspect of which is easily recognized in all individuals, in the midst of their characteristic differences; for instance, there is a state of human life in which the best individual natures contract a habit of ferocity, from which very inferior natures easily emancipate themselves, in a better state of society. The case is the same, in a political view, as our historical analysis will hereafter show. And in fact, if we were to review all the facts and reflections which establish the existence of the limits of variation, whose principle I have just laid down, we should find ourselves reproducing in succession all the proofs of the subjection of social phenomena to invariable laws; because the principle is neither more nor less than a strict application of the philosophical conception.

We cannot enlarge upon the second head: that is, the classification of modifying influences according to their respective impor- *Order of modifying influences.*

tance. If such a classification is not yet established in biology, it would be premature indeed to attempt it in social science. Thus, if the three chief causes of social variation appear to me to result from, first, race; secondly, climate; thirdly, political action in its whole scientific extent, it would answer none of our present purposes to inquire here whether this or some other is the real order of their importance. The political influences are the only ones really open to our intervention; and to that head general attention must be directed, though with great care to avoid the conclusion that that class of influences must be the most important because it is the most immediately interesting to us. It is owing to such an illusion as this that observers who believe themselves emancipated from old prejudices cannot obtain sociological knowledge, because they enormously exaggerate the power of political action. Because political operations, temporal or spiritual, can have no social efficacy but in as far as they are in accordance with the corresponding tendencies of the human mind, they are supposed to have produced what is in reality occasioned by a spontaneous evolution, which is less conspicuous, and easily overlooked. Such a mistake proceeds in neglect of numerous and marked cases in history, in which the most prodigious political authority has left no lasting traces of its well-sustained development, because it moved in a contrary direction to modern civilization; as in the instances of Julian, of Philip II., of Napoleon Bonaparte, etc. The inverse cases, unhappily too few, are still more decisive; those cases in which political action, sustained by an equally powerful authority, has nevertheless failed in the pursuit of ameliorations that were premature, though in accordance with the social movement of the time. Intellectual history, as well as political, furnishes examples of this kind in abundance. It has been sensibly remarked by Fergusson, that even the action of one nation upon another, whether by conquest or otherwise, though the most intense of all social forces, can effect merely such modifications as are in accordance with its existing tendencies; so that, in fact, the action merely accelerates or extends a development which would have taken place without it. In politics, as in science, *opportuneness* is always the main condition of all great and durable influence, whatever may be the personal value of the superior man to whom the multitude attribute social action of which he is merely the fortunate organ. The power of the individual over the race is subject to these general limits, even when the effects, for good or for evil, are as easy as possible to produce. In revolutionary times, for instance, those who are proud of having aroused anarchical passions in their contemporaries do not see that their miserable triumph is due to a spontaneous disposition, determined by the aggregate of the corresponding social state, which has produced a provisional and partial relaxation of the general harmony. As for the rest, it being ascertained that there are limits of variation among social phenomena, and modifications dependent on systematic political action; and as the scientific principle which is to describe such modifications is now known; the influence and scope of that principle must be determined in each case by the direct development of social science, applied to the appreciation of the corresponding state of circumstances. It is by such estimates, empirically attempted, that men of genius have been guided in all great and profound action upon humanity in any way whatever; and it is only thus that they have been able to rectify, in a rough way, the illusory suggestions of the irrational doctrines in which they were educated. Everywhere, as I have so often said, foresight is the true source of action.

The inaccurate intellectual habits which as yet prevail in political philosophy may induce an apprehension that, according to such considerations as those just presented, the new science of Social Physics may reduce us to mere observation of human events, excluding all continuous intervention. It is, however, certain that, while dissipating all ambitious illusions about the indefinite action of Man on civilization, the principle of rational limits to political action establishes, in the most exact and unquestionable manner, the true point of contact between social theory and practice. It is by this principle only that political art can assume a systematic character, by its release from arbitrary principles mingled with empirical notions. It is thus only that political art can pass upwards as medical art has done; the two cases being strongly analogous. As political intervention can have no efficacy unless it rests on corresponding tendencies of the political organism or life, so as to aid its spontaneous development, it is absolutely necessary to understand the natural laws of harmony and succession which determine, in every period, and under every social aspect, what the human evolution is prepared to produce, pointing out, at the same time, the chief obstacles which may be got rid of. It would be exaggerating the scope of such an art to suppose it capable of obviating, in all cases, the violent disturbances which are occasioned by impediments to the natural evolution. In the highly complex social organism, maladies and crises are necessarily even more inevitable than in the individual organism. But, though science is powerless for the moment amidst wild disorder and extravagance, it may palliate and abridge the crises, by understanding their character and foreseeing their issue, and by more or less intervention, where any is possible. Here, as in other cases, and more than in other cases, the office of science is, not to govern, but to modify phenomena; and to do this, it is necessary to understand their laws.

Thus, then, we see what is the function of social science. Without extolling or condemning political facts, science regards them as subjects of observation: it contemplates each phenomenon in its harmony with co-existing phenomena, and in its connection with the foregoing and the following state of human development: it endeavours to discover, from both points of view, the general relations which connect all social phenomena: and each of them is *explained*, in the scientific sense of the word, when it has been connected with the whole of the existing situation, and the whole of the preceding movement. Favouring the social sentiment in the highest degree, this science fulfils the famous suggestion of Pascal, by representing the whole human race, past, present, and future, as constituting a vast and eternal social unit, whose different organs, individual and national, concur, in their various modes and degrees, in the evolution of humanity. Leading us on, like every other science, with as much exactness as the extreme complexity of its phenomena allows, to a systematic prevision of the events which must result from either a given situation or a given aggregate of antecedents, political science enlightens political art, not only in regard to the tendencies which should be aided, but as to the chief means that should be employed, so as to avoid all useless or ephemeral and therefore dangerous action; in short, all waste of any kind of social force.

This examination of the general spirit of political philosophy has been much more difficult than the same process in regard to any established science. *Means of investigation.* The next step, now that this is accomplished, is to examine, according to my usual method, the means of investigation proper to Social science. In virtue of a law before recognized, we may expect to find in Sociology a more varied and developed system of resources than in any other, in proportion to the complexity of the phenomena, while yet, this extension of means does not compensate for the increased imperfection arising from the intricacy. The extension of the means is also more difficult to verify than in any prior case, from the novelty of the subject; and I can scarcely hope that such a sketch as I must present here will command such confidence as will arise when a complete survey of the science shall have confirmed what I now offer.

As Social Physics assumes a place in the hierarchy of sciences after all the rest, and therefore dependent on them, its means of investigation must be of two kinds: those which are peculiar to itself, and which may be called direct, and those which arise from the connection of sociology with the other sciences; and these last, though indirect, are as indispensable as the first. I shall review, first, the direct resources of the science. *Direct means.*

Here, as in all the other cases, there are three methods of proceeding:—by Observation, Experiment and Comparison.

Very imperfect and even vicious notions prevail at present as to what Observation can be and can effect in social science. *Observation.* The chaotic state of doctrine of the last century has extended to Method; and amidst our intellectual disorganization, difficulties have been magnified; precautionary methods, experimental and rational, have been broken up; and even the possibility of obtaining social knowledge by observation has been dogmatically denied; but if the sophisms put forth on this subject were true, they would destroy the certainty, not only of social science, but of all the simpler and more perfect ones that have gone before. The ground of doubt assigned is the uncertainty of human testimony; but all the sciences, up to the most simple, require proofs of testimony: that is, in the elaboration of the most positive theories, we have to admit observations which could not be directly made, nor even repeated, by those who use them, and the reality of which rests only on the faithful testimony of the original investigators; there being nothing in this to prevent the use of such proofs, in concurrence with immediate observations. In astronomy, such a method is obviously necessary; it is equally, though less obviously necessary even in mathematics; and, of course, much more evidently in the case of the more complex sciences. How could any science emerge from the nascent state,—how could there be any organization of intellectual labour, even if research were restricted to the utmost, if every one rejected all observations but his own? The stoutest advocates of historical scepticism do not go so far as to advocate this. It is only in the case of social phenomena that the paradox is proposed; and it is made use of there because it is one of the weapons of the philosophical arsenal which the revolutionary metaphysical doctrine constructed for the intellectual overthrow of the ancient political system. The next great hindrance to the use of observation is the empiricism which is introduced into it by those who, in the name of impartiality, would interdict the use of any theory whatever. No logical dogma could be more thoroughly irreconcilable with the spirit of the positive philosophy, or with its special character in regard to the study of social phenomena, than this. No real observation of any kind of phenomena is possible, except in as far as it is first directed, and finally interpreted, by some theory: and it was this logical need which, in the infancy of human reason, occasioned the rise of theological philosophy, as we shall see in the course of our historical survey. The positive philosophy does not dissolve this obligation, but, on the contrary, extends and fulfils it more and more, the further the relations of phenomena are multiplied and perfected by it. Hence it is clear that, scientifically speaking, all isolated, empirical observation is idle, and even radically uncertain; that science can use only those observations which are connected, at least hypothetically, with some law; that it is such a connection which makes the chief difference between scientific and popular observation, embracing the same facts, but contemplating them from different points of view: and that observations empirically conducted can at most supply provisional materials, which must usually undergo an ulterior revision. The rational method of observation becomes more necessary in proportion to the complexity of the phenomena, amidst which the observer would not know what he ought to look at in the facts before his eyes, but for the guidance of a preparatory theory; and thus it is that by the connection of foregoing facts we learn to see the facts that follow. This is undisputed with regard to astronomical, physical, and chemical research, and in every branch of biological study, in which good observation of its highly complex phenomena is still very rare, precisely because its positive theories are very imperfect. Carrying on the analogy, it is evident that in the corresponding divisions, statical and dynamical, of social science, there is more need than anywhere else of theories which shall scientifically connect the facts that are happening with those that have happened: and the more we reflect, the more distinctly we shall see that in proportion as known facts are mutually connected we shall be better able, not only to estimate, but to perceive, those which are yet unexplored. I am not blind to the vast difficulty which this requisition imposes on the institution of positive sociology,—obliging us to create at once, so to speak, observations and laws, on account of their indispensable connection, placing us in a sort of vicious circle, from which we can issue only by employing in the first instance materials which are badly elaborated, and doctrines which are ill-conceived. How I may succeed in a task so difficult and delicate, we shall see at its close; but, however that may be, it is clear that it is the absence of any positive theory which at present renders social observations so vague and incoherent. There can never be any lack of facts; for in this case even more than in others, it is the commonest sort of facts that are most important, whatever the collectors of secret anecdotes may think; but, though we are steeped to the lips in them, we can make no use of them, nor even be aware of them, for want of speculative guidance in examining them. The statical observation of a crowd of phenomena cannot take place without some notion, however elementary, of the laws of social interconnection: and dynamical facts could have no fixed direction if they were not attached, at least by a provisional hypothesis, to the laws of social development. The positive philosophy is very far from discouraging historical or any other erudition; but the precious night-watchings, now so lost in the laborious acquisition of a conscientious but barren learning, may be made available by it for the constitution of true social science, and the increased honour of the earnest minds that are devoted to it. The new philosophy will supply fresh and nobler subjects, unhoped-for insight, a loftier aim, and therefore a higher scientific dignity. It will discard none but aimless labours, without principle and without character; as in Physics, there is no room for compilations of empirical observations; and at the same time, philosophy will render justice to the zeal of students of a past generation, who, destitute of the favourable guidance which we, of this day, enjoy, followed up their laborious historical researches with an instinctive perseverance, and in spite of the superficial disdain of the philosophers of the time. No doubt, the same danger attends research here as elsewhere: the danger that, from the continuous use of scientific theories, the observer may sometimes pervert facts, by erroneously supposing them to verify some ill-grounded speculative prejudices of his own. But we have the same guard here as elsewhere,—in the further extension of the science: and the case would not be improved by a recurrence to empirical methods, which would be merely leaving theories that may be misapplied but can always be rectified, for imaginary notions which cannot be substantiated at all. Our feeble reason may often fail in the application of positive theories; but at least they transfer us from the domain of imagination to that of reality, and expose us infinitely less than any other kind of doctrine to the danger of seeing in facts that which is not.

It is now clear that social science requires, more than any other, the subordination of Observation to the statical and dynamical laws of phenomena. No social fact can have any scientific meaning till it is connected with some other social fact; without which connection it remains a mere anecdote, involving no rational utility. This condition so far increases the immediate difficulty that good observers will be rare at first, though more abundant than ever as the science expands: and here we meet with another confirmation of what I said at the outset of this volume,—that the formation of social theories should be confided only to the best organized minds, prepared by the most rational training. Explored by such minds, according to rational views of co-existence and succession, social phenomena no doubt admit of much more varied and extensive means of investigation than phenomena of less complexity. In this view, it is not only the immediate inspection or direct description of events that affords useful means of positive exploration; but the consideration of apparently insignificant customs, the appreciation of various kinds of monuments, the analysis and comparison of languages, and a multitude of other resources. In short, a mind suitably trained becomes able by exercise to convert almost all impressions from the events of life into sociological indications, when once the connection of all indications with the leading ideas of the science is understood. This is a facility afforded by the mutual relation of the various aspects of society, which may partly compensate for the difficulty caused by that mutual connection: if it renders observation more difficult, it affords more means for its prosecution.

It might be supposed beforehand that the second method of investigation, Experiment, must be wholly inapplicable in Social Science; but we shall find that the science is not entirely deprived of this resource, though it must be one of inferior value. We must remember (what was before explained) that there are

*Experiment.*

two kinds of experimentation,—the direct and the indirect: and that it is not necessary to the philosophical character of this method that the circumstances of the phenomenon in question should be, as is vulgarly supposed in the learned world, artificially instituted. Whether the case be natural or factitious, experimentation takes place whenever the regular course of the phenomenon is interfered with in any determinate manner. The spontaneous nature of the alteration has no effect on the scientific value of the case, if the elements are known. It is in this sense that experimentation is possible in Sociology. If direct experimentation had become too difficult amidst the complexities of biology, it may well be considered impossible in social science. Any artificial disturbance of any social element must affect all the rest, according to the laws both of co-existence and succession; and the experiment would therefore, if it could be instituted at all, be deprived of all scientific value, through the impossibility of isolating either the conditions or the results of the phenomenon. But we saw, in our survey of biology, that pathological cases are the true scientific equivalent of pure experimentation, and why. The same reasons apply, with even more force, to sociological researches. In them, pathological analysis consists in the examination of cases, unhappily too common, in which the natural laws, either of harmony or of succession, are disturbed by any causes, special or general, accidental or transient; as in revolutionary times especially, and above all, in our own. These disturbances are, in the social body, exactly analogous to diseases in the individual organism: and I have no doubt whatever that the analogy will be more evident (allowance being made for the unequal complexity of the organisms) the deeper the investigation goes. In both cases it is, as I said once before, a noble use to make of our reason, to disclose the real laws of our nature, individual or social, by the analysis of its sufferings. But if the method is imperfectly instituted in regard to biological questions, much more faulty must it be in regard to the phenomena of social science, for want even of the rational conceptions to which they are to be referred. We see the most disastrous political experiments for ever renewed, with only some insignificant and irrational modifications, though their first operation should have fully satisfied us of the uselessness and danger of the expedients proposed. Without forgetting how much is ascribable to the influence of human passions, we must remember that the deficiency of an authoritative rational analysis is one of the main causes of the barrenness imputed to social experiments, the course of which would become much more instructive if it were better observed. The great natural laws exist and act in all conditions of the organism; for, as we saw in the case of biology, it is an error to suppose that they are violated or suspended in the case of disease: and we are therefore justified in drawing our conclusions, with due caution, from the scientific analysis of disturbance to the positive theory of normal existence. This is the nature and character of the indirect experimentation which discloses the real economy of the social body in a more marked manner than simple observation could do. It is applicable to all orders of sociological research, whether relating to existence or to movement, and regarded under any aspect whatever, physical, intellectual, moral, or political; and to all degrees of the social evolution, from which, unhappily, disturbances have never been absent. As for its present extension, no one can venture to offer any statement of it, because it has never been duly applied in any investigation in political philosophy; and it can become customary only by the institution of the new science which I am endeavouring to establish. But I could not omit this notice of it, as one of the means of investigation proper to social science.

As for the third of those methods, Comparison, the reader must bear in mind the explanations offered, in our survey of biological philosophy, of the reasons why the comparative method must prevail in all studies of which the living organism is the subject; and the more remarkably, in proportion to the rank of the organism. The same considerations apply in the present case, in a more conspicuous degree; and I may leave it to the reader to make the application, merely pointing out the chief differences which distinguish the use of the comparative method in sociological inquiries.

*Comparison.*

It is a very irrational disdain which makes us object to

*Comparison with inferior animals.* all comparison between human society and the social state of the lower animals. This unphilosophical pride arose out of the protracted influence of the theologico-metaphysical philosophy; and it will be corrected by the positive philosophy, when we better understand and can estimate the social state of the higher orders of mammifers, for instance. We have seen how important is the study of individual life, in regard to intellectual and moral phenomena,—of which social phenomena are the natural result and complement. There was once the same blindness to the importance of the procedure in this case as now in the other; and, as it has given way in the one case, so it will in the other. The chief defect in the kind of sociological comparison that we want is that it is limited to statical consideration; whereas the dynamical are, at the present time, the preponderant and direct subject of science. The restriction results from the social state of animals being, though not so stationary as we are apt to suppose, yet susceptible only of extremely small variations, in no way comparable to the continued progression of humanity in its feeblest days. But there is no doubt of the scientific utility of such a comparison, in the statical province, where it characterizes the elementary laws of social interconnection, by exhibiting their action in the most imperfect state of society, so as even to suggest useful inductions in regard to human society. There cannot be a stronger evidence of the natural character of the chief social relations, which some people fancy that they can transform at pleasure. Such sophists will cease to regard the great ties of the human family as factitious and arbitrary when they find them existing, with the same essential characteristics, among the animals, and more conspicuously, the nearer the organisms approach to the human type. In brief, in all that part of sociology which is almost one with intellectual and moral biology, or with the natural history of Man; in all that relates to the first germs of the social relations, and the first institutions which were founded by the unity of the family or the tribe, there is not only great scientific advantage, but real philosophical necessity for employing the rational comparison of human with other animal societies. Perhaps it might even be desirable not to confine the comparison to societies which present a character of voluntary co-operation, in analogy to the human. They must always rank first in importance: but the scientific spirit, extending the process to its final logical term, might find some advantage in examining those strange associations, proper to the inferior animals, in which an involuntary co-operation results from an indissoluble organic union, either by simple adhesion or real continuity. If the science gained nothing by this extension, the method would. And there is nothing that can compare with such an habitual scientific comparison for the great service of casting out the absolute spirit which is the chief vice of political philosophy. It appears to me, moreover, that, in a practical view, the insolent pride which induces some ranks of society to suppose themselves as, in a manner, of another species than the rest of mankind, is in close affinity with the irrational disdain that repudiates all comparison between human and other animal nature. However all this may be, these considerations apply only to a methodical and special treatment of social philosophy. Here, where I can offer only the first conception of the science, in which dynamical considerations must prevail, it is evident that I can make little use of the kind of comparison; and this makes it all the more necessary to point it out, lest its omission should occasion such scientific inconveniences as I have just indicated. The commonest logical procedures are generally so characterized by their very application, that nothing more of a preliminary nature is needed than the simplest examination of their fundamental properties.

To indicate the order of importance of the forms of society which are to be studied by the Comparative Method, I begin with the chief method, which consists in a comparison of the different co-existing states of human society on the various parts of the earth's surface,—those states being completely independent of each other. By this method, the different stages of evolution may all be observed at once. Though the progression is single and uniform, in regard to the whole race, some very considerable and very various populations have, from causes which are little

*Comparison of co-existing states of society.*

understood, attained extremely unequal degrees of development, so that the former states of the most civilized nations are now to be seen, amidst some partial differences, among contemporary populations inhabiting different parts of the globe. In its relation to Observation, this kind of comparison offers the advantage of being applicable both to statical and dynamical inquiries, verifying the laws of both, and even furnishing occasionally valuable direct inductions in regard to both. In the second place, it exhibits all possible degrees of social evolution to our immediate observation. From the wretched inhabitants of Tierra del Fuego to the most advanced nations of western Europe, there is no social grade which is not extant in some points of the globe, and usually in localities which are clearly apart. In the historical part of this volume, we shall find that some interesting secondary phases of social development, of which the history of civilization leaves no perceptible traces, can be known only by this comparative method of study; and these are not, as might be supposed, the lowest degrees of evolution, which every one admits can be investigated in no other way. And between the great historical aspects, there are numerous intermediate states which must be observed thus, if at all. This second part of the comparative method verifies the indications afforded by historical analysis, and fills up the gaps it leaves: and nothing can be more rational than the method, as it rests upon the established principle that the development of the human mind is uniform in the midst of all diversities of climate, and even of race; such diversities having no effect upon anything more than the rate of progress.—But we must beware of the scientific dangers attending the process of comparison by this method. For instance, it can give us no idea of the order of succession, as it presents all the states of development as co-existing: so that, if the order of development were not established by other methods, this one would infallibly mislead us. And again, if we were not misled as to the order, there is nothing in this method which discloses the filiation of the different systems of society; a matter in which the most distinguished philosophers have been mistaken in various ways and degrees. Again, there is the danger of mistaking modifications for primary phases; as when social differences have been ascribed to the political influence of climate, instead of that inequality of evolution which is the real cause. Sometimes, but more rarely, the mistake is the other way. Indeed, there is nothing in the matter that can show which of two cases presents the diversity that is observed. We are in danger of the same mistake in regard to races; for, as the sociological comparison is instituted between peoples of different races, we are liable to confound the effects of race and of the social period. Again, climate comes in to offer a third source of interpretation of comparative phenomena, sometimes agreeing with, and sometimes contradicting the two others; thus multiplying the chances of error, and rendering the analysis which looked so promising almost impracticable. Here, again, we see the indispensable necessity of keeping in view the positive conception of human development as a whole. By this alone can we be preserved from such errors as I have referred to, and enriched by any genuine results of analysis. We see how absurd in theory and dangerous in practice are the notions and declamations of the empirical school, and of the enemies of all social speculation: for it is precisely in proportion to their elevation and generality that the ideas of positive social philosophy become real and effective,—all illusion and uselessness belonging to conceptions which are too narrow and too special, in the departments either of science or of reasoning. But it is a consequence from these last considerations that this first sketch of sociological science, with the means of investigation that belong to it, rests immediately upon the primary use of a new method of observation, which is so appropriate to the nature of the phenomena as to be exempt from the dangers inherent in the others. This last portion of the comparative method is the Historical Method, properly so called; and it is the only basis on which the system of political logic can rest.

The historical comparison of the consecutive states of humanity is not only the chief scientific device of the new political philosophy. Its rational development constitutes the substratum of the science, in whatever is essential to it. It is this

*Comparison of consecutive states.*

which distinguishes it thoroughly from biological science, as we shall presently see. The positive principle of this separation results from the necessary influence of human generations upon the generations that follow, accumulating continuously till it constitutes the preponderating consideration in the direct study of social development. As long as this preponderance is not directly recognized, the positive study of humanity must appear a simple prolongation of the natural history of Man: but this scientific character, suitable enough to the earlier generations, disappears in the course of the social evolution, and assumes at length a wholly new aspect, proper to sociological science, in which historical considerations are of immediate importance. And this preponderant use of the historical method gives its philosophical character to sociology in a logical, as well as a scientific sense. By the creation of this new department of the comparative method, sociology confers a benefit on the whole of natural philosophy; because the positive method is thus completed and perfected, in a manner which, for scientific importance, is almost beyond our estimate. What we can now comprehend is that the historical method verifies and applies, in the largest way, that chief quality of sociological science,—its proceeding from the whole to the parts. Without this permanent condition of social study, all historical labour would degenerate into being a mere compilation of provisional materials. As it is in their development especially that the various social elements are interconnected and inseparable, it is clear that any partial filiation must be essentially untrue. Where, for instance, is the use of any exclusive history of any one science or art, unless meaning is given to it by first connecting it with the study of human progress generally? It is the same in every direction, and especially with regard to political history, as it is called,—as if any history could be other than political, more or less! The prevailing tendency to speciality in study would reduce history to a mere accumulation of unconnected delineations, in which all idea of the true filiation of events would be lost amidst the mass of confused descriptions. If the historical comparisons of the different periods of civilization are to have any scientific character, they must be referred to the general social evolution : and it is only thus that we can obtain the guiding ideas by which the special studies themselves must be directed.

In a practical view, it is evident that the preponderance of the historical method tends to develop the social sentiment, by giving us an immediate interest in even the earliest experiences of our race, through the influence that they exercised over the evolution of our own civilization. As Condorcet observed, no enlightened man can think of the battles of Marathon and Salamis without perceiving the importance of their consequences to the race at large. This kind of feeling should, when we are treating of science, be carefully distinguished from the sympathetic interest which is awakened by all delineations of human life,—in fiction as well as in history. The sentiment I refer to is deeper, because in some sort personal; and more reflective, because it results from scientific conviction. It cannot be excited by popular history, in a descriptive form ; but only by positive history, regarded as a true science, and exhibiting the events of human experience in co-ordinated series which manifest their own graduated connection. This new form of the social sentiment must at first be the privilege of the choice few ; but it will be extended, somewhat weakened in force, to the whole of society, in proportion as the general results of social physics become sufficiently popular. It will fulfil the most obvious and elementary idea of the habitual connection between individuals and contemporary nations, by showing that the successive generations of men concur in a final end, which requires the determinate participation of each and all. This rational disposition to regard men of all times as fellow-workers is as yet visible in the case of only the most advanced sciences. By the philosophical preponderance of the historical method, it will be extended to all the aspects of human life, so as to sustain, in a reflective temper, that respect for our ancestors which is indispensable to a sound state of society and so deeply disturbed at present by the metaphysical philosophy.

As for the course to be pursued by this method,—it appears to me that its spirit consists in the rational use of social series; that is, in a successive estimate of the different states of humanity which shall show the growth of each disposition, physical, intellectual, moral, or political, combined with the decline of the opposite disposition, whence we may obtain a scientific prevision of the final ascendancy of the one and extinction of the other,—care being taken to frame our conclusions according to the laws of human development. A considerable accuracy of prevision may thus be obtained, for any determinate period, and with any particular views; as historical analysis will indicate the direction of modifications, even in the most disturbed times. And it is worth noticing that the prevision will be nearest the truth in proportion as the phenomena in question are more important and more general; because then continuous causes are predominant in the social movement; and disturbances have less power. From these first general aspects, the same rational certainty may extend to secondary and special aspects, through their statical relations with the first; and thus we may obtain conclusions sufficiently accurate for the application of principles.

If we desire to familiarize ourselves with this historical method, we must employ it first upon the past, by endeavouring to deduce every well-known historical situation from the whole series of its antecedents. In every science we must have learned to predict the past, so to speak, before we can predict the future; because the first use of the observed relations among fulfilled facts is to teach us by the anterior succession what the future succession will be. No examination of facts can explain our existing state to us, if we have not ascertained, by historical study, the value of the elements at work; and thus it is in vain that statesmen insist on the necessity of political observation, while they look no further than the present, or a very recent past. The present is, by itself, purely misleading, because it is impossible to avoid confounding principal with secondary facts, exalting conspicuous transient manifestations over fundamental tendencies, which are generally very quiet; and above all, supposing those powers, institutions, and doctrines, to be in the ascendant, which are, in fact, in their decline. It is clear that the only adequate corrective of all this is a philosophical understanding of the past;

that the comparison cannot be decisive unless it embraces the whole of the past; and that the sooner we stop, in travelling up the vista of time, the more serious will be the mistakes we fall into. Before our very eyes, we see statesmen going no further back than the last century, to obtain an explanation of the confusion in which we are living: the most abstract of politicians may take in the preceding century, but the philosophers themselves hardly venture beyond the sixteenth; so that those who are striving to find the issue of the revolutionary period have actually no conception of it as a whole, though that whole is itself only a transient phase of the general social movement.

The most perfect methods may, however, be rendered deceptive by misuse: and this we must bear in mind. We have seen that mathematical analysis itself may betray us into substituting signs for ideas, and that it conceals inanity of conception under an imposing verbiage. The difficulty in the case of the historical method in sociology is in applying it, on account of the extreme complexity of the materials we have to deal with. But for this, the method would be entirely safe. The chief danger is of our supposing a continuous decrease to indicate a final extinction, or the reverse; as in mathematics it is a common sophism to confound continuous variations, more or less, with unlimited variations. To take a strange and very marked example: if we consider that part of social development which relates to human food, we cannot but observe that men take less food as they advance in civilization. If we compare savage with more civilized peoples, in the Homeric poems or in the narratives of travellers, or compare country with town life, or any generation with the one that went before, we shall find this curious result,— the sociological law of which we shall examine hereafter. The laws of individual human nature aid in the result by making intellectual and moral action more preponderant as Man becomes more civilized. The fact is thus established, both by the experimental and the logical way. Yet nobody supposes that men will ultimately cease to eat. In this case, the absurdity saves us from a false conclusion; but in other cases, the complexity disguises much error in the experiment and the reasoning. In the above instance, we must resort to the laws of our nature for that verification which, taken all together, they afford to our sociological analysis. As the social phenomenon, taken as a whole, is simply a development of humanity, without any real creation of faculties, all social manifestations must be to be found, if only in their germ, in the primitive type which biology constructed by anticipation for sociology. Thus every law of social succession disclosed by the historical method must be unquestionably connected, directly or indirectly, with the positive theory of human nature; and all inductions which cannot stand this test will prove to be illusory, through some sort of insufficiency in the observations on which they are grounded. The main scientific strength of sociological demonstrations must ever lie in the accordance between the conclusions of historical analysis and the preparatory conceptions of the biological theory. And thus we find, look where we will, a confirmation of that chief intellectual character of the new science,—the philosophical preponderance of the spirit of the whole over the spirit of detail.

This method ranks, in sociological science, with that of zoological comparison in the study of individual life; and we shall see, as we proceed, that the succession of social states exactly corresponds, in a scientific sense, with the gradation of organisms in biology; and the social series, once clearly established, must be as real and as useful as the animal series. When the method has been used long enough to disclose its properties, I am disposed to think that it will be regarded as so very marked a modification of positive research as to deserve a separate place; so that, in addition to Observation, properly so called, Experiment, and Comparison, we shall have the Historical Method, as a fourth and final mode of the art of observing. It will be derived, according to the usual course, from the mode which immediately precedes it: and it will be applied to the analysis of the most complex phenomena.

*Promise of a fourth method.*

I must be allowed to point out that the new political philosophy, sanctioning the old leadings of popular reason, restores to History all its scientific rights as a basis of wise social speculation, after the metaphysical philosophy had striven to induce us to discard all large considerations of the past. In the foregoing departments of natural philosophy we have seen that the positive spirit, instead of being disturbing in its tendencies, is remarkable for confirming, in the essential parts of every science, the inestimable intuitions of popular good sense; of which indeed science is merely a systematic prolongation, and which a barren metaphysical philosophy alone could despise. In this case, so far from restricting the influence which human reason has ever attributed to history in political combinations, the new social philosophy increases it, radically and eminently. It asks from history something more than counsel and instruction to perfect conceptions which are derived from another source: it seeks its own general direction, through the whole system of historical conclusions.

Having reviewed the general character of Sociology, and its means of investigation, we must next make out its relations to the other principal sciences.

## CHAPTER IV.

### RELATION OF SOCIOLOGY TO THE OTHER DEPARTMENTS OF POSITIVE PHILOSOPHY.

THE conditions of the positive philosophy with regard to this science are not fulfilled till its relations with the other sciences are ascertained. Its establishment in its proper place in the hierarchy is a principle of such importance that it may be seen to comprehend all the philosophical requisites for its institution as a science: and it is for want of this that all attempts in our time to treat social questions in a positive manner have failed. Whether we consider the indispensable data of various kinds supplied to sociology by the other sciences, or the yet more important requisite of the sound speculative habits formed by the preparatory study of them, the daily spectacle of abortive attempts to construct a social science leaves no doubt that this grand omission is the cause of the failure, and of the wrong direction always taken, sooner or later, by minds which seemed fitted to accomplish something better. We must, then, review the relation of this last of the sciences to all the rest; but our examination of each of them, and of biology especially, has so anticipated this part of my subject, that I may pass over it very briefly.

It is a new idea that the science of society is thus connected with the rest: yet in no case is the relation more unquestionable or more marked. Social phenomena exhibit, in even a higher degree, the complexity, speciality, and personality which distinguish the higher phenomena of the individual life. In order to see how this establishes the connection in question, we must remember that in the social, as in the biological case, there are two classes of considerations:—that of Man or Humanity, which constitutes the phenomenon, and that of the medium or environment, which influences this partial and secondary development of one of the animal races. Now, by the first term of this couple, sociology is subordinated to the whole of the organic philosophy, which discloses to us the laws of human nature: and by the second, it is connected with the whole system of inorganic philosophy, which reveals to us the exterior conditions of human existence. One of the two great divisions of philosophy, in short, determines the agent concerned in sociological phenomena, and the other the medium in which it is developed. It is clear that we here take together, and treat as one, the three sections of inorganic philosophy,—chemistry, physics, and astronomy, —as they all relate equally to the social medium. It will be enough if we point out the participation of each, as the occasion arises. As to the Method, properly so called, it is, as we have seen, more and more necessary to subject studies to the graduated system of prior studies, in proportion to their increasing complexity. These are the two points we have to consider in surveying once more the encyclopedical scale, beginning, as before, with the relations which are the closest and most direct. We shall afterwards have to exhibit the reaction, scientific and logical, which sociology, once instituted, must exercise, in its turn, on the whole of the preceding sciences:—a reaction which is, as yet, even less suspected than the primary action itself.

The subordination of social science to biology is so evident that nobody denies it in statement, however it may be neglected in practice. *Relation to Biology.* This contrariety between the statement and the practice is due to something else, besides the faulty condition of social studies: it results also from the imperfection of biological science; and especially from its most conspicuous imperfection of all,—that of its highest part, relating to intellectual and moral phenomena. It is by this portion that biology and sociology are the most closely connected; and cerebral physiology is too recent, and its scientific state is too immature, to have admitted, as yet, of any proper organization of the relations of the two sciences. Whenever the time for that process arrives, the connection will be seen to bear two aspects. Under the first, biology will be seen to afford the starting-point of all social speculation, in accordance with the analysis of the social faculties of Man, and of the organic conditions which determine its character. But, moreover, as we can scarcely at all investigate the most elementary terms of the social series, we must construct them by applying the positive theory of human nature to the aggregate of corresponding circumstances,—regarding the small materials that we are able to obtain as rather adapted to facilitate and improve this rational determination than to show us what society really is at so early a period. When the social condition has advanced so far as to exclude this kind of deduction, the second aspect presents itself; and the biological theory of man is implicated with the sociological in a less direct and special manner. The whole social evolution of the race must proceed in entire accordance with biological laws; and social phenomena must always be founded on the necessary invariableness of the human organism, the characteristics of which, physical, intellectual, and moral, are always found to be essentially the same, and related in the same manner, at every degree of the social scale,—no development of them attendant upon the social condition ever altering their nature in the least, nor, of course, creating or destroying any faculties whatever, or transposing their influence. No sociological view can therefore be admitted, at any stage of the science, or under any appearance of historical induction, that is contradictory to the known laws of human nature. No view can be admitted, for instance, which supposes a very marked character of goodness or wickedness to exist in the majority of men; or which represents the sympathetic affections as prevailing over the personal ones; or the intellectual over the affective faculties, etc. In cases like these, which are more common than the imperfection of the biological theory would lead us to expect, all sociological principles must be as carefully submitted to ulterior correction as if they supposed human life to be extravagantly long, or contravened, in any other way, the physical laws of humanity; because the intellectual and moral conditions of human existence are as real and as imperative as its material conditions, though more difficult to estimate, and therefore less known. Thus, in a biological view, all existing political doctrines are radically vicious, because, in their irrational estimate of political phenomena, they suppose qualities to exist among rulers and the ruled, —here an habitual perverseness or imbecility, and there a spirit of concert or calculation,—which are incompatible with positive ideas of human nature, and which would impute pathological monstrosity to whole classes; which is simply absurd. An example like this shows what valuable resources positive sociology must derive from its subordination to biology; and especially in regard to cerebral physiology, whenever it comes to be studied as it ought.

The students of biology have, however, the same tendency to exalt their own science at the expense of that which follows it, that physicists and chemists have shown in regard to biology. The biologists lose sight of historical observation altogether, and represent sociology as a mere corollary of the science of Man; in the same way that physicists and chemists treat biology as a mere derivative from the inorganic philosophy. The injury to science is great in both cases. If we neglect historical comparison, we can understand nothing of the social evolution; and the chief phenomenon in sociology,—the phenomenon which marks its scientific originality,—that is, the gradual and continuous influence of generations upon each other,—would be disguised or unnoticed, for want of the necessary key—historical analysis. From the time that the influence of former generations becomes the cause of any modification of the social movement, the mode of investigation must accord with the nature of the phenomena; and historical analysis therefore becomes preponderant, while biological considerations, which explained the earliest movements of society, cease to be more than a valuable auxiliary and means of control. It is the same thing as when, in the study of inorganic science, men quit deduction for direct observation. It is the same thing as when, in biology, observers proceed from contemplating the organism and its medium, to analyse the ages of the individual being, as a principal means of investigation. The only difference is that the change in the instrument is the more necessary the more complex are the phenomena to be studied. This would have been seen at once, and political philosophy would have been admitted to depend on this condition for its advance, but for the prevalence of the vicious absolute spirit in social speculation, which, neglecting the facts of the case, for ever strives to subject social considerations to the absolute conception of an immutable political type, no less adverse to the relative spirit of positive philosophy than theological and metaphysical types, though less indefinite. The consequence of this error is that social modifications proper to certain periods, and passing away with them, are too often supposed to be inherent in human nature, and therefore indestructible. Even Gall, attending only to imperfect physiological considerations, and neglecting the social, wandered off into a sort of scientific declamation on the subject of war, declaring the military tendencies of mankind to be immutable, notwithstanding the mass of historical testimony which shows that the warlike disposition diminishes as human development proceeds. A multitude of examples of this kind of mistake might be presented; the most striking of which are perhaps in connection with theories of education, which are usually formed on absolute principles, to the neglect of the corresponding state of civilization.

The true nature of sociology is evident enough from what has been said. We see that it is not an appendix to biology, but a science by itself, founded upon a distinct basis, while closely connected, from first to last, with biology. Such is the scientific view of it. As to the method, the logical analogy of the two sciences is so clear as to leave no doubt that social philosophers must prepare their understandings for their work by due discipline in biological methods. This is necessary, not only to put them in possession of the general spirit of investigation proper to organic science, but yet more to familiarize them with the comparative method, which is the grand resource of investigation in both sciences. Moreover, there is a most valuable philosophical principle common to both sciences which remains to be fully developed before it can attain its final prevalence;—I mean the positive version of the dogma of final causes, discussed before in connection with the conditions of vital existence. This principle, being the necessary result of the distinction between the statical and the dynamical condition, belongs eminently to the study of living bodies, in which that distinction is especially marked, and where alone the general idea of it can properly be acquired. But, great as is its direct use in the study of individual life, it is applicable in a much more extensive and essential way in social science. It is by means of this principle that the new philosophy, uniting the two philosophical meanings of the word *necessary*, exhibits as inevitable that which first presents itself as indispensable; and the converse. There must be something in it peculiarly in harmony with social investigations, as we are led up to it by the most opposite methods of approach; one evidence of which is De Maistre's fine political aphorism, "Whatever is necessary exists."

If sociology is thus subordinated to biology, it must be scientifically related to the whole system of inorganic philosophy, because biology is so. But it is also connected with that system by immediate relations of its own.   *Relation to Inorganic philosophy.*

In the first place, it is only by the inorganic philosophy that we can duly analyse the entire system of exterior conditions, chemical, physical, and astronomical, amidst which the social evolution proceeds, and by which its rate of progress is determined. Social phenomena can no more be understood apart from their environment than those of individual life. All exterior disturbances which could affect the life of individual Man must change his social existence; and, conversely, his social existence could not be seriously disturbed by any modifications of the medium which should not derange his separate condition. I need, therefore, only refer to what I have said in regard to the influence of astronomical and other conditions on vital existence; for the same considerations bear on the case of social phenomena. It is plain that society, as well as individual beings, is affected by the circumstances of the earth's daily rotation and annual movement; and by states of heat, moisture, and electricity in the surrounding medium; and by the chemical conditions of the atmosphere, the waters, the soil, etc. I need only observe that the effect of these influences is even more marked in sociology than in biology, not only because the organism is more complex, and its phenomena of a higher order, but because the social organism is regarded as susceptible of indefinite duration, so as to render sensible many gradual modifications which would be disguised from our notice by the brevity of individual life. Astronomical conditions, above all others, manifest their importance to living beings only by passing from the individual to the social case. Much smaller disturbances would visibly affect a social condition than would disturb an individual life, which requires a smaller concurrence of favourable circumstances. For instance, the dimensions of the globe are scientifically more important in sociology than in biology, because they set bounds to the ultimate extension of population; a circumstance worthy of grave consideration in any positive system of political speculation. And this is only one case of very many. If we consider, in regard to dynamical conditions, what would be the effect of any change in the degree of obliquity of the ecliptic, in the stability of the poles of rotation, and yet more in the eccentricity of the earth's orbit, we shall see that vast changes in social life must be produced by causes which could not endanger individual existence. One of the first reflections that presents itself is that positive sociology was not possible till the inorganic philosophy had reached a certain degree of precision. The very conception of stability in human association could not be positively established till the discovery of gravitation had assured us of the permanence of the conditions of life; and till physics and chemistry had taught us that the surface of our planet has attained a natural condition, apart from accidents too rare and too partial to affect our estimate; or, at least, that the crust of the globe admits of only variations so limited and so gradual as not to interfere with the natural course of social development,—a development which could not be hoped for under any liability to violent and frequent physico-chemical convulsions of any extent in the area of human life. There is thus more room to apprehend that inorganic philosophy is not advanced enough to supply the conditions of a positive polity, than to suppose that any real political philosophy can be framed in independence of inorganic science. We have seen before, however, that there is a perpetual accordance between the possible and the indispensable. What we must have, we are able to obtain; and if there are, as in the case of the mutual action of different starry systems, cosmical ideas which are inaccessible to us, we know, in regard to sociology now, as to biology before, that they are of no practical importance to us. Wherever we look, over the whole field of science, we shall find that, amidst the great imperfection of inorganic philosophy, it is sufficiently advanced, in all essential respects, to contribute to the constitution of true social science, if we only have the prudence to postpone to a future time investigations which would now be premature.

I observed in a former chapter that no disturbing causes, acting on social development, could do more than affect its rate of progress. This is true of the operation of influences from the inorganic world, as of all others. In our review of biology we saw that the human being cannot be modified indefinitely by exterior circumstances; that such modifications can affect only the degrees of phenomena, without at all changing their nature; and again, that when the disturbing influences exceed their general limits, the organism is no longer modified, but destroyed. All this is, if possible, more eminently true of the social than of the individual organism, on account of its higher complexity and position. The course of its development must therefore be regarded as belonging to the essence of the phenomenon itself, and therefore essentially identical in all conceivable hypotheses about the corresponding medium. It is true we can easily imagine, as I said just now, that so delicate an evolution may be prevented by external disturbances, and particularly astronomical perturbations, which would not destroy the race; but as long as the evolution does proceed, it must be supposed subject to the same essential laws, and varying only in its speed, as it traverses the stages of which it is composed, without their succession or their final tendency being ever changed. Such a change would be beyond the power of even biological causes. If, for instance, we admitted some marked alterations in the human organism, or, what comes to the same thing, conceived of the social development of another animal race, we must always suppose a common course of general development. Such is the philosophical condition imposed by the nature of the subject, which could not become positive, except in as far as it could be thus conceived of; and this is much more conspicuously true in regard to inorganic causes. As to the rest, this is only another illustration of what we have so often seen in the course of our survey of the scientific hierarchy,—that if the less general phenomena occur under the necessary preponderance of the more general, this subordination cannot in any way alter their proper laws, but only the extent and duration of their real manifestations.

*Man's action on the external world.* One consideration remains, of the more importance because it applies especially to physico-chemical knowledge, which we seem to have rather neglected in this sketch for astronomical doctrine: I mean the considerations of Man's action on the external world, the gradual development of which affords one of the chief aspects of the social evolution, and without which the evolution could not have taken place as a whole, as it would have been stopped at once by the preponderance of the material obstacles proper to the human condition. In short, all human progress, political, moral, or intellectual, is inseparable from material progression, in virtue of the close interconnection which, as we have seen, characterizes the natural course of social phenomena. Now, it is clear that the action of Man upon nature depends chiefly on his knowledge of the laws of inorganic phenomena, though biological phenomena must also find a place in it. We must bear in mind, too, that physics, and yet more chemistry, form the basis of human power, since astronomy, notwithstanding its eminent participation in it, concurs not as an instrument for modifying the medium, but by prevision. Here we have another ground on which to exhibit the impossibility of any rational study of social development otherwise than by combining sociological speculations with the whole of the doctrines of inorganic philosophy.

*Necessary Education.* It cannot be necessary to repeat here that which has been established as true with regard to the other sciences, and which is more conspicuously true as each science becomes more complex,—that an adequate general knowledge of all the preceding sciences in the hierarchy is requisite to the understanding of the one that follows. In the case of sociology the absence of this preparation is the obvious cause of the failure of all attempts to regenerate the science. We desire to recognize in it a positive science, while we leave the conditions of positivity unfulfilled. We do not even form a just idea of the attributes of positivism, of what constitutes the explanation of a phenomenon, of the conditions of genuine investigation, or of the true intention in which hypotheses should be instituted and employed. We must thoroughly understand all these conditions, and use them in the natural order of the development of the sciences, venturing neither to select nor transpose, but following up the increasing complexity of the sciences, and recognizing the increase of resources which accompanies it, from astronomy with its simplicity of phenomena and of means of research, to sociology with its prodigious complexity and abundance of resources. Such discipline as this may be difficult; but it is indispensable. It is the only preparatory education which can introduce the positive spirit into the formation of social theories.

It is clear that this education must rest on a basis of mathematical philosophy, even apart from the necessity of mathematics to the study of inorganic philosophy. *Mathematical preparation.* It is only in the region of mathematics that sociologists, or anybody else, can obtain a true sense of scientific evidence, and form the habit of rational and decisive argumentation; can, in short, learn to fulfil the logical conditions of all positive speculations, by studying universal positivism at its source. This training, obtained and employed with the more care on account of the eminent difficulty of social science, is what sociologists have to seek in mathematics. As for any application of number and of a mathematical law to sociological problems, if such a method is inadmissible in biology, it must be yet more decisively so here, for reasons of which I have already said enough. The only error of this class which would have deserved express notice, if we had not condemned it by anticipation, is the pretension of some geometers to render social

*Pretended theory of chances.* investigations positive by subjecting them to a fanciful mathematical theory of chances. This error is in analogy with that of biologists who would make sociology to be a corollary or appendix to their own science by suppressing the function of historical analysis. The error of the geometers is however by far the worst of the two, in itself, as well as because mathematicians are peculiarly tenacious of error, from the abstract character of their labours, which dispenses them from the close study of nature. Gross as is the illusion, we must remember its excusable origin. It was James Bernouilli who first conceived the notion; and the notion affords evidence of the nascent need to subject social theories to some kind of positivity. None but a high order of mind could have so early felt the need; and if the expedient was vicious, there was no better way discernible by any possibility at that time. The error was much less pardonable when the notion was reproduced by Condorcet, in a more direct and systematic way; and his expectation from it, as manifested in his celebrated posthumous work, shows the fluctuating state of his mind in regard to the primary conception of social science. But there is no excuse for Laplace's repetition of such a philosophical mistake, at a time when the general human mind had begun to discern the true spirit of political philosophy, prepared as it was for the disclosure by the labours of Montesquieu and Condorcet himself, and powerfully stimulated besides by a new convulsion of society. From that time a succession of imitators has gone on repeating the fancy, in heavy algebraic language, without adding anything new, abusing the credit which justly belongs to the true mathematical spirit; so that, instead of being, as it was a century ago, a token of a premature instinct of scientific investigation, this error is now only an involuntary testimony to the absolute impotence of the political philosophy that would employ it. It is impossible to conceive of a more irrational conception than that which takes for its basis or for its operative method a supposed mathematical theory, in which, signs being taken for ideas, we subject numerical probability to calculation, which amounts to the same thing as offering our own ignorance as the natural measure of the degree of probability of our various opinions. While true mathematical theories have made great progress, for a century past, this absurd doctrine has undergone no improvement, except in some matters of abstract calculation which it has given rise to. It still abides in the midst of its circle of original errors, while mankind are learning, more and more, that the strongest proof of the reality of speculation in any science whatever is the fruitfulness of the conceptions belonging to it.

It is with a feeling of shame that I revert so often to the great maxims of philosophical pursuit, and dwell on them so long; that I should have to announce at this time of day that we must study simpler phenomena before proceeding to the more complex; and that we should acquaint ourselves with the agent of any phenomenon, and with the medium or circumstances, before we proceed to analyse it. But so different has been the course of political study pursued in the metaphysical school, that I rather apprehend that this high scientific connection will be exactly the part of my philosophical doctrine which will be least appreciated, and perhaps most contested, even after all the confirmation which I am about to offer. The reason of this apprehension is that the positive method is in direct opposition to our political habit of appealing to all sorts of minds on social questions, which they are expected to judge of, without any regular preparation, as if these problems were occasions for inspired decision. It is this consideration which makes me attach so special an importance to an explanation of the relation of Sociology to the other sciences.

To complete the account of these encyclopedic relations, we must look at the connection in an inverse way, estimating the philosophical reaction of social physics on all the foregoing sciences, in regard both to doctrine and method.—It must be at the end of the work that I must treat of Sociology as completing the whole body of philosophy, and showing that the various sciences are branches from a single trunk; and thereby giving a character of unity to the variety of special studies that are now scattered abroad in a fatal dispersion. In this place I can only point out, in a more special manner, the immediate reaction of Sociology on all the rest of natural

*Reaction of Sociology.*

philosophy in virtue of its own scientific and logical properties.

As to doctrine. In regard to the doctrine, the essential principle of this reaction is found in the consideration that all scientific speculations whatever, in as far as they are human labours, must necessarily be subordinated to the true general theory of human evolution. If we could conceive of such a thing as this theory being so perfected as that no intellectual obstacle should limit the abundance of its most exact deductions, it is clear that the scientific hierarchy would be, as it were, inverted, and would present the different sciences, in an *à priori* way, as mere parts of this single science. We have no power to realize such a state of things; but the mere supposition may enable us to comprehend the legitimate general intervention of true social science in all possible classes of human speculation. At first sight, it appears as if this high intervention must belong to the biological theory of our nature; and it was by that avenue that philosophers first caught a glimpse of the conception: and it is perfectly true that the knowledge of the individual man must exert a secret, but inevitable influence over all the sciences, because our labours bear the ineffaceable impress of the faculties which produce them. But a close examination will convince us that this universal influence must belong more to the theory of social evolution that to that of individual Man, for the reason that the development of the human mind can take place only through the social state, the direct consideration of which must therefore prevail whenever we are treating of any results of that development. This is, then, in the briefest form, the first philosophical ground of the intellectual intervention of social physics in the cultivation of all the parts of natural philosophy. There will be more to say about it hereafter.

It is evident that Sociology must perfect the study of the essential relations which unite the different sciences, as this inquiry constitutes an essential part of social statics, directly intended to disclose the laws of such a connection, in the same way as in all cases of connection between any of the elements of our civilization. The most marked instance of this operation of social science is in the direct study of social dynamics, in virtue of the principle, so familiar to us by this time, that true co-ordination must be disclosed by the natural course of the common development. All scientific men who have viewed their own particular subject in a large way have felt what important benefit might be afforded by corresponding historical information, by regulating the spontaneous expansion of scientific discoveries, and warning away from deceptive or premature attempts. I need not set forth the value that there would be in a history of the sciences, which is keenly felt by all who have made any important discovery in any science whatever: but, as my last chapter proves, no real scientific history,—no theory of the true filiation of eminent discoveries, at present exists, in any form or degree. We have only compilations of materials more or less rational, which may be of some provisional use, but which cannot be afterwards employed in the construction of any historical doctrine without strict revision, and which are certainly in their present state unfit to yield any happy scientific suggestions. When a true social science shall have been founded, such labours will assume the philosophical direction of which they are at present destitute, and will aid that development of human genius which now, in the form of unorganized erudition, they merely impede. If we remember that no science can be thoroughly comprehended till its history is understood, we shall see what special improvements this new science must introduce into each of the rest, as well as into the co-ordination of them all.

This leads us to consider the reaction of sociology on the other sciences in regard to Method. Without entering at present upon the great subject of a general theory of the positive method, I must just point out the established truth that each of the fundamental sciences specially manifests one of the chief attributes of the universal positive method, though all are present, in more or less force, in each science. The special resource of sociology is that it participates directly in the elementary composition of the common ground of our intellectual resources. It is plain that this logical co-operation of the new science is as important as that of any of the anterior sciences. We have seen that sociology adds to

*As to Method.*

our other means of research that which I have called the *historical method*, and which will hereafter, when we are sufficiently habituated to it, constitute a fourth fundamental means of observation. But, though sociology has given us this resource, it is more or less applicable to all orders of scientific speculation. We have only to regard every discovery, at the moment it is effected, as a true social phenomenon, forming a part of the general series of human development, and, on that ground, subject to the laws of succession, and the methods of investigation which characterize that great evolution. From this starting-point, indisputable in its rationality, we comprehend immediately the whole necessary universality of the historical method, thenceforth disclosed in all its eminent intellectual dignity. We can even see that, by this method, scientific discoveries become in a certain degree susceptible of rational prevision, by means of an exact estimate of the anterior movement of the science, interpreted by the laws of the course of the human mind. The historical precision can hardly become very precise; but it may furnish preparatory indications of the general direction of the contemporary progress, so as to save the vast waste of intellectual forces which is occasioned by conjectural attempts, usually doomed to failure. By this process of comparison of the present with the past, in regard to each science, it must become possible to subject the art of discovery to a kind of rational theory which may guide the instinctive efforts of individual genius, which cannot hold its course apart from the general mind, however persuaded it may be of its separation. The historical method will thus, by governing the systematic use of all other scientific methods, impart to them an amplitude of rationality in which they are now deficient, by transferring to the whole that regulated progression which at present belongs only to the details: and the choice of subjects for investigation, till now almost arbitrary, or, at least thoroughly empirical, will acquire, in a certain degree, that scientific character which now belongs only to the partial investigation of each of them.—The method itself must, if it is to accomplish these purposes, be subject to the philosophical conditions imposed by the positive spirit of sociology. It must never consider the development of each complete science, separately from the total progression of the human mind, or even from the fundamental evolution of humanity. Thus social physics, which supplies this method, must superintend its gradual application,—at least, in so far as the general conception of human development is concerned. Every partial or isolated use of this method of investigation, such as suits the desultory character of research in our day, would be either wholly ineffectual, or would realize but little good. There are some traces in existing science of this superior means of speculation, the positive method being uniform, and therefore to be found everywhere if anywhere; but its complexity and its recent origin prevent our being able to point to examples at once marked and varied enough to afford a decisive manifestation. Throughout the whole range of our positive knowledge, I know of only one unquestionable example; and that will be found, where we should naturally look for it, in mathematical science. We find it in the sublime prefatory chapters of the different sections of the "Analytical Mechanics," so little appreciated by ordinary geometers because they do not contain a single formula, but, in my opinion, proving the eminent philosophical superiority of Lagrange to all mathematicians since Descartes and Leibnitz. By his exposition of the filiation of the chief conceptions of the human mind in regard to rational mechanics, from the origin of the science to our own time, Lagrange certainly anticipated the general spirit of the historical method; because he made this estimate the basis of the whole of his own scientific speculations. These remarkable writings are admirable food for meditation not only to geometers, but to all philosophical minds, which may find here the only example of what may properly be called History, though their author made no pretension to the common title of historian.

Thus we see that the reaction of Sociology on the other sciences is as important in a logical as in a scientific view. On the one hand, positive sociology mutually connects all the sciences, and on the other hand, it adds to all resources for investigation, a new and a higher method. While, from its nature, dependent on all that went before, Social Physics repays as much as it receives by its two kinds of service towards all other knowledge. We can already perceive that such a science must form the principal band of the scientific sheaf, from its various relations, both of subordination and of direction, to all the rest. It is in this way that the homogeneous co-ordination of real sciences proceeds from their positive development, instead of being derived from any anti-scientific conceptions of a fanciful unity of different phenomena, such as have hitherto been almost exclusively resorted to.

*Speculative rank of Sociology.* Social science must always remain inferior in all important speculative respects to all the other fundamental sciences. Yet we cannot but feel, after this review of its spirit, its function, and its resources, that the abundance of its means of investigation may establish it in a higher position of rationality than the present state of the human mind might seem to promise. The unity of the subject, notwithstanding its prodigious extent, the conspicuous interconnection of its various aspects, its characteristic advance from the most general to more and more special researches, and finally the more frequent and important use of *à priori* considerations through suggestions furnished by the anterior sciences, and especially by the biological theory of human nature, may authorize the highest hopes of the speculative dignity of the science,—higher hopes than can be excited by such an imperfect realization as I propose to sketch out, the purpose of which is to embody, in a direct manner, and by sensible manifestations, the more abstract view which I have now taken of the general nature of this new political philosophy, and of the scientific spirit which should regulate its ulterior construction.

## CHAPTER V.

### SOCIAL STATICS; OR, THEORY OF THE SPONTANEOUS ORDER OF HUMAN SOCIETY.

THOUGH the dynamical part of Social Science is the most interesting, the most easily intelligible, and the fittest to disclose the laws of interconnection, still the Statical part must not be entirely passed over. We must briefly review in this place the conditions and laws of harmony of human society, and complete our statical conceptions, as far as the nascent state of the science allows, when we afterwards survey the historical development of humanity.

Every sociological analysis supposes three classes of considerations, each more complex than the preceding: viz., the conditions of social existence of the individual, the family, and society; the last comprehending, in a scientific sense, the whole of the human species, and chiefly, the whole of the white race. *Three aspects.*

Gall's cerebral theory has destroyed for ever the metaphysical fancies of the last century about the origin of Man's social tendencies, which are now proved to be inherent in his nature, and not the result of utilitarian considerations. The true theory has exploded the mistakes through which the false doctrine arose,—the fanciful supposition that intellectual combinations govern the general conduct of human life, and the exaggerated notion of the degree in which wants can create faculties. Independently of the guidance afforded by Gall's theory, there is a conclusive evidence against the utilitarian origin of society in the fact that the utility did not, and could not, manifest itself till after a long preparatory development of the society which it was supposed to have created. We shall the better see how the supposition involves us in a vicious circle if we attend *1. The Individual.*

to the character of the early ages of humanity, in which the individual advantages of association are very doubtful, if indeed we may not safely say that, in many cases, the burdens are greater than the resources, as we see only too plainly in the lowest ranks of the most advanced societies. It is thus evident that the social state would never have existed if its rise had depended on a conviction of its individual utility, because the benefit could never have been anticipated by individuals of any degree of ability, but could only manifest itself after the social evolution had proceeded up to a certain point. There are even sophists who at this day deny the utility, without being pronounced mad; and the spontaneous sociability of human nature, independent of all personal calculation, and often in opposition to the strongest individual interests, is admitted, as of course, by those who have paid no great attention to the true biological theory of our intellectual and moral nature.

Passing over some elementary considerations which belong rather to a special treatise on the physiological conditions,—such as the natural nakedness of the human being, and his helpless and protracted infancy,—which have been much exaggerated as social influences, since they exist in some animal races without producing the same social consequences,—I proceed to estimate the influence of the most important attributes of our nature in giving to society the fundamental character which belongs to it, and which remains permanent through all degrees of its development. In this view, the first consideration is of the preponderance of the affective over the intellectual faculties, which, though less remarkable in Man than in other animals, yet fixes the first essential idea of our true nature.— Though continuous action is, in all cases, an indispensable condition of success, Man, like every other animal, has a natural dislike to such perseverance, and at first finds pleasure only in a varied exercise of his activity,—the variety being of more importance to him than moderation in degree,—especially in the commonest cases, in which no strongly-marked instinct is concerned. The intellectual faculties being naturally the least energetic, their activity, if ever so little protracted beyond a certain degree, occasions in most men a fatigue which soon becomes utterly insupportable; and it is in regard to them chiefly that men of all ages of civilization relish that state of which the *dolce far niente* is the most perfect expression. Nevertheless, it is on the persevering use of these high faculties that the modifications of human life, general and individual, depend, during the course of our social development, so that we are met at once by the melancholy coincidence that Man is most in need of precisely the kind of activity for which he is the least fit. His physical imperfections and moral necessities compel him, more than any other animal, to employ his reason in amending his primitive condition; while his reason is so far from being adequate to its work that it is subject to an irresistible fatigue which can be moderated only by strong and constant stimulus. Instead of lamenting over this discordance, we must receive it as a first authentic information supplied to social science by biology, and one which must radically affect the general character of human society first, and afterwards the rate of the social evolution. The consequence which immediately concerns us here is, that almost all men are naturally unfit for intellectual labour, and devoted to material activity; so that the speculative state cannot well be produced, much less sustained, in them but by some impulse of another kind, kept up by lower but stronger propensities. However important individual differences in this respect may be, the differences are of degree only, so that the most eminent natures hold their place in the comparison; and men must be classed, in a scientific sense, by the nobleness or increasing speciality of the affective faculties by which the intellectual incitement is produced. If we observe the ascending scale of these faculties, upon Gall's theory, we see that, among the generality of men, the intellectual tension is (with some exceptions of that speculative impulse to which all human beings are liable) habitually supported only by the strong stimulus derived from the needs of the organic life, and the commonest instincts of the animal life, the organs of which lie at the back of the brain. The individual nature of man becomes lofty in proportion as the incitement proceeds from propensities which are of a higher order, more peculiar to our species, and placed, anatomically, further forward in the brain, while yet the activity of the intellectual region can never, in the noblest cases, be independent of such stimulus, unless the habit of meditation has actually become preponderant,— a case too rare to be considered in a general view.—Lest we should form a false philosophical estimate of our case, I may observe that, however we may regret the degree in which our intellectual faculties are less active than the lower, we must beware of wishing that the case was reversed. If our affective faculties were subordinated to the intellectual, all idea of improving the social organism would be merely senseless. It would be like polishing our roads, instead of merely diminishing their friction, which would not improve the accustomed locomotion, but render its mechanism contradictory to the fundamental laws of motion. For our affective faculties must preponderate, not only to rouse our reason from its natural lethargy, but to give a permanent aim and direction to its activity, without which it would be for ever lost in vague abstract speculation. Even under our actual conditions, which subject the wildest reveries to more or less control of reality, we see how the most mystical efforts of pious ecstasy to conceive of an ideal state, exempt from organic wants and from all human passions, have issued, even in the highest minds, in conceptions of a sort of transcendental idiotcy, eternally absorbed in a foolish and almost stupid contemplation of the divine majesty. Our social organism is, then, what it ought to be, except as to degree; and we must observe and remember that it is in our power, within certain narrow limits, to rectify this degree of difference; or rather, that the rectification takes place in proportion to the steady development of civilization, which tends to subordinate our propensities to our reason, more and more, without giving us any cause to apprehend a reversal of the order at any future time.

The second consideration is that, besides the preponderance of the affective over the intellectual life, the lowest and most personal propensities have, in regard to social relations, an unquestionable preponderance over the nobler. According to the sound biological theory of man, our social affections are inferior in strength and steadiness to the personal, though the common welfare must depend especially on the regular satisfaction of the former, which first originate the social state for us, and then maintain it against the divergencies of individual instincts. To understand the sociological value of this biological datum, we must observe, as in the former case, that the condition is necessary, and that it is only its degree that we have to deplore. In analogy with the former case, personal instincts must give an aim and direction to our social action. All notions of public good must be based upon those of private advantage, because the former can be nothing else than that which is common to all cases of the latter: and, under no ideal refinement of our nature, could we ever habitually desire for others anything else but what we wish for ourselves,—unless in those infinitely rare and very secondary cases in which an excessive refinement of moral delicacy, fostered by intellectual meditation, may enable a man to appreciate for another means of happiness which are of little or no value to himself. Our moral nature would then be destroyed, and not improved, if it were possible to repress our personal instincts, since our social affections, deprived of necessary direction, would degenerate into a vague and useless charity, destitute of all practical efficacy. When the morality of an advanced society bids us love our neighbours as ourselves, it embodies in the best way the deepest truth, with only such exaggeration as is required in the formation of a type, which is always fallen short of in practice. In this sublime precept, the personal instinct is the guide and measure of the social; and in no other way could the principle be presented; for in what respect and how could any one love another who did not love himself? Thus, again, we may be satisfied with the nature of Man, though not with the degree of his self-regards. We must regret that even in the best natures, the social affections are so overborne by the personal, as rarely to command conduct, in a direct way. In this sense, we may conceive, after a comparison of the two cases I have presented, that the sympathetic instinct and the intellectual activity are especially destined to compensate mutually their common social insufficiency. We may say, indeed, that if Man became more benevolent, that would be equivalent in social practice to his being more intelligent, not only because he would put his actual intelligence to better use, but because it would not be so much absorbed by the discipline which it must be constantly imposing on the strong preponderance of the personal propensities. But the converse supposition is not less exact, though it is less appreciable; for all real intellectual development is finally equivalent, in regard to the conduct of life, to a direct augmentation of natural benevolence, both by strengthening Man's empire over his passions, and by refining the habitual sense of the reactions occasioned by various social contact. If we admit, in the first case, that no great intellect can duly expand without a certain amount of universal benevolence, by which alone it can have free impulse, a lofty aim, and large exercise; so, inversely, we cannot doubt that all noble intellectual expansion fortifies general sympathy, not only by casting out selfish instigations, but by inspiring a wise predilection in favour of social order, which may, notwithstanding its ordinary coldness, concur as fortunately in the maintenance of social harmony as dispositions which are more lively and less steady. The reciprocal connection of those two chief moderators of human life, intellectual activity and the social instinct, seems thus to be unquestionable: and the first function of universal morals, in regard to the individual, consists in increasing this double influence, the gradual extension of which constitutes the first spontaneous result of the general development of humanity. And the double opposition between Man's moral and material need of intellectual toil and his dislike of it, and again, between Man's need, for his own happiness, of the social affections, and the necessary subjection of these to his personal instincts, discloses the scientific germ of the struggle which we shall have to review, between the conservative and the reforming spirit; the first of which is animated by purely personal instincts, and the other by the spontaneous combination of intellectual activity with the various social instincts.

So much for the first statical division,—the Individual. Next, we must consider the Family.

As every system must be composed of elements of the

same nature with itself, the scientific spirit forbids us to regard society as composed of individuals. The true social unit is certainly the family,— reduced, if necessary, to the elementary couple which forms its basis. This consideration implies more than the physiological truth that families become tribes, and tribes become nations: so that the whole human race might be conceived of as the gradual development of a single family, if local diversities did not forbid such a supposition. There is a political point of view from which also we must consider this elementary idea, inasmuch as the family presents the true germ of the various characteristics of the social organism. Such a conception is intermediate between the idea of the individual and that of the species, or society. There would be as many scientific inconveniences in passing it over in a speculative sense as there are dangers in practice in pretending to treat of social life without the inevitable preparation of the domestic life. Whichever way we look at it, this necessary transition always presents itself, whether in regard to elementary notions of fundamental harmony, or for the spontaneous rise of social sentiment. It is by this avenue that Man comes forth from his mere personality, and learns to live in another, while obeying his most powerful instincts. No other association can be so intimate as this primary combination, which causes a complete fusion of two natures in one. Owing to the radical imperfection of the human character, individual divergencies are too marked to admit of so close an association in any other case. The common experience of human life teaches us only too well that men must not live too familiarly together, if they are to bear, in mutual peace, the infirmities of our nature,—whether of the intellect or the affections. Even religious communities, united as they are by a special bond, were, as we know, perpetually tormented by internal dissensions, such as it is impossible to avoid if we attempt to reconcile qualities so incompatible as the intimacy and the extension of human relations. Even in the family, the intimacy is owing to the strong spontaneousness of the common end, combined with the equally natural institution of an indispensable subordination. Whatever talk there may be, in modern times, of social

2. The Family.

equality, even the most restricted society supposes, not only diversities, but inequalities; for there can be no association without a permanent concurrence in a general operation, pursued by distinct means, mutually subordinated. Now, the most entire realization possible of these elementary conditions is inherent in the family alone, where nature has supplied all the requisites of the institution. Thus, notwithstanding the temporary abuse of the family spirit in the way of excess, which has occasionally brought reproach on the institution, it is, and will ever be, the basis of the social spirit, through all the gradual modifications which it may have to undergo in the course of the human evolution. The serious assaults upon this institution which we witness in our day must, therefore, be regarded as the most alarming symptoms of our temporary tendency to social disorganization. But such a direction of the revolutionary spirit is a dangerous system only on account of the decrepitude of the belief on which the idea of the Family, like every other social idea, is made to rest. As long as the family relation has no other intellectual basis than religious doctrine, it will share whatever discredit belongs to that doctrine in the present state of human development. The Positive philosophy, which reorganizes whatever it touches, can alone re-establish the conception on an immutable foundation, by transferring all social speculation from the region of vague ideality to the ground of indisputable reality.

The constitution of the human family has undergone modifications of a progressive kind which appear to me to disclose, at each epoch of development, the exact importance of the change wrought in the corresponding social state. Thus, the polygamy of less advanced nations must give a character to the family wholly different from that which it has among nations which are capable of that monogamy to which our nature tends. In the same way, the ancient family, which consisted partly of slaves, must be very unlike the modern, which is mainly reduced to the kindred of the couple, and in which the authority of the head is comparatively small. But the estimate of these modifications will find its right place in my historical review. Our object now is to consider the elementary scientific aspect of the family; that aspect which is made common to all social cases by regarding the domestic as the basis of all social life. In this view, the sociological theory of the family is reducible to the investigation of two orders of relations, viz., the subordination of the sexes, which institutes the family, and that of ages, which maintains it. A certain amount of voluntary association takes place from that degree of the biological scale at which sex begins; and it is always occasioned by the sexual union first, and then by the rearing of progeny. If the sociological comparison must stop at the two great classes of superior animals, birds and mammifers, it is because none below them present a sufficiently complete realization of this double elementary character.

We cannot too reverently admire that universal natural disposition, on which all association is grounded, by which, in the state of marriage, however imperfect, the strongest instinct of our animal nature, at once satisfied and disciplined, occasions harmony instead of the disorder which would arise from its license. It was not to be expected that, when the revolutionary spirit was attacking everything else, it should allow marriage to escape,—connected as it has hitherto been with the theological philosophy. When the positive philosophy shall have established the subordination of the sexes, and in that, the principle of marriage and of the family, it will take its stand on an exact knowledge of human nature, followed by an appreciation of social development as a whole, and of the general phase which it now presents; and in doing this it will extinguish the fancies by which the institution is at present discredited and betrayed. No doubt Marriage, like every other human concern, undergoes modifications as human development proceeds. Modern marriage, as constituted by Catholicism, is radically different, in various respects, from Roman marriage, as that differed from the Greek, and both, in a much greater degree, from the Egyptian or Oriental, even after the establishment of monogamy. It is undisputed that these modifications have not come to any end, and that the great social reconstitution for which we are looking will establish the general character of the association, which all

*The sexual relation.*

preceding modifications have progressively developed. Meantime, the absolute spirit of the existing political philosophy mistakes such modifications for an overthrow of the institution; a state of things very analogous to that of the ancient times, when the Greek philosophy was about to make way for the Christian regeneration of the family and of society, and when fantastical errors, caused by the long intellectual interregnum gave occasion to the famous satire of Aristophanes, which we may accept as a rude rebuke of our own licentiousness.

What the ultimate conditions of marriage will be, we cannot know as yet; and if we could, this is not the place to treat of them. It is enough for our purpose to be assured that they will be consonant with the fundamental principle of the institution,—the natural subordination of the woman, which has reappeared under all forms of marriage, in all ages, and which the new philosophy will place on its right basis,—a knowledge of the individual organism first, and then of the social organism. Biological philosophy teaches us that, through the whole animal scale, and while the specific type is preserved, radical differences, physical and moral, distinguish the sexes. Comparing sex with age, biological analysis presents the female sex, in the human species especially, as constitutionally in a state of perpetual infancy, in comparison with the other; and therefore more remote, in all important respects, from the ideal type of the race. Sociology will prove that the equality of the sexes, of which so much is said, is incompatible with all social existence, by showing that each sex has special and permanent functions which it must fulfil in the natural economy of the human family, and which concur in a common end by different ways, the welfare which results being in no degree injured by the necessary subordination, since the happiness of every being depends on the wise development of its proper nature.

We have seen that the preponderance of the affective faculties is less marked in Man than in the lower animals, and that a certain degree of spontaneous speculative activity is the chief cerebral attribute of humanity, as well as the prime source of the marked character of our social organism. Now, the relative inferiority of Woman in this view is incontestable, unfit as she is, in comparison, for the requisite continuousness and intensity of mental labour, either from the intrinsic weakness of her reason or from her more lively moral and physical sensibility, which are hostile to scientific abstraction and concentration. This indubitable organic inferiority of feminine genius has been confirmed by decisive experiment, even in the fine arts, and amidst the concurrence of the most favourable circumstances. As for any functions of government, the radical inaptitude of the female sex is there yet more marked, even in regard to the most elementary state, and limited to the guidance of the mere family, the nature of the task requiring, above everything, an indefatigable attention to an aggregate of complex relations, none of which must be neglected, while the mind must be independent of the passions; in short, reasonable. Thus, the economy of the human family could never be inverted without an entire change in our cerebral organism, and the only possible result of a resistance to natural laws would be to deprive Woman of the enjoyment of her proper welfare by disturbing the family and society. Again, we have seen that, in the affective life of Man, the personal instincts overrule the sympathetic or social, which last can, and do, only modify the direction decided by the first, without becoming the habitual moving powers of practical existence. Here again, by a comparative examination, we can estimate the happy social position appropriated to the female sex. It is indisputable that women are, in general, as superior to men in a spontaneous expansion of sympathy and sociality, as they are inferior to men in understanding and reason. Their function in the economy of the family, and consequently of society, must therefore be to modify by the excitement of the social instinct the general direction necessarily originated by the cold and rough reason which is distinctive of Man. Apart from all consideration of material differences, and contemplating exclusively the noblest properties of our cerebral nature, we see that, of the two attributes which separate the human race from the brutes, the primary one indicates the necessary and invariable preponderance of the male sex, while the other points out the moderating function which is appropriate to Woman, even independently of maternal cares, which evidently constitute her most important special destination, but which are usually too exclusively insisted on, so as to disguise the direct social and personal vocation of the female sex.

*The Parental relation.* The other great element of the human family is the relation between parents and children, which, spread abroad through the whole of society, produces the natural subordination of ages. The discipline prescribed by nature in this relation is too unquestionable to admit of the same attacks of the revolutionary spirit which have been directed towards the preceding relation. The ardent champions of the political rights of women have not yet offered an analogous doctrine in regard to children, who are less able to stimulate the zeal of their special champions. Wild as are the eccentricities of our social anarchy, popular good sense, however imperfect it may still be, imposes some restraint on individual absurdities when they go so far as to shock a primary instinct.

There is certainly no natural economy more worthy of admiration than that spontaneous subordination which, first constituting the human family, then becomes the type of all wise social co-ordination. The testimony of ages has done honour to this type; and when Man has formed his conception of providential government on the most perfect direction of events that he could conceive, he has taken this institution for his model. There is no other case which offers, in the same degree, the most respectful spontaneous obedience, on the part of the inferior, without the least degradation; an obedience imposed by necessity first, and then by gratitude; and nowhere else do we see in the superior party the most absolute authority united to entire devotedness, too natural and too genial to be regarded as duty. These characteristics must become weakened in the case of wider and less intimate relations; the submission cannot be so complete and spontaneous, nor the protection so affectionate and devoted. But family life will, nevertheless, be eternally the school of social life, both for obedience and for command, which will be excellent in proportion to their approach to this model; and in the future, as in the past, the modifications of society will correspond with those which human progression must occasion in the domestic constitution. In all critical periods, however, there have been false reasoners who have argued from the inconveniences which attend this institution, like every other, against the organization itself, and who would mend it by means of a total inversion,—proposing to make society the model of the family; at a time, too, when society is in no condition to serve as a type for any kind of orderly arrangement. All domestic discipline would be impossible under a system which would take from parents the guidance and almost the acquaintance of their children, through a monstrous exaggeration of the influence of society on the education of youth; and children, of the hereditary transmission of their parents' property, accumulated on their behalf,—obedience and authority being thus successively destroyed. This work is not the place in which to examine such extravagances; but it was necessary to refer to this particular delusion in order to show the fitness of the positive polity to consolidate all the primary ideas of social order, amidst the confusion attending the decline of the theological philosophy. Here, as everywhere else, we shall find the positive philosophy subordinating all schemes of artificial order to the observation of natural order: and we shall perceive that the modifications wrought out by the social evolution are superior to any that the most eminent reformers would have ventured to conceive of beforehand,—a fact which should teach us not to interfere with the succession of different portions of the reorganization by attempting to renovate everything at once, down to the smallest details, according to the routine of modern constitutions.

We must not omit the striking property of domestic organization,—that it establishes the elementary idea of social perpetuity, by directly and irresistibly connecting the future with the past. When duly generalized, the idea and the feeling pass on from the immediate parents to ancestors, and issue in that universal respect for our predecessors which is an indispensable condition of all social economy. There is no social state which does not present evidences of it. The diminishing influence of traditions as human development proceeds, and the growing preference of written to oral transmission, must modify the expression of the sentiment among the moderns, if not the sentiment itself; but whatever point social progression may attain, it will always be supremely important that Man should not regard himself as a being of yesterday, and that the whole of his institutions and customs should connect, by a system of intellectual and material tokens, his remembrances of the entire past with his hopes for the future. The tendency of the revolutionary philosophy is to foster a disdain of the past, on account of its polities; and I need not add that the positive philosophy, which takes history for its scientific basis, which represents all the men of all times as co-operating in the same evolution, and which perseveringly connects all existing progress with the whole of antecedent human action, is thoroughly adapted to confirm the idea and sentiment of social continuity. In fact, we see that the region of the positive sciences is the only one in which this reverent co-ordination of the present with the past, has withstood the encroachments of the revolutionary philosophy, which, in every other connection, would almost have us believe that reason and justice are creations of our own day.

It is not necessary to enlarge here on the fraternal relation, though it would obtain its share of attention if we were engaged in forming a constitution of society. For our purposes here, the brotherly relation offers little subject of remark, interesting as it is from the sweetness or the bitterness which it sheds over private life. If the brothers are nearly of the same age, there is little subordination in the case; and if the difference in age is sufficient to admit of that subordination, the relation becomes, for analytical purposes, like that of parent and child. All that it is in our way to remark here is that true social science will never fail, either in studying the past, or speculating on the future, to assign the rank of absolute requisites to all elements which have, through all time, constituted an essential part of the domestic hierarchy. Discarding all Utopian fancies, and proposing to observe the economy of real society, we must bring into our scientific analysis all the arrangements which, by their steady permanence, indicate their grave importance.

The third head of our statical analysis brings us to the consideration of society, as composed of families and not of individuals, and from a point of view which commands all times and places.

The main cause of the superiority of the social to the individual organism is, according 3. Society. to an established law, the more marked speciality of the various functions fulfilled by organs more and more distinct, but interconnected; so that unity of aim is more and more combined with diversity of means. We cannot, of course, fully appreciate a phenomenon which is for ever proceeding before our eyes, and in which we bear a part; but if we withdraw ourselves in thought from the social system, and contemplate it as from afar, can we conceive of a more marvellous spectacle, in the whole range of natural phenomena, than the regular and constant convergence of an innumerable multitude of human beings, each possessing a distinct and, in a certain degree, independent existence, and yet incessantly disposed, amidst all their discordance of talent and character, to concur in many ways in the same general development, without concert, and even consciousness on the part of most of them, who believe that they are merely following their personal impulses? This is the scientific picture of the phenomenon: and no temporary disturbances can prevent its being, under all circumstances, essentially true. This reconciliation of the individuality of labour with co-operation of endeavours, which becomes more remarkable as society grows more complex and extended, constitutes the radical character of human operations when we rise from the domestic to the social point of view. The degree of association that we observe among the superior animals has something voluntary in it, but there is no organization which can make it resemble the human: and the first individual specializing of common functions is seen in our simple domestic life, which is thus a type of the social organization. The division of labour can never, however, be very marked in the family, because the members are few; and yet more because such a division would soon show itself to be hostile to the spirit of the institution; for domestic training, being founded on imitation, must dispose the children to follow parental employments, instead of undertaking new ones: and again, any very marked separation in the employments of the members must impair the domestic unity which is the aim of the association. The more we look into the subject, the more we shall see that the appropriation of employments, which is the elementary principle of general society, cannot hold anything like so important a place in the family. In fact, the domestic relations do not constitute an association, but a *union*, in the full force of the term; and, on account of this close intimacy, the domestic connection is of a totally different nature from the social. Its character is essentially moral, and only incidentally intellectual; or, in anatomical language, it corresponds more to the middle than to the anterior part of the brain. Founded chiefly upon attachment and gratitude, the domestic union satisfies, by its mere existence, all our sympathetic instincts, quite apart from all idea of active and continuous co-operation towards any end, unless it be that of its own institution. Though more or less co-ordination of different employments must exist, it is so secondary an affair that when, unhappily, it remains the only principle of connection, the domestic union degenerates into mere association, and is even too likely to dissolve altogether. In society the elementary economy presents an inverse character, the sentiment of co-operation becoming preponderant, and the sympathetic instinct, without losing its steadiness, becoming secondary. No doubt there are a multitude of men well enough organized to love their fellow-labourers, however numerous or remote they may be, and however indirect may be their co-operation; but such a sentiment, arising from the reaction of the reason upon the social feelings, could never be strong enough to guide social life. Even under the best circumstances the intellectual mediocrity of the majority of men does not allow them to form any distinct idea of relations which are too extensive, too indirect, and too foreign to their own occupations to impart any sympathetic stimulus which could be of permanent use. It is only in domestic life that Man can habitually seek the full and free expansion of his social affections; and perhaps this is the chief reason why it is the last indispensable preparation for social life; for concentration is as necessary to the feelings as generalization to the thoughts. Even the most eminent men, who direct their sympathetic instincts upon their race at large or the society in which they live, are usually impelled to this by the moral disappointments of a domestic life which has failed in some of its conditions; and however genial the imperfect compensation may be to them, this abstract love of their species admits of nothing like that satisfaction of the affections which arises from a very limited, and especially an individual attachment. However this may be, such cases are besides too evidently exceptional to affect any inquiry into the social economy. Thus, though the sympathetic instinct exists wherever there is association, more or less, the principle of co-operation is that which must prevail, when we pass on from the consideration of the family to the general co-ordination of families. To attribute to it the formation of the social state, as it was the fashion of the last century to do, is a capital error; but, when the association has once begun, there is nothing like this principle of co-operation for giving consistency and character to the combination. In the lower stages of savage life we see families combining for a temporary purpose, and then returning, almost like the brutes, to their isolated independence, as soon as the expedition, which is usually one of war or the chase, is ended, though already some common opinions, expressed in a certain uniform language, are preparing them for permanent union in tribes, more or less numerous. It is upon the principle of co-operation, then, spontaneous or concerted, that we must found our analysis of the last division of social statics.

We must include in our view of the division of employments something much more extensive than the material arrangements which the expression is usually understood to convey. *Distribution of employments.* We must include under it all human operations whatever, regarding not only individuals and classes, but also, in many ways, different nations, as participating, in a special mode and degree, in a vast common work, the gradual development of which connects the fellow-labourers with the whole series of their predecessors, and even with their successors. This is what is meant when we speak of the race being bound up together by the very distribution of their occupations; and it is this distribution which causes the extent and growing complexity of the social organism, which thus appears as comprising the whole of the human race. Man can hardly exist in a solitary state: the family can exist in isolation, because it can divide its employments and provide for its wants in a rough kind of way: a spontaneous approximation of families is incessantly exposed to temporary rupture, occasioned by the most trifling incidents. But when a regular division of employments has spread through any society, the social state begins to acquire a consistency and stability which place it out of danger from particular divergencies. The habit of partial co-operation convinces each family of its close dependence on the rest, and, at the same time, of its own importance, each one being then justified in regarding itself as fulfilling a real public function, more or less indispensable to the general economy, but inseparable from the system as a whole. In this view the social organization tends more and more to rest on an exact estimate of individual diversities, by so distributing employments as to appoint each one to the destination he is most fit for, from his own nature (which however is seldom very distinctly marked), from his education and his position, and, in short, from all his qualifications; so that all individual organizations, even the most vicious and imperfect (short of monstrosity), may be finally made use of for the general good. Such is, at least, the social type which we conceive of as the limit of the existing social order, and to which we may be for ever approximating, though without the hope of ever attaining it; and it is, in fact, a reproduction, with a large extension, of the domestic organism, with less power, in proportion to its extent, of appointing a due destination to every member; so that the social discipline must always be more artificial, and therefore more imperfect, than the domestic, which nature herself ordains and administers.

The necessities of this co-operation and distribution of special offices, cause inconvenience which I am compelled to advert to; for it is in the investigation of these that we find the scientific germ of the relation between the idea of society and that of government.

Some economists have pointed out, but in a very inadequate way, the evils of an exaggerated division of material labour; and I have indicated, in regard to the more important field of scientific labour, the mischievous intellectual consequences of the spirit of speciality which at present prevails. It is necessary to estimate directly the principle of such an influence, in order to understand the object of the spontaneous system of requisites for the continuous preservation of society. In decomposing, we always disperse; and the distribution of human labours must occasion individual divergencies, both intellectual and moral, which require a permanent discipline to keep them within bounds. If the separation of social functions developes a useful spirit of detail, on the one hand, it tends, on the other, to extinguish or to restrict what we may call the aggregate or general spirit. In the same way, in moral relations, while each individual is in close dependence on the mass, he is drawn away from it by the expansion of his special activity, constantly recalling him to his private interest, which he but very dimly perceives to be related to the public. On both grounds the inconveniences of the division of functions increase with its characteristic advantages, without their being in the same relation, throughout the spontaneous course of the social evolution. The growing speciality of habitual ideas and familiar relations must tend to restrict the understanding more and more, while sharpening it in a certain direction, and to sever more and more the private interest from a public interest which is for ever becoming more vague and indirect; while, at the same time, the social affections, gradually concentrated among individuals of the same profession, become more and more alienated from all other classes, for want of a sufficient analogy of ways and ideas. Thus it is that the principle by which alone general society could be developed and extended, threatens, in another view, to decompose it into a multitude of unconnected corporations, which almost seem not to belong to the same species; and hence it is that the gradual expansion of human ability seems destined to produce such minds as are very common among civilized peoples, and prodigiously admired by them,—minds which are very

*Inconveniences.*

able in some one respect and monstrously incapable in all others. If we have been accustomed to deplore the spectacle, among the artisan class of a workman occupied during his whole life in nothing else but making knife-handles or pins' heads, we may find something quite as lamentable in the intellectual class, in the exclusive employment of a human brain in resolving some equations, or in classifying insects. The moral effect is, unhappily, analogous in the two cases. It occasions a miserable indifference about the general course of human affairs, as long as there are equations to resolve and pins to manufacture. This is an extreme case of human automatism; but the frequency, and the growing frequency, of the evil gives a real scientific importance to the case, as indicating the general tendency, and warning us to restrain it. Thus it appears to me that the social destination of government is to guard against and restrain the fundamental dispersion of ideas, sentiments, and interests, which is the inevitable result of the very principle of human development, and which, if left to itself, would put a stop to social progression in all important respects.

Here we have, in my opinion, the basis of the elementary and abstract theory of government, regarded in its complete scientific extension; that is, as characterized by the universal necessary reaction, —first spontaneous and then regulated,— of the whole upon the parts. It is clear that the only way of preventing such a dispersion is by setting up this reaction as a new special function, which shall intervene in the performance of all the various functions of the social economy, to keep up the idea of the whole, and the feeling of the common interconnection: and the more energetically, the more individual activity tends to dissolve them. Not itself affecting any determinate social progress, it contributes to all that society can achieve, in any direction whatever, and which society could not achieve without its concentrating and protective care. The very nature of its action indicates that it cannot be merely material, but also, and much more, intellectual and moral; so as to show the double necessity of what has been called the temporal and spiritual government, the rational

*Basis of the true theory of government.*

subordination of which was the best feature of the social organization that was happily effected in its day, under the influence of the prevalent Catholicism. Moreover, this ruling function must become more, instead of less necessary, as human development proceeds, because its essential principle is inseparable from that of the development itself.—Thus, it is the habitual predominance of the spirit of the whole which constitutes government, in whatever way it is regarded. The next consideration is, how such an action arises, independently of all systematic combination, in the natural course of the social economy.

If the dispersive tendency arising from the distribution of functions naturally propagates itself, it is clear that any influence capable of neutralizing it must also be constantly expanding. In fact, an elementary subordination must always be growing out of the distribution of human operations, which gives birth to government, in the bosom of society itself, as we could easily discover by analysing any marked subdivision which has just taken place in any employment whatever. This subordination is not only material, but yet more intellectual and moral; that is, it requires, besides practical submission, a corresponding degree of real confidence in both the capacity and the probity of the special organs to whom a function, hitherto universal, is confided. Every one of us relies, even for life itself, on the aptitude and the morality of a multitude of almost unknown agents, whose folly or wickedness might affect the welfare of vast numbers of human beings. Such a condition belongs to all modes of social existence. If it is especially attributed to industrial societies, it is only because it must be most conspicuous where the division of labour goes furthest; and it is as certainly to be found in purely military societies; as the statical analysis of an army, a man-of-war, or any other active corporation shows in a moment.

*Elementary subordination.*

This elementary subordination discloses its own law; which is, that the various operations in which individuals are engaged fall naturally under the direction of those which are next above them in generality. We may easily convince ourselves of this by analysing any special occupation at the moment when it assumes a separate character:

because the task thus separated is necessarily more special than the function from which it proceeds, and to which its own fulfilment must be subordinated. This is not the occasion on which to expatiate on this law; but its political bearing concerns us here,—indicating as it does the germ of a true classification of social functions. We shall hereafter meet with a full verification of this law in regard to the industrial life of modern societies: the eminent regularity of military associations renders the law obvious at once; and when the law is once admitted, it discloses the spontaneous connection of this elementary social subordination with that political subordination, properly so called, which is the basis of government, and which presents itself as the last degree in the hierarchy formed by the subjection of the more special to the more general classes of phenomena. For, as the various particular functions of the social economy are naturally implicated in relations of greater generality, all must at length be subject to the direction of the most general function of all, which is characterized, as we have seen, by the constant action of the whole upon the parts. On the other hand, the organs of this direction must be much strengthened by the encouragement afforded to intellectual and moral inequality under a system of division of employments. It is clear that while men were obliged to do everything for themselves, they must have been confined to domestic life, devoting all their activity to supply the wants of the family; and there could be little expansion of individual ability and character. Though marked individuality must always have made itself felt, in every state of society, the division of labour, and the leisure which it brings, have been needful to the conspicuous development of that intellectual superiority on which all political ascendancy must mainly rest. We must observe, moreover, that there can be no such division of intellectual as of material labour; so that the intellectual functions must be less affected than the industrial by the dispersive tendencies of such a division. We are familiar with the effect of civilization in developing moral, and yet more, intellectual inequalities; but we must bear in mind that moral and intellectual forces do not admit, like the physical, of being accumulated and compounded: so that, eminently as they can concur, and clearly as they are the creators of social concurrence, they are much less adapted for direct co-operation. A sufficient coalition of the most insignificant individuals can easily carry any point of physical conflict, or of acquisition of wealth, against the highest superiority in an individual or a family; so that, for example, the most enormous private fortune cannot sustain any competition with the financial power of a nation, whose treasury is filled by a multitude of the smallest contributions. But, on the contrary, if the enterprise depends on a high intellectual power, as in the case of a great scientific or poetical conception, there can be no association of ordinary minds, however extensive, which can compete with a Descartes or a Shakspere. It is the same in the moral case; as, for instance, if society is in need of any great resource of devotedness, the want cannot be supplied by accumulating any amount of moderate zeal furnished by individuals. The only use of a multitude in such a case is that it improves the chance of finding the *unique* organ of the proposed function; and when that singular agent is once found, there is no degree of multitude which can weigh down its preponderance. It is through this privilege that intellectual and moral forces tend to an ever-increasing social authority, from the time when a due division of employments admits of their proper development.

Such is, then, the elementary tendency of all human society to a spontaneous government. This tendency accords with a corresponding system, inherent in us as individuals, of special dispositions towards command in some, and towards obedience in others. We must not, with regard to the first, confound the desire to rule with the fitness to do so; though the desire is one element of the fitness: and, on the other hand, there is a much stronger inclination to obedience in the generality of men than it is customary in our day to suppose. If men were as rebellious as they are at present represented, it would be difficult to understand how they could ever have been disciplined: and it is certain that we are all more or less disposed to respect any superiority,

*Tendency of society to government.*

especially any intellectual or moral elevation, in our neighbours, independently of any view to our own advantage: and this instinct of submission is, in truth, only too often lavished on deceptive appearances. However excessive the desire of command may be in our revolutionary day, there can be no one who, in his secret mind, has not often felt, more or less vividly, how sweet it is to obey when he can have the rare privilege of consigning the burdensome responsibility of his general self-conduct to wise and trustworthy guidance: and probably the sense of this is strongest in those who are best fitted for command. In the midst of political convulsion, when the spirit of revolutionary destruction is abroad, the mass of the people manifest a scrupulous obedience towards the intellectual and moral guides from whom they accept direction, and upon whom they may even press a temporary dictatorship, in their primary and urgent need of a preponderant authority. Thus do individual dispositions show themselves to be in harmony with the course of social relations as a whole, in teaching us that political subordination is as inevitable, generally speaking, as it is indispensable. And this completes the elementary delineation of Social Statics.

My sketch has perhaps been so abstract and condensed that the conceptions of this chapter may appear obscure at present; but light will fall upon them as we proceed. We may already see, however, the practical advantage which arises from the scientific evolution of human relations. The individual life, ruled by personal instincts; the domestic, by sympathetic instincts; and the social, by the special development of intellectual influences, prepare for the states of human existence which are to follow: and that which ensues is, first, personal morality, which subjects the preservation of the individual to a wise discipline; next, domestic morality, which subordinates selfishness to sympathy; and lastly, social morality, which directs all dividual tendencies by enlightened reason, always having the general economy in view, so as to bring into concurrence all the faculties of human nature, according to their appropriate laws.

# CHAPTER VI.

### SOCIAL DYNAMICS; OR, THEORY OF THE NATURAL PROGRESS OF HUMAN SOCIETY.

IF we regard the course of human develop- *Scientific view* ment from the highest scientific point of *of Human* view, we shall perceive that it consists in *progression.* educing, more and more, the characteristic faculties of humanity, in comparison with those of animality; and especially with those which man has in common with the whole organic kingdom. It is in this philosophical sense that the most eminent civilization must be pronounced to be fully accordant with nature, since it is, in fact, only a more marked manifestation of the chief properties of our species; properties which, latent at first, can come into play only in that advanced state of social life for which they are exclusively destined. The whole system of biological philosophy indicates the natural progression. We have seen how, in the brute kingdom, the superiority of each race is determined by the degree of preponderance of the animal life over the organic. In like manner, we see that our social evolution is only the final term of a progression which has continued from the simplest vegetables and most insignificant animals, up through the higher reptiles, to the birds and the mammifers, and still on to the carnivorous animals and monkeys, the organic characteristics retiring, and the animal prevailing more and more, till the intellectual and moral tend towards the ascendancy which can never be fully obtained, even in the highest state of human perfection that we can conceive of. This comparative estimate affords us the scientific view of human progression, connected, as we see it is, with the whole course of animal advancement, of which it is itself the highest degree. The analysis of our social progress proves indeed that, while the radical dispositions of our nature are necessarily invariable, the highest of them are in a continuous state of relative development, by which they rise to be preponderant powers of human existence, though the inversion of the primitive economy can never be absolutely complete. We have seen that this is the essential character of the social organism in a statical view: but it becomes much more marked when we study its variations in their gradual succession.

*Course of Man's social development.* Civilization develops, to an enormous degree, the action of Man upon his environment: and thus, it may seem, at first, to concentrate our attention upon the cares of material existence, the support and improvement of which appear to be the chief object of most social occupations. A closer examination will show, however, that this development gives the advantage to the highest human faculties, both by the security which sets free our attention from physical wants, and by the direct and steady excitement which it administers to the intellectual functions, and even the social feelings. In Man's social infancy, the instincts of subsistence are so preponderant, that the sexual instinct itself, notwithstanding its primitive strength, is at first controlled by them: the domestic affections are then much less pronounced; and the social affections are restricted to an almost imperceptible fraction of humanity, beyond which everything is foreign, and even hostile: and the malignant passions are certainly, next to the animal appetites, the mainspring of human existence. It is unquestionable that civilization leads us on to a further and further development of our noblest dispositions and our most generous feelings, which are the only possible basis of human association, and which receive, by means of that association, a more and more special culture. As for the intellectual faculties,—we see, by the habitual improvidence which characterizes savage life, how little influence reason has over men in that stage of existence. Those faculties are then undeveloped, or show some activity only in the lowest order, which relate to the exercise of the senses: the faculties of abstraction and combination are almost wholly inert, except under some transient stimulus: the rude curiosity which the spectacle of nature involuntarily inspires is quite satisfied with the weakest attempts at theological explanation; and amusements, chiefly distinguished by violent muscular activity, rising at best to a manifestation of merely physical address, are as little favourable to the development of intelligence as of social qualities. The influence of civilization in perpetually improving the intellectual faculties is even more unquestionable than its effect on moral relations. The development of the individual exhibits to us in little, both as to time and degree, the chief phases of social development. In both cases, the end is to subordinate the satisfaction of the personal instincts to the habitual exercise of the social faculties, subjecting, at the same time, all our passions to rules imposed by an ever-strengthening intelligence, with the view of identifying the individual more and more with the species. In the anatomical view, we should say that the process is to give an influence by exercise to the organs of the cerebral systems, increasing in proportion to their distance from the vertebral column, and their nearness to the frontal region. Such is the ideal type which exhibits the course of human development, in the individual, and, in a higher degree, in the species. This view enables us to discriminate the natural from the artificial part of the process of development; that part being natural which raises the human to a superiority over the animal attributes; and that part being artificial by which any faculty is made to preponderate in proportion to its original weakness: and here we find the scientific explanation of that eternal struggle between our humanity and our animality which has been recognized by all who have made Man their study, from the earliest days of civilization till now, and embodied in many forms before its true character was fixed by the positive philosophy.

This, then, is the direction of the human evolution. The next consideration is the rate at which it proceeds, apart from any differences which may result from climate, race, or other modifying causes. Taking into the account only universal causes, it is clear that the speed must be in proportion to the combined influence of the chief natural conditions relating to the human organism first, and next to its

*Rate of progress.*

medium. The invariableness,—the evident impossibility of suspending these fundamental conditions must ever prevent our estimating their respective importance, though we may have a general conviction that our spontaneous development must be hastened or retarded by any change in these elementary influences, organic or inorganic; supposing, for instance, our cerebral system to be slightly inferior, in the frontal region; or our planet to become larger or more habitable. Sociological analysis can, by its nature, reach only to accessory conditions, which are rendered susceptible of estimate by their variations.

*Ennui.* Among these secondary but permanent influences, which affect the rate of human development, *ennui* is the first which presents itself. Man, like other animals, cannot be happy without a sufficient exercise of all his faculties, intense and persistent in proportion to the intrinsic activity of each faculty. The greater difficulty experienced by man in obtaining a development compatible with the special superiority of his nature renders him more subject than the other animals to that remarkable state of irksome languor which indicates at once the existence of the faculties and their insufficient activity, and which would become equally irreconcilable with a radical debility incapable of any urgent tendency, and with an ideal vigour, spontaneously susceptible of indefatigable exercise. A disposition at once intellectual and moral, which we daily see at work in natures endowed with any energy, must have powerfully accelerated the human expansion, in the infancy of humanity, by the uneasy excitement it occasioned either in the eager search for new sources of emotion, or in the more intense development of direct human activity. This secondary influence is not very marked till the social state is sufficiently advanced to make men feel a growing need to exercise the highest faculties, which are, as we have seen, the least energetic. The strongest faculties, which are the lowest, are so easily exercised that in ordinary circumstances they can hardly generate the *ennui* which would produce a favourable cerebral reaction. Savages, like children, are not subject to much *ennui* while their physical activity, which alone is of any importance to them, is not interfered with. An easy and protracted sleep prevents them, as if they were mere animals, from feeling their intellectual torpor in any irksome way. This brief notice of the influence of *ennui* was necessary, to show what its operation really amounts to in accelerating the speed of our social evolution. But perhaps the most important of all accelerating influences is the ordinary duration of human life, which I mention in the second place. There is no denying that our social progression rests upon death. I mean, the successive steps suppose the steady renewal of the agents of the general movement, which is almost imperceptible in the course of any single life, and becomes marked only on the succession of a new generation. Here again the social resembles the individual organism,—being under the same necessity to throw off its constituent parts as they become, by the vital action itself, unfit for further use, and must be replaced by new elements. To illustrate this, we need not go so far as to suppose an indefinite duration of human life, which would presently put a stop to all progression whatever. It is enough to imagine it lengthened tenfold only, its respective periods preserving their present proportions. If the general constitution of the brain remained the same as now, there must be a retardation, though we know not how great, in our social development; for the perpetual conflict which goes on between the conservative instinct that belongs to age and the innovating instinct which distinguishes youth would be much more favourable than now to the former. From the extreme imperfection of the higher parts of our nature, even those who, in their prime, have contributed most to human progress cannot preserve their due social eminence very long without becoming more or less hostile to the further progress which they cannot assist. But an ephemeral life would be quite as mischievous as a too protracted one, by giving too much power to the instinct of innovation. The resistance which this instinct now meets with from the conservatism of age compels it to accommodate its efforts to the whole of what has been already done. Without this check, our feeble nature, which has a strong repugnance to irksome and continuous labour, would be

<small>Duration of human life.</small>

for ever proposing incomplete views and crude attempts, that could never ripen into mature projects and feasible acts: and this would be the inevitable state of things, if human life were reduced to a quarter, or even to half its present length. Such would be the consequences, in either case, if we suppose the constitution of the human brain to be much what it is now: and to suppose it essentially changed, would be to carry us over into the region of hypothesis.

No justification is however afforded by these considerations to the optimism of the advocates of final causes: for if, in this as in every other case, the actual order is necessarily more or less accordant with the course of the phenomena, it is very far from being true that the arrangement of the natural economy is as good for its purposes as we can easily conceive. The slowness of our social development is no doubt partly owing to the extreme imperfection of our organism; but it is owing nearly as much to the brevity of human life: and there would be no risk to any other great arrangement if the duration of our life, while still limited by the conditions just specified, were doubled or trebled. We have hardly thirty years (and those beset with impediments) to devote to other purposes than preparation for life or for death; and this is a very insufficient balance between what Man can devise and what he can execute. Probably no one has ever nobly devoted himself to the direct advancement of the human mind without bitterly feeling how time, employed to the utmost, failed him for the working out of more than an insignificant part of his conceptions. It will not do to say that the rapid succession of coadjutors compensates for this restriction of individual activity. Important as this compensation is, it is very imperfect, both on account of the loss of time in preparing each successor, and because the precise continuance of the work by different persons, occupying different points of view, is impossible, and the more out of the question exactly in proportion to the value of the new coadjutors. In the simplest material operations, no man's work has ever been carried on by others precisely as he would have done it himself; and the more difficult and lofty labours, which require intellectual and moral forces to complete them, are much more in need of a persistent unity in their management. These intellectual and moral forces no more admit of partition and addition by successors than by contemporaries; and, whatever the advocates of the indefinite distribution of individual efforts may say, a certain degree of concentration is necessary to the accomplishment of human progress.

Another cause which affects the rate of progress is the natural increase of population, which contributes more than any other influence to accelerate the speed. *Increase of population.* This increase has always been regarded as the clearest symptom of the gradual amelioration of the human condition; and nothing can be more unquestionable when we take the whole race into the account; or at least, all the nations which have any mutual interest: but this is not the view with which my argument is concerned. I have to consider only the progressive condensation of our species as a last general element concurring in the regulation of our rate of social progress. It is clear that by this condensation, and especially in its early stages, such a division of employments is favoured as could not take place among smaller numbers: and again, that the faculties of individuals are stimulated to find subsistence by more refined methods; and again, that society is obliged to react with a firmer and better concerted energy against the expansion of individual divergences. In view of these considerations, I speak, not of the increase of the numbers of mankind, but of their concentration upon a given space, according to the special expression which I have made use of, and which is particularly applicable to the great centres of population, whence, in all ages, human progression has started. By creating new wants and new difficulties, this gradual concentration develops new means, not only of progress but of order, by neutralizing physical inequalities, and affording a growing ascendency to those intellectual and moral forces which are suppressed among a scanty population. If we go on to inquire into the effect of a quicker or slower concentration, we shall perceive that the social movement is further accelerated by the disturbance given to the old antagonism between the conservative and the innovating instincts,—

the last being strongly reinforced. In this sense the sociological influence of a more rapid increase of population is in analogy with that which we have just been considering in regard to the duration of life; for it is of little consequence whether the more frequent renewal of individuals is caused by the short life of some, or the speedier multiplication of others; and what was said in the former case will suffice for the latter. It must be observed, however, that if the condensation and rapidity were to pass beyond a certain degree, they would not favour, but impede this acceleration. The condensation, if carried too far, would render the support of human life too difficult; and the rapidity, if extreme, would so affect the stability of social enterprises as to be equivalent to a considerable shortening of our life. As yet, however, the increase of population has never nearly reached the natural limits at which such inconveniences will begin; and we have really no experience of them, unless in a few exceptional cases of disturbance caused by migrations, ill-managed as to their extent of numbers and of time. In an extremely distant future, our posterity will have to consider the question, and with much anxiety; because, from the smallness of the globe, and the necessary limitation of human resources, the tendency to increase will become extremely important, when the human race will be ten times as numerous as at present, and as much condensed everywhere as it now is in the west of Europe. Whenever that time comes, the more complete development of human nature, and the more exact knowledge of the laws of human evolution, will no doubt supply new means of resistance to the danger; means of which we can form no clear conception, and about which it is not for us to decide whether they will, on the whole, afford a sufficient compensation.

These are not all the accelerating influences which could be mentioned; but they are the chief; and they are enough for us, in our abstract view of our subject. I have now only to exhibit the main subordination which the different aspects of human development must mutually present.

Though the elements of our social evolution are connected, and always acting on each other, one must be preponderant, in order to give an impulse to the rest, though they may, in their turn, so act upon it as to cause its further expansion. We must find out this superior element, leaving the lower degrees of subordination to disclose themselves as we proceed: and we have not to search far for this element, as we cannot err in taking that which can be best conceived of apart from the rest, notwithstanding their necessary connection, while the consideration of it would enter into the study of the others. This double characteristic points out the intellectual evolution as the preponderant principle. If the intellectual point of view was the chief in our statical study of the organism, much more must it be so in the dynamical case. If our reason required at the outset the awakening and stimulating influence or the appetites, the passions, and the sentiments, not the less has human progression gone forward under its direction. It is only through the more and more marked influence of the reason over the general conduct of Man and of society, that the gradual march of our race has attained that regularity and persevering continuity which distinguish it so radically from the desultory and barren expansion of even the highest of the animal orders, which share, and with enhanced strength, the appetites, the passions, and even the primary sentiments of Man. If the statical analysis of our social organism shows it resting at length upon a certain system of fundamental opinions, the gradual changes of that system must affect the successive modifications of the life of humanity: and this is why, since the birth of philosophy, the history of society has been regarded as governed by the history of the human mind. As it is necessary, in a scientific sense, to refer our historical analysis to the preponderant evolution, whatever it may be, we must in this case choose, or rather preserve, the general history of the human mind as the natural guide to all historical study of humanity. One consequence of the same principle,—a consequence as rigorous but less understood,—is that we must choose for consideration in this intellectual history, the most general and abstract conceptions, which require the exercise of our highest faculties. Thus it is the study of the fundamental

*The order of evolution.*

system of human opinions with regard to the whole of phenomena,— in short, the history of Philosophy, whatever may be its character, theological, metaphysical, or positive,—which must regulate our historical analysis. No other department of intellectual history, not even the history of the fine arts, including poetry, could, however important in itself, be employed for this object; because the faculties of expression, which lie nearer to the affective faculties, have always, in their palmiest days, been subordinated, in the economy of social progress, to the faculties of direct conception. The danger (which is inherent in every choice, and which is least in the choice that I have made,) of losing sight of the interconnection of all the parts of human development, may be partly guarded against by frequently comparing them, to see if the variations in any one corresponds with equivalent variations in the others. I believe we shall find that this confirmation is eminently obtainable by my method of historical analysis. This will be proved at once if we find that the development of the highest part of human interests is in accordance with that of the lowest,—the intellectual with the material. If there is an accordance between the two extremes, there must be also between all the intermediate terms.

We have indicated the general direction of the human evolution, its rate of progress, and its necessary order. We may now proceed at once to investigate the natural laws by which the advance of the human mind proceeds. The scientific principle of the theory appears to me to consist in the great philosophical law of the succession of the three states:—the primitive theological state, the transient metaphysical, and the final positive state,—through which the human mind has to pass, in every kind of speculation. This seems to be the place in which we should attempt the direct estimate of this fundamental law, taking it as the basis of my historic analysis, which must itself have for its chief object to explain and expand the general notion of this law by a more and more extended and exact application of it in the review of the entire past of human history. I hope that the frequent statement and application of this law throughout the preceding part of my work will enable me to condense my demonstration of it here, without impairing its distinctness, or injuring its efficacy in such ulterior use as we shall have to make of it.

The reader is by this time abundantly familiar with the interpretation and destination of the law. All thoughtful persons can verify for themselves its operation in individual development, from infancy to manhood, as I pointed out at the beginning of this work. We can test it, as we have tested other laws, by observation, experiment, and comparison. I have done so through many years of meditation; and I do not hesitate to say that all these methods of investigation will be found to concur in the complete establishment of this historical proposition, which I maintain to be as fully demonstrated as any other law admitted into any other department of natural philosophy. Since the discovery of this law of the three periods, all positive philosophers have agreed on its special adaptation to the particular science in which each was interested, though all have not made the avowal with equal openness. The only objections that I have encountered have related merely to the universality of its application. I hold it to be now implicitly recognized with regard to all the sciences which are positive: that is, the triple evolution is admitted in regard to all cases in which it is accomplished. It is only in regard to social science that its application is supposed to be impossible; and I believe the objection to signify nothing more than that the evolution is in this case incomplete. Social science has, with all its complexity, passed through the theological state, and has almost everywhere fully attained the metaphysical; while it has nowhere yet risen to the positive, except in this book. I shall leave the assertion of the law in regard to sociology to the demonstration which my analysis will afford: for those who cannot perceive in this volume, as a whole, the nascent realization of this last philosophical process could not be convinced by argument. Leaving the historical verification of the law therefore to the reader, I invite attention to its philosophical explanation. It is not enough that the succession of the three states is a general fact. Such generality would go for more in any other science than in sociology, because, as we

*Law of the Three Periods.*

have seen, our biological philosophy enables us to conceive of all the main relations of social phenomena *à priori*, independently of their direct investigation, and we need confirmation of our conceptions by direct knowledge of human nature and experience. An *à priori* conception of a law so important as this is of the deepest interest in the study of social dynamics; and, to confirm it, we must carefully mark the general grounds, derived from an exact knowledge, which have rendered indispensable on the one hand, and inevitable on the other, that succession of social phenomena which take their course under the operation of this law. The logical grounds have already been assigned, at the outset of the work, and repeatedly since: and it is with the moral and social that we now have to do, and we can review them without subjecting ourselves to the reproach of severing the parts of a philosophical demonstration which are in their nature bound up together.

*The Theological period.* The necessity of the intellectual evolution I assert lies in the primary tendency of Man to transfer the sense of his own nature into the radical explanation of all phenomena whatever. Philosophers tell us of the fundamental difficulty of knowing ourselves; but this is a remark which could not have been made till human reason had achieved a considerable advance. The mind must have attained to a refined state of meditation before it could be astonished at its own acts,—reflecting upon itself a speculative activity which must be at first incited by the external world. If, on the one hand, Man must begin by supposing himself the centre of all things, he must, on the other hand, next set himself up as a universal type. The only way that he can explain any phenomena is by likening them, as much as possible, to his own acts,—the only ones whose mode of production he can suppose himself, by the accompanying sensations, to understand. We may therefore set up a converse statement, and say that Man knows nothing but himself; and thus, his philosophy, in his earliest stage, consists principally in transferring this spontaneous unity, more or less fortunately, into all subjects which may present themselves to his nascent attention. It is the highest proof of his philosophical maturity when he can, at length, apply the study of external nature to his own. When I laid this down as the basis of biological philosophy, I intimated the extreme rarity of such an attainment. At the outset, under the inverse process, the universe is always subordinated to Man, in speculative as well as in active respects. We shall not have attained a truly rational position till we can reconcile these two great philosophical views, at present antagonistic, but admitting of being made mutually complementary, and, in my opinion, prepared for being so, from this time forward. Such a harmony is even now barely conceivable in the brightest insight of philosophical genius, and there could have been no choice between the two courses in the earliest days of human development. The starting-point must have been that which alone was naturally possible. This was the spontaneous origin of the theological philosophy, the elementary spirit of which consists in explaining the intimate nature of phenomena, and their mode of production, and in likening them, as much as possible, to the acts of human will, through our primary tendency to regard all beings as living a life analogous to our own, and often superior, from their greater habitual energy. This procedure is so eminently exclusive, that men are unable to emancipate themselves from it, even in the most advanced stages of evolution, except by abandoning altogether these inaccessible researches, and restricting themselves to the study of the laws of phenomena, apart from their causes. Whenever, at this day, the human mind attempts to pass these inevitable limits, it involuntary falls again into the primary errors, even in regard to the simplest phenomena, because it recurs to an aim and point of view essentially analogous, in attributing the production of phenomena to special volitions, internal, or more or less external. One case presents itself as an example, of the simplest scientific character,—that of the memorable philosophical error of the illustrious Malebranche in regard to the explanation of the mathematical laws of the elementary collision of solid bodies. If such a mind, in such an age, could explain such a theory in no other way than by an express recurrence to the continuous activity of a direct and special providence, we cannot doubt the tendency of our reason towards a radically theological philosophy whenever we attempt to penetrate, on any ground whatever, the intimate nature of phenomena.

This inevitableness of the theological philosophy is its most radical property, and the first cause of its long ascendancy. We have seen before that it was necessary, as the only possible beginning of our intellectual evolution; for the facts which must form the basis of a positive theory could not be collected to any purpose without some preliminary theory which should guide their collection. Our understanding cannot act without some doctrine, false or true, vague or precise, which may concentrate and stimulate its efforts, and afford ground for enough speculative continuity to sustain our mental activity. Our meteorological *observations*, as we call them, show us how useless may be vast compilations of facts, and how really unmeaning, while we are destitute of any theory whatever. Those who expect that the theory will be suggested by the facts, do not understand what is the course necessarily pursued by the human mind, which has achieved all real results by the only effectual method,—of anticipating scientific observations by some conception (hypothetical in the first instance) of the corresponding phenomena. Such a necessity has already been shown to be especially marked in the case of social speculations, not only from their complexity, but from the peculiarity that a long preparatory development of the human mind and of society constitutes the phenomena of the case, independently of all preparation of observers, and all accumulation of observations. It may be worth observing, that all the partial verifications of this fundamental proposition that we meet with in the different sciences confirm each other, on account of our tendency to unity of method and homogeneousness of doctrine, which would incline us to extend the theological philosophy from one class of speculations to another, even if we should not so treat each one of them separately.

The original and indispensable office of the theological philosophy is then to lead forth the human mind from the vicious circle in which it was confined by the two necessities of observing first, in order to form conceptions, and of forming theories first, in order to observe. The theological philosophy afforded an issue by likening all phenomena whatever to human acts; directly, in the first instance, by supposing all bodies to have a life more or less like our own, and indirectly afterwards, by means of the more durable and suggestive hypothesis which adds to the visible system of things an invisible world, peopled by superhuman agents, who occasion all phenomena by their action on matter, otherwise inert. The second stage is especially suitable to the human mind which begins to feel its difficulties and its needs; for every new phenomenon is accounted for by the supposition of a fresh volition in the ideal agent concerned, or, at most, by the easy creation of a new agent. However futile these speculations may now appear, we must remember that, in all times and everywhere, they have awakened human thought by offering to it the only material which it could at first accept. Besides that there was no choice, the infant reason can be interested by nothing but sublime solutions, obtained without any deep and sustained conflict of thought. We, at this day, find ourselves able, after suitable training, to devote ourselves to the study of the laws of phenomena, without heed to their first and final causes: but still we detect ourselves occasionally yielding to the infantine curiosity which pretends to a power of knowing the origin and the end of all things. But such severity of reason as we are capable of has become attainable only since the accumulation of our knowledge has yielded us a rational hope of finally discovering the natural laws that were altogether out of reach, in the early states of the human mind; and the only alternative from total inactivity was, in those days, in the pursuit of the inaccessible subjects which are represented by the theological philosophy.—The moral and social grounds of this philosophy were as necessary as the intellectual. Its moral influence was to inspire Man with confidence enough for action, by animating him with a sense of a position of supremacy. There is something astonishing in the contrast between the actual powers of Man in an infant state and the indefinite control which he aspires to exercise over external nature; just as there is in his expectation of understanding matters which are inaccessible to reason. The practical and the speculative expectation alike belong to the theological philosophy. Supposing all phenomena to be regulated by superhuman will, Man may hope to modify the universe by his desires; not by his personal resources, but by the access which he believes himself to have to the imaginary beings whose power is unlimited: whereas, if he was aware from the beginning that the universe is subject to invariable laws, the certainty that he could no more influence than understand them would so discourage him that he would remain for ever in his original apathy, intellectual and moral. We find ourselves able to dispense with supernatural aid in our difficulties and sufferings, in proportion as we obtain a gradual control over nature by a knowledge of her laws: but the early races of men were in an opposite condition. They could obtain confidence, and therefore courage, only from above, and through the illusion of an illimitable power residing there, which could, on any occasion, afford them irresistible aid. I am not referring now to any hope of a future life. We shall see presently that it was not till a much later period that that hope exercised any important social influence: and even in more recent times, we shall find that the effect of the religious spirit on the conduct of human life proceeds much more from belief in actual and special immediate aid than from the uniform perspective of a remote future existence. This seems to me the leading aspect of the remarkable state which is produced in the human brain by the important intellectual and moral phenomenon of prayer; the admirable properties of which, when it has attained its full physiological efficacy, are very manifest in the earliest stage of progress. After a long decline of the religious spirit, the notion of *miracle* was naturally formed, to characterize the events which had become exceptional, and were attributed to divine intervention: but the very conception shows that the general principle of natural laws had become familiar, and even preponderant, because the only sense of *miracle* was a transient suspension of natural laws. While the theological philosophy was all in all, there were no miracles, because everything was equally marvellous, as we see by the artless descriptions of ancient poetry, in which the commonest incidents are mixed up with the most monstrous prodigies, and undergo analogous explanations. Minerva intervenes to pick up the whip of a warrior in military games, as well as to protect him against a whole army: and in our time, the devotee is as importunate in praying for his smallest personal convenience as for the largest human interests. In all ages, the priest has been more occupied with the solicitations of his flock about immediate favours of Providence than with their care for their eternal state. However this may be, we see that it is a radical property of the theological philosophy to be the sole support and stimulus of Man's moral courage, as well as the awakener and director of his intellectual activity.—To this we must add, as another attraction of Man to this philosophy, that the affective influence comes in to fortify the speculative. Feeble as are the intellectual organs, relatively considered, the attractive moral perspective of an unbounded power of modifying the universe, by the aid of supernatural protectors, must have been most important in exciting mental action. In our advanced state of scientific progress, we can conceive of the perpetual pursuit of knowledge for the sake of the satisfaction of intellectual activity, joined to the tranquil pleasure which arises from the discovery of truth : yet it is doubtful whether such natural stimulus as this would always suffice without collateral instigations of glory, of ambition, or of lower and stronger passions, except in the case of a very few lofty minds; and with them, only after training in the requisite habits. And nothing of this kind can be supposed possible in the early days, when the intellect is torpid and feeble, and scarcely accessible to the strongest stimulus; nor yet afterwards, when science is so far advanced as to have attained some speculative success. In the working out of such speculation, the mental activity can be sustained by nothing short of the fictions of the theological philosophy about the supremacy of man and his unbounded empire over external nature; as we have seen in regard to astrology and alchemy. In our own time, when there are enlightened men who hold such delusions in regard to social speculations alone, we see how irrationally they expect to modify at will the whole course of political phenomena, in which they could not take any adequate scientific interest without such an expectation. What we see of the influence of this view in maintaining the old polities may give us some faint idea of its power when it pervaded every part of the intellectual system, and illusion beset the reason of Man, whichever way he turned. Such then was the moral operation of the theological philosophy,—stimulating Man's active energy by the offer, in the midst of the troubles of his infantine state, of absolute empire over the external world, as the prize of his speculative efforts.

*Social influences of the Theological philosophy.* The social evidences under this head will be fully treated in the following chapters, so that we may dismiss them now with a very short notice, important as they are; and the more easily, because this class of evidences is the most indisputable of the three. There are two views which must be considered, in relation to the high social office of the theological philosophy: first, its function in organizing society; and next, its provision for the permanent existence of a speculative class.—As to the first, we must perceive that the formation of any society, worthy to be so called, supposes a system of common opinions, such as may restrain individual eccentricity; and such an influence, if needful now, when men are connected together by such a concurrence of obligations as high civilization introduces, must be absolutely indispensable in the infancy of society, when families adhere to each other so feebly, by means of relations as precarious as they are defective. No concurrence of interests, nor even sympathy in sentiment, can give durability to the smallest society, if there be not intellectual unanimity enough to obviate or correct such discordance as must inevitably arise. It has been shown that, indolent as our intellectual faculties are in comparison with the others, reason must rule, not domestic but social, and yet more political life: for through it alone can there be any organization of that reaction of society on the individual which appoints the function of government, and absolutely requires a system of common opinions about nature and Man. Such a system, then, is a political necessity; and especially in the infancy of society. But, on the other hand, we must admit that the human mind, having thus furnished a basis for social organization, must depend for its further development on society itself, whose expansion is really inseparable from that of human intelligence. Here we see that society is in a vicious circle in a political, as well as a logical view, through the opposition of two equal necessities; and here, again, the only possible issue is afforded by the theological philosophy. It directs the first social organization, as it first forms a system of common opinions, and by forming such a system. Because we see it now in such a state of decomposition that its advocates lose sight of the unity of opinions that it once secured, and are themselves involved in intellectual discordance, we must not forget how, in those days of vigour by which it must be judged, it established an intellectual communion which constituted its most remarkable political function. The police consideration of a future life is wrongly attributed to this period of human society. It arose long after and was of very inferior importance to the intellectual agreement which preceded it: and its operation would not be so erroneously exaggerated, but that religion has so far faded out of men's minds as to leave no other strong habitual remembrance than of its grossest impressions.

Another way in which the theological philosophy was politically indispensable to human progress was by instituting, in the midst of society, a special class regularly devoted to speculative activity. In this view, the social supremacy of the theological philosophy has lasted to our own time. It is scarcely possible for us to form any but an indirect idea of the difficulty of establishing, in the earliest period of society, any permanent division between theory and practice, such as is effected by the existence of a class regularly occupied with speculation. Even now, amidst all the refinement of our mental habits, we find extreme difficulty in duly estimating any new operation which has no immediate practical bearing: and by this we may imperfectly understand how impossible it was, in the remotest ages, to institute among populations of warriors and slaves a corporation that should be disengaged from military and industrial employments, and whose activity should be mainly of an intellectual kind. Such a class could, in those times, have been neither established nor tolerated if

*Institution of a speculative class.*

it had not been introduced in the natural course of social movement, and invested with authority beforehand by the influence of the theological philosophy. The political function of that philosophy thus was to establish a speculative body whose social existence not only admitted of no preparatory discussion, but was itself an indispensable preparation for the regular organization of all other classes. Whatever might have been the confusion of intellectual labour, and the inanity of the leading investigations of the sacerdotal orders, it is not the less true that the human mind owes to them the first effectual separation between theory and practice, which could take place in no other manner. Mental progress, by which all other progress is directed, would certainly have been destroyed at its birth, if society had continued to be composed of families engaged in the cares of material existence, or, as the only alternative, in the excitement of a brutal military activity. Any spiritual expansion supposes the existence of a privileged class, enjoying the leisure indispensable to intellectual culture, and at the same time urged, by its social position, to develop to the utmost the kind of speculative activity compatible with the primitive state of humanity; and this description is answered by the sacerdotal institution established by the theological philosophy. Though, in the decrepitude of the old philosophy, we see the theological class sunk in mental lethargy, we must not forget that but for their activity in the days of its prime, human society would have remained in a condition much like that of a company of superior monkeys. By forming this speculative class, then, the theological philosophy fulfilled the political conditions of a further progression of the human mind.

Such are the qualities, intellectual, moral, and social, which secured the supremacy of the theological philosophy, at the outset of human progress. This is the only part of my sociological demonstration which is at all open to dispute; and this is one reason why I have dwelt so long upon it: but it is not the only reason. Another and a greater is that this view contains the radical principle of the whole demonstration, the remainder of which will not detain us long.

If this starting-point of human development has been placed beyond dispute, the final, or positive stage, does not admit of it. We have seen enough of the establishment of the positive philosophy in other departments to be satisfied of its destined prevalence in sociology. For the same reasons which explain and justify the early supremacy of the theological philosophy, we see that it must be a provisional state, for its supremacy was owing to its aptitude to meet the needs of a primitive state of humanity; and those needs are not the same, nor requiring the same philosophy to satisfy them, as those which arise in a more advanced stage of the human evolution. After having awakened human reason, and superintended its progress, in the absence of a more real philosophy, theology began to repress the human mind from the first moment of its coming into direct antagonism with the positive philosophy. And in the same way, in its moral relations, it imparted at first a consolatory confidence and active energy, which have become transmuted, by too long a duration, into oppressive terror and a faint apathy which have been too common a spectacle since it has been driven to struggle to retain its hold, instead of extending its dominion. There is no more question of the moral than of the intellectual superiority and final supremacy of the positive philosophy, capable as it is of developing in us an unshaken vigour and a deliberate steadfastness, directly derived from our own nature, without any external assistance, or any imaginary hindrance. And again, in regard to its social bearings, though the ascendancy of the theological philosophy lasted longer on this ground than on the other two, it is evident enough at present that, instead of uniting men, which was its proper function at first, it now divides them, so that after having created speculative activity, it has ended with radically hindering it. The function of reuniting, as of stimulating and directing, belongs more and more, as religious belief declines, to the conceptions of positive philosophy, which alone can establish that intellectual community all over the world on which the great future political organization is to be grounded. The intellectual destination of the two philosophies has been suffi-

*The Positive stage.*

ciently established in our review of all the departments of natural philosophy. Their moral and social destination will be illustrated in succeeding chapters of this work. My historical analysis will explain to us the continuous decline of the one and the corresponding rise of the other, from the earliest period of human progression. It may appear paradoxical to regard the theological philosophy as in a steadily declining state intellectually, at the very time that it was fulfilling its most exalted political mission; but we shall find satisfactory scientific evidence that Catholicism, its noblest social work, must necessarily be its last effort, on account of the germs of disorganization which must thenceforth grow more and more rapidly. We need here therefore only assign the general principle of the inevitable tendency of the human mind towards an exclusive positive philosophy, throughout the whole range of the intellectual system.

*Attempted union of the two philosophies.* The general, like the individual human mind, is governed by imagination first, and then, after a sufficient exercise of the faculties at large, more and more by reason. The same grounds on which the process takes place in the individual case determine that of the whole species; and with the more certainty and power on account of the greater complexity and perpetuity of the social organism. Supreme as the theological philosophy once was, it is certain that such a method of philosophizing was resorted to only because no other was possible. Wherever there has been a choice, in regard to any subject whatever, Man has always preferred the study of the laws of phenomena to that of their primary causes, though prior training, which there has been no rational education adapted to counteract, has often occasioned lapse into his old illusions. Theological philosophy has, however, never been absolutely universal. That is, the simplest and commonest facts in all classes of phenomena have always been supposed subject to natural laws, and not to the arbitrary will of supernatural agents. Adam Smith made the remark that there never was, in any age or country, a god of Weight. In more complex cases, if only the relations of phenomena are seen to be invariable, the most superficial observer recognizes the presence of law. Even among moral and social phenomena, where the entrance of positive philosophy has been interdicted, we are all obliged to act daily on the supposition of natural laws, in order to conduct the common affairs of life, for all forecast would be impossible if we supposed every incident to be ascribable to supernatural agency, and no other resource therefore possible than prayer, for influencing the course of human actions. It is even noticeable that the principle of the theological philosophy itself lies in the transference to the phenomena of external nature of the first beginnings of the laws of human action; and thus the germ of the positive philosophy is at least as primitive as that of the theological philosophy itself, though it could not expand till a much later time. This idea is very important to the perfect rationality of our sociological theory; because, as human life can never present any real creation, but only a gradual evolution, the final spread of the positive spirit would be scientifically incomprehensible, if we could not trace its rudiments from the very beginning. From that scarcely appreciable presence at the beginning, the rise of the positive spirit has been recognizable, in proportion to the extension and generalization of our observations, and the theological philosophy has been slowly but steadily driven back within the narrowing limits of phenomena whose natural laws were still unknown. Thus was the function of the old philosophy clearly a provisional one,—to maintain our mental activity by the only exercise open to it, till the positive philosophy should usher it into the wide field of universal knowledge, made accessible to the whole race. This destination has only recently exhibited itself in an unquestionable way since the disclosure of natural laws in phenomena so numerous and so various as to suggest the necessary existence of analogous laws in all other departments, however remote their actual discovery may be.

It does not follow, from anything that I have said, that the two philosophies were always visibly opposed to each other. On the contrary, the physical study must have succumbed to the theological spirit if they had seemed at the outset to be incompatible. In fact, the study of the laws of phenomena appeared, for a long course of time, to agree very well with the investigation into their causes. It was only when observations became more connected, and disclosed important relations, that the radical opposition of the two doctrines began to be felt. Before the antagonism was avowed, the positive spirit manifested its repugnance to the futile absolute explanations of the theological philosophy; and the theological spirit lavished its disdain on the circumspect march and modest investigations of the new school; while still there was no idea that the study of real laws was irreconcilable with that of essential causes. When natural laws of considerable scope were at length discovered, the incompatibility became clear between the preponderance of imagination and that of reason, between the absolute spirit and the relative; and, above all, between the ancient hypothesis of the sovereign direction of events by any arbitrary will, and the growing certainty that we can foresee and modify them by the rational access of human wisdom. It is only in our own time that the antagonism has been extended to all parts of the intellectual field: and even up to the last moment, the students of special subjects have believed that by confining themselves to the investigation of natural laws, and paying no attention to the nature of beings and mode of production of phenomena, they might find physical researches compatible with the explanations of theology; while theology made its own concessions in the form of a provisional notion of a universal providence, combined with special laws which it had imposed on itself. The conduct of Catholicism, in interdicting the habitual use of miracle and prophecy, which prevailed so largely in ancient times, seems to me to present, in religious affairs, a transient situation analogous to that which is exhibited by what is called the institution of constitutional monarchy in the political world; each being in its own way an indisputable symptom of decline. However this may be, the insufficiency of the theological philosophy manifests itself to popular observation in that form of popular evidence which can alone reach the majority of mankind,—in its comparison with its opponent in the application of means. The positive philosophy enables us to foresee and to modify natural events, and thus satisfies, more and more, as it advances, the most urgent intellectual needs of humanity, while the ancient philosophy remains barren; so that its fanciful explanations are more and more neglected, while the new philosophy obtains a perpetually firmer hold on the public reason. Those who have remained faithful in their attachment to the theological philosophy make no practical use of it in their daily life, and ground their predilection for it on its characteristic generality: so that when its antagonist shall have become systematized as fully as it is destined to be, the ancient philosophy will have lost the last attribute which has ever entitled it to social supremacy.

We have now only to take a cursory survey of the intermediate state. I have pointed out more than once before, that any intermediate state can be judged of only after a precise analysis of the two extremes. The present case is a remarkable illustration of this necessity; for, if it is once admitted that the human mind must set out from the theological state, and arrive certainly at the positive, we may easily understand how it must pass through the metaphysical, which has no other destination than to afford a transition from the one to the other. The bastard and mobile character of the metaphysical philosophy fits it for this office, as it reconciles, for a time, the radical opposition of the other two, adapting itself to the gradual decline of the one and the preparatory rise of the other, so as to spare our dislike of abrupt change, and to afford us a transition almost imperceptible. The metaphysical philosophy takes possession of the speculative field after the theological has relinquished it, and before the positive is ready for it: so that in each particular case, the dispute about the supremacy of any of the three philosophies is reduced to the mere question of opportuneness, judged by a rational examination of the development of the human mind. The method of modification consists in substituting gradually the entity for a deity when religious conceptions become so generalized as to diminish perpetually the number of supernatural agents, as well as their active intervention, and at length arrive, professedly if not really, at rigorous unity. When supernatural action loses its original

*The Metaphysical Period.*

speciality, it consigns the immediate direction of the phenomenon to a mysterious entity, at first emanating from itself, but to which daily custom trains the human mind to refer more and more exclusively the production of each event. This strange process has favoured the withdrawal of supernatural causes, and the exclusive consideration of phenomena; that is, the decline of the theological and the rise of the positive spirit. Beyond this, the general character of this philosophy is that of the theological, of which it is only a modification, though the chief. It has an inferior intellectual consistency, and a much less intense social power; so that it is much better adapted for a critical function than for any real organization: and it is those very qualities which disable it for resistance to the growth of the positive spirit. On the one hand, the increasing subtlety of metaphysical speculations is for ever reducing their characteristic entities to mere abstract denominations of the corresponding phenomena, so as to render their own impotence ridiculous when they attempt explanations: a thing which would not have been possible, in an equal degree, with purely theological forms. On the other hand, its deficiency of organizing power, in consequence of its radical inconsistency, must prevent its maintaining any such political struggle as theology maintained against the spread of positive social philosophy. However, it obtains a respite by its own equivocal and mobile nature, which enables it to escape from rational discussion even more than the theological philosophy itself, while the positive spirit is as yet too imperfectly generalized to be able to attack the only substantial ground of their common authority,—the universality which they can boast, but which it has not. However this may be, we must admit the aptitude of metaphysics to sustain, provisionally, our speculative activity on all subjects till it can receive more substantial aliment; at the same time carrying us over from the theological *régime* further and further in the direction of the positive. The same aptitude appears in its political action. Without overlooking the serious intellectual and moral dangers which distinguish the metaphysical philosophy, its transitional quality accounts to us for the universal ascendancy which it has provisionally obtained among the most advanced societies, which cannot but have an instinctive sense of some indispensable office to be fulfilled by such a philosophy in the evolution of humanity. The irresistible necessity of this temporary phase is thus, on all grounds, as unquestionable as it could be prior to the direct analysis to which it will be subjected in the course of our historical review.

During the whole of our survey of the sciences, I have endeavoured to keep in view the great fact that all the three states, theological, metaphysical, and positive, may and do exist at the same time in the same mind in regard to different sciences. I must once more recall this consideration, and insist upon it; because in the forgetfulness of it lies the only real objection that can be brought against the grand law of the three states. It must be steadily kept in view that the same mind may be in the positive state with regard to the most simple and general sciences; in the metaphysical with regard to the more complex and special; and in the theological with regard to social science, which is so complex and special as to have hitherto taken no scientific form at all. Any apparent contradiction must certainly arise, even if it could be shown to exist, from the imperfection of our hierarchical arrangement, and not from the law of evolution itself. This once fully understood, the law itself becomes our guide in further investigation, as every proved theory does, by showing us by anticipation, what phenomena to look for, and how to use those which arise: and it supplies the place of direct exploration, when we have not the necessary means of investigation. We shall find that by this law alone can the history of the human mind be rendered intelligible. Having convinced ourselves of its efficacy in regard to all other sciences, and in interpreting all that has yet come to pass in human history, we must adhere to it steadily in analysing the present, and in forming such anticipation of the future as sociology, being a real science, enables us to rely upon.

*Co-existence of the three Periods.*

To complete my long and difficult demonstration, I have only now to show that material development, as a whole, must follow a course, not only analogous, but perfectly correspondent with that of intellectual development, which, as we have seen, governs every other.

**Corresponding material development.** All political investigation of a rational kind proves the primitive tendency of mankind, in a general way, to a military life; and to its final issue in an industrial life. No enlightened mind disputes the continuous decline of the military spirit, and the gradual ascendancy of the industrial. We see now, under various forms, and more and more indisputably, even in the very heart of armies, the repugnance of modern society to a military life. We see that compulsory recruiting becomes more and more necessary, and that there is less and less voluntary persistence in that mode of life. Notwithstanding the immense exceptional development of military activity which was occasioned by anomalous circumstances at the beginning of the present century, our industrial and pacific instincts have returned to their regular course of expansion, so as to render us secure of the radical tranquillity of the civilized world, though the peace of Europe must often appear to be endangered through the provisional deficiency of any systematic organization of international relations; a cause which, though insufficient to produce war, keeps us in a state of frequent uneasiness. We need not then go over again the proof of the first and last terms of the evolution; which will be abundantly illustrated by the historical analysis that I shall offer. We have only to refer the facts of human experience to the essential laws of human nature, and the necessary conditions of social development:—a scientific procedure which has never yet been attempted.

**Primitive military life.** As long as primitive Man was averse from all regular toil, the military life alone furnished a field for his sustained activity. Apart from cannibalism, it offered the simplest means of subsistence. However deplorable the necessity, its universal prevalence and continuous development, even after subsistence might have been obtained by other means, proves that the military *régime* must have had some indispensable, though provisional office to fulfil in the progression of the race. It was indeed the only one under which human industry could make a beginning; in the same way that the scientific spirit could not have arisen without the protection of the religious. The industrial spirit supposed the existence of a considerable social development, such as could not have taken place till isolated families had been connected by the pursuits of war. The social, and yet more the political properties of military activity are, in their early stages, perfectly clear and decisive, and, in short, fully appropriate to the high civilizing function which they had to fulfil. It was thus that habits of regularity and discipline were instituted, and the families of men were brought into association for warlike expeditions or for their common defence. The objects of association could not possibly be more obvious or urgent, nor the elementary conditions of concurrence more irresistible. In no other school could a primitive society learn order; as we may see at this day in the case of those types of ancient humanity,—the exceptional individuals who cannot now be made amenable to industrial discipline. This ascendancy of the military spirit was indispensable, not only to the original consolidation of political society, but yet more to its continuous extension, which could not otherwise have taken place but with excessive slowness; and such extension was, to a certain degree, indispensable to the final development of human industry. Thus, then, we find humanity involved in the same kind of vicious circle with regard to its temporal as we saw it to be with its spiritual progress; and in both cases an issue was afforded by the fortunate expansion of a preliminary tendency. In fact, the necessary basis of the military *régime* has everywhere been the individual slavery of the producing class, by which warriors were allowed the full and free development of their activity. We shall see hereafter that the great social operation which was to be accomplished, in due time, by the continuous progression of a military system, powerfully instituted and wisely carried out, must have failed in its earliest stages. We shall also see how this ancient slavery was the necessary preparation for the final prevalence of the industrial life, by imposing on the majority of the race, irresistibly and exclusively, that toil to which Man is constitutionally averse, though an ultimate condition of laborious perseverance was in store for all. To view the case without prejudice, we must transport ourselves to those primitive times, and not regard the slavery of that age with the just horror with which we view that of modern times,—the colonial slavery of our day, which is truly a social monstrosity, existing as it does in the heart of an industrial period, subjecting the labourer to the capitalist in a manner equally degrading to both. The ancient slavery was of the producer to the warrior; and it tended to develope their respective energies, so as to occasion their final concurrence in the same social progression.

*The Military régime provisional.* Necessary as this military *régime* was, it was not the less merely provisional. While industrial activity has the fine quality of bearing the most energetic extension among all individuals and nations without making the rise of the one irreconcilable with that of the other, it is evident that the exaltation of the military life among any considerable portion of the race must occasion the restriction of all the rest; this being, in fact, the proper function of the *régime* in regard to the whole field of civilization. Thus, while the industrial period comprehends the whole term of human progress under natural laws,—that is, the whole future that we can conceive of,—the military period could last no longer than the formation of those preparatory conditions which it was its function to create. This end was attained when the chief part of the civilized world was at length united under the same rule; that is, in regard to Europe, when Rome had completed its conquests. From that time forward, military activity had neither object nor aliment; and from that time forward, therefore, it declined, so as no longer to disguise that gradual rise of the industrial spirit, which had been preparing during the interval. But, notwithstanding this connection, the industrial state was so radically different from the military as to require an intermediate term; and in the same way that, in the spiritual evolution, an intermediate term was required between the theological and the positive spirit. In both cases, the middle phase was fluctuating and equivocal. We shall see hereafter that, in the temporal case, it consisted, first, in a substitution of a defensive for an offensive military organization, and afterwards in an involuntary general subordination, more and more marked, of the military spirit to the instinct of production. This transitory phase being the one in which we live, its proper nature, vague as it is, can be estimated by indirect intuition.

Such is the temporal evolution, briefly surveyed in its three periods. No philosophical mind can help being struck by the analogy between this indisputable progression and our primary law of succession of the three states of the human mind. But our sociological demonstration requires that we should establish the connection between them by exhibiting the natural affinity which has always existed, first between the theological and the military spirit, and afterwards between the scientific and industrial; and, consequently, between the two transient functions of the metaphysicians and the legists. This elucidation will impart the last degree of precision and consistency to my demonstration, and will thus establish it as the rational basis of the entire historical analysis which will follow.

The occasional rivalry between the theological power and the military, which history presents, has sometimes disguised their radical affinity, even in the eyes of philosophers. *Affinity between the theological and military régime.* But, if we consider, there can be no real rivalry but among the different elements of the same political system, in consequence of that spontaneous emulation which, in all cases of human concurrence, must become more earnest and extensive as the end is more important and indirect, and therefore the means more distinct and independent, without the participation, voluntary or instinctive, being thereby prevented. When two powers, equally energetic, rise, increase, and decline together, notwithstanding the difference of their natures, we may be assured that they belong to the same *régime*, whatever may be their habitual conflicts. Conflict indicates radical incompatibility only when it takes place between two elements employed in analogous functions, and when the gradual growth of the one coincides with the continuous decline of the other. As to the present case, it is evident that, in any political system, there must be an incessant rivalry between the speculative and the active powers, which, through the imperfection of our nature, must often be inclined to ignore their necessary co-ordination, and to disdain the general limits of their reciprocal attributes. Notwithstanding the social affinity between science and industry, we must look for similar conflict between them hereafter, in proportion to the political ascendancy which they will obtain together. We see signs of it already in the intellectual and moral antipathy of Science to the natural inferiority of these labours of Industry which yet are the means of wealth, and in the instinctive repugnance of Industry to the abstraction which characterizes Science, and to the just pride by which it is animated.

Having despatched these objections, we may now contemplate the strong bond which unites the theological and military powers, and which has in all ages been felt and honoured by all enlightened men who have borne a part in either, notwithstanding the passions of political rivalry. It is plain that no military system could arise and endure without the countenance of the theological spirit, which must secure for it the complete and permanent subordination essential to its existence. Each period imposes equal exigencies of this sort in its special manner. At the outset, when the narrowness and nearness of the aim required a less absolute submission of mind, social ties were so weak that nothing could have been done but for the religious authority with which military chiefs were naturally invested. In more advanced times the end became so vast and remote, and the participation so indirect, that even long habits of discipline would not have secured the necessary co-operation without the aid of theological convictions occasioning blind and involuntary confidence in military superiors. It was in very ancient times that the military spirit had its great social function to fulfil; and it was in those ancient times that the two powers were usually found concentrated in the same chiefs. We must observe also that it was not every spiritual authority whatever that would have sufficiently suited the foundation and consolidation of military government, which, from its nature, required the concurrence of the theological philosophy, and no other: for instance, though natural philosophy has rendered eminent service in modern times to the art of war, the scientific spirit, which encourages habits of rational discussion, is radically incompatible with the military spirit; and we know that the subjection of their art to the principles of science has always been bitterly deplored by the most distinguished soldiers, on the introduction of every change, as a token of the decline of the military system. On this ground, then, the affinity of temporal military powers for spiritual theological powers is sufficiently accounted for. At the first glance we might suppose the converse relation to be less indispensable, since purely theocratic societies have existed, while an exclusively military one has never been known. But a closer examination will always show the necessity of the military system to consolidate, and yet more to extend, the theological authority, developed in this way by a continual political application, as the sacerdotal instinct has always been well aware. We shall see again that the theological spirit is as hostile to the expansion of industry as the military. Thus the two elements of the primitive political system have not only a radical affinity, but common antipathies and sympathies, as well as general interests; and it must be needless to enlarge further in this place on the sociological principle of the concurrence of these powers, which my historical analysis will present as constantly engaged in consolidating and correcting each other.

The latest case of political dualism is even more unquestionable than the earliest, and we are favourably circumstanced for observing it,—the two elements not having yet attained their definite ascendency, though their social development is sufficiently marked. When the time arrives for their political rivalry, it may be more difficult than now to exhibit that resemblance in origin and destination, and that conformity of principles and interests, which could not be seriously disputed as long as their common struggle against the old political system acts as a restraint upon their divergencies. The most remarkable feature that we have to contemplate in their case is the aid which each renders to the political triumph of the other, by

*Affinity between the Positive and Industrial spirit.*

seconding its own efforts against its chief antagonist. I have already noticed, in another connection, the secret incompatibility between the scientific spirit and the military. There is the same hostility between the industrial spirit, when sufficiently developed, and the theological. The most zealous advocates of the old *régime* are very far removed from the old religious point of view; but we can transport ourselves to it for a moment, and see how the voluntary modification of phenomena by the rules of human wisdom must thence appear as impious as the rational prevision of them, as both suppose invariable laws, finally irreconcilable with all arbitrary will. According to the rigorous though barbarous logic of the least civilized nations, all human intervention to improve the economy of nature is an injurious attack upon providential government. There is no doubt, in fact, that a strong preponderance of the religious spirit benumbs the industrial, by the exaggerated feelings of a stupid optimism, as has been abundantly clear on many decisive occasions. That this disastrous effect has not been more fatal is owing to priestly sagacity, which has so managed this dangerous power as to educe its civilizing influence, while neutralizing its injurious action by constant and vigilant effort, in a way which I shall presently exhibit. We cannot then overlook the political influence by which the gradual expansion of human industry must aid the progressive ascendency of the scientific spirit, in its antagonism to the religious; to say nothing of the daily stimulus which industry and science impart to each other, when once strong enough for mutual action. Thus far their office has chiefly been to substitute themselves for the ancient political powers which are yielding up their social influence; and our attention is necessarily drawn chiefly to the aid they have afforded to each other in this operation. But it is easy to perceive what force and what efficacy must reside in their connection, when it shall have assumed the organic character, in which it is at present deficient, and shall proceed to the final reorganization of modern society.

Intermediate *régime*.

Now that we have examined the two extreme states, the intermediate dualism requires little notice. The interconnection of the convergent powers, spiritual and temporal, which constitutes the transitory *régime*, is a necessary consequence of all that we have been observing. Indeed, we need but look at the labours of metaphysicians and legists to see what their affinity is, amidst their rivalries; an affinity which stakes the philosophical ascendency of the one class on the political preponderance of the other. We may, then, regard as now complete the necessary explanation required by our fundamental law of human evolution, in order to its direct application to the study of this great phenomenon. That study will be guided by the consideration of the three dualisms which I have established as the only basis of sound historical philosophy. It is worth noticing the conformity of this law of succession, at once intellectual and material, social and political, with the historical order which popular reason has instinctively established, by distinguishing the ancient and the modern world, separated and reunited by the Middle Ages. The sociological law which I have propounded may be found to have for its destination to take up a vague empirical notion, hitherto barren, and render it rational and prolific. I hail this spontaneous coincidence, as giving a sanction to my speculative labours; and I claim this confirmation, in virtue of that great aphorism of positive philosophy which I have quoted so often, which enjoins upon all sound scientific theories to start from a point sufficiently accordant with the spontaneous indications of popular reason, of which true science is simply a special prolongation.

The series of views of social dynamics sketched out in this chapter has established the fundamental law of human development, and therefore the bases of historical philosophy. We had before ascertained the spirit and method of that philosophy; and we may now therefore proceed to apply this great sociological conception to the analysis of the history of mankind.

# AN ALPHABETICAL LIST

OF BOOKS CONTAINED IN

# BOHN'S LIBRARIES.

*Detailed Catalogue, arranged according to the various Libraries, will be sent on application.*

**ADDISON'S Works.** With the Notes of Bishop Hurd, Portrait, and 8 Plates of Medals and Coins. Edited by H. G. Bohn. 6 vols. 3s. 6d. each.

**ÆSCHYLUS, The Dramas of.** Translated into English Verse by Anna Swanwick. 4th Edition, revised. 5s.

—— **The Tragedies of.** Translated into Prose by T. A. Buckley, B.A. 3s. 6d.

**ALLEN'S (Joseph, R. N.) Battles of the British Navy.** Revised Edition, with 57 Steel Engravings. 2 vols. 5s. each.

**AMMIANUS MARCELLINUS. History of Rome** during the Reigns of Constantius, Julian, Jovianus, Valentinian, and Valens. Translated by Prof. C. D. Yonge, M.A. 7s. 6d.

**ANDERSEN'S Danish Legends and Fairy Tales.** Translated by Caroline Peachey. With 120 Wood Engravings. 5s.

**ANTONINUS (M. Aurelius), The Thoughts of.** Trans. literally, with Notes and Introduction by George Long, M.A. 3s. 6d.

**APOLLONIUS RHODIUS.** 'The Argonautica.' Translated by E. P. Coleridge, B.A. 5s.

**APPIAN'S Roman History.** Translated by Horace White, M.A., LL.D. With Maps and Illustrations. 2 vols. 6s. each.

**APULEIUS, The Works of.** Comprising the Golden Ass, God of Socrates, Florida, and Discourse of Magic. 5s.

**ARIOSTO'S Orlando Furioso.** Translated into English Verse by W. S. Rose. With Portrait, and 24 Steel Engravings. 2 vols. 5s. each.

**ARISTOPHANES' Comedies.** Translated by W. J. Hickie. 2 vols. 5s. each.

**ARISTOTLE'S Nicomachean Ethics.** Translated, with Introduction and Notes, by the Venerable Archdeacon Browne. 5s.

—— **Politics and Economics.** Translated by E. Walford, M.A., with Introduction by Dr. Gillies. 5s.

**ARISTOTLE'S Metaphysics.** Translated by the Rev. John H. M'Mahon, M.A. 5s.

—— **History of Animals.** Trans. by Richard Cresswell, M.A. 5s.

—— **Organon;** or, Logical Treatises, and the Introduction of Porphyry. Translated by the Rev. O. F. Owen, M.A. 2 vols. 3s. 6d. each.

—— **Rhetoric and Poetics.** Trans. by T. Buckley, B.A. 5s.

**ARRIAN'S Anabasis of Alexander,** together with the Indica. Translated by E. J. Chinnock, M.A., LL.D. With Maps and Plans. 5s.

**ATHENÆUS. The Deipnosophists;** or, the Banquet of the Learned. Trans. by Prof. C. D. Yonge, M.A. 3 vols. 5s. each.

**BACON'S Moral and Historical Works,** including the Essays, Apophthegms, Wisdom of the Ancients, New Atlantis, Henry VII., Henry VIII., Elizabeth, Henry Prince of Wales, History of Great Britain, Julius Cæsar, and Augustus Cæsar. Edited by J. Devey, M.A. 3s. 6d.

—— **Novum Organum and Advancement of Learning.** Edited by J. Devey, M.A. 5s.

**BASS'S Lexicon to the Greek Testament.** 2s.

**BAX'S Manual of the History of Philosophy.** for the use of Students. By E. Belfort Bax. 5s.

**BEAUMONT and FLETCHER,** their finest Scenes, Lyrics, and other Beauties, selected from the whole of their works, and edited by Leigh Hunt. 3s. 6d.

**BECHSTEIN'S Cage and Chamber Birds,** their Natural History, Habits, Food, Diseases, and Modes of Capture. Translated, with considerable additions on Structure, Migration, and Economy, by H. G. Adams. Together with SWEET BRITISH WARBLERS. With 43 coloured Plates and Woodcut Illustrations. 5s.

**BEDE'S (Venerable) Ecclesiastical History of England.** Together with the ANGLO-SAXON CHRONICLE. Edited by J. A. Giles, D.C.L. With Map. 5s.

**BELL (Sir Charles). The Anatomy and Philosophy of Expression,** as connected with the Fine Arts. By Sir Charles Bell, K.H. 7th edition, revised. 5s.

**BERKELEY (George), Bishop of Cloyne, The Works of.** Edited by George Sampson. With Biographical Introduction by the Right Hon. A. J. Balfour, M.P. 3 vols. 5s. each.

**BION.** See THEOCRITUS.

**BJÖRNSON'S Arne and the Fisher Lassie.** Translated by W. H. Low, M.A. 3s. 6d.

**BLAIR'S Chronological Tables** Revised and Enlarged. Comprehending the Chronology and History of the World, from the Earliest Times to the Russian Treaty of Peace, April 1856. By J. Willoughby Rosse. Double vol. 10s.

—— **Index of Dates.** Comprehending the principal Facts in the Chronology and History of the World, alphabetically arranged; being a complete Index to Blair's Chronological Tables. By J. W. Rosse. 2 vols. 5s. each.

**BLEEK,** Introduction to the Old Testament. By Friedrich Bleek. Edited by Johann Bleek and Adolf Kamphausen. Translated by G. H. Venables, under the supervision of the Rev. Canon Venables. 2 vols. 5*s*. each.

**BOETHIUS'S** Consolation of Philosophy. King Alfred's Anglo-Saxon Version of. With a literal English Translation on opposite pages, Notes, Introduction, and Glossary, by Rev. S. Fox, M.A. 5*s*.

**BOHN'S** Dictionary of Poetical Quotations. 4th edition. 6*s*.

**BOHN'S** Handbooks of Games. New edition. In 2 vols., with numerous Illustrations 3*s*. 6*d*. each.

Vol. I.—TABLE GAMES:—Billiards, Chess, Draughts, Backgammon, Dominoes, Solitaire, Reversi, Go-Bang, Rouge et Noir, Roulette, E.O., Hazard, Faro.

Vol. II.—CARD GAMES:—Whist, Solo Whist, Poker, Piquet, Ecarté, Euchre, Bézique, Cribbage, Loo, Vingt-et-un, Napoleon, Newmarket, Pope Joan, Speculation, &c., &c.

**BOND'S** A Handy Book of Rules and Tables for verifying Dates with the Christian Era, &c. Giving an account of the Chief Eras and Systems used by various Nations; with the easy Methods for determining the Corresponding Dates. By J. J. Bond. 5*s*.

**BONOMI'S** Nineveh and its Palaces. 7 Plates and 294 Woodcut Illustrations. 5*s*.

**BOSWELL'S** Life of Johnson, with the TOUR IN THE HEBRIDES and JOHNSONIANA. Edited by the Rev. A. Napier, M.A. With Frontispiece to each vol. 6 vols. 3*s*. 6*d*. each.

**BRAND'S** Popular Antiquities of England, Scotland, and Ireland. Arranged, revised, and greatly enlarged, by Sir Henry Ellis, K.H., F.R.S., &c., &c. 3 vols. 5*s*. each.

**BREMER'S** (Frederika) Works. Translated by Mary Howitt. 4 vols. 3*s*. 6*d*. each.

**BRIDGWATER TREATISES.**

Bell (Sir Charles) on the Hand. With numerous Woodcuts. 5*s*.

Kirby on the History, Habits, and Instincts of Animals. Edited by T. Rymer Jones. With upwards of 100 Woodcuts. 2 vols. 5*s*. each.

Kidd on the Adaptation of External Nature to the Physical Condition of Man. 3*s*. 6*d*.

Chalmers on the Adaptation of External Nature to the Moral and Intellectual Constitution of Man. 5*s*.

**BRINK** (B. ten) Early English Literature. By Bernhard ten Brink. Vol. I. To Wyclif. Translated by Horace M. Kennedy 3*s*. 6*d*.

Vol. II. Wyclif, Chaucer, Earliest Drama Renaissance. Translated by W. Clarke Robinson, Ph.D. 3*s*. 6*d*.

Vol. III. From the Fourteenth Century to the Death of Surrey. Edited by Dr. Alois Brandl. Trans. by L. Dora Schmitz. 3*s*. 6*d*.

—— Five Lectures on Shakespeare. Trans. by Julia Franklin. 3*s*. 6*d*.

**BROWNE'S** (Sir Thomas) Works Edited by Simon Wilkin. 3 vols. 3*s*. 6*d*. each.

**BURKE'S Works.** 8 vols. 3s. 6d. each.

    I.—Vindication of Natural Society—Essay on the Sublime and Beautiful, and various Political Miscellanies.

    II.—Reflections on the French Revolution — Letters relating to the Bristol Election — Speech on Fox's East India Bill, &c.

    III.—Appeal from the New to the Old Whigs—On the Nabob of Arcot's Debts—The Catholic Claims, &c.

    IV.—Report on the Affairs of India, and Articles of Charge against Warren Hastings.

    V.—Conclusion of the Articles of Charge against Warren Hastings—Political Letters on the American War, on a Regicide Peace, to the Empress of Russia.

    VI.—Miscellaneous Speeches—Letters and Fragments—Abridgments of English History, &c. With a General Index.

    VII. & VIII.—Speeches on the Impeachment of Warren Hastings; and Letters. With Index. 2 vols. 3s. 6d. each.

——— Life. By Sir J. Prior. 3s. 6d.

**BURNEY'S Evelina.** By Frances Burney (Mme. D'Arblay). With an Introduction and Notes by A. R. Ellis. 3s. 6d.

——— Cecilia. With an Introduction and Notes by A. R. Ellis. 2 vols. 3s. 6d. each.

**BURN (R.) Ancient Rome and its Neighbourhood.** An Illustrated Handbook to the Ruins in the City and the Campagna, for the use of Travellers. By Robert Burn, M.A. With numerous Illustrations, Maps, and Plans. 7s. 6d.

**BURNS (Robert), Life of.** By J. G. Lockhart, D.C.L. A new and enlarged Edition. Revised by William Scott Douglas. 3s. 6d.

**BURTON'S (Robert) Anatomy of Melancholy.** Edited by the Rev. A. R. Shilleto, M.A. With Introduction by A. H. Bullen, and full Index. 3 vols. 3s. 6d. each.

**BURTON (Sir R. F.) Personal Narrative of a Pilgrimage to Al-Madinah and Meccah.** By Captain Sir Richard F. Burton, K.C.M.G. With an Introduction by Stanley Lane-Poole, and all the original Illustrations. 2 vols. 3s. 6d. each.

    \*\*\* This is the copyright edition, containing the author's latest notes.

**BUTLER'S (Bishop) Analogy of Religion, Natural and Revealed,** to the Constitution and Course of Nature; together with two Dissertations on Personal Identity and on the Nature of Virtue, and Fifteen Sermons. 3s. 6d.

**BUTLER'S (Samuel) Hudibras.** With Variorum Notes, a Biography, Portrait, and 28 Illustrations. 5s.

——— or, further Illustrated with 60 Outline Portraits. 2 vols. 5s. each.

**CÆSAR. Commentaries on the Gallic and Civil Wars,** Translated by W. A. McDevitte, B.A. 5s.

**CAMOENS' Lusiad**; or, the Discovery of India. An Epic Poem. Translated by W. J. Mickle. 5th Edition, revised by E. R. Hodges, M.C.P. 3s. 6d.

**CARAFAS (The) of Maddaloni.** Naples under Spanish Dominion. Translated from the German of Alfred de Reumont. 3s. 6d.

**CARLYLE'S French Revolution.** Edited by J. Holland Rose, Litt.D. Illus. 3 vols. 5s. each.

—— Sartor Resartus. With 75 Illustrations by Edmund J. Sullivan. 5s.

**CARPENTER'S (Dr. W. B.) Zoology.** Revised Edition, by W. S. Dallas, F.L.S. With very numerous Woodcuts. Vol. I. 6s.
[*Vol. II. out of print.*]

**CARPENTER'S Mechanical Philosophy, Astronomy, and Horology.** 181 Woodcuts. 5s.

—— Vegetable Physiology and Systematic Botany. Revised Edition, by E. Lankester, M.D., &c. With very numerous Woodcuts. 6s.

—— Animal Physiology. Revised Edition. With upwards of 300 Woodcuts. 6s.

**CASTLE (E.) Schools and Masters of Fence**, from the Middle Ages to the End of the Eighteenth Century. By Egerton Castle, M.A., F.S.A. With a Complete Bibliography. Illustrated with 140 Reproductions of Old Engravings and 6 Plates of Swords, showing 114 Examples. 6s.

**CATTERMOLE'S Evenings at Haddon Hall.** With 24 Engravings on Steel from designs by Cattermole, the Letterpress by the Baroness de Carabella. 5s.

**CATULLUS, Tibullus, and the Vigil of Venus.** A Literal Prose Translation. 5s.

**CELLINI (Benvenuto). Memoirs of,** written by Himself. Translated by Thomas Roscoe. 3s. 6d.

**CERVANTES' Don Quixote de la Mancha.** Motteaux's Translation revised. 2 vols. 3s. 6d. each.

—— Galatea. A Pastoral Romance. Translated by G. W. J. Gyll. 3s. 6d.

—— Exemplary Novels. Translated by Walter K. Kelly. 3s. 6d.

**CHAUCER'S Poetical Works.** Edited by Robert Bell. Revised Edition, with a Preliminary Essay by Prof. W. W. Skeat, M.A. 4 vols. 3s. 6d. each.

**CHESS CONGRESS of 1862.** A Collection of the Games played. Edited by J. Löwenthal. 5s.

**CHEVREUL on Colour.** Translated from the French by Charles Martel. Third Edition, with Plates, 5s.; or with an additional series of 16 Plates in Colours, 7s. 6d.

**CHILLINGWORTH'S Religion of Protestants.** A Safe Way to Salvation. 3s. 6d.

**CHINA, Pictorial, Descriptive, and Historical.** With Map and nearly 100 Illustrations. 5s.

**CHRONICLES OF THE CRUSADES.** Contemporary Narratives of the Crusade of Richard Cœur de Lion, by Richard of Devizes and Geoffrey de Vinsauf; and of the Crusade at St. Louis, by Lord John de Joinville. 5s.

**CICERO'S Orations.** Translated by Prof. C. D. Yonge, M.A. 4 vols. 5s. each.

CICERO'S Letters. Translated by Evelyn S. Shuckburgh. 4 vols. 5s. each.

—— On Oratory and Orators. With Letters to Quintus and Brutus. Translated by the Rev. J. S. Watson, M.A. 5s.

—— On the Nature of the Gods, Divination, Fate, Laws, a Republic, Consulship. Translated by Prof. C. D. Yonge, M.A., and Francis Barham. 5s.

—— Academics, De Finibus, and Tusculan Questions. By Prof. C. D. Yonge, M.A. 5s.

—— Offices; or, Moral Duties. Cato Major, an Essay on Old Age; Lælius, an Essay on Friendship; Scipio's Dream; Paradoxes; Letter to Quintus on Magistrates. Translated by C. R. Edmonds. 3s. 6d.

**CORNELIUS NEPOS.**—*See* JUSTIN.

**CLARK'S (Hugh) Introduction to Heraldry.** 18th Edition, Revised and Enlarged by J. R. Planché, Rouge Croix. With nearly 1000 Illustrations. 5s. Or with the Illustrations Coloured, 15s.

**CLASSIC TALES,** containing Rasselas, Vicar of Wakefield, Gulliver's Travels, and The Sentimental Journey. 3s. 6d.

**COLERIDGE'S (S. T.) Friend.** A Series of Essays on Morals, Politics, and Religion. 3s. 6d.

—— Aids to Reflection, and the CONFESSIONS OF AN INQUIRING SPIRIT, to which are added the ESSAYS ON FAITH and the BOOK OF COMMON PRAYER. 3s. 6d.

—— Lectures and Notes on Shakespeare and other English Poets. Edited by T. Ashe. 3s. 6d.

**COLERIDGE'S Biographia Literaria;** together with Two Lay Sermons. 3s. 6d.

—— Table-Talk and Omniana. Edited by T. Ashe, B.A. 3s. 6d.

—— Miscellanies, Æsthetic and Literary; to which is added, THE THEORY OF LIFE. Collected and arranged by T. Ashe, B.A. 3s. 6d.

**COMTE'S Positive Philosophy.** Translated and condensed by Harriet Martineau. With Introduction by Frederic Harrison. 3 vols. 5s. each.

**COMTE'S Philosophy of the Sciences,** being an Exposition of the Principles of the *Cours de Philosophie Positive*. By G. H. Lewes. 5s.

**CONDÉ'S History of the Dominion of the Arabs in Spain.** Translated by Mrs. Foster. 3 vols. 3s. 6d. each.

**COOPER'S Biographical Dictionary.** Containing Concise Notices (upwards of 15,000) of Eminent Persons of all Ages and Countries. By Thompson Cooper, F.S.A. With a Supplement, bringing the work down to 1883. 2 vols. 5s. each.

**COXE'S Memoirs of the Duke of Marlborough.** With his original Correspondence. By W. Coxe, M.A., F.R.S. Revised edition by John Wade. 3 vols. 3s. 6d. each.

\*\*\* An Atlas of the plans of Marlborough's campaigns, 4to. 10s. 6d.

—— History of the House of Austria (1218-1792). With a Continuation from the Accession of Francis I. to the Revolution of 1848. 4 vols. 3s. 6d. each.

**CRAIK'S (G. L.) Pursuit of Knowledge under Difficulties.** Illustrated by Anecdotes and Memoirs. Revised edition, with numerous Woodcut Portraits and Plates. 5s.

**CRUIKSHANK'S Punch and Judy.** The Dialogue of the Puppet Show; an Account of its Origin, &c. With 24 Illustrations, and Coloured Plates, designed and engraved by G. Cruikshank. 5s.

**CUNNINGHAM'S Lives of the Most Eminent British Painters.** A New Edition, with Notes and Sixteen fresh Lives. By Mrs. Heaton. 3 vols. 3s. 6d. each.

**DANTE. Divine Comedy.** Translated by the Rev. H. F. Cary, M.A. 3s. 6d.

—— Translated into English Verse by I. C. Wright, M.A. 3rd Edition, revised. With Portrait, and 34 Illustrations on Steel, after Flaxman.

**DANTE. The Inferno.** A Literal Prose Translation, with the Text of the Original printed on the same page. By John A. Carlyle, M.D. 5s.

—— **The Purgatorio.** A Literal Prose Translation, with the Text printed on the same page. By W. S. Dugdale. 5s.

**DE COMMINES (Philip), Memoirs of.** Containing the Histories of Louis XI. and Charles VIII., Kings of France, and Charles the Bold, Duke of Burgundy. Together with the Scandalous Chronicle, or Secret History of Louis XI., by Jean de Troyes. Translated by Andrew R. Scoble. With Portraits. 2 vols. 3s. 6d. each.

**DEFOE'S Novels and Miscellaneous Works.** With Prefaces and Notes, including those attributed to Sir W. Scott. 7 vols. 3s. 6d. each.

    I.—Captain Singleton, and Colonel Jack.

    II.—Memoirs of a Cavalier, Captain Carleton, Dickory Cronke, &c.

    III.—Moll Flanders, and the History of the Devil.

    IV.—Roxana, and Life of Mrs. Christian Davies.

    V.—History of the Great Plague of London, 1665; The Storm (1703); and the True-born Englishman.

    VI.—Duncan Campbell, New Voyage round the World, and Political Tracts.

    VII.—Robinson Crusoe.

**DEMMIN'S History of Arms and Armour,** from the Earliest Period. By Auguste Demmin. Translated by C. C. Black, M.A. With nearly 2000 Illustrations. 7s. 6d.

**DEMOSTHENES' Orations.** Translated by C. Rann Kennedy. 5 vols. Vol. I., 3s. 6d.; Vols. II.-V., 5s. each.

**DE STAËL'S Corinne or Italy.** By Madame de Staël. Translated by Emily Baldwin and Paulina Driver. 3s. 6d.

**DEVEY'S Logic,** or the Science of Inference. A Popular Manual. By J. Devey. 5s.

**DICTIONARY of Latin and Greek Quotations;** including Proverbs, Maxims, Mottoes, Law Terms and Phrases. With all the

Quantities marked, and English Translations. With Index Verborum (622 pages). 5s.

DICTIONARY of Obsolete and Provincial English. Compiled by Thomas Wright, M.A., F.S.A., &c. 2 vols. 5s. each.

DIDRON'S Christian Iconography: a History of Christian Art in the Middle Ages. Translated by E. J. Millington and completed by Margaret Stokes. With 240 Illustrations. 2 vols. 5s. each.

DIOGENES LAERTIUS. Lives and Opinions of the Ancient Philosophers. Translated by Prof. C. D. Yonge, M.A. 5s.

DOBREE'S Adversaria. Edited by the late Prof. Wagner. 2 vols. 5s. each.

DODD'S Epigrammatists. A Selection from the Epigrammatic Literature of Ancient, Mediæval, and Modern Times. By the Rev. Henry Philip Dodd, M.A. Oxford. 2nd Edition, revised and enlarged. 6s.

DONALDSON'S The Theatre of the Greeks. A Treatise on the History and Exhibition of the Greek Drama. With numerous Illustrations and 3 Plans. By John William Donaldson, D.D. 5s.

DRAPER'S History of the Intellectual Development of Europe. By John William Draper, M.D., LL.D. 2 vols. 5s. each.

DUNLOP'S History of Fiction. A new Edition. Revised by Henry Wilson. 2 vols. 5s. each.

DYER (Dr. T. H.). Pompeii: its Buildings and Antiquities. By T. H. Dyer, LL.D. With nearly 300 Wood Engravings, a large Map, and a Plan of the Forum. 7s. 6d.

—— The City of Rome: its History and Monuments. With Illustrations. 5s.

DYER (T. F. T.) British Popular Customs, Present and Past. An Account of the various Games and Customs associated with Different Days of the Year in the British Isles, arranged according to the Calendar. By the Rev. T. F. Thiselton Dyer, M.A. 5s.

EBERS' Egyptian Princess. An Historical Novel. By George Ebers. Translated by E. S. Buchheim. 3s. 6d.

EDGEWORTH'S Stories for Children. With 8 Illustrations by L. Speed. 3s. 6d.

ELZE'S William Shakespeare. —See SHAKESPEARE.

EMERSON'S Works. 5 vols. 3s. 6d. each.
 I.—Essays and Representative Men.
 II.—English Traits, Nature, and Conduct of Life.
 III.—Society and Solitude—Letters and Social Aims — Addresses.
 VI.—Miscellaneous Pieces.
 V.—Poems.

ENNEMOSER'S History of Magic. Translated by William Howitt. 2 vols. 5s. each.

EPICTETUS, The Discourses of. With the ENCHEIRIDION and Fragments. Translated by George Long, M.A. 5s.

EURIPIDES. A New Literal Translation in Prose. By E P. Coleridge, M.A. 2 vols. 5s. each.

**EUTROPIUS.**—*See* JUSTIN.

**EUSEBIUS PAMPHILUS**, Ecclesiastical History of. Translated by Rev. C. F. Cruse, M.A. 5s.

**EVELYN'S Diary and Correspondence.** Edited from the Original MSS. by W. Bray, F.A.S. With 45 engravings. 4 vols. 5s. each.

**FAIRHOLT'S Costume in England.** A History of Dress to the end of the Eighteenth Century. 3rd Edition, revised, by Viscount Dillon, V.P.S.A. Illustrated with above 700 Engravings. 2 vols. 5s. each.

**FIELDING'S Adventures of Joseph Andrews and his Friend Mr. Abraham Adams.** With Cruikshank's Illustrations. 3s. 6d.

—— History of Tom Jones, a Foundling. With Cruikshank's Illustrations. 2 vols. 3s. 6d. each.

—— Amelia. With Cruikshank's Illustrations. 5s.

**FLAXMAN'S Lectures on Sculpture.** By John Flaxman, R.A. With Portrait and 53 Plates. 6s.

**FOSTER'S (John) Life and Correspondence.** Edited by J. E. Ryland. 2 vols. 3s. 6d. each.

—— Critical Essays. Edited by J. E. Ryland. 2 vols. 3s. 6d. each.

—— Essays: on Decision of Character; on a Man's writing Memoirs of Himself; on the epithet Romantic; on the aversion of Men of Taste to Evangelical Religion. 3s. 6d.

—— Essays on the Evils of Popular Ignorance; to which is added, a Discourse on the Propagation of Christianity in India. 3s. 6d.

**FOSTER'S Essays** on the Improvement of Time. With NOTES OF SERMONS and other Pieces. 3s. 6d.

**GASPARY'S History of Italian Literature.** Translated by Herman Oelsner, M.A., Ph.D. Vol. I. 3s. 6d.

**GEOFFREY OF MONMOUTH**, Chronicle of.—*See Old English Chronicles.*

**GESTA ROMANORUM**, or Entertaining Moral Stories invented by the Monks. Translated by the Rev. Charles Swan. Revised Edition, by Wynnard Hooper, B.A. 5s.

**GILDAS**, Chronicles of.—*See Old English Chronicles.*

**GIBBON'S Decline and Fall of the Roman Empire.** Complete and Unabridged, with Variorum Notes. Edited by an English Churchman. With 2 Maps and Portrait. 7 vols. 3s. 6d. each.

**GILBART'S History, Principles, and Practice of Banking.** By the late J. W. Gilbart, F.R.S. New Edition, revised by A. S. Michie. 2 vols. 10s.

**GIL BLAS, The Adventures of.** Translated from the French of Lesage by Smollett. With 24 Engravings on Steel, after Smirke, and 10 Etchings by George Cruikshank. 6s.

**GIRALDUS CAMBRENSIS' Historical Works.** Translated by Th. Forester, M.A., and Sir R. Colt Hoare. Revised Edition, Edited by Thomas Wright, M.A., F.S.A. 5s.

**GOETHE'S Faust.** Part I. German Text with Hayward's Prose Translation and Notes. Revised by C. A. Buchheim, Ph.D. 5s.

**GOETHE'S Works.** Translated into English by various hands. 14 vols. 3s. 6d. each.
- I. and II.—Autobiography and Annals.
- III.—Faust. Two Parts, complete. (Swanwick.)
- IV.—Novels and Tales.
- V.—Wilhelm Meister's Apprenticeship.
- VI.—Conversations with Eckermann and Soret.
- VIII.—Dramatic Works.
- IX.—Wilhelm Meister's Travels.
- X.—Tour in Italy, and Second Residence in Rome.
- XI.—Miscellaneous Travels.
- XII.—Early and Miscellaneous Letters.
- XIV.—Reineke Fox, West-Eastern Divan and Achilleid.

**GOLDSMITH'S Works.** A new Edition, by J. W. M. Gibbs. 5 vols. 3s. 6d. each.

**GRAMMONT'S Memoirs of the Court of Charles II.** Edited by Sir Walter Scott. Together with the BOSCOBEL TRACTS, including two not before published, &c. New Edition. 5s.

**GRAY'S Letters.** Including the Correspondence of Gray and Mason. Edited by the Rev. D. C. Tovey, M.A. Vols. I. and II. 3s. 6d. each.

**GREEK ANTHOLOGY.** Translated by George Burges, M.A. 5s.

**GREEK ROMANCES of Heliodorus, Longus, and Achilles Tatius**—viz., The Adventures of Theagenes & Chariclea ; Amours of Daphnis and Chloe ; and Loves of Clitopho and Leucippe. Translated by Rev. R. Smith, M.A. 5s.

**GREGORY'S Letters on the Evidences, Doctrines, & Duties of the Christian Religion.** By Dr. Olinthus Gregory. 3s. 6d.

**GREENE, MARLOWE, and BEN JONSON.** Poems of. Edited by Robert Bell. 3s. 6d.

**GRIMM'S TALES.** With the Notes of the Original. Translated by Mrs. A. Hunt. With Introduction by Andrew Lang, M.A. 2 vols. 3s. 6d. each.

—— Gammer Grethel; or, German Fairy Tales and Popular Stories. Containing 42 Fairy Tales. Trans. by Edgar Taylor. With numerous Woodcuts after George Cruikshank and Ludwig Grimm. 3s. 6d.

**GROSSI'S Marco Visconti.** Translated by A. F. D. The Ballads rendered into English Verse by C. M. P. 3s. 6d.

**GUIZOT'S History of the English Revolution of 1640.** From the Accession of Charles I. to his Death. Translated by William Hazlitt. 3s. 6d.

—— History of Civilisation, from the Fall of the Roman Empire to the French Revolution. Translated by William Hazlitt. 3 vols. 3s. 6d. each.

**HALL'S (Rev. Robert) Miscellaneous Works and Remains.** 3s. 6d.

**HAMPTON COURT: A Short History of the Manor and Palace.** By Ernest Law, B.A. With numerous Illustrations. 5s.

**HARDWICK'S History of the Articles of Religion.** By the late C. Hardwick. Revised by the Rev. Francis Procter, M.A. 5s.

**HAUFF'S Tales.** The Caravan—The Sheik of Alexandria—The Inn in the Spessart. Trans. from the German by S. Mendel. 3s. 6d.

**HAWTHORNE'S Tales.** 4 vols. 3s. 6d. each.
- I.—Twice-told Tales, and the Snow Image.
- II.—Scarlet Letter, and the House with the Seven Gables.
- III.—Transformation [The Marble Faun], and Blithedale Romance.
- IV.—Mosses from an Old Manse.

**HAZLITT'S Table-talk.** Essays on Men and Manners. By W. Hazlitt. 3s. 6d.

—— Lectures on the Literature of the Age of Elizabeth and on Characters of Shakespeare's Plays. 3s. 6d.

—— Lectures on the English Poets, and on the English Comic Writers. 3s. 6d.

—— The Plain Speaker. Opinions on Books, Men, and Things. 3s. 6d.

—— Round Table. 3s. 6d.

—— Sketches and Essays. 3s. 6d.

—— The Spirit of the Age; or, Contemporary Portraits. Edited by W. Carew Hazlitt. 3s. 6d.

—— View of the English Stage. Edited by W. Spencer Jackson. 3s. 6d.

**HEATON'S Concise History of Painting.** New Edition, revised by Cosmo Monkhouse. 5s.

**HEGEL'S Lectures on the Philosophy of History.** Translated by J. Sibree, M.A.

**HEINE'S Poems,** Complete. Translated by Edgar A. Bowring, C.B. 3s. 6d.

—— Travel-Pictures, including the Tour in the Harz, Norderney, and Book of Ideas, together with the Romantic School. Translated by Francis Storr. A New Edition, revised throughout. With Appendices and Maps. 3s. 6d.

**HELP'S Life of Christopher Columbus,** the Discoverer of America. By Sir Arthur Helps, K.C.B. 3s. 6d.

—— Life of Hernando Cortes, and the Conquest of Mexico. 2 vols. 3s. 6d. each.

—— Life of Pizarro. 3s. 6d.

—— Life of Las Casas the Apostle of the Indies. 3s. 6d.

**HENDERSON (E.) Select Historical Documents of the Middle Ages,** including the most famous Charters relating to England, the Empire, the Church, &c., from the 6th to the 14th Centuries. Translated from the Latin and edited by Ernest F. Henderson, A.B., A.M., Ph.D. 5s.

**HENFREY'S Guide to English Coins,** from the Conquest to the present time. New and revised Edition by C. F. Keary, M.A., F.S.A. 6s.

**HENRY OF HUNTINGDON'S History of the English.** Translated by T. Forester, M.A. 5s.

**HENRY'S (Matthew) Exposition of the Book of the Psalms.** 5s.

**HELIODORUS. Theagenes and Chariclea.**—*See* GREEK ROMANCES.

**HERODOTUS.** Translated by the Rev. Henry Cary, M.A. 3s. 6d.

—— Notes on, Original and Selected from the best Commentators. By D. W. Turner, M.A. With Coloured Map. 5s.

—— Analysis and Summary of By J. T. Wheeler. 5s.

**HESIOD, CALLIMACHUS, and THEOGNIS.** Translated by the Rev. J. Banks, M.A. 5s.

**HOFFMANN'S (E. T. W.) The Serapion Brethren.** Translated from the German by Lt.-Col. Alex. Ewing. 2 vols. 3s. 6d. each.

**HOLBEIN'S Dance of Death and Bible Cuts.** Upwards of 150 Subjects, engraved in facsimile, with Introduction and Descriptions by Francis Douce and Dr. Thomas Frognall Dibdin. 5s.

**HOMER'S Iliad.** Translated into English Prose by T. A. Buckley, B.A. 5s.

—— **Odyssey.** Hymns, Epigrams, and Battle of the Frogs and Mice. Translated into English Prose by T. A. Buckley, B.A. 5s.

—— *See also* POPE.

**HOOPER'S (G.) Waterloo: The Downfall of the First Napoleon:** a History of the Campaign of 1815. By George Hooper. With Maps and Plans. 3s. 6d.

—— **The Campaign of Sedan:** The Downfall of the Second Empire, August – September, 1870. With General Map and Six Plans of Battle. 3s. 6d.

**HORACE.** A new literal Prose translation, by A. Hamilton Bryce, LL.D. 3s. 6d.

**HUGO'S (Victor) Dramatic Works.** Hernani—Ruy Blas—The King's Diversion. Translated by Mrs. Newton Crosland and F. L. Slous. 3s. 6d.

—— **Poems, chiefly Lyrical.** Translated by various Writers, now first collected by J. H. L. Williams. 3s. 6d.

**HUMBOLDT'S Cosmos.** Translated by E. C. Otté, B. H. Paul, and W. S. Dallas, F.L.S. 5 vols. 3s. 6d. each, excepting Vol. V. 5s.

**HUMBOLDT'S Personal Narrative of his Travels to the Equinoctial Regions of America during the years 1799-1804.** Translated by T. Ross. 3 vols. 5s. each.

—— **Views of Nature.** Translated by E. C. Otté and H. G. Bohn. 5s.

**HUMPHREYS' Coin Collector's Manual.** By H. N. Humphreys. with upwards of 140 Illustrations on Wood and Steel. 2 vols. 5s. each.

**HUNGARY:** its History and Revolution, together with a copious Memoir of Kossuth. 3s. 6d.

**HUTCHINSON (Colonel).** Memoirs of the Life of. By his Widow, Lucy; together with her Autobiography, and an Account of the Siege of Lathom House. 3s. 6d.

**HUNT'S Poetry of Science.** By Richard Hunt. 3rd Edition, revised and enlarged. 5s.

**INGULPH'H Chronicles of the Abbey of Croyland,** with the CONTINUATION by Peter of Blois and other Writers. Translated by H. T. Riley, M.A. 5s.

**IRVING'S (Washington) Complete Works.** 15 vols. With Portraits, &c. 3s. 6d. each.
  I.—Salmagundi, Knickerbocker's History of New York.
  II.—The Sketch-Book, and the Life of Oliver Goldsmith.
  III.—Bracebridge Hall, Abbotsford and Newstead Abbey.
  IV.—The Alhambra, Tales of a Traveller.
  V.—Chronicle of the Conquest of Granada, Legends of the Conquest of Spain.

IRVING'S (WASHINGTON) COMPLETE WORKS *continued*.
VI. & VII.—Life and Voyages of Columbus, together with the Voyages of his Companions.
VIII.—Astoria, A Tour on the Prairies.
IX.—Life of Mahomet, Lives of the Successors of Mahomet.
X.—Adventures of Captain Bonneville, U.S.A., Wolfert's Roost.
XI.—Biographies and Miscellaneous Papers.
XII.-XV.—Life of George Washington. 4 vols.
—— Life and Letters. By his Nephew, Pierre E. Irving. 2 vols. 3s. 6d. each.

ISOCRATES, The Orations of. Translated by J. H. Freese, M.A. Vol. I. 5s.

JAMES'S (G. P. R.) Life of Richard Cœur de Lion. 2 vols. 3s. 6d. each.

JAMESON'S (Mrs.) Shakespeare's Heroines. Characteristics of Women: Moral, Poetical, and Historical. By Mrs. Jameson. 3s. 6d.

JESSE'S (E.) Anecdotes of Dogs With 40 Woodcuts and 34 Steel Engravings. 5s.

JESSE'S (J. H.) Memoirs of the Court of England during the Reign of the Stuarts, including the Protectorate. 3 vols. With 42 Portraits. 5s. each.

—— Memoirs of the Pretenders and their Adherents. With 6 Portraits. 5s.

JOHNSON'S Lives of the Poets. Edited by Mrs. Alexander Napier, with Introduction by Professor Hales. 3 vols. 3s. 6d. each.

JOSEPHUS (Flavius), The Works of. Whiston's Translation, revised by Rev. A. R. Shilleto, M.A With Topographical and Geographical Notes by Colonel Sir C. W. Wilson, K.C.B. 5 vols. 3s. 6d. each.

JOYCE'S Scientific Dialogues. With numerous Woodcuts. 5s.

JUKES-BROWNE (A. J.), The Building of the British Isles: a Study in Geographical Evolution. Illustrated by numerous Maps and Woodcuts. 2nd Edition, revised, 7s. 6d.

JULIAN, the Emperor. Containing Gregory Nazianzen's Two Invectives and Libanus' Monody, with Julian's extant Theosophical Works. Translated by C. W. King, M.A. 5s.

JUNIUS'S Letters. With all the Notes of Woodfall's Edition, and important Additions. 2 vols. 3s. 6d. each.

JUSTIN CORNELIUS NEPOS, and EUTROPIUS. Translated by the Rev. J. S. Watson, M.A. 5s.

JUVENAL, PERSIUS. SULPICIA and LUCILIUS. Translated by L. Evans, M.A. 5s.

KANT'S Critique of Pure Reason. Translated by J. M. D. Meiklejohn. 5s.

—— Prolegomena and Metaphysical Foundations of Natural Science. Translated by E. Belfort Bax. 5s.

KEIGHTLEY'S (Thomas) Mythology of Ancient Greece and Italy. 4th Edition, revised by Leonard Schmitz, Ph.D., LL.D. With 12 Plates from the Antique. 5s.

**KEIGHTLEY'S Fairy Mythology,** illustrative of the Romance and Superstition of Various Countries. Revised Edition, with Frontispiece by Cruikshank. 5s.

**LA FONTAINE'S Fables.** Translated into English Verse by Elizur Wright. New Edition, with Notes by J. W. M. Gibbs. 3s. 6d.

**LAMARTINE'S History of the Girondists.** Translated by H. T. Ryde. 3 vols. 3s. 6d. each.

—— **History of the Restoration of Monarchy in France** (a Sequel to the History of the Girondists). 4 vols. 3s. 6d. each.

—— **History of the French Revolution of 1848.** 3s. 6d.

**LAMB'S (Charles) Essays of Elia and Eliana.** Complete Edition. 3s. 6d.

—— **Specimens of English Dramatic Poets of the Time of Elizabeth.** 3s. 6d.

—— **Memorials and Letters of Charles Lamb.** By Serjeant Talfourd. New Edition, revised, by W. Carew Hazlitt. 2 vols. 3s. 6d. each.

—— **Tales from Shakespeare** With Illustrations by Byam Shaw. 3s. 6d.

**LANE'S Arabian Nights' Entertainments.** Edited by Stanley Lane-Poole, M.A., Litt.D. 4 vols. 3s. 6d. each.

**LANZI'S History of Painting in Italy,** from the Period of the Revival of the Fine Arts to the End of the Eighteenth Century. Translated by Thomas Roscoe. 3 vols. 3s. 6d. each.

**LAPPENBERG'S History of England under the Anglo-Saxon Kings.** Translated by B. Thorpe, F.S.A. New edition, revised by E. C. Otté. 2 vols. 3s. 6d. each.

**LECTURES ON PAINTING,** by Barry, Opie, Fuseli. Edited by R. Wornum. 5s.

**LEONARDO DA VINCI'S Treatise on Painting.** Translated by J. F. Rigaud, R.A., With a Life of Leonardo by John William Brown. With numerous Plates. 5s.

**LEPSIUS'S Letters from Egypt, Ethiopia, and the Peninsula of Sinai.** Translated by L. and J. B. Horner. With Maps. 5s.

**LESSING'S Dramatic Works,** Complete. Edited by Ernest Bell, M.A. With Memoir of Lessing by Helen Zimmern. 2 vols. 3s. 6d. each.

—— **Laokoon, Dramatic Notes, and the Representation of Death by the Ancients.** Translated by E. C. Beasley and Helen Zimmern. Edited by Edward Bell, M.A. With a Frontispiece of the Laokoon group. 3s. 6d.

**LILLY'S Introduction to Astrology.** With a GRAMMAR OF ASTROLOGY and Tables for Calculating Nativities, by Zadkiel. 5s.

**LIVY'S History of Rome.** Translated by Dr. Spillan, C. Edmonds, and others. 4 vols. 5s. each.

**LOCKE'S Philosophical Works.** Edited by J. A. St. John. 2 vols. 3s. 6d. each.

—— **Life and Letters:** By Lord King. 3s. 6d.

**LOCKHART (J. G.)**—See BURNS.

**LODGE'S Portraits of Illustrious Personages of Great Britain,** with Biographical and Historical Memoirs. 240 Portraits engraved on Steel, with the respective Biographies unabridged. 8 vols. 5s. each.

**LONGFELLOW'S Prose Works.** With 16 full-page Wood Engravings. 5s.

**LOUDON'S (Mrs.) Natural History.** Revised edition, by W. S. Dallas, F.L.S. With numerous Woodcut Illus. 5s.

**LOWNDES' Bibliographer's Manual of English Literature.** Enlarged Edition. By H. G. Bohn. 6 vols. cloth, 5s. each. Or 4 vols. half morocco, 2l. 2s.

**LONGUS. Daphnis and Chloe.** —See GREEK ROMANCES.

**LUCAN'S Pharsalia.** Translated by H. T. Riley, M.A. 5s.

**LUCIAN'S Dialogues of the Gods, of the Sea Gods, and of the Dead.** Translated by Howard Williams, M.A. 5s.

**LUCRETIUS.** Translated by the Rev. J. S. Watson, M.A. 5s.

**LUTHER'S Table-Talk.** Translated and Edited by William Hazlitt. 3s. 6d.

—— **Autobiography.** — See MICHELET.

**MACHIAVELLI'S History of Florence,** together with the Prince, Savonarola, various Historical Tracts, and a Memoir of Machiavelli. 3s. 6d.

**MALLET'S Northern Antiquities,** or an Historical Account of the Manners, Customs, Religions and Laws, Maritime Expeditions and Discoveries, Language and Literature, of the Ancient Scandinavians. Translated by Bishop Percy. Revised and Enlarged Edition, with a Translation of the PROSE EDDA, by J. A. Blackwell. 5s.

**MANTELL'S (Dr.) Petrifactions and their Teachings.** With numerous illustrative Woodcuts. 6s.

—— **Wonders of Geology.** 8th Edition, revised by T. Rupert Jones, F.G.S. With a coloured Geological Map of England, Plates, and upwards of 200 Woodcuts. 2 vols. 7s. 6d. each.

**MANZONI. The Betrothed:** being a Translation of 'I Promessi Sposi.' By Alessandro Manzoni. With numerous Woodcuts. 5s.

**MARCO POLO'S Travels;** the Translation of Marsden revised by T. Wright, M.A., F.S.A. 5s.

**MARRYAT'S (Capt. R.N.) Masterman Ready.** With 93 Woodcuts. 3s. 6d.

—— **Mission;** or, Scenes in Africa. Illustrated by Gilbert and Dalziel. 3s. 6d.

—— **Pirate and Three Cutters.** With 8 Steel Engravings, from Drawings by Clarkson Stanfield, R.A. 3s. 6d.

—— **Privateersman.** 8 Engravings on Steel. 3s. 6d.

—— **Settlers in Canada.** 10 Engravings by Gilbert and Dalziel. 3s. 6d.

—— **Poor Jack.** With 16 Illustrations after Clarkson Stansfield, R.A. 3s. 6d.

—— **Peter Simple.** With 8 full-page Illustrations. 3s. 6d.

—— **Midshipman Easy.** With 8 full page Illustrations. 3s. 6d.

**MARTIAL'S Epigrams,** complete. Translated into Prose, each accompanied by one or more Verse Translations selected from the Works of English Poets, and other sources. 7s. 6d.

**MARTINEAU'S (Harriet)** History of England, from 1800–1815. 3s. 6d.

—— History of the Thirty Years' Peace, A.D. 1815–46. 4 vols. 3s. 6d. each.

—— See Comte's Positive Philosophy.

**MATTHEW PARIS'S** English History, from the Year 1235 to 1273. Translated by Rev. J. A. Giles, D.C.L. 3 vols. 5s. each.

**MATTHEW OF WESTMINSTER'S** Flowers of History, from the beginning of the World to A.D. 1307. Translated by C. D. Yonge, M.A. 2 vols. 5s. each.

**MAXWELL'S** Victories of Wellington and the British Armies. Frontispiece and 5 Portraits. 5s.

**MENZEL'S** History of Germany, from the Earliest Period to 1842. 3 vols. 3s. 6d. each.

**MICHAEL ANGELO AND RAPHAEL**, their Lives and Works. By Duppa and Quatremere de Quincy. With Portraits, and Engravings on Steel. 5s.

**MICHELET'S** Luther's Autobiography. Trans. by William Hazlitt. With an Appendix (110 pages) of Notes. 3s. 6d.

—— History of the French Revolution from its earliest indications to the flight of the King in 1791. 3s. 6d.

**MIGNET'S** History of the French Revolution, from 1789 to 1814. 3s. 6d.

**MILL (J. S.).** Early Essays by John Stuart Mill. Collected from various sources by J. W. M. Gibbs. 3s. 6d.

**MILLER (Professor).** History Philosophically Illustrated, from the Fall of the Roman Empire to the French Revolution. 4 vols. 3s. 6d. each.

**MILTON'S** Prose Works. Edited by J. A. St. John. 5 vols. 3s. 6d. each.

—— Poetical Works, with a Memoir and Critical Remarks by James Montgomery, an Index to Paradise Lost, Todd's Verbal Index to all the Poems, and a Selection of Explanatory Notes by Henry G. Bohn. Illustrated with 120 Wood Engravings from Drawings by W. Harvey. 2 vols. 3s. 6d. each.

**MITFORD'S (Miss)** Our Village Sketches of Rural Character and Scenery. With 2 Engravings on Steel. 2 vols. 3s. 6d. each.

**MOLIÈRE'S** Dramatic Works. A new Translation in English Prose, by C. H. Wall. 3 vols. 3s. 6d. each.

**MONTAGU.** The Letters and Works of Lady Mary Wortley Montagu. Edited by her great-grandson, Lord Wharncliffe's Edition, and revised by W. Moy Thomas. New Edition, revised, with 5 Portraits. 2 vols. 5s. each.

**MONTAIGNE'S** Essays. Cotton's Translation, revised by W. C. Hazlitt. New Edition. 3 vols. 3s. 6d. each.

**MONTESQUIEU'S** Spirit of Laws. New Edition, revised and corrected. By J. V. Pritchard, A.M. 2 vols. 3s. 6d. each.

**MORPHY'S** Games of Chess. Being the Matches and best Games played by the American Champion, with Explanatory and Analytical Notes by J. Löwenthal. 5s.

**MOTLEY (J. L.).** The Rise of the Dutch Republic. A History. By John Lothrop Motley. New Edition, with Biographical Introduction by Moncure D. Conway. 3 vols. 3s. 6d. each.

**MUDIE'S British Birds**; or, History of the Feathered Tribes of the British Islands. Revised by W. C. L. Martin. With 52 Figures of Birds and 7 Coloured Plates of Eggs. 2 vols.

**NEANDER (Dr. A.). History of the Christian Religion and Church.** Trans. from the German by J. Torrey. 10 vols. 3s. 6d. each.

—— **Life of Jesus Christ.** Translated by J. McClintock and C. Blumenthal. 3s. 6d.

—— **History of the Planting and Training of the Christian Church by the Apostles.** Translated by J. E. Ryland. 2 vols. 3s. 6d. each.

—— **Memorials of Christian Life in the Early and Middle Ages**; including Light in Dark Places. Trans. by J. E. Ryland. 3s. 6d.

**NIBELUNGEN LIED.** The Lay of the Nibelungs, metrically translated from the old German text by Alice Horton, and edited by Edward Bell, M.A. To which is prefixed the Essay on the Nibelungen Lied by Thomas Carlyle. 5s.

**NEW TESTAMENT (The) in Greek.** Griesbach's Text, with various Readings at the foot of the page, and Parallel References in the margin; also a Critical Introduction and Chronological Tables. By an eminent Scholar, with a Greek and English Lexicon. 3rd Edition, revised and corrected. Two Facsimiles of Greek Manuscripts. 900 pages. 5s.

The Lexicon may be had separately, price 2s.

**NICOLINI'S History of the Jesuits**: their Origin, Progress, Doctrines, and Designs. With 8 Portraits. 5s.

**NORTH (R.) Lives of the Right Hon. Francis North, Baron Guildford, the Hon. Sir Dudley North, and the Hon. and Rev. Dr. John North.** By the Hon. Roger North. Together with the Autobiography of the Author. Edited by Augustus Jessopp, D.D. 3 vols. 3s. 6d. each.

**NUGENT'S (Lord) Memorials of Hampden, his Party and Times.** With a Memoir of the Author, an Autograph Letter, and Portrait. 5s.

**OLD ENGLISH CHRONICLES,** including Ethelwerd's Chronicle, Asser's Life of Alfred, Geoffrey of Monmouth's British History, Gildas, Nennius, and the spurious chronicle of Richard of Cirencester. Edited by J. A. Giles, D.C.L. 5s.

**OMAN (J. C.) The Great Indian Epics**: the Stories of the RAMAYANA and the MAHABHARATA. By John Campbell Oman, Principal of Khalsa College, Amritsar. With Notes, Appendices, and Illustrations. 3s. 6d.

**ORDERICUS VITALIS' Ecclesiastical History of England and Normandy.** Translated by T. Forester, M.A. To which is added the CHRONICLE OF ST. EVROULT. 4 vols. 5s. each.

**OVID'S Works, complete.** Literally translated into Prose. 3 vols. 5s. each.

**PASCAL'S Thoughts.** Translated from the Text of M. Auguste Molinier by C. Kegan Paul. 3rd Edition. 3s. 6d.

**PAULI'S (Dr. R.) Life of Alfred the Great.** Translated from the German. To which is appended Alfred's ANGLO-SAXON VERSION

OF OROSIUS. With a literal Translation interpaged, Notes, and an ANGLO-SAXON GRAMMAR and GLOSSARY, by B. Thorpe. 5s.

PAUSANIAS' Description of Greece. Newly translated by A. R. Shilleto, M.A. 2 vols. 5s. each.

PEARSON'S Exposition of the Creed. Edited by E. Walford, M.A. 5s.

PEPYS' Diary and Correspondence. Deciphered by the Rev. J. Smith, M.A., from the original Shorthand MS. in the Pepysian Library. Edited by Lord Braybrooke. 4 vols. With 31 Engravings. 5s. each.

PERCY'S Reliques of Ancient English Poetry. With an Essay on Ancient Minstrels and a Glossary. Edited by J. V. Pritchard, A.M. 2 vols. 3s. 6d. each.

PERSIUS.—See JUVENAL.

PETRARCH'S Sonnets, Triumphs, and other Poems. Translated into English Verse by various Hands. With a Life of the Poet by Thomas Campbell. With Portrait and 15 Steel Engravings. 5s.

PHILO-JUDÆUS, Works of. Translated by Prof. C. D. Yonge, M.A. 4 vols. 5s. each.

PICKERING'S History of the Races of Man, and their Geographical Distribution. With AN ANALYTICAL SYNOPSIS OF THE NATURAL HISTORY OF MAN by Dr. Hall. With a Map of the World and 12 coloured Plates. 5s.

PINDAR. Translated into Prose by Dawson W. Turner. To which is added the Metrical Version by Abraham Moore. 5s.

PLANCHÉ. History of British Costume, from the Earliest Time to the Close of the Eighteenth Century. By J. R. Planché, Somerset Herald. With upwards of 400 Illustrations. 5s.

PLATO'S Works. Literally translated, with Introduction and Notes. 6 vols. 5s. each.
I.—The Apology of Socrates, Crito, Phædo, Gorgias, Protagoras, Phædrus, Theætetus, Euthyphron, Lysis. Translated by the Rev. H. Carey.
II.—The Republic, Timæus, and Critias. Translated by Henry Davis.
III.—Meno, Euthydemus, The Sophist, Statesman, Cratylus, Parmenides, and the Banquet. Translated by G. Burges.
IV.—Philebus, Charmides, Laches, Menexenus, Hippias, Ion, The Two Alcibiades, Theages, Rivals, Hipparchus, Minos, Clitopho, Epistles. Translated by G. Burges.
V.—The Laws. Translated by G. Burges.
VI.—The Doubtful Works. Translated by G. Burges.
—— Summary and Analysis of the Dialogues. With Analytical Index. By A. Day, LL.D. 5s.

PLAUTUS'S Comedies. Translated by H. T. Riley, M.A. 2 vols. 5s. each.

PLINY'S Natural History. Translated by the late John Bostock, M.D., F.R.S., and H. T. Riley, M.A. 6 vols. 5s. each.

PLINY. The Letters of Pliny the Younger. Melmoth's translation, revised by the Rev. F. C. T. Bosanquet, M.A. 5s.

PLOTINUS, Select Works of. Translated by Thomas Taylor. With an Introduction containing the substance of Porphyry's Plotinus. Edited by G. R. S. Mead, B.A., M.R.A.S. 5s.

**PLUTARCH'S Lives.** Translated by A. Stewart, M.A., and George Long, M.A. 4 vols. 3s. 6d. each.

—— **Morals.** Theosophical Essays. Translated by C. W. King, M.A. 5s.

—— **Morals.** Ethical Essays. Translated by the Rev. A. R. Shilleto, M.A. 5s.

**POETRY OF AMERICA.** Selections from One Hundred American Poets, from 1776 to 1876. By W. J. Linton. 3s. 6d.

**POLITICAL CYCLOPÆDIA.** A Dictionary of Political, Constitutional, Statistical, and Forensic Knowledge; forming a Work of Reference on subjects of Civil Administration, Political Economy, Finance, Commerce, Laws, and Social Relations. 4 vols. 3s. 6d. each.

**POPE'S Poetical Works.** Edited, with copious Notes, by Robert Carruthers. With numerous Illustrations. 2 vols. 5s. each.

—— **Homer's Iliad.** Edited by the Rev. J. S. Watson, M.A. Illustrated by the entire Series of Flaxman's Designs. 5s.

—— **Homer's Odyssey**, with the Battle of Frogs and Mice, Hymns, &c., by other translators. Edited by the Rev. J. S. Watson, M.A. With the entire Series of Flaxman's Designs. 5s.

—— **Life**, including many of his Letters. By Robert Carruthers. With numerous Illustrations. 5s.

**POUSHKIN'S Prose Tales:** The Captain's Daughter—Doubrovsky—The Queen of Spades—An Amateur Peasant Girl—The Shot—The Snow Storm—The Postmaster — The Coffin Maker — Kirdjali—The Egyptian Nights—Peter the Great's Negro. Translated by T. Keane. 3s. 6d.

**PRESCOTT'S** Conquest of Mexico. Copyright edition, with the notes by John Foster Kirk, and an introduction by G. P. Winship. 3 vols. 3s. 6d. each.

—— **Conquest of Peru.** Copyright edition, with the notes of John Foster Kirk. 2 vols. 3s. 6d. each.

—— **Reign of Ferdinand and Isabella.** Copyright edition, with the notes of John Foster Kirk. 3 vols. 3s. 6d. each.

**PROPERTIUS.** Translated by Rev. P. J. F. Gantillon, M.A., and accompanied by Poetical Versions, from various sources. 3s. 6d.

**PROVERBS, Handbook of.** Containing an entire Republication of Ray's Collection of English Proverbs, with his additions from Foreign Languages and a complete Alphabetical Index; in which are introduced large additions as well of Proverbs as of Sayings, Sentences, Maxims, and Phrases, collected by H. G. Bohn. 5s.

**PROVERBS, A Polyglot of Foreign.** Comprising French, Italian, German, Dutch, Spanish, Portuguese, and Danish. With English Translations & a General Index by H. G. Bohn. 5s.

**POTTERY AND PORCELAIN,** and other Objects of Vertu. Comprising an Illustrated Catalogue of the Bernal Collection of Works of Art, with the prices at which they were sold by auction, and names of the possessors. To which are added, an Introductory Lecture on Pottery and Porcelain, and an Engraved List of all the known Marks and Monograms. By Henry G. Bohn. With numerous Wood Engravings, 5s.; or with Coloured Illustrations, 10s. 6d.

**PROUT'S (Father) Reliques.** Collected and arranged by Rev. F. Mahony. New issue, with 21 Etchings by D. Maclise, R.A. Nearly 600 pages. 5s.

**QUINTILIAN'S Institutes of Oratory**, or Education of an Orator. Translated by the Rev. J. S. Watson, M.A. 2 vols. 5s. each.

**RACINE'S (Jean) Dramatic Works.** A metrical English version. By R. Bruce Boswell, M.A. Oxon. 2 vols. 3s. 6d. each.

**RANKE'S History of the Popes**, their Church and State, and especially of their Conflicts with Protestantism in the 16th and 17th centuries. Translated by E. Foster. 3 vols. 3s. 6d. each.

—— **History of Servia and the Servian Revolution.** With an Account of the Insurrection in Bosnia. Translated by Mrs. Kerr. 3s. 6d.

**RECREATIONS in SHOOTING.** By 'Craven.' With 62 Engravings on Wood after Harvey, and 9 Engravings on Steel, chiefly after A. Cooper, R.A. 5s.

**RENNIE'S Insect Architecture.** Revised and enlarged by Rev. J. G. Wood, M.A. With 186 Woodcut Illustrations. 5s.

**REYNOLD'S (Sir J.) Literary Works.** Edited by H. W. Beechy. 2 vols. 3s. 6d. each.

**RICARDO on the Principles of Political Economy and Taxation.** Edited by E. C. K. Gonner, M.A. 5s.

**RICHTER (Jean Paul Friedrich).** Levana, a Treatise on Education: together with the Autobiography (a Fragment), and a short Prefatory Memoir. 3s. 6d.

—— **Flower, Fruit, and Thorn Pieces**, or the Wedded Life, Death, and Marriage of Firmian Stanislaus Siebenkaes, Parish Advocate in the Parish of Kuhschnapptel. Newly translated by Lt. Col. Alex. Ewing. 3s. 6d.

**ROGER DE HOVEDEN'S Annals of English History**, comprising the History of England and of other Countries of Europe from A.D. 732 to A.D. 1201. Translated by H. T. Riley, M.A. 2 vols. 5s. each.

**ROGER OF WENDOVER'S Flowers of History**, comprising the History of England from the Descent of the Saxons to A.D. 1235, formerly ascribed to Matthew Paris. Translated by J. A. Giles, D.C.L. 2 vols. 5s. each.

**ROME in the NINETEENTH CENTURY.** Containing a complete Account of the Ruins of the Ancient City, the Remains of the Middle Ages, and the Monuments of Modern Times. By C. A. Eaton. With 34 Steel Engravings. 2 vols. 5s. each.

—— *See* BURN and DYER.

**ROSCOE'S (W.) Life and Pontificate of Leo X.** Final edition, revised by Thomas Roscoe. 2 vols. 3s. 6d. each.

—— **Life of Lorenzo de' Medici**, called 'the Magnificent.' With his poems, letters, &c. 10th Edition, revised, with Memoir of Roscoe by his Son. 3s. 6d.

**RUSSIA. History of**, from the earliest Period, compiled from the most authentic sources by Walter K. Kelly. With Portraits. 2 vols. 3s 6d. each.

**SALLUST, FLORUS, and VELLEIUS PATERCULUS.** Translated by J. S. Watson, M.A. 5s.

**SCHILLER'S Works.** Translated by various hands. 7 vols. 3s. 6d. each:—

    I.—History of the Thirty Years' War.

SCHILLER'S WORKS *continued.*

II.—History of the Revolt in the Netherlands, the Trials of Counts Egmont and Horn, the Siege of Antwerp, and the Disturbances in France preceding the Reign of Henry IV.

III.—Don Carlos, Mary Stuart, Maid of Orleans, Bride of Messina, together with the Use of the Chorus in Tragedy (a short Essay).

These Dramas are all translated in metre.

IV.—Robbers (with Schiller's original Preface), Fiesco, Love and Intrigue, Demetrius, Ghost Seer, Sport of Divinity.

The Dramas in this volume are translated into Prose.

V.—Poems.

VI.—Essays, Æsthetical and Philosophical.

VII.—Wallenstein's Camp, Piccolomini and Death of Wallenstein, William Tell.

SCHILLER and GOETHE. Correspondence between, from A.D. 1794-1805. Translated by L. Dora Schmitz. 2 vols. 3s. 6d. each.

SCHLEGEL'S (F.) Lectures on the Philosophy of Life and the Philosophy of Language. Translated by the Rev. A. J. W. Morrison, M.A. 3s. 6d.

—— Lectures on the History of Literature, Ancient and Modern. Translated from the German. 3s. 6d.

—— Lectures on the Philosophy of History. Translated by J. B. Robertson. 3s. 6d.

SCHLEGEL'S Lectures on Modern History, together with the Lectures entitled Cæsar and Alexander, and The Beginning of our History. Translated by L. Purcell and R. H. Whitelock. 3s. 6d.

—— Æsthetic and Miscellaneous Works. Translated by E. J. Millington. 3s. 6d.

SCHLEGEL (A. W.) Lectures on Dramatic Art and Literature. Translated by J. Black. Revised Edition, by the Rev. A. J. W. Morrison, M.A. 3s. 6d.

SCHOPENHAUER on the Fourfold Root of the Principle of Sufficient Reason, and On the Will in Nature. Translated by Madame Hillebrand. 5s.

—— Essays. Selected and Translated. With a Biographical Introduction and Sketch of his Philosophy, by E. Belfort Bax. 5s.

SCHOUW'S Earth, Plants, and Man. Translated by A. Henfrey. With coloured Map of the Geography of Plants. 5s.

SCHUMANN (Robert). His Life and Works, by August Reissmann. Translated by A. L. Alger. 3s. 6d.

—— Early Letters. Originally published by his Wife. Translated by May Herbert. With a Preface by Sir George Grove, D.C.L. 3s. 6d.

SENECA on Benefits. Newly translated by A. Stewart, M.A. 3s. 6d.

—— Minor Essays and On Clemency. Translated by A. Stewart, M.A. 5s.

SHAKESPEARE DOCUMENTS. Arranged by D. H. Lambert, B.A. 3s. 6d.

SHAKESPEARE'S Dramatic Art. The History and Character of Shakespeare's Plays. By Dr. Hermann Ulrici. Translated by L. Dora Schmitz. 2 vols. 3s. 6d. each.

SHAKESPEARE (William). A Literary Biography by Karl Elze, Ph.D., LL.D. Translated by L. Dora Schmitz. 5s.

SHARPE (S.) The History of Egypt, from the Earliest Times till the Conquest by the Arabs, A.D. 640. By Samuel Sharpe. 2 Maps and upwards of 400 Illustrative Woodcuts. 2 vols. 5s. each.

SHERIDAN'S Dramatic Works, Complete. With Life by G. G. S. 3s. 6d.

SISMONDI'S History of the Literature of the South of Europe. Translated by Thomas Roscoe. 2 vols. 3s. 6d. each.

SMITH'S Synonyms and Antonyms, or Kindred Words and their Opposites. Revised Edition. 5s.

—— Synonyms Discriminated. A Dictionary of Synonymous Words in the English Language, showing the Accurate signification of words of similar meaning. Edited by the Rev. H. Percy Smith, M.A. 6s.

SMITH'S (Adam) The Wealth of Nations. Edited by E. Belfort Bax. 2 vols. 3s. 6d. each.

—— Theory of Moral Sentiments. With a Memoir of the Author by Dugald Stewart. 3s. 6d.

SMYTH'S (Professor) Lectures on Modern History. 2 vols. 3s. 6d. each.

SMYTH'S (Professor) Lectures on the French Revolution. 2 vols. 3s. 6d. each.

SMITH'S (Pye) Geology and Scripture. 2nd Edition. 5s.

SMOLLETT'S Adventures of Roderick Random. With short Memoir and Bibliography, and Cruikshank's Illustrations. 3s. 6d.

SMOLLETT'S Adventures of Peregrine Pickle. With Bibliography and Cruikshank's Illustrations. 2 vols. 3s. 6d. each.

—— The Expedition of Humphry Clinker. With Bibliography and Cruikshank's Illustrations. 3s. 6d.

SOCRATES (surnamed 'Scholasticus'). The Ecclesiastical History of (A.D. 305-445). Translated from the Greek. 5s.

SOPHOCLES, The Tragedies of. A New Prose Translation, with Memoir, Notes, &c., by E. P. Coleridge, M.A. 5s.

SOUTHEY'S Life of Nelson. With Portraits, Plans, and upwards of 50 Engravings on Steel and Wood. 5s.

—— Life of Wesley, and the Rise and Progress of Methodism. 5s.

—— Robert Southey. The Story of his Life written in his Letters. Edited by John Dennis. 3s. 6d.

SOZOMEN'S Ecclesiastical History. Translated from the Greek. Together with the ECCLESIASTICAL HISTORY OF PHILOSTORGIUS, as epitomised by Photius. Translated by Rev. E. Walford, M.A. 5s.

SPINOZA'S Chief Works. Translated, with Introduction, by R. H. M. Elwes. 2 vols. 5s. each.

STANLEY'S Classified Synopsis of the Principal Painters of the Dutch and Flemish Schools. By George Stanley. 5s.

STARLING'S (Miss) Noble Deeds of Women. With 14 Steel Engravings. 5s.

STAUNTON'S Chess-Player's Handbook. 5s.

—— Chess Praxis. A Supplement to the Chess-player's Handbook. 5s.

**STAUNTON'S Chess - player's Companion.** Comprising a Treatise on Odds, Collection of Match Games, and a Selection of Original Problems. 5*s*.

—— **Chess Tournament of 1851.** With Introduction and Notes. 5*s*.

**STOCKHARDT'S Experimental Chemistry.** Edited by C. W. Heaton, F.C.S. 5*s*.

**STOWE (Mrs. H. B.) Uncle Tom's Cabin.** Illustrated. 3*s*. 6*d*.

**STRABO'S Geography.** Translated by W. Falconer, M.A., and H. C. Hamilton. 3 vols. 5*s*. each.

**STRICKLAND'S (Agnes) Lives of the Queens of England,** from the Norman Conquest. Revised Edition. With 6 Portraits. 6 vols. 5*s*. each.

—— **Life of Mary Queen of Scots.** 2 vols. 5*s*. each.

—— **Lives of the Tudor and Stuart Princesses.** With Portraits. 5*s*.

**STUART and REVETT'S Antiquities of Athens,** and other Monuments of Greece. With 71 Plates engraved on Steel, and numerous Woodcut Capitals. 5*s*.

**SUETONIUS' Lives of the Twelve Cæsars** and **Lives of the Grammarians.** Thomson's translation, revised by T. Forester. 5*s*.

**SWIFT'S Prose Works.** Edited by Temple Scott. With a Biographical Introduction by the Right Hon. W. E. H. Lecky, M.P. With Portraits and Facsimiles. 12 vols. 3*s*. 6*d*. each.
[*Vols. I.-X. ready.*
   I.—A Tale of a Tub, The Battle of the Books, and other early works. Edited by Temple Scott. With a Biographical Introduction by W. E. H. Lecky.

SWIFT'S PROSE WORKS *continued.*
   II.—The Journal to Stella. Edited by Frederick Ryland, M.A. With 2 Portraits and Facsimile.
   III. & IV.—Writings on Religion and the Church.
   V.—Historical and Political Tracts (English).
   VI.—The Drapier's Letters. With facsimiles of Wood's Coinage, &c.
   VII.—Historical and Political Tracts (Irish).
   VIII.—Gulliver's Travels. Edited by G. R. Dennis. With Portrait and Maps.
   IX.—Contributions to Periodicals.
   X.—Historical Writings.
   XI.—Literary Essays.
[*In preparation.*
   XII.—Index and Bibliography.
[*In preparation.*

**TACITUS. The Works of.** Literally translated. 2 vols. 5*s*. each.

**TALES OF THE GENII.** Translated from the Persian by Sir Charles Morell. Numerous Woodcuts and 12 Steel Engravings. 5*s*.

**TASSO'S Jerusalem Delivered.** Translated into English Spenserian Verse by J. H. Wiffen. With 8 Engravings on Steel and 24 Woodcuts by Thurston. 5*s*.

**TAYLOR'S (Bishop Jeremy) Holy Living and Dying.** 3*s*. 6*d*.

**TEN BRINK.**—*See* BRINK.

**TERENCE and PHÆDRUS.** Literally translated by H. T. Riley, M.A. To which is added, Smart's Metrical Version of Phædrus. 5*s*.

**THEOCRITUS, BION, MOSCHUS, and TYRTÆUS.** Literally translated by the Rev. J. Banks, M.A. To which are appended the Metrical Versions of Chapman. 5*s*.

**THEODORET and EVAGRIUS.** Histories of the Church from A.D. 332 to A.D. 427; and from A.D. 431 to A.D. 544. Translated. 5s.

**THIERRY'S History of the Conquest of England by the Normans.** Translated by William Hazlitt. 2 vols. 3s. 6d. each.

**THUCYDIDES. The Peloponnesian War.** Literally translated by the Rev. H. Dale. 2 vols. 3s. 6d. each.

—— An Analysis and Summary of. By J. T. Wheeler. 5s.

**THUDICHUM (J. L. W.) A Treatise on Wines.** Illustrated. 5s.

**URE'S (Dr. A.) Cotton Manufacture of Great Britain.** Edited by P. L. Simmonds. 2 vols. 5s. each.

—— Philosophy of Manufactures. Edited by P. L. Simmonds. 7s. 6d.

**VASARI'S Lives of the most Eminent Painters, Sculptors, and Architects.** Translated by Mrs. J. Foster, with a Commentary by J. P. Richter, Ph.D. 6 vols. 3s. 6d. each.

**VIRGIL.** A Literal Prose Translation by A. Hamilton Bryce, LL.D. With Portrait. 3s. 6d.

**VOLTAIRE'S Tales.** Translated by R. B. Boswell. Containing Bebouc, Memnon, Candide, L'Ingénu, and other Tales. 3s. 6d.

**WALTON'S Complete Angler.** Edited by Edward Jesse. With Portrait and 203 Engravings on Wood and 26 Engravings on Steel. 5s.

—— Lives of Donne, Hooker, &c. New Edition revised by A. H. Bullen, with a Memoir of Izaak Walton by Wm. Dowling. With numerous Illustrations. 5s.

**WELLINGTON, Life of.** By 'An Old Soldier.' From the materials of Maxwell. With Index and 18 Steel Engravings. 5s.

**WELLINGTON, Victories of.** *See* MAXWELL.

**WERNER'S Templars in Cyprus.** Translated by E. A. M. Lewis. 3s. 6d.

**WESTROPP (H. M.) A Handbook of Archæology, Egyptian, Greek, Etruscan, Roman.** Illustrated. 5s.

**WHITE'S Natural History of Selborne.** With Notes by Sir William Jardine. Edited by Edward Jesse. With 40 Portraits and coloured Plates. 5s.

**WHEATLEY'S A Rational Illustration of the Book of Common Prayer.** 3s. 6d.

**WHEELER'S Noted Names of Fiction, Dictionary of.** 5s.

**WIESELER'S Chronological Synopsis of the Four Gospels.** Translated by the Rev. Canon Venables. 3s. 6d.

**WILLIAM of MALMESBURY'S Chronicle of the Kings of England.** Translated by the Rev. J. Sharpe. Edited by J. A. Giles, D.C.L. 5s.

**XENOPHON'S Works.** Translated by the Rev. J. S. Watson, M.A., and the Rev. H. Dale. In 3 vols. 5s. each.

**YOUNG (Arthur). Travels in France during the years 1787, 1788, and 1789.** Edited by M. Betham Edwards. 3s. 6d.

—— Tour in Ireland, with General Observations on the state of the country during the years 1776–79. Edited by A. W. Hutton. With Complete Bibliography by J. P. Anderson, and Map. 2 vols. 3s. 6d. each.

**YULE-TIDE STORIES.** A Collection of Scandinavian and North-German Popular Tales and Traditions. Edited by B. Thorpe. 5s.

# THE YORK LIBRARY

A NEW SERIES OF REPRINTS ON THIN PAPER.

The volumes are printed in a handy size ($6\frac{1}{2} \times 4\frac{1}{4}$ in.), on thin but opaque paper, and are simply and attractively bound.

Price, in cloth, 2s. net ; in leather, 3s. net.

'The York Library is noticeable by reason of the wisdom and intelligence displayed in the choice of unhackneyed classics. . . . A most attractive series of reprints. . . . The size and style of the volumes are exactly what they should be.'—*Bookman.*

'These books should find their way to every home that owns any cultivation.'—*Notes and Queries.*

*The following volumes are now ready:*

CHARLOTTE BRONTË'S JANE EYRE.

BURNEY'S EVELINA. Edited, with an Introduction and Notes, by ANNIE RAINE ELLIS.

BURNEY'S CECILIA. Edited by ANNIE RAINE ELLIS. 2 vols.

BURTON'S ANATOMY OF MELANCHOLY. Edited by the Rev. A. R. SHILLETO, M.A., with Introduction by A. H. BULLEN. 3 vols.

BURTON'S (SIR RICHARD) PILGRIMAGE TO AL-MADINAH AND MECCAH. With Introduction by STANLEY LANE-POOLE. 2 vols.

CERVANTES' DON QUIXOTE. MOTTEUX'S Translation, revised. With LOCKHART'S Life and Notes. 2 vols.

CLASSIC TALES : JOHNSON'S RASSELAS, GOLDSMITH'S VICAR OF WAKEFIELD, STERNE'S SENTIMENTAL JOURNEY, WALPOLE'S CASTLE OF OTRANTO. With Introduction by C. S. FEARENSIDE, M.A.

COLERIDGE'S AIDS TO REFLECTION, and the Confessions of an Inquiring Spirit.

COLERIDGE'S FRIEND. A series of Essays on Morals, Politics, and Religion.

COLERIDGE'S TABLE TALK AND OMNIANA. Arranged and Edited by T. ASHE, B.A.

DRAPER'S HISTORY OF THE INTELLECTUAL DE-VELOPMENT OF EUROPE. 2 vols.

GEORGE ELIOT'S ADAM BEDE.

EMERSON'S WORKS. A new edition in 5 volumes, with the Text edited and collated by GEORGE SAMPSON.

FIELDING'S TOM JONES. 2 vols.

GASKELL'S SYLVIA'S LOVERS.

## The York Library—continued.

**GESTA ROMANORUM,** or Entertaining Moral Stories invented by the Monks. Translated from the Latin by the Rev. CHARLES SWAN. Revised edition, by WYNNARD HOOPER, M.A.

**GOETHE'S FAUST.** Translated by ANNA SWANWICK, LL.D. Revised edition, with an Introduction and Bibliography by KARL BREUL, Litt.D., Ph.D.

**HAWTHORNE'S TRANSFORMATION** (THE MARBLE FAUN).

**IRVING'S SKETCH BOOK.**

**JAMESON'S SHAKESPEARE'S HEROINES.** Characteristics of Women: Moral, Poetical, and Historical.

**LAMB'S ESSAYS.** Including the Essays of Elia, Last Essays of Elia, and Eliana.

**MARCUS AURELIUS ANTONINUS, THE THOUGHTS OF.** Translated by GEORGE LONG, M.A. With an Essay on Marcus Aurelius by MATTHEW ARNOLD.

**MARRYAT'S MR. MIDSHIPMAN EASY.** With 8 Illustrations by E. T. WHEELER.

**MARRYAT'S PETER SIMPLE.** With 8 Illustrations by F. A. FRASER.

**MONTAIGNE'S ESSAYS.** Cotton's translation. Revised by W. C. HAZLITT. 3 vols.

**MORE'S UTOPIA.** With the Life of Sir Thomas More, by William Roper, and his Letters to Margaret Roper and others. Edited, with Introduction and Notes, by GEORGE SAMPSON. [*In the Press.*

**MOTLEY'S RISE OF THE DUTCH REPUBLIC.** With a Biographical Introduction by MONCURE D. CONWAY. 3 vols.

**PASCAL'S THOUGHTS.** Translated from the Text of M. AUGUSTE MOLINIER by C. KEGAN PAUL. Third edition.

**PLUTARCH'S LIVES.** Translated, with Notes and a Life by AUBREY STEWART, M.A., and GEORGE LONG, M.A. 4 vols.

**SWIFT'S GULLIVER'S TRAVELS.** Edited, with Introduction and Notes, by G. R. DENNIS, with facsimiles of the original illustrations.

**SWIFT'S JOURNAL TO STELLA.** Edited, with Introduction and Notes, by F. RYLAND, M.A.

**TROLLOPE'S THE WARDEN.** With an Introduction by FREDERIC HARRISON.

**TROLLOPE'S BARCHESTER TOWERS.**

**TROLLOPE'S DR. THORNE.**

**TROLLOPE'S FRAMLEY PARSONAGE.**

**TROLLOPE'S SMALL HOUSE AT ALLINGTON.** 2 vols.

**TROLLOPE'S LAST CHRONICLE OF BARSET.** 2 vols.

**ARTHUR YOUNG'S TRAVELS IN FRANCE,** during the years 1787, 1788, and 1789. Edited with Introduction and Notes, by M. BETHAM EDWARDS.

*Other Volumes are in Preparation.*

# BELL'S HANDBOOKS
## OF
# THE GREAT MASTERS
## IN PAINTING AND SCULPTURE.

Edited by G. C. WILLIAMSON, Litt.D.

Post 8vo.  With 40 Illustrations and Photogravure Frontispiece.  5s. net each.

*The following Volumes have been issued:*

BOTTICELLI.  By A. Streeter.  2nd Edition.
BRUNELLESCHI.  By Leader Scott.
CORREGGIO.  By Selwyn Brinton, M.A.  2nd Edition.
CARLO CRIVELLI.  By G. McNeil Rushforth, M.A.
DELLA ROBBIA.  By the Marchesa Burlamacchi.  2nd Edition.
ANDREA DEL SARTO.  By H. Guinness.  2nd Edition.
DONATELLO.  By Hope Rea.  2nd Edition.
GERARD DOU.  By Dr. W. Martin.  Translated by Clara Bell.
GAUDENZIO FERRARI.  By Ethel Halsey.
FRANCIA.  By George C. Williamson, Litt.D.
GIORGIONE.  By Herbert Cook, M.A.
GIOTTO.  By F. Mason Perkins.
FRANS HALS.  By Gerald S. Davies, M.A.
BERNARDINO LUINI.  By George C. Williamson, Litt.D.  3rd Edition.
LEONARDO DA VINCI.  By Edward McCurdy, M.A.
MANTEGNA.  By Maud Cruttwell.
MEMLINC.  By W. H. James Weale.
MICHEL ANGELO.  By Lord Ronald Sutherland Gower, M.A., F.S.A.
PERUGINO.  By G C. Williamson, Litt.D.  2nd Edition.
PIERO DELLA FRANCESCA.  By W. G. Waters, M.A.
PINTORICCHIO.  By Evelyn March Phillipps.
RAPHAEL.  By H. Strachey.  2nd Edition.
REMBRANDT.  By Malcolm Bell.  2nd Edition.
RUBENS.  By Hope Rea.
LUCA SIGNORELLI.  By Maud Cruttwell.  2nd Edition.
SODOMA.  By the Contessa Lorenzo Priuli-Bon.
TINTORETTO.  By J. B. Stoughton Holborn, M.A.
VAN DYCK.  By Lionel Cust, M.V.O., F.S.A.
VELASQUEZ.  By R. A. M. Stevenson.  3rd Edition.
WATTEAU.  By Edgcumbe Staley, B.A.
WILKIE.  By Lord Ronald Sutherland Gower, M.A., F.S.A.

*Others to follow.*

# THE CHISWICK SHAKESPEARE.

*Illustrated by BYAM SHAW*

WITH INTRODUCTIONS AND GLOSSARIES BY JOHN DENNIS.

Printed at the Chiswick Press, pott 8vo., price 1s. 6d. net per volume; also a cheaper edition, 1s. net per volume; or 2s. net in limp leather; also a few copies, on Japanese vellum, to be sold only in sets, price 5s. net per volume.

*Now Complete in 39 Volumes.*

ALL'S WELL THAT ENDS WELL.
ANTONY AND CLEOPATRA.
AS YOU LIKE IT.
COMEDY OF ERRORS.
CORIOLANUS.
CYMBELINE.
HAMLET.
JULIUS CÆSAR.
KING HENRY IV. Part I.
KING HENRY IV. Part II.
KING HENRY V.
KING HENRY VI. Part I.
KING HENRY VI. Part II.
KING HENRY VI. Part III.
KING HENRY VIII.
KING JOHN.
KING LEAR.
KING RICHARD II.
KING RICHARD III.
LOVE'S LABOUR'S LOST.
MACBETH.
MEASURE FOR MEASURE.
MERCHANT OF VENICE.
MERRY WIVES OF WINDSOR.
MIDSUMMER-NIGHT'S DREAM.
MUCH ADO ABOUT NOTHING.
OTHELLO.
PERICLES.
ROMEO AND JULIET.
THE TAMING OF THE SHREW.
THE TEMPEST.
TIMON OF ATHENS.
TITUS ANDRONICUS.
TROILUS AND CRESSIDA.
TWELFTH NIGHT.
TWO GENTLEMEN OF VERONA.
WINTER'S TALE.
POEMS.
SONNETS.

'A fascinating little edition.'—*Notes and Queries.*

'A cheap, very comely, and altogether desirable edition.'—*Westminster Gazette.*

'But a few years ago such volumes would have been deemed worthy to be considered *éditions de luxe*. To-day, the low price at which they are offered to the public alone prevents them being so regarded.'—*Studio.*

'Handy in shape and size, wonderfully cheap, beautifully printed from the Cambridge text, and illustrated quaintly yet admirably by Mr. Byam Shaw, we have nothing but praise for it. No one who wants a good and convenient Shakespeare—without excursuses, discursuses, or even too many notes—can do better, in our opinion, than subscribe to this issue: which is saying a good deal in these days of cheap reprints.'—*Vanity Fair.*

'What we like about these elegant booklets is the attention that has been paid to the paper, as well as to the print and decoration; such stout laid paper will last for ages. On this account alone, the 'Chiswick' *should easily be first* among pocket Shakespeares.'—*Pall Mall Gazette.*

\*\*\* *The Chiswick Shakespeare may also be had bound in 12 volumes, full gilt back, price 36s. net.*

New Editions, fcap. 8vo. 2s. 6d. each net.

# THE ALDINE EDITION

OF THE

# BRITISH POETS.

'This excellent edition of the English classics, with their complete texts and scholarly introductions, are something very different from the cheap volumes of extracts which are just now so much too common.'—*St. James's Gazette.*

'An excellent series. Small, handy, and complete.'—*Saturday Review.*

---

**Akenside.** Edited by Rev. A. Dyce.

**Beattie.** Edited by Rev. A. Dyce.

**Blake.** Edited by W. M. Rossetti.

**Burns.** Edited by G. A. Aitken. 3 vols.

**Butler.** Edited by R. B. Johnson. 2 vols.

**Campbell.** Edited by His Son-in-law, the Rev. A. W. Hill. With Memoir by W. Allingham.

**Chatterton.** Edited by the Rev. W. W. Skeat, M.A. 2 vols.

**Chaucer.** Edited by Dr. R. Morris, with Memoir by Sir H. Nicolas. 6 vols.

**Churchill.** Edited by Jas. Hannay. 2 vols.

**Coleridge.** Edited by T. Ashe, B.A. 2 vols.

**Collins.** Edited by W. Moy Thomas.

**Cowper.** Edited by John Bruce, F.S.A. 3 vols.

**Dryden.** Edited by the Rev. R. Hooper, M.A. 5 vols.

**Goldsmith.** Revised Edition by Austin Dobson. With Portrait.

**Gray.** Edited by J. Bradshaw, LL.D.

**Herbert.** Edited by the Rev A. B. Grosart.

**Herrick.** Edited by George Saintsbury. 2 vols.

**Keats.** Edited by the late Lord Houghton.

**Kirke White.** Edited, with a Memoir, by Sir H. Nicolas.

**Milton.** Edited by Dr. Bradshaw. 2 vols.

**Parnell.** Edited by G. A. Aitken.

**Pope.** Edited by G. R. Dennis. With Memoir by John Dennis. 3 vols.

**Prior.** Edited by R. B. Johnson. 2 vols.

**Raleigh and Wotton.** With Selections from the Writings of other COURTLY POETS from 1540 to 1650. Edited by Ven. Archdeacon Hannah, D.C.L.

**Rogers.** Edited by Edward Bell, M.A.

**Scott.** Edited by John Dennis. 5 vols.

**Shakespeare's Poems.** Edited by Rev. A. Dyce.

**Shelley.** Edited by H. Buxton Forman. 5 vols.

**Spenser.** Edited by J. Payne Collier. 5 vols.

**Surrey.** Edited by J. Yeowell.

**Swift.** Edited by the Rev. J. Mitford. 3 vols.

**Thomson.** Edited by the Rev. D. C. Tovey. 2 vols.

**Vaughan.** Sacred Poems and Pious Ejaculations. Edited by the Rev. H. Lyte.

**Wordsworth.** Edited by Prof. Dowden. 7 vols.

**Wyatt.** Edited by J. Yeowell.

**Young.** 2 vols. Edited by the Rev. J. Mitford.

# THE ALL-ENGLAND SERIES.
## HANDBOOKS OF ATHLETIC GAMES.

The only Series issued at a moderate price, by Writers who are in the first rank in their respective departments.

'The best instruction on games and sports by the best authorities, at the lowest prices.'—*Oxford Magazine*.

Small 8vo. cloth, Illustrated. Price 1s. each.

Cricket. By FRED C. HOLLAND.
Cricket. By the Hon. and Rev. E. LYTTELTON.
Croquet. By Lieut.-Col. the Hon. H. C. NEEDHAM.
Lawn Tennis. By H. W. W. WILBERFORCE. With a Chapter for Ladies, by Mrs. HILLYARD.
Squash Tennis. By EUSTACE H. MILES. Double vol. 2s.
Tennis and Rackets and Fives. By JULIAN MARSHALL, Major J. SPENS, and Rev. J. A. ARNAN TAIT.
Golf. By H. S. C. EVERARD. Double vol. 2s.
Rowing and Sculling. By GUY RIXON.
Rowing and Sculling. By W. B. WOODGATE.
Sailing. By E. F. KNIGHT, dbl.vol. 2s.
Swimming. By MARTIN and J. RACSTER CORBETT.
Camping out. By A. A. MACDONELL. Double vol. 2s.
Canoeing. By Dr. J. D. HAYWARD. Double vol. 2s.
Mountaineering. By Dr. CLAUDE WILSON. Double vol. 2s.
Athletics. By H. H. GRIFFIN.
Riding. By W. A. KERR, V.C. Double vol. 2s.
Ladies' Riding. By W.A.KERR, V.C.
Boxing. By R. G. ALLANSON-WINN. With Prefatory Note by Bat Mullins.

Fencing. By H. A. COLMORE DUNN.
Cycling. By H. H. GRIFFIN, L.A.C., N.C.U., C.T.C. With a Chapter for Ladies, by Miss AGNES WOOD. Double vol. 2s.
Wrestling. By WALTER ARMSTRONG. New Edition.
Broadsword and Singlestick. By R. G. ALLANSON-WINN and C. PHILLIPPS-WOLLEY.
Gymnastics. By A. F. JENKIN. Double vol. 2s.
Gymnastic Competition and Display Exercises. Compiled by F. GRAF.
Indian Clubs. By G. T. B. CORBETT and A. F. JENKIN.
Dumb-bells. By F. GRAF.
Football—Rugby Game. By HARRY VASSALL.
Football—Association Game. By C. W. ALCOCK. Revised Edition.
Hockey. By F. S. CRESWELL. New Edition.
Skating. By DOUGLAS ADAMS. With a Chapter for Ladies, by Miss L. CHEETHAM, and a Chapter on Speed Skating, by a Fen Skater. Dbl. vol. 2s.
Baseball. By NEWTON CRANE.
Rounders, Fieldball, Bowls, Quoits, Curling, Skittles, &c. By J. M. WALKER and C. C. MOTT.
Dancing. By EDWARD SCOTT. Double vol. 2s.

## THE CLUB SERIES OF CARD AND TABLE GAMES.

'No well-regulated club or country house should be without this useful series of books.
Small 8vo. cloth, Illustrated. Price 1s. each. *Globe*.

Bridge. By 'TEMPLAR.'
Whist. By Dr. WM. POLE, F.R.S.
Solo Whist. By ROBERT F. GREEN.
Billiards. By Major-Gen. A. W. DRAYSON, F.R.A.S. With a Preface by W. J. Peall.
Hints on Billiards. By J. P. BUCHANAN. Double vol. 2s.
Chess. By ROBERT F. GREEN.
The Two-Move Chess Problem. By B. G. LAWS.
Chess Openings. By I. GUNSBERG.
Draughts and Backgammon. By 'BERKELEY.'
Reversi and Go Bang. By 'BERKELEY.'

Dominoes and Solitaire. By 'BERKELEY.'
Bézique and Cribbage. By 'BERKELEY.'
Écarté and Euchre. By 'BERKELEY.'
Piquet and Rubicon Piquet. By 'BERKELEY.'
Skat. By LOUIS DIEHL.
\*\*\* A Skat Scoring-book. 1s.
Round Games, including Poker, Napoleon, Loo, Vingt-et-un, &c. By BAXTER-WRAY.
Parlour and Playground Games. By Mrs. LAURENCE GOMME.

The Best Practical Working Dictionary of the English Language.

# WEBSTER'S INTERNATIONAL DICTIONARY.

<u>2348 PAGES.</u>     <u>5000 ILLUSTRATIONS.</u>

## NEW EDITION, REVISED THROUGHOUT WITH A NEW SUPPLEMENT OF 25,000 ADDITIONAL WORDS AND PHRASES.

---

The Appendices comprise a Pronouncing Gazetteer of the World, Vocabularies of Scripture, Greek, Latin, and English Proper Names, a Dictionary of the Noted Names of Fiction, a Brief History of the English Language, a Dictionary of Foreign Quotations, Words, Phrases, Proverbs, &c., a Biographical Dictionary with 10,000 names, &c., &c.

---

**Dr. MURRAY,** *Editor of the 'Oxford English Dictionary,'* says:—' In this its latest form, and with its large Supplement and numerous appendices, it is a wonderful volume, which well maintains its ground against all rivals on its own lines. The 'definitions,' or more properly, 'explanations of meaning' in 'Webster' have always struck me as particularly terse and well-put; and it is hard to see how anything better could be done within the limits.'

**Professor JOSEPH WRIGHT,** M.A., Ph.D., D.C.L., LL.D., *Editor of the 'English Dialect Dictionary,'* says:—' The new edition of "Webster's International Dictionary" is undoubtedly the most useful and reliable work of its kind in any country. No one who has not examined the work carefully would believe that such a vast amount of lexicographical information could possibly be found within so small a compass.'

**Professor A. H. SAYCE,** LL.D., D.D., says:—' It is indeed a marvellous work; it is difficult to conceive of a Dictionary more exhaustive and complete. Everything is in it—not only what we might expect to find in such a work, but also what few of us would ever have thought of looking for.'

**Rev. JOSEPH WOOD,** D.D., *Head Master of Harrow,* says:—' I have always thought very highly of its merits. Indeed, I consider it to be far the most accurate English Dictionary in existence, and much more reliable than the "Century." For daily and hourly reference, "Webster" seems to me unrivalled.'

---

*Prospectuses, with Prices and Specimen Pages, on Application.*

---

LONDON: GEORGE BELL & SONS, YORK HOUSE,
PORTUGAL STREET, W.C.

50,000.  S. & S. 11.06.

# BELL'S CATHEDRAL SERIES.

*Profusely Illustrated, cloth, crown 8vo. 1s. 6d. net each.*

ENGLISH CATHEDRALS. An Itinerary and Description. Compiled by JAMES G. GILCHRIST, A.M., M.D. Revised and edited with an Introduction on Cathedral Architecture by the Rev. T. PERKINS, M.A., F.R.A.S.

    BANGOR. By P. B. IRONSIDE BAX.
    BRISTOL. By H. J. L. J. MASSÉ, M.A.
    CANTERBURY. By HARTLEY WITHERS. 5th Edition.
    CARLISLE. By C. KING ELEY.
    CHESTER. By CHARLES HIATT. 3rd Edition.
    CHICHESTER. By H. C. CORLETTE, A.R.I.B.A. 2nd Edition.
    DURHAM. By J. E. BYGATE, A.R.C.A. 3rd Edition.
    ELY. By Rev. W. D. SWEETING, M.A. 2nd Edition.
    EXETER. By PERCY ADDLESHAW, B.A. 2nd Edition, revised.
    GLOUCESTER. By H. J. L. J. MASSÉ, M.A. 3rd Edition.
    HEREFORD. By A. HUGH FISHER, A.R.E. 2nd Edition, revised.
    LICHFIELD. By A. B. CLIFTON. 2nd Edition.
    LINCOLN. By A. F. KENDRICK, B.A. 3rd Edition.
    MANCHESTER. By Rev. T. PERKINS, M.A.
    NORWICH. By C. H. B. QUENNELL. 2nd Edition.
    OXFORD. By Rev. PERCY DEARMER, M.A. 2nd Edition, revised.
    PETERBOROUGH. By Rev. W. D. SWEETING. 2nd Edition, revised.
    RIPON. By CECIL HALLETT, B.A.
    ROCHESTER. By G. H. PALMER, B.A. 2nd Edition, revised.
    ST. ALBANS. By Rev. T. PERKINS, M.A.
    ST. ASAPH. By P. B. IRONSIDE BAX.
    ST. DAVID'S. By PHILIP ROBSON, A.R.I.B.A.
    ST. PATRICK'S, DUBLIN. By Rev. J. H. BERNARD, M.A., D.D. 2nd Edition.
    ST. PAUL'S. By Rev. ARTHUR DIMOCK, M.A. 3rd Edition, revised.
    ST. SAVIOUR'S, SOUTHWARK. By GEORGE WORLEY.
    SALISBURY. By GLEESON WHITE. 3rd Edition, revised.
    SOUTHWELL. By Rev. ARTHUR DIMOCK, M.A. 2nd Edition, revised.
    WELLS. By Rev. PERCY DEARMER, M.A. 3rd Edition.
    WINCHESTER. By P. W. SERGEANT. 3rd Edition.
    WORCESTER. By E. F. STRANGE. 2nd Edition.
    YORK. By A. CLUTTON-BROCK, M.A. 3rd Edition.

*Uniform with above Series. Now ready. 1s. 6d. net each.*

ST. MARTIN'S CHURCH, CANTERBURY. By the Rev. CANON ROUTLEDGE, M.A., F.S.A.
BEVERLEY MINSTER. By CHARLES HIATT.
WIMBORNE MINSTER and CHRISTCHURCH PRIORY. By the Rev. T. PERKINS, M.A.
TEWKESBURY ABBEY AND DEERHURST PRIORY. By H. J. L. J. MASSÉ, M.A.
BATH ABBEY, MALMESBURY ABBEY, and BRADFORD-ON-AVON CHURCH. By Rev. T. PERKINS, M.A.
WESTMINSTER ABBEY. By CHARLES HIATT.
STRATFORD-ON-AVON CHURCH. By HAROLD BAKER.

## BELL'S HANDBOOKS TO CONTINENTAL CHURCHES.

*Profusely Illustrated. Crown 8vo, cloth, 2s. 6d. net each.*

AMIENS By the Rev. T. PERKINS, M.A.
BAYEUX. By the Rev. R. S. MYLNE.
CHARTRES: The Cathedral and Other Churches. By H. J. L. J. MASSÉ, M.A.
MONT ST. MICHEL. By H. J. L. J. MASSÉ, M.A.
PARIS (NOTRE-DAME). By CHARLES HIATT.
ROUEN: The Cathedral and Other Churches. By the Rev. T. PERKINS, M.A.

www.ingramcontent.com/pod-product-compliance
Lightning Source LLC
Chambersburg PA
CBHW030402230426
43664CB00007BB/712